A DICTIONARY OF PROTESTANT CHURCH MUSIC

by

James Robert Davidson

The Scarecrow Press, Inc.
Metuchen, N.J.   1975

Library of Congress Cataloging in Publication Data

Davidson, James Robert, 1942-
   A dictionary of Protestant church music.

   Includes bibliographies and index.
    1. Church music--Protestant churches--Dictionaries.
I. Title.
ML102.C5D33   783'.026   74-30101
ISBN 0-8108-0788-2

To the One I Love

TABLE OF CONTENTS

PREFACE

The present "Dictionary of Protestant Church Music" is the first phase in the author's projected "Dictionary of Church Music." It was undertaken upon the recommendation and encouragement of Dr. G. Maurice Hinson, Professor of Church Music, The Southern Baptist Theological Seminary, Louisville, Kentucky.

For the professional assistance given the researcher at various phases of the project by the faculty members of the School of Church Music at the seminary, and especially by Dr. Jay W. Wilkey, chairman of the graduate committee, heartfelt gratitude is extended. Likewise, to Dr. Carlton R. Young of Perkins School of Theology, Southern Methodist University, and to the University Carilloneur, Albert C. Gerken of the University of Kansas, the author expresses his appreciation for their prompt, reliable information. The author is indebted to the librarians of the James P. Boyce Centennial Library of The Southern Baptist Theological Seminary, the Hardin Library of Tift College, the Music Library of Carnegie Library, Pittsburgh, Pennsylvania, the New York Public Library and the Library of Congress for their aid in guiding him to rare and valuable sources of information.

INTRODUCTION

Presently, whenever a person wants information on terms used in Protestant church music, particularly a clear definition, many different sources have to be consulted and then usually the resources have to be combined for a good working definition. To date, only one volume, G. W. Stubbings' A Dictionary of Church Music, 1949, which claims to define terms of church music, has been published in English. In that work, the author clearly stated that he "has not hesitated to express his own opinions." A volume of the nature of the present one, written from a historical perspective, thus seems long overdue. "A Dictionary of Protestant Church Music" seeks to provide the musical amateur, student and scholar with accurate and pertinent information on musical and liturgical topics related to Protestant church music.

How broad is the concept of "Protestant church" and what is church music? The Protestant church is to be interpreted as any Christian church other than those of the Roman Catholic, Old Catholic or Eastern traditions. "Church music" has come about in at least three ways. The first is by functional association. This would include music which is not related to any religious text or tune associated with a text. For example, the preludes and fugues (not based on chorales or hymn tunes) written for the organ and commonly used as preludes or postludes in a service of worship could be considered church music by association. Second, music is considered "church music" through liturgical function. Here, music designed for a particular place in the worship service or liturgy provide the obvious examples: e. g., a setting of the Te Deum laudamus, by the late Healey Willan (1880-1968), sung at Morning Prayer. Third, and somewhat overlapping with the previous, is the consideration of music as "church music" through religious textual association. Vivid illustrations from history show how Martin Luther (1483-1546) took the folk songs of his day,

changed the texts, and made Reformation chorales out of
them.   Are they not church music?   With this interpretation as a common point of departure, the title of the present work therefore implies a lexicon of terms peculiar to
the music and worship of non-Catholic (or Orthodox) Christian churches, accurately defined and delineated in their historical perspective.

Readers interested in a survey of the developments,
movements and events in Protestant church music from the
Reformation to the present are directed to the entry herein,
History of Protestant Church Music.

From the earliest musical dictionary, the 11th-cen-
tury Vocabularium Musicum, to the present day, little attention has been given to a lexicon of terms used in church
music.   Lloyd Hibberd's article, "Dictionaries of Music,"
in the Harvard Dictionary of Music[1] (p. 233) cites only
two such works, both in German: S. Kümmerle, Encyclo-
pedie der evangelischen Kirchenmusik (1888-1895, 4 vols.),
and A. Weissenbaech, Sacra Musica: Lexikon der katho-
lischen Kirchenmusik (1937).   Omitted from the revision of
the above article is the more practical than the scholarly
Stubbings Dictionary, which is greatly slanted toward the
administration and functions of the Church of England.   It
also contains terms applicable to music in general and
terms specifically related to organ nomenclature.   (The latter is adequately dealt with by Stevens Irwin in the Dictionary of Pipe Organ Stops.)

Similar works of a lexicographical nature which have
made their place as definitive reference volumes in music
have been studied or evaluated in preparation for the present work.   Among these is the Grove's Dictionary of Music
and Musicians.[2]   In this source of reference most entries
of terms give a brief etymology, definition and historical
perspective, and a brief bibliography.   As the title states,
this work also contains authoritative articles on musicians.
The Harvard Dictionary of Music[1] is designed to provide
concise authoritative information on all musical topics.   Its
most distinctive trait is its restriction to musical topics;
i.e., it omits biographical entries.

Having studied the composition of the Harvard Dictionary of Music and having come to appreciate its useful-
ness as a tool for research, the present author has taken
it as a model for "A Dictionary of Protestant Church Music."

As with the Apel volume, this work does not include biographical articles as separate entries, since there appear
to be other sources of this nature readily available in the
English language. [2,3] Biographical material is included only
as it relates to the topics, and then, within the articles
themselves.

At the conclusion of this work an index is provided
containing names of persons and institutions, as well as
titles of books and various musical works, that are cited
throughout the dictionary in numerous contexts.   This index
will provide the reader with a further method of tracing
specific terms of interest throughout the entire work, as
each term relates to several entries.

ENTRY.   Each entry has been evaluated as to its
relevance to Protestant church music, and only when found
meaningful has it been included.   All entries are alphabetically arranged.   When an alternate spelling is common,
the alternate form has been given an entry with a cross-
reference leading to the form of the term most commonly
used in the present English language, under which the
article appears.

ETYMOLOGY.   Derivations of the terms have been
guided, as much as possibly, by two current authoritative
sources: Webster's Third New International Dictionary of
the English Language Unabridged (P. Gove, ed. , 1965) and
The Random House Dictionary of the English Language (J.
Stein, ed. , 1966).

ARTICLE.   The articles contain, first and foremost,
a concise definition of the entry.   Except for minor terms,
the definition is followed by a brief historical summary of
its application from its origins to the present day.   Information for this has been derived from primary source materials, when available, or from definitive secondary materials.   As much as possible, personal opinions and reactions have been minimized.

EXAMPLES.   When meaningful and expedient, musical examples, facsimiles or illustrations have been included
with an entry to illustrate or clarify the term.

BIBLIOGRAPHY.   At the conclusion of an entry a
brief bibliography containing both primary and secondary
source materials usually appears.   Often, references to an

item in this bibliography have appeared in the article--e.g.,
"(King, 159)", meaning page 159 of the book by King to be
found in the brief bibliography at the end of the entry. The
reader is further advised to consult other obvious lexicographical volumes appropriate to various terms. Such works
include Julian's Dictionary of Hymnology, [4] Hartford and
Stevenson's Prayer Book Dictionary, [5] Blume's Die Musik in
Geschichte und Gegenwart, [6] and Thompson's International
Encyclopedia of Music and Musicians, [7] as well as the previously mentioned Grove's and Harvard dictionaries. [2,1] Also,
standard music histories--such as those by Grout[8] and
Crocker[9] of recent years in addition to the older volumes
such as those by Lang[10] and Adler[11]--have not been listed
in the present articles, but can provide much useful information for the reader.

NOTES

1. Apel, Willi, ed. Harvard Dictionary of Music, 2d
ed. Cambridge, Mass.: Belknap Press of Harvard University Press, 1969.
2. Grove's Dictionary of Music and Musicians, 5th ed.,
ed. by Eric Blom. New York: St. Martin's Press, 1954.
9 vols.
3. Baker's Biographical Dictionary of Musicians, 5th
ed., ed. by Nicholas Slonimsky. New York: G. Schirmer,
1958. With 1971 supplement, ed. by Slonimsky.
4. Julian, John, ed. Dictionary of Hymnology. New
York: Dover Publications, 1957.
5. Hartford, George, and Morley Stevenson, eds. The
Prayer Book Dictionary. London: Pitman and Sons, 1912.
6. Blume, Friedrich, ed. Die Musik in Geschichte
und Gegenwart. Kassel: Bärenreiter, 1951-1968. 14 vols.
7. Sabin, Robert, ed. The International Encyclopedia
of Music and Musicians, 9th ed. New York: Dodd, Mead,
1964.
8. Grout, Donald J. A History of Western Music.
New York: W. W. Norton, 1960.
9. Crocker, Richard. A History of Musical Style.
New York: McGraw-Hill, 1966.
10. Lang, Paul H. Music in Western Civilization.
New York: W. W. Norton, 1941.
11. Adler, Guido, ed. Handbuch der Musikgeschichte.
Berlin-Wilmersdorf: H. Keller, 1930. 2 vols.

TABLE OF ABBREVIATIONS

Books and Periodicals

ACM   Arnold, Samuel (ed.). Cathedral Music. 4 vols. 1790.

AHM   Adler, Guido. Handbuch der Musikgeschichte. 2 vols. 1930.

AM   Annales Musicologiques, Neuilly-sur-Seine, 1952- .

AMI   Acta Musicologica, Kassel, 1929- .

AMW   Archiv für Musikwissenschaft. Trossingen, 1943- .

BCP   Book of Common Prayer, 1945.

BGA   Bach-Gesamtausgabe. 46 vols. 1851-1899.

BH   Sims, Walter Hines (ed.). Baptist Hymnal. 1956.

CdMI   I Classici della Musica Italiana. 36 vols. 1919-1921.

CEKM   Apel, Willi (ed.). Corpus of Early Keyboard Music. 1963- .

CH   Noss, Luther (ed.). Christian Hymns. 1963.

CM   Boyce, William (ed.). Cathedral Music. 3 vols. 1788.

CS   Ewerhart, Rudolf (ed.). Cantio Sacra. 1955.

Cw   Blume, Friedrich and Kurt Gudewill (eds.). Das Chorwerk. 1929- .

DdT   Denkmäler deutscher Tonkunst. 65 vols. 1892-1931.

DED   Das Erbe deutsche Musik. 1935- .

DT	Denkmäler der Tonkunst. 6 vols. 1869-1871.
DTOe	Denkmäler der Tonkunst in Osterreich, 1959- .
ECM	The Treasury of English Church Music. 5 vols. 1965.
EECM	Early English Church Music. 1963- .
EngCM	English Church Music, Croydon, Surrey, 1930- .
GD	Blom, Eric (ed.). Grove's Dictionary of Music and Musicians. 5th ed. 1954.
GMB	Schering, Arnold (ed.). Geschichte der Musik in Beispielen. 1931.
HAM	Davison, Archibald and Willi Apel (eds.). Historical Anthology of Music. 2 vols. 1950.
Hymnal 1940	The Hymnal of the Protestant Episcopal Church in the United States. 1940.
JAMS	Journal of the American Musicological Society, Richmond, Virginia, 1948- .
JCM	Journal of Church Music, Philadelphia, 1959- .
JeF-S	Journal of English Folk-Song Society, London, 1900?- .
MA	Marrocco, W. Thomas and Harold Gleason (eds.). Music in America. 1964.
MB	Lewis, Anthony (ed.). Musica Britannica. 1951- .
MK	Musik und Kirche, Kassel, 1929- .
ML	Music and Letters, London, 1919- .
MM	Parrish, C. and J. F. Ohl (eds.). Masterpieces of Music Before 1750. 1951.
MMG	Monatshefte für Musik-Geschichte, Berlin, 1869-1905.
MQ	Musical Quarterly, New York, 1915- .
MS 8182	Manuscript catalog no. of some works by Graun in the Offentliche wissenschaftliche Bibliothek, Berlin.
OBC	Dearmer, Percy, Ralph Vaughan Williams and Martin Shaw (eds.). Oxford Book of Carols. 1928.

PRMA   <u>Proceedings of the Royal Musical Association,</u> London, 1872- .

TCM   <u>Tudor Church Music.</u> 10 vols. 1922-1929, 1948.

TEM   Parrish, Carl (ed.). <u>A Treasury of Early Music.</u> 1958.

ZGO   Ritter, A. (ed.). <u>Zur Geschichte des Orgelspiels.</u> 2 vols. 1884.

ZM   <u>Zeitschrift für Musikwissenschaft,</u> Leipzig, 1918-1935.

ZMG   <u>Zeitschrift für Musik und Gottesdienst,</u> Zürich, 1947- .

Signs and Symbols

*	preceding a word in the text, indicates this is a subject covered in a separate entry; in the etymology portion of an entry, use of the asterisk indicates that an etymology of a certain word is given elsewhere in an entry beginning with that word.
A	alto (as in SATB)
a5[4, 7, etc]	5 voice parts (or 4 or 7 etc.)
acc.	accusative
adv.	adverb
AF.	Anglo-French
Av.	Avestan
b.	born
B	bass (as in SATB)
c.	circa
cf.	compare with
C.M.	common meter
compar.	comparative
D.	Dutch; also descant (as in DATB)
Dan.	Danish
dim.	diminutive

E.	English
F.	French
fr.	from
Fris.	Frisian
G.	German
Goth.	Gothic
Gr.	Greek
H.	Hebrew
imper.	imperative
ind.	indicative
intens.	intensive
It.	Italian
L.	Latin
L. GR.	Late Greek
lit.	literally
LL.	Late Latin
L. M.	long meter
ME.	Middle English
MF.	Middle French
MHG.	Middle High German
ML.	Medieval Latin
MLG.	Middle Low German
n. d.	no date (i. e., of publication: none shown)
neut.	neuter
NL.	New Latin
n. p.	no publisher (i. e., none identifiable); also, no place (i. e., of publication: none shown)
OE.	Old English
OF.	Old French
OHG.	Old High German
ON.	Old Norse
ONF.	Old Norman French

orig.	originally
OS.	Old Saxon
part.	participle
per.	person
perh.	perhaps
pl.	plural
Pr.	Provencal
prob.	probable, probably.
pron.	pronoun
pub.	published
R. S. C. M.	Royal Society of Church Music (British)
S	soprano (as in SATB)
Skr.	Sanskrit
S. M.	short meter
S. P. C. K.	Society for the Promotion of Christian Knowledge (British)
Sw.	Swedish
T	tenor (as in SATB)
uncert.	uncertain
VL.	Vulgate Latin
W.	Welsh

THE DICTIONARY

ABENDMUSIK (G. evening music)

The evening musical performances of a quasi-sacred character, given mainly during the Advent season and primarily in the Protestant churches of Northern Germany during the 17th and 18th centuries, have become known as Abendmusiken. The term is particularly associated with the famous religious concerts of Dietrich Buxtehude (1637-1707) at Marienkirche in Lübeck (although the term was used by his predecessor, Franz Tunder (1614-1667) in the 1640's). The concerts occurred following the afternoon service on the last Sunday after Trinity, the Sunday before Advent, and the second, third, and fourth Sundays in Advent, and consisted of organ, orchestral and vocal compositions. While no complete musical setting of any of these services is extant, they appear to have been quite long and varied. They have been likened to a loosely woven *oratorio with *dialogues, *arias, *chorales and polyphonic choruses accompanied by organ and orchestra. The "colossal Baroque" enjoyed its last glories at these sumptuous performances. At the height of these musical events stood the masterful organ playing and improvization of Buxtehude. The fame of his Abendmusiken attracted musicians from all over Germany, including Handel and Bach.

Karstädt, Georg. Die "Extraordinarien" Abendmusiken Dietrich Buxtehude. Lübeck: Verlag Max Schmidt-Romhild, 1962.
Michel, Josef. "Die Abendmusik als Möglichkeit evangelischen Verkindigung," MK, 29:65-77, March-April, 1959.
Pirro, André. Dietrich Buxtehude. Paris: Librairie Fischbacher, 1913. Pp. 248-289.
Seiffert, Max, ed. Dietrich Buxtehude und Kirchenkantaten. Rev. by Hans Joachim Moser. DdT, XIV. Wiesbaden:
Stahl, Wilhelm. Die Lübecker Abendmusiken im 17. und 18. Jahrhundert. Lübeck: n.p., 1937.

A CAPPELLA   (It. cappella chapel, or alla cappella in the
        church style); see *chapel)

        Primarily, a cappella refers to a composition for
several voices performed without instrumental accompaniment. Earlier in history this term was employed when the
instruments, having no independent part, doubled the voice
parts in unisons or octaves. This latter meaning is now
obsolete.
        With the masses of Ockeghem and Josquin a period
typified by a cappella (unaccompanied) singing became established in the church. The model composer for this type
of music, however, is considered to be Palestrina. German composers during the early Reformation adopted this
style of music particularly when setting the *passion narrative, *psalms and other biblical texts, a practice seen in
the 20th-century works of such composers as Hugo Distler
(1908-1942) and Ernst Pepping (b. 1901). The *anthem in its
early development, when it differed from the *motet mainly
in language, was considered an a cappella form, a concept
which changed as it developed into a multi-sectioned form.

Dorian, Frederick. The History of Music in Performance.
        New York: W. W. Norton, 1942. Part I.
Handschin, J. Die Grundlagen des a-cappella-Stils. Zürich:
        Hans Hausermann und der Häusermannsche Privatchor,
        1929.
Kroyer, Theodore. "A cappella oder conserto?" in: Fest-
        schrift Hermann Kretzschmar. Leipzig: n.p., 1918.

"ACHTLIEDER-BUCH"

        Commonly known as the Wittenburg Gesangbuch, the
"Achtlieder-buch" is the first collection of Lutheran hymns.
The first song book of the Reformation (see *Hymnody
(German)) was originally entitled: Etlich christlich lider
Lobgesang ... in der Kirchen zu singen. It contained eight
poems to four melodies and was produced by Martin Luther
(1483-1546) and his friend Johann Walther (1496-1570).
Only the melodies of the tunes were given as the congrega-
tion sang in unison. The printer was Jobst Gutkneckt of
Nürnberg.

Das Achtliederbuch (Nürnberg 1523/4). Ed. by Konrad
        Amelin. Kassel: n.p., 1957. (Facsimile ed.)
Strunk, Oliver. Source Readings in Music History: The

Renaissance. New York: W. W. Norton, 1965. Pp.
151-152.

AGNUS DEI (L. Lamb of God)

Originally inserted into the Roman service of Holy
Communion by Pope Sergius I (687-701) to accompany the
breaking of the bread, the Agnus Dei has also been found
in various Protestant services throughout history. In
Luther's *Deutsche Messe (1525) it retained its position at
the end of the service. However, the German Agnus Dei
could take the form of the *chorale, Christe, du Lamm
Gottes" or "O Lamm Gottes unschuldig." It found its place
into the 1549 *Book of Common Prayer, but was omitted
in the 1552 edition. Meanwhile because of continued use it
has been restored to the Anglican service.
The Agnus Dei has traditionally maintained its position of being the final item of the *ordinary of the *mass or
*service of Holy Communion (see *Communion service).

Reed, Luther D. The Lutheran Liturgy. Philadelphia:
Muhlenberg Press, 1947. Pp. 368-371.

AINSWORTH PSALTER

The Book of Psalms, Englished both in Prose and
Metre was prepared by Henry Ainsworth (1517-1622) in
1612 and has become known as the Ainsworth Psalter. This
psalter was prepared for the English Separatists in Holland
and was published in Amsterdam. It enjoyed a total of
six editions, the last in 1690.
In the original edition (1612), 39 different tunes appeared for use with the 150 psalms, many of which were
borrowed from the Genevan Psalter (see *Psalmody, metri-
cal--The Continent) and the Sternhold and Hopkins Psalter
(the Old Version--also see *Psalmody, metrical as above).
The melodies were printed with the diamond-shaped notes
of the period with no bar lines. These tunes, which contain considerable metrical variety and rhythmic freedom,
are claimed to be the "cornerstone of America's music" in
folk traditions, international background and musical freedom (Chase, p. 16).

Chase, Gilbert. America's Music: from the Pilgrims to the
Present. Rev. ed. New York: McGraw-Hill, 1966.
Chapter 1.

Smith, Carlton Sprague. Early Psalmody in America.
Series I. The Ainsworth Psalter. New York: New
York Public Library, 1938. (Facsimile ed.)

ALLELUIA (L. form of H. hallelujah praise ye the Lord)

An ejaculation used frequently in religious worship
in festival seasons, particularly *Eastertide, is the alleluia.
Like the other Hebrew word, *"amen," alleluia, or hallelujah, came into the Christian liturgy very early. It is found
in many psalms as a shout of joy and triumph.
The alleluia is appropriately placed in the Lutheran
service as an acclamation to the hearing of the *Gospel.
During Lent it is exchanged for the sentence: "Christ hath
humbled himself, and become obedient unto death: even the
death of the cross."
In the *Book of Common Prayer (1549) the alleluia
was appointed to be said after the first *Gloria Patri at
*Morning Prayer and Evening Prayer (*Vespers) during the
Easter season. The 1552 Book of Common Prayer replaced
it with a *versicle and *response.

Reindall, Walter. "Das Hallelujah," Kirchenchordienst, 5:
33-37, March-April, 1935.
Thomas, Wilhelm. "Das österliche Hallelujah," Kirchenchordienst, 1:30-31, March-April, 1935.
Wellesz, Egon. "Gregory the Great's Letter on the Alleluia," AM, 2:7-26, 1954.

ALTARGESANG (G.)

Materials chanted in the German tongue by the officiant at the altar in the German Lutheran Church are called
Altargesänge. The word may also denote similar chantings
in the Roman church.

Ameln, Konrad and Christhard Mahrenholz, eds. Der Altargesang. Vol. I of Handbuch der deutschen evangelischen Kirchenmusik. Göttingen: Vandenhoeck und
Ruprecht, 1941.

AMEN (H. firm, established, as adv. certainly, assuredly)

The ejaculatory response to a prayer of ascription of

praise derived from the Hebrew genoite (so be it) is the
amen. Found as a formula of concurrence in the Old Testament (Numbers 5:22; Deuteronomy 27:15) the amen was used
in synagogue worship and was adopted into the worship of the
early Christians. The Apostle Paul speaks of the amen of
the assembly at the giving of thanks (I Corinthians 14:16) and
Justin Martyr (100?-165?) reports of the people saying amen
after prayer and thanksgiving.

Musically, in the settings of the *masses and *oratorios of the 17th and 18th centuries the affirming character
of the amen often inspired extensive fugal writing for the
grand finale, called amen-fugues, because of the reiteration
of the word. The practice is reported to have first occurred
with Antonio Bertali (1605-1669) (see AHM, I:516).

Reindell, Walter. "Das 'Amen', " Kirchenchordienst, 5:18-
    21, March-April, 1939.

ANAMNESIS (Gr. anamnesis, fr. anaminneskein to recall
    to memory)

The prayer immediately after the Consecration, containing the assurance that the church is mindful of the injunction, "Do this in commemoration of Me" (I Corinthians
11:24), is called the Anamnesis. In the *Book of Common
Prayer (1549) it was incorporated into Anglican worship, but
omitted in the 1552 revision. However, numerous other revisions, e.g., American and Scottish, have retained it.

Shepard, Massey Hamilton, Jr. The Oxford American
    Prayer Book Commentary. New York: Oxford University Press, 1950. Pp. 80-81.

ANGLICAN CHANT (ML. Anglicanus, fr. Anglicus English,
    fr. Angli the English; OF. chanter, fr. L. cantare
    fr. canere to sing)

[Contents: (general); Early development; Later development; (bibliography).] The simple type of harmonized
melody employed by the Anglican Church (and by other English-speaking Protestant churches of similar communion)
for the singing of psalms and canticles and other unmetrical

texts is Anglican chant. Its main principles are those of the
psalm tones of Gregorian chant with the usual exclusion of
the intonation. Thus, a short harmonized melody is repeated
for each verse (or set of verses) of the text, the reciting
tone at the opening of each line being flexible to accommodate the varying numbers of syllables in the different lines.
The number of syllables sung on the reciting tone is determined by the two cadences, the mediation and the final,
which are usually sung syllabically. The basic purpose of
the Anglican chant is to make possible the singing of unmetrical texts in a free manner, preserving the irregular
rhythm of the words. Typically, Anglican chant consists of
a seven-measure harmonized melody, with a two-phrase
division of three and four measures.

Early Development

        The harmonizing of psalm tones in the practice known
as *fauxbourdon was quite common in the 16th century, as
seen in the works of Josquin des Prez and Vittoria.   Instances of this are also evident in the psalm tunes of Ravenscroft.   In England, many leading Elizabethan composers
(Tallis, Morley, Byrd, and Gibbons) produced fine examples
of fauxbourdon in their settings of the prose *psalms and
*canticles.   Yet, exactly when and who was responsible for
this phenomenon in Anglican church music cannot be accurately determined.
        Immediately after the Restoration, as choirs and
organs were reinstated into the service, cathedrals began
publishing works to explain the character of its service, including the use of harmonized *plainsong in the manner of
single Anglican chants.   Among these works were Lowe's
Short Directions of the Performance of the Cathedral Service
(1661), Clifford's The Divine Services and Anthems usually
sung in the Cathedrals and Collegiate Churches of the Church
of England (1664) and Playford's Restoration edition of Introduction to the Skill of Music (1674).   Most of the chants of
this period basically were the Anglicanization of the Gregorian
tones with the melody in the tenor.   Within a century, however, the plainsong tunes began to appear in the soprano part
as seen in Dr. Boyce's Cathedral Music (1760).

Later Development

        By the 18th century composers began producing their
own chant melodies.   This resulted in the weakening of good
chanting as bar-lines and definite time-values began to be

indicated along with the melody. Yet a certain amount of
elasticity was maintained in the performance to accommodate
the different lengths of the prose verses. In actual practice,
however, the music and texts became pressed into an accepted rigid accentuation where certain points of the chant
were invariably stressed, which method received the name,
the "Anglican thump." At this time, double chants (of 14-
measure lengths) became well known, their origin being
traceable to the Allison's Psalter (1599) and before. Their
use was to accommodate two verses of text instead of one,
thus providing greater variety. In more recent times,
triple and quadruple chants have been composed for use with
two or more psalms, a practice which created great complexity and confusion.

There also has existed a small quantity of "change-
able chants, " so called because of the flexible nature of the
mode which may be major or minor according to the mood
of the psalm or canticle.

Until the *Oxford Movement in the 19th century,
Anglican chanting was the sole property of the choirs in the
cathedrals and collegiate churches. However, with the introduction of surpliced choirs and the desire for a fully
choral service, brought about by the Oxford Movement in
the early and mid-19th century, the chanting slowly became
the property of almost every village church. This brought
about a need for a method of indicating to the ordinary
choirs which portions of the verse were to be recited and
which inflected. In 1837 the first attempt to solve this
problem was presented in printed form. The author was
Robert James, organist of Ely Cathedral. Other early attempts at directing the singers of Anglican chant through
asterisks, syllables printed in heavy type and bar-lines were
Hullah's Psalms with Chants (1844), the Psalter of the
S. P. C. K., edited by Turle (1865), the English Psalter
(1865), and the Psalter Accented (1872). However, with all
the confusion brought about by the many versions of pointing
and accentuation, each choir usually preferred and practiced
its own traditional way. With the introduction of local choir
festivals strong influence was brought upon the need for a
standard of uniform pointing. The most prominent and widely
used version then became The Cathedral Psalter (1875) in
which Sir John Stainer and Sir Joseph Barnby were among
the editors. During the 18th and 19th centuries many different versions of the chants by various composers appeared,
often with grave distortions to the texts. It would appear
that those composers had envisioned the chant as a composition to which words were fitted rather than a musical setting
serving the words.

At this time a second movement arose in the English
church with regard to chanting. This movement, headed by
Pickering, Redhead, Dyce, and Oakley, sought the reinstatement of plainsong. Attempts were made to revise and continue the work of John Merbecke (The Booke of Common
Praier Noted, 1550).

However, the renaissance of Anglican chant gained
its major impetus from Poet Laureate Robert Bridges, who
in 1912 wrote a pamphlet promoting the writing of chant
music fitted to the text. In his writings he provided a detailed analysis of the verbal rhythms of the English psalms
in light of the structure of Anglican chant. His efforts
gained practical support from Sir Hugh Allen who put Bridges'
principles to work at the New Oxford College chapel. By
1925 the Psalter Newly Pointed, published by the S.P.C.K.,
became the pioneering publication to promote this improved
style of chanting. Other psalters followed, the Oxford Psalter (1929) and the English Psalter, giving helpful suggestions
for chanting in village churches. Thus, a method for over-
hauling the metrical Anglican chant of the 18th and 19th centuries has become a moving force in the 20th century as
this style of chanting seeks to return to a more natural
speech rhythm and an effective communication of the psalms
in English as a mode of worship.

Ellinwood, Leonard, "Anglican Chant: Past and Present,"
    Church Music, 69.1 [sic]:14-18, 1969.
Honeychurch, Fred Arthur. "The Anglican Chant; A History
    of the Development of Harmonized Chanting." Unpub-
    lished M.S.M. thesis, Union Theological Seminary,
    New York, 1951.
Kelk, A. H. Singing of the Psalms and Canticles to Angli-
    can Chant. Shorter Papers of the Church Music So-
    ciety, No. 6. London: Oxford University Press, n.d.
Pearce, Charles William. "Futility of Anglican Chant," MQ,
    6:118-126, January, 1920.

ANTHEM (ME. antem, antefne, fr. OE. antefn, antefen,
    fr. ML. antefana, fr. L. GR. pron. of Gr. antiphona,
    neut. pl. of antiphonon antiphon, or anthem, fr. anti-
    phonos sounding contrary, returning a sound, fr. anti
    over against + phone sound, voice)

[Contents: (general); Origin, and early background;
Tudor Church music era (1500-1649); Commonwealth and
Restoration eras (1650-1730); Handelian era (1730-1800);

Early 19th-century anthem era (1800-1875); Victorian era
(1875-1920); America; 20th century (to the present); (bibliography).] In the broadest sense, any sacred choral composition, usually sung by a church choir, with words of a religious nature and of a relatively short duration can be classified as an anthem. More specifically, an anthem is a musical composition, accompanied or unaccompanied, of more
than one part (all parts being more complex than those of a
*hymn) with a sacred text in English, and an official but not
liturgical position in the service of the Anglican Church; a
position similar to that of the *motet in the Roman rite.
        According to form and style the anthem is divided into
two main categories: full anthems and *verse anthems. In
the category of full anthems, any anthem written for a whole
undivided choir, in polyphonic style (similar to the 16th-
century Latin motet) is considered a motet-anthem. However, if the choir is divided into groups and used in alternation, the nomenclature is antiphonal-anthem. Among the types
of verse anthems, those whose major text is presented by a
solo voice or voices with the chorus in a supporting role are
considered declamatory-anthems. While the same may be
true of the sectional-anthem, it will also have its sections
marked by some musical means as style or key. The largest type of this form is the *cantata-anthem which bears the
influence of the 17th- and 18th-century church *cantatas.
With this type the sectional-anthem is extended by means of
instrumental interludes, overtures, arias, recitatives, duets,
etc.

Origin and Early Background

        The anthem may be said to be the successor of the
*motet from which it developed. In fact, in its earliest
stages during the Reformation, many anthems were simply
translations of motets from Latin to English. Thus, the
history of this English phenomenon dates from the Reformation to the present, with a period of drought during the Civil
War. Following the belief of Luther, who thought music to
be second only to divinity, rather than Calvin, the anthem
was permitted as a part of the church service from the 16th
century. However, it was not until the 1662 revision of the
*Book of Common Prayer, during the reign of King Charles
II, that the rubric stood as it does today--after the third
*collect in *Morning Prayer and *Evening Prayer "in Quires
and Places where they sing, here followeth the Anthem."

Tudor Church Music Era (1500-1649)

The major portion of this period (1500-1625) is referred to as the contrapuntal unaccompanied anthem or motet
period. Two main sources surviving the upheavals of the
16th and 17th centuries are the British Museum Appendix
74-76 (containing 12 anthems) and the Wanley Manuscript.
From these materials, the anthems show a largely contrapuntal style with various phrases of the text set forth polyphonically by successive points of imitation, with the words
from the earliest voices being proportioned to terminate all
voices together at the end of the phrase, as in the motet.
During this period a conflict of styles is apparent between
musicians and churchmen; the former preferring the flexibility of the contrapuntal style, while the latter desired the
note-against-note structure for textual clarity.   Probably
the first printed collection of English Church Music is from
this period and style, John Day's Mornyng and Evenyng
Praier and Communion set forth ... (1565).
The performance practice of the day was mostly *a
cappella singing, though organ books for anthems were not
uncommon. However, they usually doubled the voice-parts,
sometimes only the outer voices. So, nothing would be lost
if the accompaniment was omitted.
The antiphonal-anthem, consisting of interspersed
passages for both sections of the choir and also passages
that would alternate between the two choruses in antiphonal
style, are characteristic of this period. For these anthems
the two semi-choruses, usually constituted in the same way
(SATB), were seated in two different choir stalls: one side,
the *cantoris, seated on the north side by the *precentor,
and the other, the *decani, seated on the south or dean's
side.
During this period, one of vicissitude from the Reformation, musicians found protection in the monarch's own
Chapel Royal, which provided the best opportunities for
music.
Early composers of this period, Robert Fayrfax
(c. 1460-1521) and John Tavener (c. 1495-1545), were concerned with pure melodic inventiveness, independence of imitative voices, and particularly long irregularly shaped phrases. Written in mostly "a5" and "a6" these modal anthems
no longer use a given melody to add unity.
On January 21, 1549, with the Act of Uniformity and
the complete break with the Roman Catholic Church in worship (including the use of Latin), a real need for new church
music arose in England. To meet this need, Christopher Tye

(c.1500-1572/3) became one of the finest Tudor composers
to write a number of high quality anthems. Because of his
understanding and use of counterpoint and the high standard
which he set for this form, Tye has been called the "father
of the anthem." It was he who gave the English motet-anthem its simple form with direct expression of idea, as con-
trasted with the Latin motet with its complex form containing
an indirect expression of ideas. Thus, the motet-anthem is
characterized by its predominant use of four voice-parts, in
motet-, familiar-, and mixed-styles, set syllabically with
simple harmonies and homo-rhythms, being directed toward
the understanding of the congregation rather than toward
heaven (King, 54-55). The division of the text into short
sections and the handling of each section in a note-against-
note style of canonic imitation, with regular harmonic cadences, further distinguish the English anthem. The technique of word-painting is also prominent.

Following Tye, Thomas Tallis (c. 1505-1585) refined
the anthem melodically, rhythmically and, to some extent,
formally. The "father of English church music," as he is
called, and the teacher of William Byrd incorporated more
daring harmonies (ascending sevenths resolving upward,
cross-relation) and achieved greater rhythmic flexibility
("Wherewithal shall a young man cleanse his way?" ECM,
II:8).

Possibly derived from the antiphonal anthems of
earlier English composers and the polychoral idea of the
Venetian School, the verse anthem (or solo anthem) emerged,
necessitating the use of accompanying instruments. The foremost pioneer of this form was William Byrd (1534-1623)--
see TCM, II--who is credited with the first verse anthem in
print. Twelve such anthems of his are extant ("Teach me,
O Lord," ECM, II:60). For his day he was a real innova-
tor, harmonically (skillfully using the augmented sixth
chords), rhythmically (through the employment of alternating
meters), and stylistically (being a master of word-painting).
It was from the experiments with this form by Tudor church
musicians (more marked changes in texture for musical contrast, addition of several movements for chorus, and an improved orchestra) that the *cantata-anthem of half a century
later was to evolve. At his highest level of expression,
Byrd surpassed all Tudor composers and dominated the entire field of music both on the Continent and in England during his life-time (King, 142).

Up to this time musicians were writing for both the
Roman and Anglican churches. With Orlando Gibbons (1583-
1625) this was not true; thus, giving him the title, "the father

of purely Anglican music." His anthems contain more expressions of action and human emotions than mysticism ("See, see, the Word is incarnate," ECM, II:198). His full anthems reveal more notes, more words, and more parts than any of the other composers of this era. He, with Byrd, further developed the anthem toward the rondo form (ABACA). During this time, the *verse-anthem usually followed this form: (1) each verse was introduced by a short instrumental section, often in stretto; (2) the solo voice (or voices) enters using the same subject, though not always; and (3) the chorus repeats, in whole or part, the words (King, 159).

Known more for his madrigals than his anthems, Thomas Weelkes (c.1575-1623) wrote some 45 extant anthems, most of which are in verse style. With his preference for a massive texture, he wrote usually for "a5 to a7" voices, rarely "a4" ("Give ear, O Lord," ECM, II:166). He excelled in the subject-answer relationships of the motet-style, foreshadowing the fugue. Yet, his anthems are most striking. Weelkes was in the precarious position of having to look backward as well as forward, concluding one era and anticipating another.

Another transitional composer was Thomas Tompkins (1572-1656), whose *Musica Deo Sacra (1668) contained 94 anthems. His full anthems varied widely in voicing, from "a3" to "a12," and his verse-anthems required a high standard of solo singing and virtuoso organ-playing. Known for his excellent wedding of text and music, Tompkins often repeated the last words of the phrase ends. ("Arise, O Lord unto thy resting place," ECM, II:143).

In 1641 Barnard's Church Music was published, being the first collection of anthem repertory in print.

Commonwealth and Restoration Eras (1650-1730)

From the influences of the secular music of the Commonwealth era--the use of independent movements for concerted instruments and the rise of the *aria for the vast solo sections in the *verse-anthem--the *cantata-anthem was destined to appear later in this era. Contributing to its arrival was Pelham Humphrey (1647-1674). His "O Lord my God, why hast Thou forsaken me" (ECM, III:36) illustrates the idiosyncrasy of the Restoration verse anthem to have several voices proclaim passages in quick succession. Other mannerisms of his anthems are the repetition of single words in an ejaculatory manner and the obtrusive use of the appoggiatura. His declamatory anthems are marked by virtuoso effects. In general, the Restoration anthems show a sensitivity

of musical rhythm dictated by text, an affective style of
melody, an enriched sonority and harmony, and a preference
to the concerto style (verse, chorus, verse, chorus) (King,
251).

John Blow (1648-1708) wrote anthems in each of the
styles of the day: full and verse (declamatory, sectional
and cantata). His full anthems ("Let my prayer come up, "
ECM, III:68) usually combined the motet and homophonic
styles in a basically syllabic treatment of the text. They
are pure vocal music without accompaniment and use slower
note values. Of his anthems, the declamatory type use
prose rather than poetic texts. They show a lack of melo-
diousness in favor of verbal directness, a peculiarity of
Restoration church music ("O Lord, Thou has searched me
out, " CM, III:239). Similar to the recitative and aria of
opera, the contrasting sections of declamation and lyricism
mark Blow's sectional anthems ("We will rejoice in thy salvation"). In these he will often change meter. Designed
for special occasions, such as coronations, the cantata-
anthems of Blow made use of the multi-sections and instrumental ritornelli and sinfonia of the Continental church cantatas ("God spake sometimes in various ways, " MB, VII:1).
This truly "concerted" music incorporated faster note values,
more melismas, mixed meters, and more daring harmonies;
truly dramatic in effect.

Contemporary with Blow was Henry Purcell (1658-
1695), who wrote 13 full anthems and 49 verse-anthems.
Through his anthems Purcell established two important links:
(1) his full anthems are in the polyphonic style of the inflec-
tional principles of the Elizabethans; and (2) his music served
as Handel's model in developing his English style (King, 303).
He added a new dimension in the English anthem, that of the
dramatic character of combining solo, ensemble and instrumental interludes in his verse-anthems together with superb
word-painting.   ("I will give thanks unto the Lord, " ECM,
III:95). This naturally demanded and gave rise to the virtuoso singer. The usual form of Purcell's verse anthems
became

Overture (lengthy duple, then triple)
Verse (usually men's voices, solo and combined)
Chorus
Ritornello
Verse
Ritornello
Repeat of opening symphony
Verse
Final chorus

Lesser composers of the Restoration Era were William Croft (1678-1727)--"O Lord, rebuke me not" (ECM, III:24); John Weldon (1676-1736)--"In Thee, O Lord, have I put my trust" (CM, II:202); Jeremiah Clarke (1673/4-1707)-- "He shall send down from on high" (ECM, III:122); and Dr. Benjamin Rogers (1614-1698)--"Teach me, O Lord" (CM, II:105).

Handelian Era (1730-1800)

While John Weldon was engrossed in the full anthem, Maurice Green (1696-1755) wrote almost exclusively in the verse-anthem style ("O clap your hands, " ECM, III:171). The custom of concluding with a chorus in fugal form (borrowed from the oratorio) was beginning to come into vogue. This was practically the only use of the ensemble since the solo sections were becoming the most important, to the near exclusion of the choir.

The chief contributions of George Frideric Handel (1685-1759) to anthem literature are the 12 Chandos Anthems, the "Coronation Anthem" (1727) and the two wedding anthems. The Chandos Anthems (1718-1720), are an example of Handel's frequent use of adaptation, parodying and expansion of pre-existing materials. These 12 anthems are neither typical of previous features of anthem construction nor of the future course of anthem literature. They are more like the German cantatas with a strong Italian influence in the solo sections. Handel even incorporated the use of chorales in three of them (Wienandt, 165-170).

The compiler of the valuable three-volume work, Cathedral Music, William Boyce (1710-1779) composed many anthems (full and verse) and much service music for the Anglican Church. He, like Greene, continued in the line of Purcell, though not so skillfully ("The heavens declare the glory of God, " ECM, III:204).

Written with theatrical considerations and for vocal display were the solo anthems of Henry Purcell ("Sing to the Lord") and Jeremiah Clark ("O Be Joyful"). Other composers contributing anthems to this era were Jonathan Battishill (1738-1801)--"O Lord, look down from heaven" (ECM, IV:9); William Hayes (1707-1777); James Kent (1700-1776); James Nares (1715-1783)--"The souls of the righteous" (ECM, III:225); Benjamin Cooke (1734-1793); and Samuel Arnold (1740-1802).

Early 19th-Century Anthem Era (1800-1875)

During the early 19th century the distinction of verse

and full anthems begins to change. Now, the full anthem incorporates the use of solo voices, however, within the continuous flow of the materials and not set apart by sections.
     With William Crotch (1775-1847) there was the begin-
nings of a written accompaniment. In his Ten Anthems
(after 1800) he went to the trouble of writing an organ part
in a few places, with the remainder left to a continuo part
as had been the custom. By the time of the anthems of
Thomas Attwood (1765-1838) an organ part is found ("Come
Holy Ghost," ECM, IV:21). However, in the case of Attwood's Cathedral Music, the accompaniments were arranged
by his godson, Thomas Attwood Walmisley (1814-1856). But
by the mid-19th century, written organ accompaniments were
commonplace, even when simply *colla parte. Attwood was
followed by Sir John Goss (1800-1880) and Samuel Sebastian
Wesley (1810-1876), both of whom made great strides toward
a new type of anthem--simple, forthright, uncomplicated for
the choir, yet challenging for the soloist. Basically syllabic,
traditional 19th-century harmony, rarely using solo material,
with the principal-melody in the top voice of the choir and
accompaniment, the anthems of this time met the needs of
the limited choral facilities in the churches. Both Attwood
and Goss are credited with the stabilizing of English church
music before a period when it would be tested by traditional-
ists (Wienandt, 347).
     Most prolific of this period is Sir Frederick Arthur
Gore Ouseley (1825-1889), who wrote at least seventy anthems. He favored the full anthem with no solos, often
writing for eight voice parts. Several of these eight-part
anthems are for double chorus (*cantoris and *decani) ("O
Saviour of the world," ECM, IV:130). All of his accompaniments are *colla parte.
     Though the texts for the anthems of this period came
largely from the Scriptures or other liturgical materials, a
new source of texts became available to this generation of
composers: the hymn, thus giving birth to the *hymn-anthem. Both Samuel S. Wesley ("Thou Judge of quick and
dead") and T. A. Walmisley used texts by Charles Wesley
and Isaac Watts (Wienandt, 348).

Victorian Era (1875-1920)

     This period of anthem history bears the influence of
three Continental composers: Mendelssohn, Gounod and
Spohr, whose seductive harmonies and incessant use of chro-
maticism induced the sensations of prettiness and sentimental
emotionalism to English church-goers. Not only were their

harmonies adopted as models for compositions, but excerpts from their oratorios were frequently used as anthems. Writing under this influence was John Stainer (1875-1901) whose "How beautiful upon the mountains" (ECM, IV:151) exemplifies the dominance of simple, sweet melodies over the text. Of lesser importance are the anthems of Sir Arthur Sullivan (1842-1900), who considered church music secondary to the theater ("O taste and see").

Of major importance is the renaissance of the church anthem started by C. Hubert H. Parry (1848-1918) and Charles Villiers Stanford (1852-1924). They reinstated the 16th- and 17th-century forms of the full and verse-anthems, returned to the dominance of the text and skillfully incorporated text-painting. Parry's "Hear my words, ye people" (ECM, IV:158) illustrates this craftsmanship as does Stanford's "The Lord is my Shepherd" (Fellows, 241-243). Later, Charles Wood (1866-1921) continued in the efforts of trying to raise the whole standard of cathedral music as the Victorian era came to a close.

Under the influence of the *Oxford Movement the anthem began employing both texts and tunes of the hymn, thus becoming the counterpart of the German chorale. Yet, many composers would still use only the texts (Noble's "Jesus, the very thought of Thee"). It was here that the hymn-anthem was firmly established and from which it was to grow in America.

America

The truly American anthem has its beginnings in a rather colloquial manner with the works of William Billings (1746-1800). His Bostonian primitivism, now treasured, shows a healthy vigor and rugged denial of European sophistication and polish ("When Jesus wept, " MA, 111). This trend was followed in the first American collection of original choral music, *Urania, by James Lyon. The materials contained within it mainly included psalm-tunes, *fuging tunes and anthems of popularity. The melody remained in the tenor (Wienandt, 349-350).

In opposition to Billings and Lyon were Andrew Law (1748-1821), who introduced shape-notes and lifted the melody to the soprano, and Oliver Holden (1765-1844) and Samuel Holyoke (1762-1820), trying to silence the exciting style of the fuging tune with their musically conservative collections of hymns and anthems (Daniel, 130). However, neither of these streams really lasted, since the genteel European tradition and training became quickly and strongly entrenched.

Imported from Bohemia, the American Moravian tradition fostered another line of anthem development. This
tradition of fine musical artistry produced many good anthems for chorus and orchestra--John Antes (1740-1811)
"Go, congregation, go!"; John Friedrick Peter (1746-1813)
"It is a precious thing." Being so ingrown, however, it
died out without influencing American composition.

To help America form its musical culture, Lowell
Mason (1792-1872) started compiling music by European
composers, putting English religious texts to them and calling them anthems. Thus, for him, the word "anthem" came
to mean "any religious part-song that is more extended than
a hymn" (Wienandt, 354).

America's first native-born choral composer was
Dudley Buck (1839-1909). His anthems carried the mark
of their day in church music--the long solo sections with
organ accompaniments, an outgrowth of the *quartet choir
(Wienandt, 354). A student of Buck was Harry Rowe Shelley
(1858-1947) who expanded the quartet anthem to its limits
("The King of Love, my Shepherd is"). Less influenced by
this phenomenon are the several anthems of Horatio Parker
(1863-1919).

20th Century (to the present)

With the increased popularizing of music in the church
service, particularly in America, the production of anthems
has become open to almost anyone. As a result, the caliber
of composition has not been equal to former generations.
Thus, many of the major composers have turned their backs
on the anthems as a form of composition.

In England, the names of Gustav Holst (1874-1934);
e.g., "Turn back, o man") and Ralph Vaughan Williams
(1892-1958; e.g., "O taste and see") are noteworthy of a
high standard of anthem. Outstanding examples on the
American scene are Leo Sowerby (1895-1968; e.g., "I will
lift up mine eyes"), Jean Berger (b.1901; e.g., "O give
thanks unto the Lord") and Alan Hovhaness (b.1911; e.g.,
"From the ends of the earth").

A particular growth in the teaching of new hymns and
*hymn tunes to the American congregations has produced a
growing interest in the *hymn-anthem. Whether it be good
or bad, it is present and seemingly fulfills its purpose.

In the mid-20th century much experimentation and innovation has entered the anthem form. Outstanding for the
promotion of jazz in church anthems is the *Twentieth Century Church Light Music Group; e.g., Malcolm Williamson

(b. 1913), "Procession of Palms" and "Come, ye thankful people come. " In another area of newness is the "Praise to God" by Knut Nystedt (b. 1915) which incorporates tone-clusters and choral <u>Sprechstimme</u>. Electronic and aleatory music can be seen in some of the anthems of R. Felciano ("Pentecost, " 1967). Whether these innovations will be accepted and developed in future years or left as they are, must be the decision of coming generations.

Daniel, Ralph T. <u>The Anthem in New England before 1800.</u>
      Evanston, Ill.: Northwestern University Press, 1966.
      _____. "English Models for the First American Anthems, " JAMS, 12:49-58, January, 1960.
Fellows, Edmund H. <u>English Cathedral Music</u>. London: Methuen, 1945.
Foster, Myles B. <u>Anthems and Anthem Composers</u>. London: Novello, 1901.
King, William Joseph. "The English Anthem from the Early Tudor Period through the Restoration Era. " Unpublished Ph.D. dissertation, Boston University Graduate School, Boston, Massachusetts, 1962.
Wienandt, Elwyn and Robert Young. <u>The Anthem in England and America</u>. New York: The Free Press, 1970.
      _____. <u>Choral Music of the Church</u>. New York: The Free Press, 1965.

ANTIPHON (ML. <u>antiphona</u>, fem. sing., fr. Gr. <u>antiphona</u>
      musical accord., sounding in response)

     The sacred text, generally a sentence taken from the scriptures, sung before and after a *psalm or *canticle as a refrain emphasizing the application of the psalm or canticle to the particular service is the antiphon.

     Historically, the antiphon probably originated from the method of presenting the psalms in early Hebrew worship. In the A.D. 100's, St. Ignatius introduced its use to the Western church, envisioning the angels singing in alternate choirs. It may be related also to the chorus in Greek drama or the Roman citharoedic chant. In the fourth century Ambrose, Bishop of Milan, produced a compilation of texts suitable for antiphonal singing. However, it was the antiphonaries, the collections or antiphons, compiled under Pope Gregory the Great that standardized the antiphons in the Roman church.

     With the Reformation, the use of the antiphon in the Lutheran church is attested to by the collection of hymns and

antiphons by Sixtus Dietrich (c. 1490-1548), one of the earliest outstanding composers for the Protestant liturgy. The
Anglican Church, on the other hand, abolished the use of
antiphons from its services, leaving nothing in the choral
portions of the service but the *anthem to mark the great
church festivals. However, with the advent of the *Oxford
Movement the antiphon slowly made its way back into the
Anglican liturgy. Many of the antiphons, particularly the
seven greater antiphons to the Blessed Virgin Mary, began
to appear in English translations for use as hymns. The
first of these was in John Newman's (1801-1890) Tracts for
the Time, No. 75, in 1837. The work of John Mason Neale
(1818-1866) reveals a similar trend in his translation and
compilation of several 12th-century antiphons into the hymn,
"Veni, veni Emanuel" ("O come, o come, Emanuel, " CH,
70).
        According to the American Book of Common Prayer
antiphons are prescribed for use in the office of *Morning
Prayer before and after the *Venite.
        Musically, the antiphon is an integral part of the
psalm, being sung to the same *psalm-tone. On festival
occasions the antiphons are "doubled, " i.e., they are sung
in their entirety before and after the psalm or canticle.
Otherwise, only the first few words of the antiphon introduce
the psalm, the complete antiphon being sung at the conclusion by all.

Neale, John M. Essays on Liturgiology and Church History.
        2d ed. London: R. F. Littledale, 1869.

ANTIPHONAL CHANT   (*antiphon + *chant)

        The singing of a *chant by two parts of a choir alter-
nately is called antiphonal chant. It is a common practice
in the Anglican Church for presenting the *psalms. However, when the alternation occurs between the officiant and
the choir the result is called "responsorial" chant.

Wellesz, Egon. Eastern Elements in Western Chant. Lon-
        don: Oxford University Press, 1947.

APOSTLE (ME. apostle, postle, fr. OF. apostle, aspostele,
        fr. apostolus fr. Gr. apostolus one sent forth or
        away, fr. apostellein to send away, fr. apo from +
        stellein to send)

Term used in early services for "epistle":   see
*Epistle.

ARIA   (It.: OF. air, G. aire, fr. L. aer air)

In opera, *oratorio, *cantata and *passion literature,
the accompanied vocal composition, usually for solo voice
and instrumental accompaniment, in which musical expres-
siveness dominates the text, is known as an aria; this being
in contrast to the heightened speech qualities of the *recitative.   The aria is often used to portray moments of contemplation, temporarily interrupting the dramatic motion.

The oratorios of Giacomo Carissimi (1605-1674) contained arias of a lyric character inclined toward the bel
canto style.   With the concentration on the virtuoso and
castrati the bel canto aria with its emphasis on the purely
musical aspects developed.   This is readily seen in the
Bologna and Modena composers among the oratorios of Alessandro Stradella (1642-1682) and Giovanni Barrista Vitali
(c. 1644-1692).

The development of the da capo aria, on the other
hand, is ascribed to Alessandro Scarlatti (1660-1725), student of Carissimi.   In the years after 1710, the aria normally appeared in three large sections, with the third part
like the first and the second of a distinctive character; thus
the third part was not written out but indicated by the words,
da capo ("from the beginning").

In the choral works of the Lutheran Reformation the
da capo aria found its place in the cantatas, oratorios and
passions.   The lyrical aria struggled with the *chorale for
predominance and won.   The key composers of this early
da capo aria in the cantata were Johann Kuhnau (1660-1722)
and Friedrich Wilhelm Zachow (1663-1712).   However, it
was in the masterful craftsmanship of J. S. Bach (1685-
1750), whose incorporation of the pietistic texts of Erdmann
Neumeister (1671-1756), that this form was brought to its
fullness.   Illustrative of this is the tenor aria, "Ich hore
mitten in dem Leiden," from Cantata 38, "Aus tiefer Not
schrei' ich zu dir" (BGA, VII:241f.).

Also bearing the expressive lyricism of the Italian
da capo aria were the arias of G. F. Handel's (1685-1759)
oratorios.   These show the last major usage of the form in
Protestant church music since the opera became the chief
musical form to employ the aria, and then in a differing
manner.

Godefroy, J. V. L. "Some Aspects of the Aria." ML,
    17:200, 1936.
Kretzschmar, Hermann. Geschichte des neuen deutsches
    Liedes. Vol. I. Leipzig: Breitkopf und Härtel, 1911.

ARIOSO (It. like an aria)

        A style of vocal music which is a compromise of the
*recitative and *aria is termed arioso up to and including
the time of J. S. Bach. Bach uses this form along with the
aria in the St. Matthew Passion (BGA, IV:1) to create an
ethereal and tender mood amid the dramatic tragedy of the
crucifixion.

Spitta, Philipp. Johann Sebastian Bach. Vol. I. New
    York: Dover Publications, 1951.

ASCRIPTION (L. ascriptio, fr. ascribere to ascribe, fr.
    ad to + scribere to write)

        The prescribed text following the *Preface of the
communion service and preceding the *Sanctus is the Ascription: "Therefore with Angels and Archangels, and with
all the company of heaven, we laud and magnify thy glorious
Name, evermore praising thee, and saying:".

Reed, Luther D. The Lutheran Liturgy. Philadelphia:
    Muhlenberg Press, 1947.

AUSBUND (G.)

        "A selected group of fine Christian songs, composed
in the Rassan Castle prison by the Swiss brethren, and by
other evangelical Christians here and there." This is the
full title (translated) of the first edition of the Swiss Anabaptist Hymnal (1564) which is commonly referred to by its ab-
breviated title, Ausbund. Contained in the second edition
(1583) were martyr songs by some of the early Anabaptist
leaders among its 130 hymns.
        According to Duerksen's study, the origin of the 73
tunes in the Ausbund breaks down in the following manner:
seven from plainsong, five from sequences, four from
*Leisen, three from Minnesinger repertoire, three from

Meistersinger songs, 41 from Lutheran sources, several
Marienlieder and an extensive use of folk tunes (Duerksen,
74f.). The melodic style of the monophonic unaccompanied
tunes, similar to the Lutheran *chorale, usually was limited
to an octave range. However, the texts tended to be quite
lengthy, up to 45 four-line stanzas. It is characteristic for
the Ausbund hymns to open with a declamation (look, behold,
listen, etc.) and to close with a benediction or doxology.
    The Anabaptist movement being a folk religion ex-
pressed itself in a folk-styled music, often lacking the artistic sense present in the hymn writing of the Lutherans.
However, it depicted the major doctrinal beliefs, musical
tastes and abilities of a large segment of Reformation peoples. The Ausbund has continued its tradition into the 20th
century remaining the basic hymnbook of the Amish community (Duerksen, 157).

Das Ausbund: Etliche schöne Christiche Lieder ... 13th ed.
    Lancaster County, Pa.: Verlag von den Amischen
    Gemeinden, 1962.
Bender, Harold S. "The First Edition of Ausbund," The
    Mennonite Quarterly Review, 3, April, 1929, 147-148.
Duerksen, Rosella R. "Anabaptist Hymnody of the Sixteenth
    Century." Unpublished D.S.M. dissertation, Union
    Theological Seminary, New York, 1955.

AUTOHARP (Gr. auto, fr. autos self, same + ME. harpe,
    fr. OE. hearpe)

    An autoharp is a zither-like instrument used primarily
for accompanying simple folk-type melodies. The simple
chord-sounds are achieved by depressing one of the special
bars provided, dampening all the strings except those required for the chord, and strumming all the strings with a
finger or plectrum. The most popular varieties come with
12 or 15 bars. Melodies may be plucked by more competent
performers.
    Invented by Charles Zimmerman, an immigrant to
Philadelphia in 1881, the "automatic harp" (as it was originally called) was to be a musical instrument that would be
easy for most people to play.
    Because of its portable nature and easiness to learn
to play the autoharp became an important American folk instrument. It has been used in homes for entertainment and
recreation, by itinerant preachers for congregational singing
among the mountain-folk (known to them as the "mountain
piano"), and by teachers for singing in the classroom.

With the multiple choir ministries in the mid-20th-
century Protestant churches, the autoharp has become a
helpful tool especially among the children's choirs.

Peterson, Meg. The Many Ways to Play the Autoharp.
    2 vols. Union, N.J.: Oscar Schmidt-International,
    1966.

BALLAD (ME. balade, fr. OF. balade, fr. Pr. balada a
    dancing song, fr. balar to dance, fr. LL. ballare)

A song which relates a story in simple verse and
tune of anonymous authorship, being sustained through oral
tradition is a ballad. Its main distinction from the *carol
is that it lacks the *burden which is so characteristic of
the carol.
    While the ballad and its associated dancing were
largely expressive of non-Christian themes and attitudes,
the Christian ideas slowly made their way into the ballad
as Northern Europe experienced the conversion (c. seventh
century) by the Roman Catholic Church. Realizing the
power and potential of folklore, Gregory the Great (c. 540-
604) instructed his missionaries to adapt the existing native
customs and to instill in them Christian teaching. Thus,
the monks responded with sacred legends in ballad form,
stories from the Bible and the Apocrypha. This use of
secular song baptized for the purposes of the missionary-
evangelist has been a familiar one throughout history: the
*fa-so-la white spirituals of the *camp meeting, the *con-
trafacta of Luther's Reformation, and the *spirituals of the
Negro.
    Among the oldest ballads influenced by Christian lit-
erature are the 13th-century "Judas" and the 15th-century
"St. Stephen and Herod" (Wells, 180). One of the best
known Christianized ballads is "The Cherry Tree Carol"
(OBC 66), which was associated with the 15th-century mystery plays. The ballads existed not only in Europe but also
in the rural settlements of America where the influence of
the revivalist was so strongly felt. "The Little Family" is
one such naive expression, centered around the life of Jesus
(Wells, 190).

Bryant, Frank E. A History of English Balladry. Boston:
    R. G. Badger, 1913.

Jackson, George Pullen. White Spirituals in the Southern
    Uplands. Chapel Hill: University of North Carolina
    Press, 1933. Chapter 16.
Schinham, Jan Philip, ed. The Music of the Ballads. Dur-
    ham, N.C.: Duke University Press, 1957.
Sharp, Cecil J. English Folk Songs from the Southern
    Appalachians. Ed. by Maud Karpeles. 2 vols. Lon-
    don: Oxford University Press, 1932.
Wells, Evelyn Kendrick. The Ballad Tree: A Study of
    British and American Ballads, Their Folklore, Verse,
    and Music. London: Methuen, 1950.

BASSO CONTINUO (It.) see THOROUGH-BASS

BASSO SEQUENTE (It.)

        The organ part (accompaniment) which duplicates in
detail the lowest sounding voice part in a composition is
known as the basso sequente. It came into use in the late
16th century. However, it was a common practice in the
17th-century English *verse-anthems of Aldrich, Humfrey,
Turner, and Blow. (Cf. *thorough-bass.)

Keller, Hermann. Thoroughbass Method. Trans. and ed.
    by Carl Parrish. New York: W. W. Norton, 1965.
Schneider, Max. Die Anfänge des Basso continuo and seiner
    Bezifferung. Leipzig: Breitkopf and Härtel, 1918.

BAY PSALM BOOK

        "The Whole Booke of Psalms Faithfully Translated
into English Metre ... 1640." This title denotes the book
known as the Bay Psalm Book or New England Psalm Book.
It was basically the work of John Cotton, John Eliot, Robert
Mather and Thomas Welde. The Bay Psalm Book was the
first book to be published in the American colonies. It was
not until the ninth edition (1698) that it appeared with tunes,
this edition being the first extant book with music printed in
North America. This edition contained 13 tunes, mostly in
two-part harmony and in common meter. (See also *psalmody, metrical (America).)

The Bay Psalm Book. Chicago: University of Chicago
    Press, 1956 (facsimile ed.).

Heraszti, Zoltan. The Enigma of the Bay Psalm Book.
     Chicago: University of Chicago Press, 1956.

BEICHT-VESPER (G.)

     The service of confession preparatory to the recep-
tion of the Holy Communion in the 19th century, offered as
an attempt by churchly communities to restore the observance of several of the historical *Canonical Hours is known
as the Beicht-Vesper. This 19th-century revival of the ancient office of *Vespers to Lutheran schools and deacones-
ses' institutions, and less generally to congregations developed the use of the *litany instead of the *Magnificat.

Reed, Luther D. Worship. Philadelphia: Muhlenberg
     Press, 1959.

BENEDICITE OMNIA OPERA (L.)

     The Benedicite omnia opera is the *canticle from the
"Song of the Three Holy Children," verses 35-65 of the
ninth book of the Apocrypha, which is usually sung in the
office of *Morning Prayer of the Anglican Church from Septuagesima Sunday to Easter and often during Advent as an
alternative to the *Te Deum laudamus. These two canticles
are the only portions of their kind in the Anglican services
not taken from the canonized Scriptures.

     "O all ye works of the Lord, bless ye the Lord:
     praise him, and magnify him for ever. O ye Angels
     of the Lord, bless ye the Lord: praise him, and
     magnify him for ever.

     "O ye Heavens, bless ye the Lord: praise him and
     magnify him for ever. O ye Waters that be above the
     firmament, bless ye the Lord: praise him, and mag-
     nify him for ever. O all ye powers of the Lord, bless
     ye the Lord: praise him and magnify him for ever.
     O ye Sun and Moon, bless ye the Lord: praise him
     and magnify him for ever. O ye Stars of heaven, bless
     ye the Lord: praise him and magnify him for ever.
     O ye Showers and Dew, bless ye the Lord: praise him,
     and magnify him for ever. O ye Winds of God, bless
     ye the Lord: praise him, and magnify him for ever.
     O ye Winter and Summer, bless ye the Lord: praise
     him, and magnify him for ever. O ye Dews and Frosts,

bless ye the Lord: praise him, and magnify him for
ever. O ye Frosts and Cold, bless ye the Lord:
praise him, and magnify him for ever. O ye Ice and
Snow, bless ye the Lord: praise him, and magnify
him for ever. O ye Nights and Days, bless ye the
Lord: praise him, and magnify him for ever. O ye
Light and Darkness, bless ye the Lord: praise him,
and magnify him for ever. O ye Lightnings and
Clouds, bless ye the Lord: praise him, and magnify
him for ever.

"O let the Earth bless the Lord: yea, let it praise
him, and magnify him for ever. O ye Mountains and
Hills, bless ye the Lord: praise him, and magnify
him for ever. O all ye Green Things upon the earth,
bless ye the Lord: praise him, and magnify him for
ever. O ye Wells, bless ye the Lord: praise him,
and magnify him for ever. O ye Seas and Floods,
bless ye the Lord: praise him, and magnify him for
ever. O ye Whales, and all that moves in the waters,
bless ye the Lord: praise him, and magnify him for
ever. O all ye Fowls of the air, bless ye the Lord:
praise him, and magnify him for ever. O all ye
Beasts and Cattle, bless ye the Lord: praise him,
and magnify him for ever. O ye Children of Men,
bless ye the Lord: praise him, and magnify him for
ever.

"O let Israel bless the Lord: praise him, and magnify
him for ever. O ye Priest of the Lord, bless the
Lord: praise him and magnify him for ever. O ye
Servants of the Lord, bless ye the Lord: and Souls
of the Righteous, bless ye the Lord: praise him, and
magnify him for ever. O ye holy and humble Men of
heart, bless ye the Lord: praise him, and magnify
him for ever.

"Let us bless the Father, and the Son, and the Holy
Ghost: praise him, and magnify him for ever" [BCP].

Proctor, Francis and W. H. Frere. A New History of the
    Book of Common Prayer. London: Macmillan, 1955.
    PP. 380-384.

BENEDICTION (L. Benedictio, fr. benedicere to bless, fr.
    bene well + dicere to say)

    The form of blessing of prayer pronounced upon the

faithful at the conclusion of a worship service is commonly
called a benediction. It is usually and most often said by a
minister. In the Lutheran liturgy the Aaronic benediction
(Numbers 6:24-26) is used as instituted by Martin Luther in
his *Deutsche Messe (1526). The Swedish liturgy follows the
Aaronic form with a Trinitarian formula ("In the Name of
the Father, and of the Son, and of the Holy Ghost"), which
has been incorporated into the common liturgy of 1958.

   The Anglican *Book of Common Prayer uses the
Pauline benediction (Philippians 4:7) amplified with "And the
Blessing of God Almighty ..." for the service of Holy Communion, and the 2 Corinthians 13:14ff. for *Morning Prayer
and Evening Prayer (*Vespers).

   Among less liturgical congregations the final prayer
invoking God's blessing upon the faithful before departing is
referred to as the benediction or dismissal prayer.

Reed, Luther D. The Lutheran Liturgy. Philadelphia:
      Muhlenberg Press, 1947.
Shepherd, Massey Hamilton, Jr. The Oxford American
      Prayer Book Commentary. New York: Oxford Uni-
      versity Press, 1950.

BENEDICTUS (L.)

   (1) The song of Zacharias taken from Luke 1:68-79
is the Gospel *canticle for the office of *Matins and *Morning Prayer. In Matins it is the substitute for the *Te Deum,
while in Morning Prayer it may be alternated with the *Jubilate (Deo). It is traditionally sung to ancient *psalm-tones
or to double *Anglican chants.

      "Blessed be the Lord God of Israel; for he hath visited
      and redeemed his people; And hath raised up a mighty
      salvation for us, in the house of his servant David; As
      he spake by the mouth of his holy Prophets, which have
      been since the world began; That we should be saved
      from our enemies, and from the hand of all that hate
      us.

      "To perform the mercy promised to our forefathers,
      and to remember his holy covenant; To perform the
      oath which he sware to our forefather Abraham, that
      he would give us; That we being delivered out of the
      land of our enemies might serve him without fear; In
      holiness and righteousness before him, all the days of
      our life. And thou, child, shalt be called the prophet

of the Highest: for thou shalt go before the face of the
Lord to prepare his ways; To give knowledge of salvation unto his people for the remission of their sins,
Through the tender mercy of our God: whereby the
day-spring from on high hath visited us; To give light
to them that sit in darkness, and in the shadow of
death, and to guide our feet unto the way of peace"
[BCP].

(2) The Benedictus qui venit, also called the Benedictus, is from Matthew 21:9 and comprises the second portion of the *Sanctus in the service of Holy Communion.
Though originally a part of the Anglican service in the *Book
of Common Prayer (1549), it was omitted in the 1552 revision. The *Deutsche Messe (1526) of Martin Luther secured
its place in Lutheran liturgy. As an *anthem it has been a
fruitful text for Palm Sunday. "Blessed is He that cometh in
the Name of the Lord; Hosanna in the highest. "

Proctor, Francis and W. H. Frere. A New History of the
     Book of Common Prayer. London: Macmillan, 1955.
Reed, Luther D. The Lutheran Liturgy. Philadelphia:
     Muhlenberg Press, 1947.

"BLACK RUBRIC"

The declaration by the Order of Council (1552) after
the rubrics at the end of the communion service in the Anglican *Book of Common Prayer (1549) on kneeling, stating that
kneeling was the proper posture for receiving communion;
and also on the communion elements, stating that "corporal
presence" be substituted for "real and essential presence, "
became known as the "Black Rubric. " It came about, in
part, as a reaction to the unofficial communion practices of
John Knox and his strong preaching against kneeling to receive communion. The inclusion of this order in the Second
Book of Common Prayer (1552) under Edward VI had several
other reactions, not the least of these being the deletion of
singing in the church service. This had the long-lasting
effect of silencing Merbecke's new services in The Booke of
Common Praier Noted (1550), a work which during the Tractarian movement finally received its due recognition.

Proctor, Francis and W. H. Frere. A New History of the
     Book of Common Prayer. London: Macmillan, 1955.
Stevenson, Robert M. Patterns of Protestant Church Music.
     Durham, N.C.: Duke University Press, 1953. Ch. 3.

BOOK OF COMMON PRAYER

The book required for the performance of the services in the Church of England and other Anglican churches is the Book of Common Prayer (or, Prayer Book). Basically there were two major influences upon the construction of the Book of Common Prayer: the long history of the Roman Catholic liturgies and liturgical books, and the long series of Lutheran Kirchenordnungen inaugurated by Martin Luther in 1523. Among the greatest of the Roman influences has been the *Sarum Use of Salisbury Cathedral.

With the creation and use of the "Bible in English" (c.1535), the desire for the liturgy to be in the vernacular was a logical progression. Already the new edition of the Sarum Breviary (1541) carried distinct marks of England's break with Rome. Thus, work began on a liturgy expressive of the Church of England. The first change by Archbishop Cranmer came in 1544 with the *litany in English. Following several experimental publications (among them being King Henry's Primer, 1545), an order for communion was approved (1548). In 1549 the first Book of Common Prayer was finally adopted and placed into service through the Act of Uniformity, 1549.

The contents of this first Prayer Book replaced the several liturgical volumes necessary in the Roman Church. The offices of *Morning Prayer and Evening Prayer (*Vespers) corresponded to the breviary; the contents of the communion office to the missal; special offices (baptism, burial, etc.) to the manual; and the table of lessons and the full text of the psalms replaced the lectionary and psalter. All of the above plus a calendar of main feast days was included in this first volume.

Because of the close association of music with the old Latin services, a strong desire for a musical setting of the first Prayer Book was soon felt. The syllabic simplification of the traditional plainsong melodies for these English texts was achieved by John Merbecke in The Booke of Common Praier Noted, 1550.

Because of much controversy and the failure of uniformity, a second Prayer Book was produced in 1552. Its contents were not drastically altered from the first book, but it included simple changes and additions in order and theology. This new version and its adoption stifled the acceptance of Merbecke's newly published setting, leaving it to the late 19th century to be resurrected to a position of integrity. (This resurrection was initiated by John Stainer's Cathedral Prayer Book, 1891.)

Upon the death of Edward VI, one year later, the Book of Common Prayer was declared void as Mary ascended the throne. However, with the reign of Elizabeth beginning in 1558, the Prayer Book gained a more firm foothold in England than when it was first introduced. During this period and for the next century, the Book of Common Prayer was to undergo only minor variations.

That musical settings of the Anglican services were published is attested to by John Day's Certain Notes set forth in foure and three parts to be song (1560), and his Morning and Evening Prayer and Communion set forthe in foure parts to be song in churches. However, no one setting of the services received any official sanction. Following another stormy period of rebellion the Prayer Book was again introduced and revised, this time in 1662 during the reign of Charles II. This volume, containing some 600 alterations over the previous version, brought a greater unity to the Anglican Church not previously achieved, being translated into over 100 different languages. Among the dissenters, however, were the churches of Scotland, Ireland and America. The latter two, mostly for political reasons, revised the 1662 edition of the Prayer Book and issued their own. The Church of Ireland completed their version in 1877; whereas the American Prayer Book was printed in 1786, three years before the United States Constitution, (revised in 1892).

Brightman, F. E. The English Rite. London: Rivingtons, 1915.

Procter, Francis and Walter Howard Frere. A New History of the Book of Common Prayer. London: Macmillan, 1955.

Shepherd, Massey Hamilton, Jr. The Oxford American Prayer Book Commentary. New York: Oxford University Press, 1950.

BOY CHOIRS (ME. boi, perh. akin to D. boef, Fris. boi, boy, G. bube, ON. bofi rogue + *choir)

The incorporation of young unchanged male voices in choral music for unison (soprano) or part-singing (soprano and alto) is known as the boy choir. Currently three types of choirs incorporating boys' voices exist: the choir of men and boys, the boys' choir within the church, and the concert boys' choir.

Historically boy choirs can be traced back to 476 B.C.

when they were used to honor the winners of the 14th Olympic
Games. The choirs in temple and early Christian worship
were comprised of all male voices. Tradition states that
Pope Sylvester (reigned 314-335) established a school to edu-
cate boy choristers in the fourth century (Tuten, 1). However, St. Hilary, Bishop of Rome (461-467) is credited with
establishing the first schola cantorum. The duty of these
choristers was primarily that of singing in the church choir.
The idea of the clear young male voice in chorus quickly
spread from Rome throughout western Europe. In England,
in particular, resident and non-resident choir schools and
collegiate choirs were established in the cathedrals. Among
the oldest existing boy choirs were those of St. Thomaskirche,
Leipzig and Salisbury Cathedral, both dating from the 13th
century.

The earliest establishment of the male choir in the
United States was recorded to have been at Trinity Church,
New York, in 1761 (unvested) and at St. Michaels, Charles-
ton, South Carolina, in 1798 (vested) (Tuten, 2). However,
it was during 1840-1860 and following, under the influence
of the *Oxford Movement, that the boy choir system of the
Church of England was adopted into the Anglican churches of
America, as at the Church of the Advent, Boston.

In the 20th century the boy choir movement has existed
in a state of flux, many of the church choirs having been dissolved for one reason or another. However, one of the key-
notes of this century has been the Wa-Li-Ro Choir School
(founded 1933), a summer camp devoted to the training of boy
choristers. Since the advent of the Vienna Boychoir American tours (the first in 1932) a number of concert boy choirs
have organized in the United States, including the Columbus
Boychoir (1937), the Mitchell Boychoir (c.1940), the Texas
Boy Choir (1946), the Atlanta Boy Choir (1956) and the Berk-
shire Boy Choir (1967) (Root, 116).

Of special interest is the emphasis on training the
cambiata voice, fostered by Irving Cooper.

Cooper, Irving. Letters to Pat. New York: Carl Fischer,
    1953.
The Diapason, 59, April, 1968 (devoted to the boy choir
    movement).
Moritz, James. "Boychoir Discography," Music AGO /RCCO,
    4:28-32, August, 1970.
Nicholson, S. H. Boy Choirs. London: Paterson Publica-
    tions, n.d.
Noble, T. Tertius. The Training of the Boy Chorister.
    New York: G. Schirmer, Inc., 1943.

Norden, N. Lindsay. "Boy-Choir Fad," MQ, 3:189-197,
     April, 1917.
Parish, Carl. "A Renaissance Music Manual for Choirboys,"
     Aspects of Medieval and Renaissance Music, ed. Jan
     LaRue. New York: W. W. Norton, 1966.
Root, Arlene V. Root. "Boychoirs: A Brief History,"
     Choristers Guild Letters, 20:107, February, 1969.
Tuten, Elizabeth Armes. "The Boy Choir in the Non-Litur-
     gical Church." Unpublished M.S.M. thesis, Union
     Theological Seminary, New York, 1942.

BRASS CHOIRS

        The performing ensemble composed of three or more
brass instruments may be termed a brass choir or brass
ensemble (in German, Stadtpfeifer, city pipers, Posaunenchor, trombone choir). Originating from the use of brass
instruments for signal purposes, military marches and festive occasions, the Stadtpfeifer or Türmer (tower musicians)
of the 15th and 16th centuries slowly gained a place of recognition in Protestant church music. The suggested year for
the commencement of responsible tower-playing is 1584. The
music performed was primarily four-part chorale settings,
specially composed sonatas or groups of dance movements
(Ode, 4). Outstanding composers for the Baroque Stadtpfeifer
music were Johann Pezel (1639-1695) and Gottfried Reiche
(1667-1734). Pezel's writings for tower playing are readily
available (Türmmusiken, DdT, LXIII); whereas, the only extant brass music of Reicha is the 24 Neue Quatricinia, four-
part compositions in fugal style for one cornet and three
trombones (published in Buffalo: Ensemble Publications).
Throughout the Baroque period the quantity of vocal and instrumental music from the Lutheran church has provided a
monumental legacy for church music.
        With the ebbing of the church as a patron of the arts
in the Classic and Romantic eras, the brass instruments
followed the major movement of music from the church to
the concert hall. However, in 1843 a Posaunenchor (one
keyed bugle and three trombones) was organized in West-
phalia. This marked the beginning of a movement of amateur brass instrumentalists who sought to return the use of
instruments in worship. Since these amateur musicians possessed limited technique their basic repertoire was primarily
songs and *hymns in a vocal style (Ode, 6). With its growth
in the 20th century the Posaunenchor movement has become
of increasing importance in German Evangelical church music.

Its new repertoire consists of processionals and recessionals, preludes and postludes, chorale settings and accompaniments for organ, choir and congregation. For nearly two centuries (1660-1860) in England the instrumental music in the village churches was primarily the task of the *Old Church Gallery Minstrels, whose ensembles included brass instruments as well as other types. In America, on the other hand, it was the brass choirs of the Lutheran and Moravian congregations (in particular, the trombone choir of the Moravian church at Bethlehem, Pennsylvania) which maintained these instruments in Protestant worship. Twentieth-century American Protestant churches are continuing to realize the growing potential of the brass choir in the life of the church as a means to praise God. Thus, more literature is becoming readily available.

Honemeyer, K. Die Posaunenchor im Gottesdienst. Gütersloh: Rufer-Verlag, 1951.
Mergenthaler, Wilhelm, Paul Beinhauer and Richard Lorcher. Handreichungen für Posaunenbläser. Wuppertal: Aussaat, 1964.
Ode, James. Brass Instruments in Church Services. Minneapolis: Augsburg Publishing House, 1970.
Schieber, Ernst. "Blasmusik im Gottesdienst, " MK, 11: 174-178, July-August, 1939.

BREVIARY see SARUM BREVIARY

BURDEN (ME. burdown the bass in music, fr. OF. bourdon, fr. ML. burdo drone, bumblebee)

The *chorus or motto to a *stanza of a carol is a burden. It denotes the basic distinction between the *ballad and the *carol, the former being without the burden. Often the burden is in the language of the day.

CAESURA (L. a cutting off, a division, stop, fr. cadere, caesum to cut off)

The pause or break marking the rhythmic point of division in a melodic line or line of a hymn is the caesura. As a rule, each of the first three lines in a stanza of a

Sapphic-metered hymn (11.11.11. 5) normally has a caesura after the fifth syllable; thus, the meter is essentially 5. 6 5. 6 5. 6 5. Basically, the caesura has been intended to indicate what generally can be sung in one breath.

CALL TO PRAYER (ME. callen, fr. OE. caellian; akin to
        OHG. kallen to call + Me. preire, fr. OF. preiere,
        fr. assumed VL. precaria, fr. L. precarius got by
        prayer, fr. precari to pray)

A sentence, such as "The Lord is nigh unto them that call upon Him in truth, " sung by the choir before the pastoral prayer, acting as its preparation is spoken of as the call to prayer.

CALL TO WORSHIP (Me. callen, fr. OE. Ceallian; akin to
        OHG. kallon to call + *worship)

A spoken (by the minister) or sung (chorally) phrase addressed to the congregation, inviting them to share in the service of worship is a call to worship (cf. *introit). The call to worship usually begins with an ascription to the majesty of God.

CAMP MEETING (F. , fr. It. campo, fr. L. campus plain,
        field, depression + fr. OE. mot, gemot meeting)

The socio-religious institution initiated around the turn of the 19th century which presented the message of repentance and "the new life" to the frontier society of America through a four-or-more-day encampment, each person or family providing for his own physical needs--food and lodging--has received the name camp meeting.
        Among the forerunners of the camp meeting were the early out-door Methodist meetings called "fielding meetings" and the grosse Versammlungen of the German-speaking Lutherans and Methodists in frontier Pennsylvania. It was a natural outgrowth, as well, of the gatherings and protracted meetings of the itinerant preachers who traveled the countryside on horseback. The earliest known use of the term "camp meeting" in print was in 1775 by John Waller, a Baptist preacher.
        However, the first genuine camp meeting occurred in July of 1800 at Gasper River in Logan County, Kentucky, a

meeting lasting from Saturday evening to Tuesday morning.
Under the leadership of the Presbyterian preacher, James
McGready, and his associates, this four-day meeting with
the Lord's Supper observed on Sunday set the norm for all
encampments of this "Second Great Awakening" (Sims, 24).
Among the standard elements which composed these meetings
were the presence of multitudes of people, impassioned
preaching in the open air, emotional demonstrations among
the congregation, a frantic seeking and finding of salvation,
and "camping-out" by families. Many of the participants
gathered from as far as one hundred miles, arriving by
horseback and wagon. Once at the site, they arranged the
camp in a square, the platform and pulpit in the center,
hewn logs arranged in rows around the platform for seating,
and the wagons on the outside, in the fashion of a "wagon
city." These non-denominational and interracial gatherings
grew to enormous sizes of 25,000 people with 30 preachers
(Hooper, 86). The camp meetings of the "Kentucky Revival"
(1800-1805), having spread all over the United States from
North to South, caused such a growth in the various denominations that the Baptists, Methodists, and Presbyterians began to become self-sufficient and to conduct their own denominational camp meetings, the forerunner of the summer
conferences. By 1840, with the innovations of the wooden
auditorium, dining rooms and two-story cottages, at the
"New Fashioned Camp Meeting" in the eastern states, the
preaching became more organized and the congregational behavior more subdued (Sims, 83). As the late 19th and early
20th centuries came the camp meetings gave way to the pro-
tracted meetings, thus, fading from view. In Illinois as
well as other sections of the Midwest camp meetings have
continued to exist among various denominations, particularly
at conference grounds.

The camp meeting resulted from conditions thought by
religious leaders to be prevalent in America and similar to
those in England at the time of the Wesley Revival: the
lower-class citizens were being neglected by the institutional
church; society was in a state of moral depravity and spiritual
misery; the established religious institutions appeared indifferent or inactive to society; and the message of the church
was being clothed in sentimentalism.

From the beginning of the encampment movement
singing played an important role, not only as a vehicle of
communication but also as an emotional release. Often the
singing and praying was accompanied by dancing exercises
such as the "jerk" and "falling," particularly at the time of
conversion and infilling of the Spirit. The style of singing

is reported to have been very loud, the men singing the tune with the women "harmonizing" a subordinant part an octave higher. Since musical knowledge was limited, variations from the printed page were the norm in the performance of the songs, particularly as the emotional level of the meeting heightened.

Exactly what songs were sung at the first camp meetings is nowhere recorded. However, Gilbert Chase speculates that The Pocket Hymn Book (Philadelphia, 1797) was probably used (Chase, 208). Among the early collections of the evangelical hymnody used at the encampments were Henry Allison's Hymns and Spiritual Songs (1802), David Mintz's Spiritual Song Book (1805), John C. Totten's A Collection of the most admired hymns and spiritual songs, with the choruses affixed as usually sung at camp-meetings (1809) and Thomas S. Hinde's The Pilgrim Songster (1810). The latter book, being one of the best-known camp song books, shows great variation of both tunes and texts among its different editions; thus, indicating reliance on oral tradition by which the songs were transmitted in the frontier country (Johnson, 194, 195). Despite the vast quantity of song books being published there was a shortage. Thus, the leaders would often cut up the hymnbooks and distribute the pages for memorization. They also practiced the art of "*lining-out the hymn" a technique which aided the illiterate greatly.

Among the early hymns are found works of Watts and Wesley, but the homespun hymnody of the people was more satisfying to the new religious conditions of the camp meeting. These were such things as religious ballads, hymns of praise and revival spirituals. The religious ballads, not new to history, were composed for the soloist who sought to relate some biblical narrative, scriptural giant, or even his own personal religious experience, frequently sung during the altar call (the mourner's song). Abounding in joy, the hymns of praise related the evangelical fervor of the converts and communicants as they might sing "Come, thou fount of every blessing, tune my heart to sing thy grace." The brand new song of the camp meeting, however, was the revival spiritual, a result of textual simplification. Often spontaneous, these rhythmic and graphic religious folksongs combined common religious phrases with the everyday language of the people. The contagious nature of them was due in part to their extensive use of repetition and reliance on old British folk tunes common to all (Johnson, 196-201).

Of the types of revival spirituals, those incorporating a shortened stanza of a traditional 18th-century hymn with an added chorus of the same length represent the least change from traditional hymnody.

On Jordan's stormy banks I stand...
I'm bound for the promised land....

Thus, it became possible for all to join in the chorus while
only a few might sing the stanza (Johnson, 201-203). This
idea is seen modified in the call-response type where the
chorus is interpolated after each verse-line.

Call: Remember sinful youth, you must die!
Response: You must die! etc.

A simpler form was the stanza with much repetition, requiring a change of one word or phrase of poetry for subsequent stanzas. These songs centered on persons and biblical
heroes.

Oh where is good old Noah? (three times)
Safe in the promised Land.

The dialogue or antiphonal songs provide the congregation
with a set reply to the verse-form question of the leader,
a technique of alternation reminiscent of the "lining-out"
practice.

Leader: "Hail you! and where are you bound for?
Hallelujah!
Response: Oh, I'm bound for the land of Canaan,
Hallelujah!"

Among the later song books to continue the homespun
hymnody of the frontier camp meeting were John Wyeth's
Repository of Sacred Music (1810), William Walker's Southern
Harmony (1835) and B. F. White's Sacred Harp (1844). Many
of these oblong-shaped collections were found in the cabins of
the frontier where they were used in the family prayer service.
Few, if any, camp meeting hymnody texts have survived in the present-day hymnody. However, many of the
tunes have been incorporated into worship as well as having
been the inspiration for larger symphonic works by contemporary composers.

Chase, Gilbert. America's Music: from the Pilgrims to
the Present. Rev. 2d ed. New York: McGraw-Hill,
1966. Chapter 11.
Hooper, William Lloyd. Church Music in Transition. Nash-
ville: Broadman Press, 1963.
Jackson, George Pullen. Spiritual Folk-Songs of Early
America. New York: J. J. Augustin Publishers, 1937.
Johnson, Charles A. The Frontier Camp Meeting; Religion's
Harvest Time. Dallas: Southern Methodist University
Press, 1955.

Sims, John N.   "The Hymnody of the Camp Meeting Tradition." Unpublished D.S.M. dissertation, Union Theological Seminary, New York, 1960.

CANONICAL HOURS

In the Roman Catholic Church the services of Scripture and prayer, said or sung eight times a day at prescribed hours, are known as daily hours, office hours, divine office, or Canonical Hours--Matins, Lauds, Prime,
Terce, Sext, None, Vespers and Compline. Among the
Protestant churches of the Anglican and Lutheran communions, however, the term (in German, Stundenofficium) refers to the two services of prayer and praise known as
*Morning Prayer and Evening Prayer (Evensong), or *Matins
and *Vespers.

The history of the office hours can be traced back to
the Jewish observance of the hours of prayer at the third,
sixth and ninth hours of the day. With the development of
monastic communities the number of services increased as
did their complexity. By the end of the fifth century the
system of office hours was complete in the West, though it
went through some modification.

At first the Hours were simple, consisting mainly of
the reading or chanting of the psalter, lessons from Scripture, hymns and prayers. Under the influence of monastic
ingenuity the services became overloaded with intricate detail
and made a burdensome daily obligation. Seeing genuine
value in the Hours, the Reformers encouraged a simplified
version of two, Matins and Vespers, for daily use in the
church schools and with the congregations on Sundays and
festival days.

With the breach between England and Rome, the English church took opportunity to reform its worship. Archbishop Cranmer, realizing the value of Lauds and Vespers
(the only Hours traditionally attended by the people), incorporated their orders into the worship of the Church of England using the vernacular terms, "Matins" and "Evensong,"
in the Book of Common Prayer, 1549. In the 1552 edition
he changed the terms to *Morning Prayer and Evening
Prayer. The basic objective of this reform simplified the
complex system, making it available to the laity, and recovered an orderly continuous reading of the Bible and psalter
through a series of lessons. In the cathedrals and collegiate
churches chanting was retained as was the practice of intoning the entire psalter once every month. While the Anglican

Hours have had a long uninterrupted history, the Lutheran Matins and Vespers, as established by Luther, were restored in 1888 following general abandonment caused by war, Pietism, and Rationalism.

Morning Prayer resulted from assimilating the three morning hours of the Roman rite: Matins, Lauds and Prime. From Matins came the opening sentences, *Venite, *Te Deum laudamus and the lessons; from Lauds the *Benedictus, *Benedicite and *collect for the day were extracted; and from Prime came the Creed, lesser litany, *Lord's Prayer, *versicles and third collect.

Evensong, the combination of Vespers and Compline, received the *Magnificat and collect for the day from the former and the "Nunc dimittis, Creed, preces and collect for night from the latter.

The Canonical Hours as used in the Anglican Church evolved in three sections. The first section (the Sentence, Exhortation, Confession and Absolution) was an addition to the English Prayer Book in 1552. The third section (the Final Prayer with the Prayer of St. Chrysostom and the Grace) was a 1662 addition. The remainder was originally established in the first *Book of Common Prayer (1549).

Choral settings of these services have been common throughout history, the basic materials being the canticles. The harmonized or plainsong chanting really does not begin until the *Invitatory and *Venite. Among the composers of choral (non-chant) settings of these services are Tallis, Gibbons, Blow, Purcell, Boyce, Stanford, Noble and Howells.

Concerning the construction of the Canonical Hours, the Anglican offices begin with an introduction and preparation basically consisting of confession and absolution. This addition to the office proper can be traced to the correction of an omission of this act of worship in the 1549 Book of Common Prayer. It also may be related to confession placed at the opening of the service by the French Reformers in the book of Pollanus. In the Lutheran services the act of confession is included in The Prayer which includes the *Kyrie eleison.

Psalmody and the Scripture lessons compose a major portion of the Hour services, a principal feature of both Jewish and early Christian worship. The medieval practice of chanting the entire psalter each week has been modified in the cathedral and collegiate chapels of the Anglican rite to once every month. With the development of vernacular hymnody, the interest in chanting the psalms diminished in the Lutheran churches. The Scripture lessons follow a prescribed order for both Lutheran and Anglican Hours, the Anglican usually providing more extended texts.

A very important feature of the Lutheran Hours, hymnody, reflects the influence of the Benedictine Rule, which provided a wealth of Latin office hymns. With the encouragement of vernacular hymnody, the Lutheran church developed a vast heritage of hymnological materials for use during the Hours and the mass. The Anglican Church of England, under the Reform influence of Calvin and Zwingli, broke the history of hymn singing in the Hours until the late 17th century when metrical psalms and hymns were reinstated.

Developed in the Gallican church and later adopted by Rome, the *responsory was incorporated into the Lutheran offices of Matins and Vespers with its characteristic liturgical patterns of combined verses and response from Scripture selected for the season or feast day. Its name probably has been derived from the arrangement of the text or its musical setting. Traditionally sung after each lesson, the Lutheran Reformers simplified its use for after the last lesson only. With the period of Pietism and Rationalism the responsory was omitted, only to be restored in the English Lutheran Liturgy in America in 1888. Many composers, including the eminent Max Reger, have written choral settings of the responsories. The Anglican Church has excluded them from their worship.

The *canticles, hymn-like scriptural passages, form an important aspect in the Canonical Hours as they have throughout the history of the Christian church.

Regarding the collects, these prayers originally followed each psalm or canticle in the ancient services. The Collect for the Day, placed at the end of the office, was a later addition being extracted from the mass. With the incorporation of various versicles and responses along with the Kyrie, Lord's Prayer and other materials, the suffrages eventually developed. These traditionally have fashioned the close of the Anglican Hours. The prayers of the Lutheran Hours, with the Kyrie, Lord's Prayer, Collect for the Day and other collects, conclude Matins with the Collect of Grace and Vespers with the Collect for Peace.

Proctor, Francis and Walter Howard Frere. A New History of the Book of Common Prayer. London: Macmillan, 1955.

Reed, Luther D. The Lutheran Liturgy. Philadelphia: Muhlenberg Press, 1959. Chapter 23.

_____. Worship: A Study of Corporate Devotion. Philadelphia: Muhlenberg Press, 1959. Chapter 8.

Shepherd, Massey Hamilton, Jr. The Oxford American Prayer

Book Commentary. New York: Oxford University Press, 1950. Pp. 3-34.

CANTATA (It., fr. cantare to sing, fr. L. cantare, intens. of canere to sing)

[Contents: (general); German church cantata; 19th-century sacred cantata; 20th-century sacred cantata; (bibliography).] A composite vocal form initiating in the Baroque era, the Protestant cantata is a multi-sectioned composition of recitatives, solos, choruses and instrumental accompaniment which is based on a religious or quasi-religious text, and which may or may not be based on a *chorale or *hymn tune. In size it is smaller than the *oratorio. The term appeared soon after 1600 as the third product of the mondic style (opera and oratorio), replacing the madrigal. At first the term simply distinguished a vocal composition (cantata) from an instrumental one (sonata). But soon it became the solo cantata of Italy, a grouping of arias and recitatives of contrasting character with sections often separated by instrumental sinfonia. Alessandro Scarlatti, composer of more than 600 such works, is a prime example. Through a century of refinement, the Italian solo cantata gave only the name and sectional form to the German cantata.

German Church Cantata

In the German Lutheran tradition the church cantata held a similar position as the anthem in the Anglican Church; it was desirable, though not essential, to include within the corporate worship; religious, but not liturgical. The position was normally before the sermon and between the reading of the Gospel lesson and the singing of the chorale, "Wir glauben all' an einen Gott" (the Creed chorale), by the congregation. Placed thusly, or divided before and after the sermon, it often served as a sermon-motet or a reflection on the Gospel of the day, causing composers to identify such compositions by the liturgical calendar, as "Dom XVI:p: Trin." (16th Sunday after Trinity). From Schütz to even as late as Bach's time, the principal choral music of the service was not designated cantata (still meaning solo cantata), but rather with neutral terms like Kirchenmusik and Stück. Other more specific terms commonly used were aria, concerto, dialogo, motetto, ode, and psalm.

Though strictly not in the line of the cantata, Heinrich Schütz (1585-1672) shows a firm understanding of the

concertato style for the German service in his Symphoniae
Sacrae (1629). His concerto for three voices and trio sonata, "O Herr hilf" (MM, 137), is an early example of the
kind of treatment Schütz's contemporaries were to develop.
Following a brief sinfonia, the voices enter imitating the
rhythmic pattern of the instruments. In the triple section,
voices and instruments alternate in a concertato style, not
to return to the opening idea. With the unique German contribution, the chorale, it was not long before it was incorporated into the concertato style. John Hermann Schein
(1586-1630) used two voices as counterparts of the treble in
a trio sonata with a continuo in his chorale concerto, "Ers-
chienen ist der herrliche Tag" (TEM, 220).
          Among the larger collections of early German con-
certed church music is Andreas Hammerschmidt's (1612-
1675) two-volume Musicalische Gespräche über die Evangelia
("Musical Conversations on the Gospels"--1665-1656). This
work contains 59 pieces in varied styles and arrangements
for vocal and instrumental groups; none of which are called
cantatas but merely Kirchenmusik. The form is that of a
dialogue with chorus, incorporating a chorale as a part of
the dialogue itself as well as the concluding chorus. Even
this early, the conscious attention of the composers to the
appropriateness and consistency of the text is evident.
          As can be seen in the Musicalische Gespräche and
throughout Baroque German Protestantism, two distinct types
of texts are found in Kirchenmusik: strophic and madrigalian.
The chorale exemplifies the former, while free rhymed prose
and biblical passages the latter. Neither type is used to the
exclusion of the other. In fact, in the mature German church
cantata of the Baroque period, the strophic and madrigalian
verses alternate fairly regularly as a succession of recitatives, arias, choruses and chorales are set off by varied
orchestra interludes.
          Continuing in the development toward the chorale can-
tata, Franz Tunder (1614-1667), Buxtehude's predecessor at
Marienkirche, Lübeck, set the strophic limitations of the
chorale in the variation form popular to organ composition.
These chorale variations for voices ("Ein' feste Burg ist unser
Gott"--DdT, III:42) treat each stanza of the chorale text in a
manner fitting its character and mood.
          Though most German composers were now making ex-
tensive use of the chorale types, Matthias Weckmann (1621-
1674) preferred the madrigalian verse. Yet, he continued
the use of the concertato style.
          Johann Rudolph Ahle (1625-1673) influenced by the
dialogue technique, as in the words of Hammerschmidt, carried

it one step further into polychoral composition. "Wir glauben all' an einen Gott" (DdT, V:125) shows this use as the
chorale text is divided between two separate choruses.
       The structure of Buxtehude's *Abendmusik yields a
tendency for the return of familiar materials. Each section
of his structures is separated by an instrumental ritornello.
Often his opening chorus is repeated at the end in a da capo
fashion. His use of a solo for each stanza provides good
contrast (see DdT, XIV:15-38; 107-138). The chorale as an
appropriate vehicle of expression is masterfully handled by
Buxtehude.
       Influenced strongly by his Italian training, yet res-
ponding to his German heritage, Johann Philip Krieger (1649-
1725), composer of some two thousand works of the cantata
type, is a central figure in the development of the cantata.
Limitless in variety, Krieger's works range from simple solo
dialogues to those with colossal double choruses and double
orchestras, reminiscent of Orazio Benevoli. In the late
1690's there is evidence of Krieger's urge to incorporate the
fully developed aria into the German sacred concerto tradition. However, it was not until the court poet, Erdmann
Neumeister (1671-1756), provided suitable texts that the cantata with full-fledged arias could emerge. His only extant
cantata incorporating this new form is "Rufet nicht die Weis-
heit?" ("Doth wisdom not call?"--DdT, LIII-IV:275). Thus,
the cantata has come into its mature form with the inclusion
of distinct recitatives and arias.
       While Krieger's work was more or less isolated at
Weissenfal, Johann Kuhnau (1661-1722) and Friedrich Wilhelm
Zachow (1663-1712) generated great interest around Leipzig.
Kuhnau, whose total output is unknown, was capable of producing
magnificent cantatas for festive occasions. "Wenn ihr fröhlich
seid an euren Festen" ("When you are joyful on your festivals"--DdT, LVIII-LIX:244) requires an expanded orchestra of
four trumpets and timpani, paired violins, violas, bassoon
and continuo and shows a similarity to the French overture.
With no strophic texts in this cantata, Kuhnau freely employs
the modern Italian idioms of the aria, concerted sections, as
well as an exciting fugue. As for the chorale cantata, Kuhnau's "Wie schön leuchtet der Morgenstern" (How brightly
shines the morning star"--DdT, LVIII-IX:292) always attempts
to keep the memory of the tune before the listener through
the use of the characteristic leaps, actually quoting the tune
in the opening and closing sections of the piece. His use of
motto beginnings for the aria and chorus is a strong unifying
feature. Yet, with all of his creativeness, Kuhnau's recitatives remain in the arioso form of the older church cantatas.

In the works of Zachow three distinct uses of the chorale can be seen: (1) the Schlusschoral, or summary of the cantata's doctrinal message; (2) as a commentary on the message, the chorale being used in the course of the composition; and (3) the chorale verses fencing the entire composition, even being used to make up the entire substance of the cantata on occasion (Wienandt, 259). All this he could do incorporating the Italian style into it--"Dies ist der Tag" ("This is the day"--DdT, XXI-II:236).

Before moving to the master of the German church cantata, one more different chorale treatment should be observed, that of Christopher Graupner (1683-1760). In his "Ach wie nichtig, ach wie fluchtig" ("Ah, how empty; ah, how fleeting"--DdT, LI-II:108), Graupner uses the chorale in a broken style with each phrase of the text presented separately, first in free-style then in block-chords (very similar to the madrigalian settings).

Turning now to the pinnacle of the German Baroque church cantata, the five complete "year books" of church cantatas by Johann Sebastian Bach (1685-1750) compose the nucleus of his cantata writing. With 59 cantatas for each year, his output in this form must be around 259 cantatas; all but 29 having been written in Leipzig. (Only 208 survive today.) For his textual inspirations, Bach turned mainly to the poetic works of Neumeister, Franck, Picander and Henrici. The latter wrote especially for Bach and at his request.

Bach's trial cantata at Leipzig was "Jesus nahm zu sich die Zwölfe" ("Jesus said unto the twelve"--BGA, V^1:62) written for Quinquagesima Sunday. It reflects the Gospel of the day; how Jesus, with his disciples, was heading toward Jerusalem to await his passion, seeing a blind man, restores his sight. The cantata consists of an arioso for tenor and bass with SATB chorus, an aria for alto, a recitative for bass, a tenor aria, and a closing chorale ("Ertodt uns durch dein' Gute"). One of the chief innovations of Bach to the cantata at Leipzig was the church cantata in two parts, a method used by oratorio composers whose works were destined to be presented before and after the sermon in Catholic worship. In "Die Elender sollen essen, das sie satt werden" ("The poor shall eat and be satisfied"--BGA, XVIII:149) a reflection of the rich man and Lazarus, Bach uses the chorale "Was Gott thut, das ist wohlgethan" ("Whate'er our God ordains is right") as the focal point for unity of the two parts. Part one ends with a chorale-fantasy statement by the chorus and orchestra; part two begins with a sinfonia by the strings with a trumpet statement of the chorale. The closing chorale section of part one further unifies part two by being repeated at its conclusion.

Throughout the works of Bach, especially his cantatas and other compositions based on chorales, there is evidence of a long tradition of word-painting and intensification of text by means of musical symbolism. These symbols may be melodic, rhythmic, diagrammatic or reiterative, conveying ideas of grief, joy, angels, demons, the cross or bells. To deny symbolism existing in Bach's cantatas is to miss a portion of his genius in setting the texts. However, the idea of word-painting can be taken to extreme limits of tedium.

Written for the government at Mühlhausen in 1708 "Gott ist mein König" ("God is my King"--BGA, XVIII:3) shows Bach's knowledge of Venetian practice. The opening chorus is set for the alternation of coropleno sections with the smaller senza ripieni. With the full chorus a complete orchestral accompaniment is used; with the smaller vocal ensemble usually one instrumental-section and continuo is employed. Thus, a series of dynamic levels are automatically instituted. Another innovation in this cantata is in the duo for soprano and tenor. In the tenor, the principal text is presented, while the soprano sings, in obbligato fashion, an ornamented chorale which complements the text of the tenor.

An outstanding example of Bach's treatment of the chorale cantata in variation form is the Easter cantata, "Christ lag in Todesbanden" ("Christ lay in death's dark prison"--BGA, I:97). His masterful handling of seven stanzas of the same chorale to avoid monotony and still maintain a thread of unity surpasses his predecessors, Tunder and Krieger. Each of Luther's seven stanzas is set in a distinctive style. Unity is handled in part with the arch-form, evident in the selection of voices for the successive divisions of the piece.

                              chorus
                                IV
                          III   solo V
                   II   duo   VI
            I   chorus   VII

The choruses stand as the foundation and keystone of the arch, while the solos and duos form the pillars. The tune itself is everywhere present throughout the sinfonia and each stanza (Wienandt, 267).

The cantata for the Sunday after the Feast of Circumcision, "Ach Gott, wie manches Herzelied" ("O God, how many a pang of heart"--BGA, XII²:135) is an example of a

Bach cantata without the use of a chorus. In fact, Bach labeled it a "concerto in dialogo." Written for soprano and bass the solo arias and recitatives are framed by duettos in which the soprano states the chorale over the bass commentary. The cantatas not based on chorales are usually based on some scriptural text, such as Psalm 38:3, "Es ist nichts gesundes an meinem Leibe" ("There is no soundness in my flesh"--BGA, V¹:155). The penitential text is set forth in the opening chorus as a double fugue, whose themes are related to a penitential chorale. True to his genius, Bach uses this chorale ("Ach Herr mich armen Sunder") in an interrupted fashion as a portion of the accompaniment, played by flutes, cornets and trombones. The depth of expression produced by the combination of the lamenting scriptural text and the invisible text of this penitential chorale is unfathomable. Following expressive arias by the bass and soprano, Bach concludes the work with a simple and moving four-part chorale.

A younger contemporary of Bach, Karl Heinrich Graun (1704-1759) is known more for his passion oratorio, Der Tod Jesu (The Death of Jesus) than his cantatas. For festival services his works often demand a full chorus and orchestra ("O come, let us praise the Lord"), while for services of lesser significance Graun reduces forces to strings and selected soloists (the chorus singing the simple chorale setting at the close). The latter is the case with "O Gott du Brinquell aller Liebe" ("O God, thou wellspring of all kindness," MS 8182), which requires tenor and bass soloists.

Following the mid-18th century, composers were turning from the church to other sources (opera and chamber music) for their livelihood. The church had lost its attractiveness and could not provide the creativity and inspiration of the society outside its walls. Thus, the importance of the cantata as a creative form declined.

19th-Century Sacred Cantata

Few attempts were made on the Continent in cantata writing during the 19th century. Of the most notable ones two are by Felix Mendelssohn (1809-1847). A veritable prayer, "As the Hart Pants" (1838) is a setting of Psalm 42 for soprano and chorus. The "Gutenberg Fest-Cantata" (1840) written for the unveiling of Gutenberg's statue in the public square, uses as its Schlusschoral "Nun danket alle Gott." Of note in France is the cantata, "Mary Magdalen" (1873) by Jules Emile Frederic Massenet (1842-1912). First performed at the Odéon (Paris) it is set in five scenes for solo and chorus.

Turning to England, which was still engrossed in oratorio-worship, two composers come to the forefront of cantata composition. Alfred Robert Gaul (1837-1913) is remembered for his "Ruth" and "The Holy City." Sir John Stainer (1840-1901), however, is known for his lenten cantata, "The Crucifixion" (1887), which is still performed today. This and his other two cantatas ("The Daughter of Jarius" and "St. Mary Magdalene") make use of hymn texts often to be sung by choir and congregation.

"Nebuchadnezzar" (1847), a biblical cantata by James Monroe Deems (1818-1901) is considered one of the first American sacred cantatas. Only the alto part-book is extant. A prolific composer of music for use in the average American church by people with little or no training is George Frederick Root (1820-1895) (Kent, 117). At least two of his works, "Under the Palm, or The Flower Feast" and "Florence, The Pilgrim, or The Children of the Plain," are written for soli, Sunday school chorus and piano. Though much of his music is trite, he met the people's musical taste where it was, in hopes to elevate it later.

Dudley Buck, Jr. (1839-1909) contributed a series of five cantatas called the Christian Year between 1892 and 1896. Each is centered around some phase of Christ's birth or passion--"The Story of the Cross," "The Triumph of David," "The Coming of the King," "The Song of the Night" and "Christ the Victor." His compositions show a consistency of style written for the average choral group (Kent, 185).

A student of Buck, Harry Rowe Shelly (1858-1946) has three cantatas which are credited to him. "Vexilla Regis" (1893), "The Inheritance Divine" (1895) and "Death and Life" (1915) are all in a style similar to those of his teacher.

Lesser cantatas of this period in American history are "The Pilgrim's Progress" (1871) by James Cox Beckel (1811-?); "Saint John" (1890) by James C. D. Parker (1828-1916); "Prayer and Praise" (1888) by William Wallace Gilchrist (1846-1916); "Lazarus" (1894) and "The Fatherhood of God" (1900) by Peter August Schnecker (1850-1903); and "David" by George W. Marston (1840-1901). Belonging to this period, but composed in the early 20th century, are the two cantatas by Horatio Parker (1863-1919), "The Holy Child" and "The Shepherd's Vision" (1906), both well suited for the average choral group with soloists.

20th-Century Sacred Cantata

Turning again to Germany, one finds an active revival of the sacred cantata in a Baroque style with different harmonic treatment. The following are only examples of the diversity within this form today. The use of chorales set against dissonant counterpoint is seen in the a capella work, "Die Weinachtsgeschichte" ("The Christmas Cantata"--1930) by Hugo Distler (1908-1942). The soli narratives are chanted in a style similar to Schütz. Distler's "Nun danket all' und bringet Ehr" ("Now bring thanks and glorify") for soli, chorus, organ and strings is a fine example of the German chorale cantata in the 20th century. Similarly, Hans Friedrich Micheelsen (b. 1902) and Friedrich Zipp (b. 1914) make use of the chorale. In Micheelsen's "Lutherchoralkantate" (1953) four familiar chorales are employed, each given a movement where it is developed in variation form. Zipp's "Such, wer da will, ein ander Zeil" ("Let him who chooses seek another goal"--1939?) incorporates unison congregation singing. Written in the style of Buxtehude, Heinrich Spitta's (b. 1902) "From Heaven Above, Ye Angels All" (1945) is based on the Christmas chorale, "Vom Himmel hoch, O Englein kommt." Ernst Pepping (b. 1901) shows the influence of the motet style in his "Die Weihnachtsgeschichte des Lukas" ("The Christmas Story according to St. Luke"--1959) for four to seven voices. Each of its five sections is written with a distinct style and texture. Representative of a more popular style Heinz Werner Zimmermann (b. 1937) has written his "Psalmkonzert" (1957) incorporating jazz. It is written in five sections for baritone, five-voice choir, children's choir, three trumpets, vibraphone and contrabass. The final section quotes the chorale, "Nun danket all' ein Gott."

Elsewhere on the Continent, Darius Milhaud (b. 1892) has set three stories about Daniel in his "Miracles of Faith" (1953). Employing dissonant counterpoint, Flor Peeters (b. 1903) wrote a Christmas cantata for soli and two equal voices accompanied, "To Bethlehem" (1955), quoting part of "Adeste Fidelis" at its conclusion.

England and particularly America have become the market centers for cantatas in the 20th century. Church choirs in both centuries, regardless of size, are almost compelled to perform a cantata at Christmas and Easter because their congregations have come to expect it. With this vast market one cannot expect all compositions to be of an equally high caliber. Thus, in the discussion to follow, a representative sampling of the major areas of cantata composition will be presented.

Looking first to England, the cantata, "The Hymn of
Jesus" (1917), by Gustav Holst (1874-1934), is an example
of the use of chant. It opens with the beautiful chanting of
the Vexilla regis. This work is for double chorus, orchestra and piano. Based on the harvest hymn by Claudius,
Harold Edwin Darke's (b. 1888) "The Sower" depicts the biblical parable of the "Sower and the Seed." In a similar
vein, Eric Harding Thiman (b. 1900) composed "The Parables"
(1931), using three parables from the Gospels and incorporating into the work several chorales and hymns. Outstanding
in English music is the name and works of Benjamin Britten
(b. 1913). Three of his cantatas are "A Boy Was Born"
(1933)--a theme and six variations based on ancient English
carols; "Rejoice in the Lamb" (1943)--a festival cantata on
a text by Christopher Smart; and "St. Nicholas" (1948). Another important British composer is Ralph Vaughan Williams
(1872-1958). His "This Day" (1954) is a cantata for STB
soloists and chorus suitable for Christmas. "Pilgrim's
Journey" was published posthumously and is an adaptation
for soli and double chorus from his "morality," Pilgrim's
Progress (1949). Also to be mentioned are "The Garden and
the Cross" (1949?) by Alec Rowley (b. 1892) and "The New-
born King" (1960) by Gordon Jacobs (b. 1895). Of interest
is Gerald Finzi's (1901-1956) small Christmas cantata, "In
Terra Pax" (1954). His style is one of excited rhythmic in-
tensity. The text is woven from some poems of Robert
Bridges and Luke 2. Jazz, too, has influenced the 20th-cen-
tury English cantata in the works of Malcolm Williamson and
others in the *Twentieth Century Church Light Music Group.
Williamson's "Procession of Psalms" carries a dignified beat
as it presents "Ride on, ride on in majesty."
    The 20th-century American sacred cantata is a prime
example of diversity. In writing "The Seven Words of Christ
from the Cross" (1956) Richard Wienhorst (b. 1917) produces
a style similar to Schütz but with dissonant counterpoint and
the use of chorales. Harald Rohlig (b. 1928) based his
"Christ Is Arisen" (1964) on a 12th-century "Leisen Christ
ist erstanden" and the chorale "Christ lag in Todesbanden."
Alan Hovhaness (b. 1911) shows the influence of the Oriental
musical systems in his "Easter Cantata" (1958) for soprano,
chorus and chamber orchestra. Three cantatas are representative of Daniel Pinkham's (b. 1923) work--"Wedding Cantata" (1956), "Christmas Cantata" (1957) and "Easter Cantata" (1962). In the latter, for mixed chorus, brass and
percussion, he uses an exciting canon in 12/8 rhythm to
communicate "Go quickly and tell to all." Also making use
of driving rhythms, Peter Mennin (b. 1923) has written "The

Christmas Story" (1950), an effective work for soprano and
tenor soloists, mixed chorus and chamber orchestra. Win-
ning a Pulitzer Prize in 1945, "Canticle of the Sun" (1944)
by Leo Sowerby (1895-1968) is a setting of the words of St.
Francis for mixed chorus and orchestra. His "Christ Re-
born" (1951), an extended work, is based on a relevant text
for Christmas.

Writing for the average church choir in America,
Joseph Clokey (b. 1890) has produced many cantatas. His
"Christ Is Born" (1935) and "Childe Jesus" (1922) are examples of his writing, the latter being based largely on Christmas carols. Robert Graham has written several cantatas
especially for children's choirs--"Lo! A Star" and "What
Gift Have I?"--as well as those for adult choirs--"Golgotha"
(1962). Using choral narration in antiphonal style, choral
recitative, hymns and canticles, Talmadge Dean (b. 1915) composed an unusual cantata, "The Word Was Made Flesh"
(1963). Influenced by hymns of the shaped-note tradition
Lewis Henry Horton composed "The White Pilgrim" (1940)
and "An Appalachian Nativity" (1955) for soli, chorus and
accompaniment. Including the use of aleatory techniques,
Fred Prentice has given a forward look to the cantata through
"The Day of Resurrection" (1968). This work designed for
Easter, requiring mixed chorus, two readers, congregation,
brass and percussion, may well indicate a new trend for cantata composition.

John W. Peterson is a prolific composer of a type of
cantata, making great use of hymns and hymn tunes. His
"Hallelujah, What a Savior!" and "Night of Miracles" are
typical of his popular style. The youth-oriented cantatas
which developed in the late 1960's reflect the folk idiom, as
John Wilson's "Shepherds, Rejoice" (1968) and the so-called
pop idiom, as Phillip Landgrave's "Purpose" (1968) and
Ralph Carmichael's "Tell It Like It Is" (1969). (See also
*"Pop, " Gospel.)

Kent, Ralph McVety. "A Study of Oratorio and Sacred Can-
    tata Composers in America before 1900." Unpublished
    dissertation, State University of Iowa, Iowa City, Iowa,
    1954.
Scheriz, Arnold. Über Kantaten J. S. Bachs. Leipzig:
    n. p. , 1942.
Schmitz, Eugen. Geschichte der Kantate und die geistliche
    Konzerts. Leipzig: Breitkopf and Härtel, 1914.
Terry, Charles Sanford. Cantatas and Oratorios. 2 vols.
    London, n. p. , 1915-1921.
Whittaker, W. Gillies. The Cantatas of Johann Sebastian

Bach. 2 vols. London: Oxford University Press, 1959.

Wienandt, Elwyn. Choral Music of the Church. New York: The Free Press, 1965.

CANTATA-ANTHEM (*cantata + *anthem)

The cantata-anthem is an extension of the multisectional English *anthem making it into a larger form through the expansion of each section into a completely separate movement: some movements being solely instrumental, some choral or small solo ensembles, and others being for vocal solos. This form, resembling the church cantata of the Continent, flourished from the Restoration period of England, during the reigns of Charles II and James II. It approximated the cantata in its employment of the new theatrical idea of recitative, aria and small vocal ensembles. Through the efforts of John Blow the cantata-anthem was brought to a type of composition with its numerous short sections unified more textually and musically. Purcell achieved more complete integration through his use of repetition of complete vocal sections, as well as the recapitulation of instrumental ritornelli. Generally, the form was limited to non-liturgical occasions, as its foremost purpose seemed to be exploitation of the particular vocal and instrumental resources of the locality. After the turn of the 18th century the cantata-anthem tradition continued mainly in works for special occasions such as coronations, weddings, victories or royal birthdays.

Handel's Chandos Anthems are good examples of cantata-anthems.

Lam, Basil. "The Church Music," in: Handel: A Symposium. Ed. by Gerald Abraham. London: Oxford University Press, 1954.

Wienandt, Elwyn and Robert Young. The Anthem in England and America. New York: The Free Press, 1970.

CANTATA DA CHIESA (It. church singing)

The term, cantata da chiesa, reflective of early 17th-century Italian musical developments, refers to the application of the principle of the nuove musiche, the alternating of recitatives and arias, to the *cantata. It was first applied to church music in the sacred cantatas of G. Carissimi (1605-1674). (Example: "Domine, Deus meus," for soprano and basso continuo, CS, VIII.)

CANTATE DOMINO   (L.)

"O sing unto the Lord a new song for he hath done marvelous things" (Psalm 98) is called by its Latin heading, Cantate Domino. It may be substituted for the *Magnificat following the first lesson in the Anglican office of Evening Prayer (*Vespers) as instituted by the Prayer Book 1552.

CANTICA DE MOBILE   (L. moveable songs)

Within churches oriented to the liturgical ordering of the *Christian Year, the hymns which are selected by the minister or cantor that are not designed for a specific season or day, but are moveable, are considered cantica de mobile. (Cf. *Cantica de tempore.)

CANTICA DE TEMPORE   (L. songs for a time)

*Hymns or *chorales that were written with definite bearing on the *Gospel of the day or have become appropriate to a specific season or day in the *Christian Year and, thus, whose usage has become ecclesiastical tradition, have been termed cantica de tempora (cf. *Cantica de mobile). This term stems from the Lutheran hymnic practice of providing a hymn with a definite bearing for most of the Gospel readings in the church calendar. Thus, in time each Sunday came to have its own respective chorale. This practice included all the hymns by Luther and selected ones by authors of the Lutheran tradition.

CANTICA NOVA   (L. new song)

The term used by Luther to describe the wholesome vocal music of a sacred character in his efforts to promote vernacular church song is cantica nova. He likened this music to the "new songs" in the Book of Psalms.

CANTICLE   (L. canticilum a little song, dim. of canticum song, fr. canere, cantum to sing)

Biblical songs, hymn-like in character and similar to the psalms, but found elsewhere in the Scriptures are classified thusly. Divided into two kinds, the cantica minor

(lesser canticles) are the Old Testament songs and the cantica major (greater canticles) are those occurring in the Gospels. These songs are used in liturgical services, usually
during *Morning Prayer and Evening Prayer (or *Vespers).
The practice of their use can be attributed to the influence
of the Roman Hour services and the Jewish hours of prayer.
     The Benedictus es, Domine ("Blessed art though, O
Lord, God of our Fathers") is a portion of the "Song of
Three Holy Children" from the ninth book of the Apocrypha,
verses 29-34. It was included in the 1928 revision of the
Book of Common Prayer for use during the service of Morning Prayer. The Benedicite, omnia opera ("O all ye works
of the Lord, bless ye the Lord; praise Him and magnify Him
forever") is also from the "Song of the Three Holy Children, "
verses 35-65. It was originally prescribed for use during
the Lenten season in 1549. In the Anglican service, one of
these or the *Te Deum is sung after the First Lesson.
     Following the Second Lesson, the *Benedictus ("Blessed
be the Lord, God of Israel") is sung. It is from Luke 1:68,
the Song of Zacharias, and appeared in Edward's first prayer
book. Either this or the *Jubilate (Deo) (Psalm 100) is used.
In the Lutheran liturgy, the Benedictus, which, like the other
New Testament canticles, commemorates the Incarnation, is
used in the service of Matins following the address. With its
reference to light--the "Dayspring from on High"--it is proper
to alternate with the Te Deum during Advent and from Septuagesima to Palm Sunday.
     The *Magnificat ("My soul doth magnify the Lord") is
the Song of Mary--Luke 1:46-55. Since the fourth century it
has maintained the place given it by St. Benet, that of following the first lesson in Vespers or Evening Prayer. Though
it bears similarities to the Song of Hannah (I Samuel 2:10)
and to certain Psalm verses, the Magnificat contains its own
character of exaltation from a humble spirit, giving thanks to
God for the Incarnation and for His mercy upon "all them
that fear him from generation to generation. " In the Anglican order of Evening Prayer it may be alternated with the
*Cantate Domino (Psalm 98) or the Bonum est confiteri (Psalm
92) after the First Lesson.
     After the Second Lesson, the last canticle the *Nunc
Dimittis ("Lord, now lettest thou thy servant depart in
peace"), is presented. It is the Song of Simeon--Luke 2:29-
32--upon seeing the Christ Child. Being so placed in the
service of Evening Prayer, this song of parting and prayer
for peace and rest is perfectly fitted. These two canticles
were appointed to their respective positions in the Anglican
order in 1549. However, in 1552, the *Deus misereatur

(Psalm 67) or the Benedic anima mea (Psalm 103) were permitted as alternates. In the Lutheran service of Vespers,
the Magnificat and the Nunc Dimittis alternate, the latter
being particularly appropriate during Advent, Lent and the
Trinity season.

   Other canticles which serve a lesser function in the
services of the Anglican and Lutheran orders are basically
from the Old Testament--Song of Miriam and Moses (Exodus
15); Prayer of Habakkuk (Habakkuk 3--Domine audivi); Prophet's Song (Isaiah 12); Song of Hannah (I Samuel 2:1-10); Song
of Moses (Deuteronomy 32--Audite caeli). The Song of Solomon, commonly used, in part for motets, is referred to as
Canticum canticorum, Dunstables' Quam pulchra es being a
fine example. Though sometimes considered a canticle, the
Te Deum, being non-biblical, is more properly a hymn (see
*Hymnody).

   While settings of the canticles in anthem form are
numerous, particularly from 19th-century England, chant
settings are normally used in services.

   More recently, the British composer, Benjamin Britten
(b. 1913), defines canticle as an extended song for solo voice
or voices, with piano, on religious or quasi-religious texts.
Thus, he has composed three such canticles (1947, 1952,
1954).

Kelk, A. H. Singing of the Psalms and Canticles to Anglican
     Chant, Shorter Papers of the Church Music Society,
     No. 6. London: Oxford University Press, n.d.
Pocknee, C. E. "The Place of the Canticles in Public Wor-
     ship," EngCM, 30:7-10, February, 1960.
Proctor, Francis and H. Frere. A New History of the Book
     of Common Prayer. London: Macmillan, 1955.
Reed, Luther. Worship. Philadelphia: Muhlenberg Press,
     1959.

CANTIONAL see KANTIONAL

CANTOR (ME. precentor, chanter, G. Cantor, Kantor, fr.
     L. a singer, fr. canere to sing)

   In the cathedral, collegiate and monastic churches of
England the official in charge of the music was the cantor,
who was second in rank to the dean of the cathedral. His
duties involved the directing of the musical portions of the
service in general, and in particular, the intoning of the

psalms and *canticles. He sat in the first return-stall, on the north side of the choir, facing the altar; thus, the north side was called the *cantoris or chanter's side, in contrast to the decani or deacon's side. More recently, the cantor is generally responsible for supervising all the singing, selecting the music, and preparing for its proper performance.

In the German Lutheran tradition the musical head of the educational institution with a choir-school, attached to a church was called a cantor (e.g., J. S. Bach at St. Thomas Schule, Leipzig). The first Lutheran cantor was J. Walther (1496-1570), Luther's musical advisor.

Krickeberg, Dieter. Das protestantische Kantorat in 17. Jahrhundert. Berlin: Merseburger, 1965.
Luther, Wilhelm Martin. "Die gesellschaftliche und wirtschaftliche Stellung des protestantischen Kantor," MK, 19:33-40, January-February, 1949.
Müller, Karl Ferdinand. Der Kantor: Sein Amt und seine Dienste. Gütersloh: Gütersloher Verlagshaus, 1964.
Werner, Arno. Vier Jahrhunderte im Dienste der Kirchenmusik. Leipzig: C. Merseburger, 1932.

CANTORIS

In the English tradition of the *anthem and service, cantoris indicated that section of the choir which sat on the north side of the chancel, the same side as the *precentor. (See *Cantor.) The opposite section is known as the *decani choir. The purpose achieved by this division magnified the antiphonal nature of the psalm chants and frequently of the anthems and services.

CANTUS FIRMUS (ML. fixed song)

A melody which is derived from any preexisting source and incorporated as the basis of a polyphonic composition through the addition of other voices is a cantus firmus. In terms of origin, cantus firmi can be categorized as follows: (1) plainsong melodies, (2) Protestant *chorales, (3) secular melodies and (4) abstract melodic materials. The discussion below is solely that of group two, the Protestant chorale.

The early use of the cantus firmus in the Protestant Reformation was nurtured by Jan Pieterszoon Sweelinck (1562-1621) through his organ variations of chorales and psalm tunes (see *Chorale prelude). Unlike the Roman

Catholic composers who felt organistic variation of sacred
cantus firmi to be irreverent, Sweelinck and the other Protestant German composers of the period felt a sense of liturgical dignity through this treatment of the cantus firmus.
The cantus firmus technique was also used in vocal compositions as the *chorale motet, the *chorale concertato, the
*cantata, the *passion and the *oratorio.   This is quite evi-
dent in the chorale motets and cantatas of J. S. Bach (1685-
1750), the choral and organ works of Johannes Brahms
(1777-1856) and Max Reger (1873-1916) and in the neo-Ba-
roque technique of such 20th-century composers as Hugo
Distler (1908-1942) and J. N. David (b. 1895).

Blume, Friedrich. Das monodische Prinzip in der protes-
    tant Kirchenmusik. Leipzig: Breitkopf und Härtel,
    1925.
Winterfeld, C. von. Der evangelische Kirchengesang und
    sein Verhältnis zur Kunst des Tonsatzes.   3 vols.
    Hildesheim: Olms, 1966 (orig. ed. 1843-47).

CAPELLMEISTER see KAPELLMEISTER

CARILLON (Fr., fr. L. quadrilio a set of four)

       In the broadest sense a carillon can be any set of
bells (originally four) hung "fixed" in a tower and played
manually by means of a clavier or automatically be a clockwork mechanism. However, the accepted definition of a
carillon is a musical instrument consisting of 23 or more
cup-shaped bronze bells, tuned chromatically, and played
either by means of a clavier of levers operated by hands
and feet, or electronically by an ivory keyboard; a set of
bells smaller in number is called a "chime."
       The use of bells in the praise of God can be traced
to the Bible where references to King David playing bells
can be found. Historically, though, the carillon can be
traced to the ancient Orient where its possibilities were revealed thousands of years ago. The early carillons contained small bells which were sounded by the performers
tapping upon them with a prepared hammer. The use of the
mechanical clockwork appeared in the 13th century. (The
English word clock is derived from the Dutch Klok meaning
bell.)
       During the 15th century in what is presently known as
Belgium and Holland the musical practice of rendering melo-

dies together with harmony evolved for use with church bells.
After centuries of experimentation, in the 14th century the
overtone series forming a minor triad proved the most agree-
able in combinations with other tones. This has stood the
test of time for over 500 years. The early 16th century
marked the use of the keyboard for playing the bells (Aude-
narde, 1510). However, it was in Europe during the 15th to
18th centuries that the art of campanology was firmly established. Among the great names of bell-founders were the
Hemony brothers, the van den Gheyn family and the Dumery
family. During the 19th century carillons spread to England
and America. In the present century bell-foundaries are
found in America, England, Holland and France. Acclaimed
as the largest carillons are those at the University of Chicago Chapel, Riverside Church of New York and Kirk in the
Hills, Bloomfield, Michigan.

Traditionally, the carefully manufactured bells (usually
30 to 50) of the carillon are hung in a fixed manner within
an enclosed tower. The clappers inside each bell are connected with wires to a clavier of round wooden keys and
pedals. The keys are of oak and arranged much like the
keyboard of the piano. The sharp keys are in an upper row,
projecting 3-1/2 inches; the naturals are in the lower row,
projecting 6-1/2 inches. Because of the weight of the clappers the entire hand is employed to sound each note and it
requires great strength. Modern campanology has developed
several advanced performing techniques such as tremolando,
arpeggiando and rapid passages. Electronic consoles have
replaced manual claviers in some American-made instruments of recent years.

Following the destruction of the Napoleonic armies,
the restoration and renaissance of the carillon was no small
task. With the determined efforts of Jef Denyn (1862-1941),
the son of a municipal carillonneur, the bells were improved
in quality and a new perfection of musical performance became infused with the formal evening carillon recitals inaugurated by him. Denyn also established the first school for
campanology in 1922, the Beiaardschool, Mechelin, Belgium.
In 1936 the Guild of Carillonneurs of North America was
formed fostering the carillon art on this continent.

Among the outstanding early composers of carillon
music are Matthias van den Gheyn (1721-1785) and Potthoff
(1726-?). Contemporary composers include Jef Denyn (1862-
1941), J. A. F. Wagenaar (1862-1941), Jef van Hoof (1886-
1959), Johan Franco (b.1908), John Cage (b.1912) and Daniel
Pinkham (b.1923).

Archer, J. Stuart, "On Carillon Music," ML, 18:179, 1937.

Bigelow, Arthur Lynds. English Type Carillonic Bells; Their History and Music. Sellersville, Pa.: Schulmerick Electronics, 1949.

Elewijick, Christian van. Anciens Collection ... d'clavecinistes flamandes. N.p., n.p., 1877 (Music).

Heuven, Engelbert Wiegman van. Acoustical Measurements on Church-bells and Carillons. The Hague: n.p., 1949.

Price, Percival. The Carillon. London: Oxford University Press, 1933.

Rice, W. Gorham. Carillon Music and Singing Towers of the Old World and the New. New York: Dodd, Mead, 1931.

Westcott, Wendell. An Introduction to Carillon Technique and Arranging. Aarle-Tixtel, Netherlands: Petit Futsen, 1956.

_____. "The Carillon and Its Christian Tradition," A.G.O. Quarterly, 10:99-100, July, 1965.

CAROL (M.E. carol, carole a dance or round accompanied by singing, fr. OF carole, fr. caroler to dance, prob. fr. L. choraules, choraula a flute player who accompanied the chorus on the flute, fr. Gr. choros dance + aulein to play on the flute, fr. aulos flute)

[Contents: (general); Early history; The golden age (15th and 16th centuries); The revival; (bibliography).] A song, usually of a joyful character, on any subject with uniform *stanzas and a *burden defines the carol around 1550 in England (in French, noël; in German, Weihnachtslied). When incorporating a narrative quality it is referred to as the ballad-carol (cf. *Ballad). Throughout the centuries it has been maintained as an expression springing from the common life of the people, sometimes being related to a song or dance that is entertaining. With the late 19th- and 20th-century reinstatement of the carol into Christian worship, it must be redefined as a quasi-religious song of folklike spirit with reference to the joyful observance of something new in the life of Christ.

Early History

As can be seen in the etymology of the word carol, dance and music were closely related to this term in ancient history--pre-Christian, early Christian and pagan. Man has

sought some joyous expression for his emotions in worship,
and in this has turned to music and dance. With the rise of
monasticism, the exuberance exhibiting the spontaneous religious emotions of the people were squelched. Likewise, the
joyful carol-like utterances for the celebration of the new
were doomed.

This silencing of religious folk-song was broken in
the Middle Ages with the revival of drama within the church.
As monasticism thrived, it developed a more elaborate and
intricate ritual surrounding the liturgical services, giving
rise to dramatics which synthesized music, movement, sound
and color. Decorative, melismatic alleluias accompanied the
festal rites. These wordless carolings became the basis for
the tropes and sequences of the ninth century and, thus, the
beginnings of medieval hymns and carols. The first tropes,
used in procession at Eastertide and later at Christmas, developed an increasing amount of dramatic action in the service. As the momentum grew, it evolved into liturgical
drama and the mysteries. The narrative music accompanying
the action in these dramas marked the beginning of carolry
in the church (Keefe, 20).

Another medieval impulse to the creation of carols
were the folk dramas, ludi, of village feasts. These were
primarily seasonal observances consisting of games, processions, pantomime, dancing and music centered around the
death-resurrection motif. The jongleurs and troubadours
often served as musical leaders of these folkways.

In the 13th century St. Francis of Assisi is said to
have added a new lyrical beauty to the rather crude character of the carol, as did Jacopone da Todi. This 13th-cen-
tury Latin carol could be considered the progenitor of the
ballad carol (Routley, 46). The *macaronic verse style--
i.e., the intermingling of Latin and the vernacular--charac-
terized the 14th-century German carol, as exhibited in "In
dulci Jubilo" (OBC, 86).

Fifteenth- and 16th-century English history reveals
the use of carols as an important feature of the mystery
plays. At times, the carolers received a more enthusiastic
ovation from the audience than did the actors. The enthusiasm for caroling at these performances sometimes grew
to the point of processions through the streets by the musicians and the audience singing carols. Thus, it was but a
small step from this custom to the independent singing of
carols during this period.

These early carols, prior to 1550, were written in
manuscript form and not perpetrated by oral tradition. Thus,
a rather literate society can be associated with them. These

medieval songs were disciplined in form, being written in
the form of the processional dance, didactic in text and
vigilant in content (Routley, 44).

The Golden Age (15th and 16th centuries)

Considering the form of the English ballad carol, the
major portion of what is called carol literature today, its
origins may be linked to the French Christmas songs, *noëls.
For the most part, the stanzas were the basic material with
no burden and few refrains. However strong this influence
may have been the 15th-century English carol can be directly
connected with the ballad, a short-stanza poem graphically
narrating some popular story. It arose in an age of Chau-
cerian influence and wide-spread humanism, when people
were seeking a less severe song than the old Latin office
hymn and a more vivacious one than plainsong melody. The
form of the English ballads given the ballad-carols was traditionally one of great length, sometimes 400 or more stanzas, but normally in the meter of the "fourteeners" (8.6.8.6.).
Occasionally the meter might vary to Long Meter and the
rhythm to triple time. Included in the "fourteeners" are
couplets containing two lines in which 14 syllables were not
always found. Examples of tripping extra syllables and
shifting accents were inalienable properties of these ballads.
It was these fourteeners of ballad literature which provided
a connection between the carol and the modern hymn. This
became evident in Thomas Sternhold's invention of the *psalms
in English ballad verse, the beginning of the Old Version of
the psalter.
        The writers of the 15th- and 16th-century ballad-carol
were the minstrels, who from the time of Cromwell were
resident musicians in English villages. Their employment
furnished songs and dances for almost every festive occasion,
including those of the church. The purpose of the songs was
to tell a story and the most dramatic narratives came from
the Christmas stories, thus, the quantity of carols recounting
the Gospel narratives of the Nativity. Many of this type of
carol concluded each stanza with a refrain which permitted
the people to join in the singing ("God rest you merry gentle-
men," OBC, 12). Some of the ballad-carols show the influence of the legendary homiletical stories preached by the
friars blended with the Gospel stories ("The Cherry Tree
Carol," OBC, 66). Dialogue has been another method used
to convey the narrative in carolry. Typical of this were
conversations between Mary and Jesus ("The holy well,"
OBC, 56). A very common form of the ballad-carol is the

"lullaby carol" ("This endrys night," OBC, 39). This type
is prominent among the medieval manuscript carols and
French noëls as well as the ballads (Routley, 58).

Apart from the legendary ballad-carols of the Nativity,
those of redemption and other church doctrines were provided by the carol-makers who found a new sense of drama
and imagination in this material. Though these carols may
center on one aspect of the redemptive act (as the passion),
they generally also proclaimed the other aspect (the joyful
message)--("Awake, awake, ye drowsy souls," OBC, 44).
Thus, the solemn and the merry have been juxtaposed.

Another form of folk-song influence on the carol is
the numerical mnemonic verse. This is a conversational
cataloguing, by number or topic of some basic theme. The
carol, "Welcome Yule" (OBC, 174), is a catalogue of the
days during the Christmas season. The idea is as ancient
as Hebrew civilization but it presents an effective means of
remembering ("The seven joys of Mary," OBC, 70).

Beginning with the mid-17th century in England, the
festival of Christmas was observed by law as a day of fasting. Under this somber order of Puritanism, the beauties
of carolry were silenced, living only in the memory of the
people. Even during the Restoration period, the carol remained subdued. This resulted, in part, from the rise of
contrapuntal music, motets and madrigals and later by larger
musical forms, as music became more an art for the aris-
tocracy. Carolry maintained this relatively insignificant role
until the mid-19th century when it achieved new recognition,
a rebirth.

The singing of the early carols was very flexible.
There were no "proper" tunes; thus, whatever tune was
known and appropriate might be used, be it a church tune,
folk tune, dance or minstrel song. If instruments were
available, the carols would be performed with accompaniment; however, unaccompanied singing was the norm.

The Revival

The heralding of the revival of carolry occurred with
Davies Gilberts' (1769-1839) Some Ancient Christmas Carols
with the tunes to which they were formerly sung in the West
of England (1822) and William Sandys' (1792-1874) Christmas
Carols New and Old (1833). This was the result, in part,
of the spirit of the *Oxford Movement with its reverence for
things ancient. One of the leaders of the Oxford Movement,
John Mason Neale, also aided the revival of the carol with
his finding and translating of the Swedish collection, Piae

Cantiones.   Neale and Rev. T. Helmore produced this volume of Carols for Christmas-tide and Easter-tide in 1853
and 1854.   However, the first successful attempt at a collection of carols reasonably representing all known traditions,
and the real key to the carol revival was Christmas Carols
New and Old (1871) by Henry R. Bramley and John Stainer.
This collection of 42 carols (enlarged to 70 in 1878) has
rightly been called the "Hymns A & M of carols." Another
influential and educational volume was R. R. Chope's
(1830-?) Carols for Use in Church (1875) which contained
112 carols.   In his 1894 edition the number of carols grew
to 215.
        Though the carol revival was an English phenomenon,
realized by the publication of collections of carolry and the
incorporation of carols into church worship, the carolry was
by no means limited to this country.   This is evidenced with
the inclusion of carols from many nationalities in the Oxford
Book of Carols.   From Sweden came the 15th-century "Unto
us a boy is born" (OBC, 92); from Germany, the 16-th century "Es ist ein' Ros' entsprungen" (OBC, 76); Poland and
Czechoslovakia contributed the "Rocking Carol" (OBC, 87);
from Holland, "A Child is born in Bethlehem" (OBC, 73);
and from France, "Willie take your little drum" (OBC, 82).
In America, the carol revival brought similar results as it
did in England, with carol services, out-of-door caroling
through the streets and the publishing of carol collections.
One of America's contributions to carol literature is J. H.
Hopkin's "We three kings of Orient are" (OBC, 196).
        The continuation of the carol revival into the 20th
century has produced a classic reference source.   Under
the editorship of Percy Dearmer, Ralph Vaughan Williams
and Martin Shaw The Oxford Book of Carols (1928) was presented, an anthology of carolry from all times and nationalities.   The preface of this volume serves as a fine summary
of the form, function and history of this musical form.   Even
in the 20th century, new carols are being written and being
incorporated into collections.   Such a carol is Frances Ches-
terton's "How far is it to Bethlehem?" (OBC, 142).   Similar
work is evident in the carols of Sydney Carter (e.g., "Every
star shall sing a carol") as contained in the Peter Smith collections Faith, Folk and Clarity; Faith, Folk and Nativity and
Faith, Folk and Festivity.
        With the enthusiasm of carol singing in churches,
homes, institutions and commercial establishments at Christmas time, and with the traditional service of the Festival of
Nine Lessons and Carols at King's Chapel, Cambridge, borrowed and adapted by churches all over the globe, carolry appears to be at the apex of fashion at the present time.

Dearmer, Percy, R. Vaughan Williams and Martin Shaw.
    The Oxford Book of Carols. London: Oxford Univer-
    sity Press, 1928.
Greene, Richard Leighton. The Early English Carol. Ox-
    ford, Eng.: Clarendon Press, 1935.
Keefe, Mildred Jones. "Carols: Their Origin and Connec-
    tion with Dramatic Ritual and Folkways." Unpublished
    M.A. thesis, Boston University, Boston, Massachusetts,
    1936.
Phillips, William J. Carols: Their Origin, Music and Con-
    nection with Mystery-Plays. London: George Rout-
    ledge, 1921.
Routley, Erik. The English Carol. London: Herbert Jen-
    kins, 1958.
_____ (ed.). University Carol Book. Brighton, Eng.:
    H. Freeman & Co., 1961.
Stevens, John (ed.). "Medieval Carols," Vol. IV,
    Musica Britannica. London: Stainer & Bell, 1958.

CATHEDRAL MUSIC

    The music written for the choirs of the English cathe-
drals, consisting chiefly of *services and *anthems, is referred to as cathedral music. Two collected editions of this
music were compiled by Boyce (1710-1779) and Arnold (1740-
1802). (See *Editions, historical.)

Barnett, W. A. "Music in Cathedrals," PRMA, 3:84, 1877.
Bumpus, John S. A History of English Cathedral Music
    (1549-1889). 2 vols. London: T. Werner Laurie,
    1908.
Fellows, E. W. Forty Years of Cathedral Music. London:
    Oxford University Press, 1940.
Rippon, Bishop of. "Cathedral Music," ML, 3:162-166,
    April, 1922.
Shaw, H. W. Eighteenth-century Cathedral Music. (Papers
    of the Church Music Society, No. 21.) London: Ox-
    ford University Press, 1952.

CHANGE-RINGING (OF. changier, f. LL. cambiare to ex-
    change + OE. hringan)

    The art of bell-ringing peculiar to England in which
a set of bells of various numbers are sounded singly one
after the other in a prescribed mathematical manner is known

as change-ringing. It was developed in 17th-century England,
a development parallel to that of the *carillon on the Continent. A set of bells comprising a change could vary in number from five to 12, usually tuned to notes of the major
scale. The largest bell, the tenor, is the tonic; the smallest
bell is called the treble and is indicated as "1". In change-
ringing each order of bell strikes is called a "change." The
original change which initiates all the possible permutations
is called "rounds." A set of changes is not completed until
"rounds" reappears.

Known as the first treatise on change-ringing is
Fabiam Stedman's Tintinnologia (1668, Cambridge).

Change ringing was practiced where tower bells were
so arranged that their colored woolen bell ropes form a circle with their neighbors. Experienced bell ringers set the
bells in motion at the proper moment by causing each bell
to sing alternately in opposite directions with his pull.

Since many of the peals were quite lengthy and practice was necessary indeed, *handbells were devised as a
convenient means of practicing change-ringing.

Wilson, Wilfrid G. The Art and Science of Change-Ringing
    on Church and Handbells. New York: October House,
    1965.

CHANT (OF. chanter, fr. L. cantare, fr. canare to sing)

A simple monophonic setting or formula used to convey the *psalms and other Scriptural materials is termed a
chant. Historically, it is derived from the word meaning
the prayerful singing of the choir before the altar. (See
*Anglican chant and *Plainsong.)

Ramsbotham, A. "On Psalm-chanting," ML, 1:208-217,
    July, 1920:
Thomas, Wilhelm. "Deutschen Sprechgesang im Gottes-
    dienst," MK, 4:59-66, March-April, 1932.

CHAPEL (ME., fr. OF. chapele, fr. LL. cappella, orig.
    a short cloak, or hood, dim. of cappa cloak. The
    place where St. Martin's cloak was preserved as a
    precious relic was called a cappella, hence the name
    of other similar places of worship)

Originally, the building where St. Martin's cloak was

preserved was called a cappella, a term which came to be
applied to other places containing revered relics of the
saints.   Later the term was expanded to include private
places of worship that were not churches.   Quite prominent
is the institution of worship for sovereigns, called Chapel
Royal.   Places of worship in institutional campuses are often referred to as chapels.   In cathedrals and large churches
a smaller room with its own altar is also known by this title.
      The Chapel Royal of the English monarchs has upheld
a high musical standard and played an invaluable role in the
development and cultivation of English Church Music through
the employment of musicians known as the "musicians of the
Chapel Royal" (almost an institution in themselves).

LeHuray, Peter.   Music and the Reformation in England
      1549-1660.   London: Herbert Jenkins, 1967.   Chap-
      ter 3.
Tremmel, Phyllis.   "Ye Men of Olden Quires and Pypes, "
      Music: The A.G.O. and R.C.C.O. Magazine, 4:28-
      33, February, 1970.

CHOIR (OE, quire, fr. ME. quer, fr. OF. cuer, fr. L.
      chorus, a choral dance, chorus, choir, fr. Gr.
      choros, orig. dancing place)

      (1)   The body of singers who participate in the ser-
vice of public worship is called a choir, as opposed to its
secular counterpart "the chorus. "   From the Reformed tradition, the role of the choir is two-fold: to lead the congregational singing and to sing compositions which add beauty to
the service in praise of God.

      (2)   The part of the church where the singers per-
form; in the medieval cruciform church, it is the altar or
east end.

      (3)   A division of the organ designed for accompani-
ment purposes is the choir.

Harris, Clement A.   "Church Choirs in History, " ML,
      17:210-217, July, 1936.
Kobelt, J.   "Der Kirchenchor, seine Stellung und Aufgabe in
      unserer Kirche, " ZMG, 3:1,3, 1950.
Rainbow, Bernarr.   The Choral Revival in the Anglican
      Church (1839-1892).   London: Oxford University Press,
      1970.

CHOIR-BOOK (fr. G. <u>chorbuch</u>)

The large-sized manuscript of 15th- and 16th-century polyphonic choral music with all the parts present on the open page in the arrangement shown here is a choir-book. The choir members then would gather around the stand upon which the music was placed to perform the work.

S	A
T	B

Though dating from about 1480, the *part-book did not receive wide acceptance until the mid-16th century. The method of printing for these was one in which each voice part was printed in a separate volume.

With the development of orchestral music around 1600, the printing of the complete score intact became the accepted practice, though instances of part-book writing still continued.

Apel, Willi. The Notation of Polyphonic Music 900-1600. 5th ed. Cambridge, Mass.: Mediaeval Academy of America, 1961.
Schröder, O. "Das eisenacher Cantorenbuch," ZM 12:173-179, December, 1931.

CHOIRMASTER (*choir + ME. <u>maister</u>, fr. OE. <u>magister</u> and fr. OF <u>maistre</u>, fr. L. <u>magister</u>, orig. a double comparative from the root of <u>magnus</u>, great)

The church official who is solely responsible for the training and functioning of the *choir(s) and the selection of the music which the ensemble sings is the choirmaster or choir director. (Cf. *Kapellmeister.)

Klink, Waldeman. Der Chormeister. Mainz: Schott, 1931.

CHOIR PARENTS (*choir + OF., fr. L. <u>parena</u>, <u>-entis</u>, fr. <u>parere</u> to bring forth)

The mothers and fathers of the children and young people who comprise the membership of the various choirs in the music ministry within a church are the choir parents or choir sponsors. These persons can be of invaluable assistance to the *choirmaster. Their tasks often include enrollment, orientation of new members, notification to parents of choir policies, transportation problems, clerical work,

robing and social functions.   In some instances these parents
are organized into a "Choir Parents' Guild."

Kettring, Donald D.   Steps Toward a Singing Church.   Phila-
    delphia: The Westminster Press, 1948.   Pp. 65-69.

CHOOSING NOTES   (ME. chesen, chosen, fr. OE. cēosan;
    akin to L. gustare to taste + OF., fro. L. nota a
    mark, sign)

    The compositional technique common in the tunes of
William Billings (1689-1750) in which an extra note(s) appears in a given voice so that the singer may decide which
note to sing is termed the choosing note.   Billings in The
Singing Master's Assistant, put it this way: "When you meet
with 2 or 3 Notes standing one over the other, they are
called Choosing notes, and signify that you may sing which
you please, or all if your part has performers enough, and
remember that they add not to the time; but to the variety."
When used, choosing notes appeared most often in the soprano, alto and bass parts but seldom, if ever, in the tenor
(which was the tune).   When a choice is given in the bass it
is most often the octave.

Garrett, Allen M.   "Performance Practices in the Music of
    William Billings," JAMS, 5:147-148, Spring, 1953.

CHORALE   (F. or ML.; F. choral, fr. ML. choralis, fr.
    L. chorus chorus, fr. Gr. choros dance)

    [Contents: (general); Medieval ancestry; The Johann
Crüger era (1600-1660); The Freylinghausen era (c. 1644-1756);
The rational era (1750-1817); The revival era (1817 to the
present); (bibliography).]   The hymn tunes of the German
Protestant Church from the 16th to the mid-18th centuries,
which correspond to the metrical psalm tunes of the Calvinists and the Church of England, are called chorales.   This
nomenclature is indebted to the Roman Church Gregorian
chorale or ancient chant which served as the *cantus firmus
for much polyphonic service music as did the Reformation
chorale.   This usage is seen in the *chorale preludes, *cantatas and motets of Dietrich Buxtehude (1637-1707), J. S.
Bach (1685-1750), Johannes Brahms (1777-1856), Helmut
Walcha (b. 1907) and Ernst Pepping (b. 1901).
    As will be seen below, the chorale was wedded to the

gesungenes Wort principle, in which the text and tune are
conceived almost simultaneously, since each chorale text is
associated with its own appropriate text (Riedel, 10). Among
the most prevalent forms of the chorale is the old bar-form
of the Meistersingers with its two Stollens and an Abgesang
(AAB).

Medieval Ancestry

Reflective of the dominance of the church in the Middle Ages, the various predecessors of the chorale provided
a rich heritage of sacred song. Among these from the
Roman liturgy were the various tropes for the ordinary of
the *mass as well as the sequences, *antiphons and other
chants of the proper of the mass, the office antiphons and
*canticles, and the Latin hymns. Of the better known ante-
cedent tunes is the Kyrie fons bonitatis of the second mass
reproduced in the Lutheran liturgy as "Kyrie, Gott Vater in
Ewigkeit" ("Kyrie, God the Father in heaven above"). Because of his emphasis on *congregational singing it was only
logical for Martin Luther (1483-1546) and the other German
reformers to turn to the Latin plainsong as a ready source
of information. Prior to the Reformation, the Protestant
chorale developed from its medieval predecessors to the established form which composed a major source of inspiration
during the Baroque era. Martin Luther, along with the musical assistance of Johann Walther (1496-1570) created and
adapted a vast number of hymns to new and existing melodies which were to become the nucleus of German *hymnody.
Considered the first hymnal of the evangelical church was
Luther's *Achtlieder-buch (1524). It was soon followed by
other small hymnals containing similar materials. Among
the major characteristics of the robust chorales created during this period was the bar-form of the German Meistersingers (e.g., "Allein Gott in der Höh sei Ehr"--ab, ab,
cab--CH, 5). Another device of the Reformation chorale
was the distinctive complex polyrhythmic quality, involving
the 3:2 relationship of hemiola (e.g., "Es ist ein' Ros' entsprungen," CH, 59). Although a preserver of the past,
Luther also pressed forward by the use of the Ionian mode
(the major mode of today) for certain hymns ("Ein' feste
Burg ist unser Gott," CH, 2). These tunes were designed
to encourage singing, not passive listening, once again showing Luther as a creative pedagogical genius, adapting the familiar to instruct in the unfamiliar. After all, the chorale
was a vehicle to convey church doctrine.
Also involved in the Luther tradition of the 16th-century

chorale were two important poet-composers, Nicolaus Hermann (c.1480-1561) and Philipp Nicolai (1556-1608). The
latter's "Wie shön leuchtet der Morgenstern" ("How brightly
shines the morning star," CH, 78) has become one of the
magnificent examples of this era.

The Johann Crüger Era (1600-1660)

During this period, which included the devastation of
the Thirty Years' War but yet produced many inventive minds
such as Newton, Shakespeare, and Rembrandt, the chorale
underwent two distinctive changes. First, the Reformation
concept of poet-composer gave way to the separate specialist,
poet or composer. The outstanding poetic authors of German
hymns for this period were Paul Gerhardt (1607-1676) and
Johann Rist (1607-1667). Secondly, the unison style of congregational singing of the chorales gave way to the *Kantional style of four-part homophonic writing with the melody
in the soprano (Riedel, 56).

Among the numerous composers who developed the
style of this post-Reformation period were Melchior Vulpius
(1560-1615), Melchior Teschner (1584-1635) and Johann G.
Ebeling (1637-1676).

Regarding the characteristics of this era of chorale
composition, the hüpfend rhythm (♩♩♩♩) is frequently
present giving a simplicity and persistence common to some
folk spirituals. Expansion of the simple joy of triple meter
to a four-fold meter or even alternating duple and triple
meters during this period was quite common, as seen in
Ebeling's "Warum sollt ich mich deen Grämen" ("All my
heart this night rejoices," CH, 8). The tendency for composers to devise tonal progressions to underline and portray
the word meanings, i.e., pictorialism, ever so common in
the *chorale preludes of J. S. Bach, can be seen with the
emergence of strong tonal devices of these Kantional chorales.

The major contribution of this era, though, was Johann Crüger (1598-1662), whose hymnbook, Praxis Pietatis
Melica (The practice of piety through music, 1647), containing many texts by his good friend, Paul Gerhardt, underwent 45 editions and reprints in a 90-year period. His two
great tunes, "Nun danket alle Gott" ("Now thank we all our
God," CH, 68) and "Herzliebster Jesu" ("Ah, Holy Jesus,"
CH, 4) reflect the influence of French Calvinism upon him
in that these chorales begin with the triple hammer stroke
common to the metrical tunes of the French Psalter. However, it should not be assumed that Crüger was influenced
only by the new. He skillfully blended modality and tonality

in his melodies as well as retaining the bar-form and some of the rhythmic drive of the former period.

The Freylinghausen Era (c. 1644-1756)

With the dawning of the Age of Enlightenment or Reason, another style of chorale developed, one which was influenced by the individualism and pietism of the day. The chorale was now being turned from a corporate expression to that of the individual, as seen in the employment of the soloist accompanied by the keyboard and bass instrument in basso continuo (*thorough-bass) style. Evidence of this can be found in Johann Anastasius Freylinghausen's (c. 1670-1739) Geistreiches Gesangbuch which ultimately contained 750 hymns and 250 melodies (see CH, 57). This style, along with the style galant, gave both the singers and players latitude to ornament and improvise as they performed the melodies of the old and new chorales. Thus, as exemplified in the chorales and work of Johann Mattheson (1681-1764) the chorale became the property of the amateur soloist and accompanist. Because of the melodic, linear emphasis, many chorales of the Baroque era with their simplicity and beauty have survived not only in hymnals but also in other compositions for which they have served as motivic material.

Specific characteristics of the "Freylinghausian" chorales included clearly tonal melodies and harmonies with an emphasis upon the triad. Pictorialism continues while rhythms become more dance-like with triple meters, reflective of the spreading ornamental Italian music.

Thus, the chorales of this time might be called chorale arias or "private music" as they were not intended for congregational use but for domestic and private meditation which is also noticed in the highly personalized texts by the leading poet of the day, Joachim Neander (1650-1680).

The consummation of this era came with the harmonizations of the chorales by J. S. Bach (1685-1750), which again are not considered congregational but choral.

The Rational Era (1750-1817)

Influenced by the world around it, the church and consequently the chorale felt the pressures of rationalistic thinking. The major results on the chorale were few lasting texts and tunes, and the divesting of the ornamentation and driving rhythms from the existing tunes. Thus, the plodding movement of the equal-note duration which exists in many hymnals today stems from this era.

The Revival Era (1817 to the Present)

With the coming of the 19th century, a spirit of Reformation evangelism arose which has carried into the 20th century as well. This revival movement was founded by Professor Ernest Ardt (1769-1829) a leader for renewed interest in hymnology. His "Von dem Wort und dem Kirchenliede" ("The Word and the Hymn," 1819) served as the impetus for this evangelical hymnological revival. During this period new hymnals were compiled and the monumental catalogues of chorales--Johannes Zahn's Die Melodien der deutschen evangelischen Kirchenlieder, 6 vols., 1889-1893, and Albert Fischer's Evangelische Kirchenlied des 17. Jahrhunderts, 6 vols., 1904-1916--were published.

It continues to be a slow painful process for the Christian church everywhere to reinstate the original rhythms and the original ornamentations of the chorales.

Liemohn, Edwin. The Chorale. Philadelphia: Muhlenberg
    Press, 1953.
Mahrenholz, Christhard and Oskar Söhngen (eds.). Hand-
    buch zum Evangelischen Kirchengesangbuch. 3 vols.
    Göttingen: Vandenhoeck, n.d.
Precht, Fred L. "The Historical Development of the
    Lutheran Chorale," Church Music, 66.1[sic]:6-12,
    1966.
Reidel, Johannes. The Lutheran Chorale: Its Basic Tradi-
    tions. Minneapolis: Augsburg Publishing House, 1967.
Zahn, Johannes. Die Melodien der deutschen evangelischen
    Kirchenlieder aus den Quellen geschöpft und mitgeteilt.
    6 vols. Hildesheim: Olms, 1963. (1904-1916)

CHORALE CANTATA (*chorale + *cantata)

A *cantata which employs the text and melody of an existing *chorale in one or more movements is termed a chorale cantata. Primarily a Baroque technique (in German, Choralkantate), it is masterfully exhibited in the cantatas of J. S. Bach ("Christ lag in Todesbanden," "Nun danket alle Gott" and "Wachet auf"). Predecessors in this practice were Franz Tunder (1614-1667), Johann Rosenmüller (c.1620-1684), Johann Pachelbel (1653-1706) and Johann Kuhnau (1660-1722).

Terry, C. S. J. S. Bach, Cantata Texts. London: Oxford
    University Press, 1926.
Whittaker, W. G. The Cantatas of Johann Sebastian Bach:

Sacred and Secular. 2 vols. London: Oxford University Press, 1959.

CHORALE CONCERTATO (*chorale + *concertato)

The setting of a *hymn tune or *chorale for choir, organ, congregation and instrument(s) in which each stanza of the *hymn is treated in a different manner musically is a chorale concertato. This 20th-century form relates to the 16th- and 17th-century practice of alternatim singing of hymns by the choir and congregation.

CHORALE FANTASY

An organ composition in which the *chorale melody is employed in a fragmented manner accompanied by rhapsodic figurations in a free improvisatory style is a chorale fantasy. (Cf. *Chorale prelude.)

CHORALE FUGUE (*chorale + *fugue)

An organ composition in which the first phrase of a *chorale melody appears as the subject of a fugue is a chorale fugue. (Cf. *Chorale prelude.)

CHORALE MOTET (*chorale + *motet)

(1) The polyphonic choral composition based on a *chorale with an associated biblical or religious text, with instrumental accompaniment optional, and with sectional imitative contrapuntal development is a chorale motet.

From the beginning the chorale motet was a tool of the church, seeking to accomplish two tasks: to articulate Reformation theology through hymnody and to familiarize the German peoples with the chorale melodies. Among the early Protestant masters of this form were Gregor Meyer (c.1510-1576), Sixt Dietrich (c.1490-1548), George Rhaw (c.1488-1548) and Ludwig Senfl (c.1492-1555). With the chorale cantus in the tenor, the remaining voices (usually two to four parts) employed contrapuntal imitation which varied with each phrase of the cantus firmus. In Senfl's "Sancte pater" (DED, XIII:3-16) the chorale appears in canon between the tenor and discantus secundus as well as being separated into phrases by interludes.

By the time of the chorale motets of Michael Praetorius (1571-1621) and Samuel Scheidt (1587-1654) the form
had developed to the points of a soprano-oriented cantus
(rather than tenor-), juxtaposed homophonic and polyphonic
style and the introduction of polychoral and instrumental
technique. However, because of the influence of the *concertato style (or stile concertato), which was difficult to
fuse into the settled form of the chorale motet, Scheidt,
Schein and Hammerschmidt moved the chorale into the direction of the dialogue, the chorale concertato. Tunder and
Buxtehude, on the other hand, guided the chorale toward the
cantata, which J. S. Bach (1685-1750) brought to completion.

Though the chorale motet declined in use as a compositional form in and of itself after 1650, its influence has
remained in the various movements of cantatas which possess pure chorale motet characteristics (see, e.g., Bach's
"Christ lag in Todesbanden," verses 1 & 4, BGA, I:96-124).
Also, it has remained present in the organ *chorale preludes
of the German Baroque period, which might be called chorale
motets "without words."

(For the English equivalent to the chorale motet see
*Anthem.)

(2) In organ composition the form in which the successive phrases of a *chorale are used as the basis for the
successive points of imitation, in the manner of a *motet,
is called a chorale motet. (Cf. *Chorale prelude.)

Morgan, Wesley K. "The Chorale Motet from 1650-1750."
   Unpublished Ph.D. dissertation, University of Southern
   California, Los Angeles, 1956.
Seaich, John E. "Leichtentritt's History of the Motet: A
   Study and Translation (Chapters 7-15)." Unpublished
   Ph.D. dissertation, University of Utah, Salt Lake City,
   1958.

CHORALE PARTITA

An organ composition consisting of a set of variations
upon a *chorale melody is a chorale partita. (Cf. *Chorale
prelude.)

CHORALE PRELUDE

In its broadest concept an organ composition in a

polyphonic style which is based upon and presents in varied
forms a chorale melody is considered a chorale prelude
(also, choral prelude; in German, Choralvorspiel).

More specifically it is a polyphonic composition for
organ (or other instruments) based on a chorale melody,
designed to be performed before the singing of the chorale
by the congregation.

The chorale prelude, a term peculiar to Protestant
Church music, differs from the broader term, organ chorale,
which historically includes the closely related polyphonic
organ settings of hymns of the Roman Catholic Church. The
latter served as musical substitutes for plainsong, inheriting
a liturgical function. Thus, the background for the development of the chorale prelude lies in the heritage of the organ
hymn as transmitted by the Paumann Fundamentum Organi-
sandi (1452), the Buxheimer Orgelbuch (c. 1460-70), the
Schlick Tabulaturen etlicher Lobgesang und Lidlein (1512)
and the Mulliner Book (c. 1560), to mention a few collections.

Through the insistence of Luther to teach his followers
by means of congregational song (the chorale) and his encouragement of the use of the organ during worship, the development of one of the most beautiful art forms of the
Baroque period--the chorale prelude--was evident. Coinci-
dentally with the congregational singing of the chorale came
the organist's duty to play the chorale as an introduction,
often embellished in such a way as to create an artistic
work known as the chorale prelude. At first, these compositions followed their Roman Catholic models with the long-
note cantus-firmus remaining the tenor. However, it was
not long before the chorale melodies began to appear in the
soprano, sometimes with expressive ornamentation. Among
the first collections illustrative of this development were
E. Nicolaus Ammerbach's Orgel oder Instrument Tabulatur
(1571, 1583) and Augustus Normiger's Tabulaturbuch auff dem
Instrumente (1598), both collections being essentially homophonic settings of chorales interspersed with polyphonic elements.

Developing during the 16th century from the model of
the vocal motet, the *chorale motet employed the principle
of multi-sections resulting from the successive points of imitation representing each phrase of the chorale (Michael Praetorius' complex chorale-motet on Wir glauben all). During
the 17th century other types of chorale preludes developed.
Having the soprano sustain the tune in clear perceptibility,
the melody chorale incorporates contrapuntal writing in the
accompanying lower parts. The ornamented chorale enriched
the melody by expressive ornamentation. Similar to the imi-

tative style of the chorale motet, the chorale fugue utilized
only one theme which is derived from the opening phrase of
the chorale. The chorale canon employs the melody in close
imitation in two voice parts, as in a canon. The most free
and fanciful in character of all chorale preludes is the
chorale fantasy whose character is of an improvisatory nature. Also to be mentioned are the choral partitas (variations) in which the chorale melody is placed in numerous
expressive contrapuntal settings.

The development of the chorale variation, influenced
by the variation principles of the late 16th-century Italian
instrumentalists, was initiated primarily by Jan Pieterszoon
Sweelinck (1562-1621), the Dutch organist and composer.
Each contrapuntal variation of the chorale melody (the versus)
differed in two ways, by figuration or change of character,
the number of voices often varying. However, the cantus
firmus being rarely dissolved by variation was clearly recognizable though it changed voice positions. Thus, the clear
contrast of timbre demanded by this style of writing brought
about the tonal design of the Baroque organ. Samuel Scheidt's
(1587-1654) variations expanded Sweelinck's figurative variations by changing the rhythmic patterns or motives with each
phrase of the chorale melody within the versus. (Scheidt,
"Variations on Warum betrubst du dich?" HAM, 196). Other
composers to employ this Baroque form were Scheidemann,
Tunder, Buxtehude and Pachelbel. Certain examples by composers show an attempt at the pictorialism of each chorale
stanza with successive variations. One such remarkable
work is Franz Tunder's variations on "Jesus, Christus unser
Heiland" (K. Straube, Choralvorspiele alte Meister, 1951,
p. 130). In the mid-17th century the chorale variation
evolved into the more extended chorale partita. This favored
form of many Baroque composers permitted them to reveal
their individuality. To this form Johann Pachelbel (1653-
1706) brought his virtuoso spirit, George Böhm (1661-1733)
contributed the elegance and grace of French keyboard music,
and J. G. Walther (1684-1748) exploited full sonorities while
maintaining solid contrapuntal style. In the variations on
"Auf meinen lieben Gott" by D. Buxtehude the fusion of the
chorale variation with the suite is achieved as the chorale
melody is molded into the allemande, sarabande, courante
and gigue. This served as a model for the 20th-century
variations on "Ja ich glaub an Jesum Christum" (Op. 13) by
Ernst Křenek (b. 1900).

Derived from Sweelinck's model of the chorale variation and the chorale motet is the chorale fantasy as seen in
Scheidt's "Fantasia super Ich ruf zu dir, Herr Jesus Christ"

(DdT, I). This form developed mainly among the composers
of the North German school who applied the brilliant rhapsodic elements of extensive ornamentation of the chorale, run-
ning passages and arpeggios to fragments of the cantus firmus. Among the earliest examples of extended chorale
fantasies are two works by Johannes Stephanni (CEKM, 17).
Main contributors to this form were Scheidemann, Tunder,
Reinken and Buxtehude. In Buxtehude's chorale fantasies the
toccata is ever present with fragments of the chorale melody
emerging and disappearing amid a turbulent accompaniment
("Wie schön leuchtet"). Reinken, on the other hand, reveals
the German predilection for polyphony amid virtuosity through
the use of double pedal. ("An Wasserflüssen Babylon, "
CEKM, 16.)
        Often termed as a chorale motet, the chorale fugue
was predominantly a form of the central German school. In
it the initial phrase of the chorale melody became the fugue
subject, with the remainder of the melody introduced either
as a cantus firmus or in a chain of fughettas (phrase by
phrase). Among the earliest representatives is Heinrich
Bach's (1615-1692) "Erbarm dich mein" (ZGO II:101). To
this form Pachelbel brought a thoroughly instrumental character, while J. G. Walther provided strength with the late
Baroque harmonies.
        The specific form known as the chorale prelude with
the clearly recognizable melody, usually being in the soprano, is related to the chorale partita, being an extension of
a single variation. The melody, either plain or ornamented,
was accompanied in a contrapuntal manner. Usually each
phrase of the chorale melody was introduced by a short, imitative anticipatory motive in the other voices. The real
groundwork for the development of this form by J. S. Bach
was laid by Buxtehude and Pachelbel. The highly personal
interpretation of the chorale by the former was consummated
by Bach.
        J. S. Bach (1685-1750), the keystone of the Baroque,
brought to culmination all the basic forms of the chorale
prelude. From the more than 150 chorale preludes of Bach
the following illustrate each type: cantus-firmus chorale--
"Jesus Christus, unser Heiland (BG, III:234); chorale motet--
"Wenn wir in hochsten Noten sein" (BG, XXV:145); chorale
fuge--"Allein Gott in der Höh sei Ehr" (BG, XL:45); chorale
prelude (melody type)--most of the preludes of the Orgelbüchlein; ornamented chorale--"Wenn wir in höchsten Nöten
sein" (BG, XXV:57); chorale canon--"Liebster Jesu, wir sind
hier" (BG, XXV:49); choral fantasy--"Ein' feste Burg ist
unser Gott" (BG, XL:57); and chorale partitas--"Sei gegrüsset,
Jesu gütig" (BG, XL:122).

Following the death of Bach, the role of the church in music and, thus, the attractiveness of organ composition declined. Along with this decrease of organ music was that of the chorale prelude. Mendelssohn's (1809-1847) Organ Sonatas (Op. 65) marked the beginning of a renaissance of the use of the chorale in organ composition. Johannes Brahms (1833-1897) ended his creative musical output with 11 chorale preludes (Op. 122) in a style similar to that of Bach. Following his German heritage, Max Reger (1873-1916) contributed numerous preludes, both short and extended in development. Similarly S. Karg-Elert (1877-1933) produced substantial contribution to chorale prelude literature with his 66 Chorale Improvisations (Op. 65).

In the 20th century a continued revival of the chorale prelude is found through the contributions of men like Johann Nepomuk David (b. 1895), Ernst Pepping (b. 1901), Helmut Walcha (b. 1907), Joseph Ahrens (b. 1904), Cor Kee (b. 1900), Flor Peeters (b. 1903) and Healey Willan (1880-1968). With the rising importance of the hymn in this century the logical union of the hymn with the chorale prelude has produced a vast amount of hymn preludes. Outstanding contributions to this form have come from Healey Willan and Flor Peeters, as well as Leo Sowerby, Seth Bingham and Jan Bender, to mention only a few.

Edson, Jean Slater. Organ Preludes. 2 vols. Metuchen, N. J.: Scarecrow Press, 1970. Supplement, 1974.
Macpherson, Charles. "Chorale Preludes, Ancient and Modern," PRMA, 39, 1913.
Morgan, Wesley. "The Chorale Motet from 1650-1750." Unpublished dissertation, University of Southern California, Los Angeles, 1956.
Pack, Carol J. "The Chorale Preludes of Ernst Pepping as Compared with their Historical Antecedents." Unpublished M.M. thesis, Baylor University, Waco, Texas, 1965.

CHORALE VARIATIONS

An organ composition consisting of a set of variations (versus) upon a chorale is a chorale variation. It is also termed *chorale partita. (Cf. *Chorale prelude.)

Sego, Charles M. "The Chorale Variation Technique of Jan Pieterszoon Sweelinck." Unpublished M.M. thesis, Southern Methodist University, Dallas, Texas, 1959.

CHORALITER   (fr. F. choral, fr. ML. choralis)

The singing of *psalms, *hymns and *chorales by the chorus-of-the-whole, i.e. the congregation, in union or octaves, is called choraliter.   It was the musical practice observed in the Lutheran commune throughout the 16th century. After 1600 simple four-part settings were provided for the congregation.   However, it should be noted that as early as 1524 three- to five-part settings of chorales were available (J. Walther's Geystliche Gesangk Büchleyn).

In the 17th century choraliter was employed during services on ordinary Sundays while *figuraliter was reserved for festival days.

Adlung, Jacob. Anleitung zu der musikalischen Gelahrtheit
    (1758).   Ed. by Hans Joachim Moser.   Kassel:
    Bärenreiter, 1953.   (Facsimile ed.)

CHORISTER   (fr. F. choriste, fr. ML. chorista, fr. Gr.
    choros)

The senior boy member of the choir in the English cathedral is called a chorister.   He has received training in the singing of church music provided through the existence of endowed choirs in the cathedral establishments.   History has provided evidence to labeling of these choirs as the "nurseries" of British musical composition, in that many esteemed British composers have emerged from this system, e.g., Blow, Humphrey, Purcell.   (Cf. *Boy choirs.)   It was the choristers that set the level of attainment for the younger singers, the singing-boys (the future choristers) and the probationers (the youngest boys, the novices).

Nicholson, Sydney H. Quires and Places Where They Sing.
    London: S.P.C.K., 1932.

CHORUS   (L. a dance in a ring, a dance accompanied with
    song, a chorus, a band of dancers and singers, fr.
    Gr. choros)

(1)   In hymnody, the one or two identical lines recurring at the end of each *stanza of a *hymn may be called a chorus.   Unlike the *refrain, the chorus is not essential to the meaning of the text, and often appears to be tacked on (cf. *Burden).   It is associated with the *gospel song and

hymn from the American revival era.   (See "Wonderful
Words of Life," BH, 181).

(2)   Also from the American revival era and Sunday
school movement, the shortened form of the *gospel song
containing a simple truth, directly stated and made easy to
remember, is called a chorus.   It is thought to have originated in the early 20th century with the evangelistic campaigns of Charles H. Alexander and others.   The earliest
extant publication of choruses is the Alexander Gospel Songs
(1909).

Sydnor, James Rawlings.   The Hymn and Congregational
    Singing.   Richmond, Va.:   John Knox Press, 1960.
    Chapter 6.

CHRISTIAN YEAR   (L. christianus, fr. Gr. christianos +
    ME. yer, yeer, zer, fr. OE. gear, fr. Gr. hora
    a season of the year, horos a year, Av. yare year)

The annual cycle of religious seasons into which the
church calendar is arranged commonly is called the Christian Year (or church year or liturgical year).   Its meaningful observance in every generation aims to unite each Christian with the persons, events, and emotions associated with
the life of Christ and the development of the early Christian
Church.
    The distinct characteristics of the seasons of the
Christian Year, its feasts and facts, are historically rooted
in the Hebrew people who, like their pagan neighbors, built
their religious observances around the seasonal cycles of
nature and the heavenly bodies, yet reinterpreting the calendar as containing days of historical commemoration.   Passover, thus, became associated with the first new moon of
spring, a time of the ingathering of the first-fruits of the
spring harvest.
    Supplying the link between the Jewish calendar and
the Christian calendar is the Passover celebration when
Jesus of Nazareth, the Paschal Lamb, was slain and rose
again the third day.   Thus, from the beginning of Christianity, this event has been seen as the culmination of one historical era and the beginning of a new age, a commemoration of past events and the anticipation of future ones.
    The primacy of the Easter festival is seen in the
fact that almost the entire Christian Year depends upon it
for dating.   This "royal feast of feasts," lasting 50 days to

Pentecost, was originally the only festival observed by the Church universal during the first three centuries of its history. As a period of joy and songs of alleluias, the season included not only the Lord's Passion and Resurrection but also the Ascension and coming of the Holy Spirit. During the fourth century, the days of Holy Week were broken off and Ascension Day was established as 40 days after Easter. (This resulted from the investigations by Constantine and his mother into the historical sites of the Biblical stories in Palestine.)

Originating from the baptism and first communion of new converts into the church on Easter, a period of preparation and intensive study for these novices evolved into the season of Lent. By the time of the Council of Nicea, A.D. 325, the prayer and fasting of these was joined by all the faithful and set at 40 days or six weeks, corresponding to the Lord's wilderness retreat.

It was during the sixth century that the Roman church sought to set apart the three Sundays preceding Lent as special days to invoke God's aid and protection against war, famine and plague. For them these pre-Lenten days (Quinquagesima, Sexagesima and Septuagesima) have traditionally been an extension of the Lenten discipline. Protestant churches, however, feeling the Lenten season sufficiently long, have tended to consider the pre-Lent Sundays as major festivals in the calendar, or have omitted them.

The second cycle of the Christian Year, the one focusing on the Incarnation, owes its origin to the influence of the Gentile festivals of savior-gods' birthdays. Beginning in the early third century, Christians in Egypt are known to have celebrated the "Manifestation" of the Redeemer in the world on January 6th. This festival which originally supplanted the Egyptian birthday festival of Osiris was accepted almost throughout the Western church by the mid-fourth century as the feast of Epiphany associating the Matthew account of the visit of the Magi to the infant Christ with it. In Rome, however, in the early fourth century, December 25th was chosen as the celebration of Christ's birth to counter the major pagan festival of the Unconquered Sun. By the fifth century the Eastern and Western churches had adopted each other's festivals of Incarnation and Manifestation.

As with the Easter cycle, a period of preparation developed prior to the Christmas cycle. The period of penitence for the coming of the Christ, the Advent, was adopted into the Western church by the sixth century and limited to four Sundays before Christmas.

Though the Christmas and Easter cycles progress

from Advent Sunday through Whitsunday, many weeks of summer and autumn remain. This season has become known as
the season of Trinity, after the English festival associated
with St. Thomas Becket's consecration as Archbishop of Can-
terbury on Trinity Sunday in 1162. The emphasis of Trinity
has traditionally been one of instruction in Christian growth
and living. Thus, in a way, it is a period of preparation for
the next Advent-Whitsunday cycle, the coming of our Savior
anew. In the mid-20th century there has been a move among
the Methodist and Presbyterian churches of America to di-
vide Trinity into two seasons: Pentecost, beginning with
Pentecost Sunday and continuing through the next to the last
Sunday of August, and Kingdomtide, beginning with the last
Sunday of August and continuing until Advent.

Stanley, Vernon. The Liturgical Year; An Explanation of
    the Origin, History and Significance of the Festival
    Days and Fasting Days of the English Church. Lon-
    don: Mowbray, 1901.

CHRISTMASTIDE

    The season of the *Christian Year beginning with
Christmas Day, December 25, and continuing until the eve
of Epiphany, January 5, is known as Christmastide.

Wetzler, Robert and Helen Huntington. Seasons and Sym-
    bols: A Handbook on the Church Year. Minneapolis:
    Augsburg Publishing House, 1962.

CHURCH ORCHESTRA see ORCHESTRAL INSTRUMENTS

COLLA PARTE ACCOMPANIMENT (It., with the part)

    Colla parte accompaniment indicates that the instru-
ment parts are to be a literal duplication of the vocal lines.

COLLECT (OF. collecta, fr. L. ecclesia collecta an early
    Roman gathering for worship and prayer, akin L.
    collecta a collection in money, and assemblage, fr.
    colligere to bind together)

    The brief stylized prayer peculiar to the day or

festival which preceded liturgical *lessons in the eucharistic
services is the collect. This formal prayer also occurs in
the daily services of prayer (see *Canonical Hours).

As a literary form, the collect is in five sections:
(1) the invocation, (2) the relative clause to God's attributes,
(3) the petition, (4) the reason for the petition, and (5) the
ending, a pleading in Christ's name.

In use among believers for nearly 15 centuries, the
collects composed during the Reformation era and later have
become more extended in form and more specific in thought
than those of earlier composition. (The most ancient known
collection of these prayers is the Leonine, named for Pope
Leo the Great, 440-461.) The Reformers, in fact, translated, adapted and combined many of the ancient Latin collects for use in their vernacular services, as seen in Luther's Taufbüchlein and in the *Book of Common Prayer
(1549).

Although often intoned by the 16th-century Reformed
ministers, the collects generally are recited today.

Reed, Luther D. The Lutheran Liturgy. Philadelphia:
    Muhlenberg Press, 1947. Pp. 278-287.
Strodach, Paul Z. The Collect for the Day. Philadelphia:
    V.L.P.H., 1935.

COMMON WAY (ME. commun, comon, fr. OF. comun,
    commun, fr. L. communis + ME. wey, way, fr.
    OE. weg)

The late 17th- and 18th-century style of *congregational singing occurring among the New England communities
and associated with the rural folk tradition in which psalm
tunes were sung according to the manner of each congregation
--ornamented and varied, but not notated--is referred to as
the "common way" or the "usual way" or the "early New
England folk style." It is in opposition to the notated style
of the reformers of early New England psalmody, called
"regular singing" or "singing by note."

Among the characteristics of the "common way" were
the very slow singing, the abundant use of ornaments, arbi-
trary alteration of pitch and time values, and non-synchroni-
zation among voices. A vital part of this style was the
principle of *lining-out, the "call-and-response" pattern so
basic to folk-song tradition.

Gilbert Chase. America's Music: From the Pilgrims to the

Present. 2d. ed. New York: McGraw-Hill, 1966.
Chapter 2.

COMMUNION SERVICE (F. or L.; F. communion, fr. L.
communio + *service)

The musical settings of the office of Holy Communion
is called a communion service (Anglican). Because of doctrinal differences, this service has not been a mere English
setting of the Roman Mass. Basically only the Kyrie and
the Credo were set musically by the Tudor church musicians,
the Gloria, Sanctus and Agnus Dei having been omitted.
Archbishop Cranmer, in the second edition of the
Prayer Book (1552), moved the Gloria from its traditional
location following the Kyrie to the end of the service. Introducing the Ten Commandments into the beginning of the
service he gave the Kyrie the role of a penitential response
to the Law: after each of the first nine commandments
came the response, "Lord, have mercy upon us, and incline
our hearts to keep this law"; following the tenth, "Lord,
have mercy upon us, and write all these laws in our hearts,
we beseech Thee."
Settings of the Gloria slowly returned to the service
during the 17th century, taking their place at the end of the
service, following the post-communion Thanksgiving. However, the late 16th- and 17th-century communion services
consisted basically of the Kyrie and Nicene Creed, as is the
case with the William Byrd (1543-1623) fourth service,
known as the Great Service (TCM, II:123-222). By the Restoration the Sanctus reappeared with greater regularity, as
in William Croft's (1687-1727) Morning Service in B Minor
(ACM, I:151-186).
With the introduction of the rubric (1789), permitting
a communion hymn during the receiving of the sacraments,
the Agnus Dei regained entry into the communion service,
being commonly sung at this point.
The communion service along with settings of services
of *Morning Prayer and Evening Prayer (*Vespers) belong to
the *full service. (For the Lutheran equivalent see *Deutsche
Messe.)

Arnold, J. H. The Music of the Holy Communion. Papers
    of the Church Music Society, No. 16. London: Oxford
    University Press, 1946.
Titcomb, Everett. Anglican Ways. New York: H. W.
    Gray, 1962.

Weinandt, Elwyn A. Choral Music of the Church. New
    York: The Free Press, 1965.

COMPLINE (L. completorium)

    The last of the *Canonical Hours, completing the
daily cycle in the Roman Church, incorporated into the Anglican liturgy in the Revised Prayer Book (1928), is called
Compline. The *preces from this office compose the evening *suffrages which may be used in connection with *Vespers in the Lutheran Church.

Shepherd, Massey H., Jr. The Oxford American Prayer
    Book Commentary. New York: Oxford University
    Press, 1950.

CONCERTATO STYLE (fr. It. concerto, fr. concertare, fr.
    L. concertare to contend, disbute, debate, fr. con +
    certare to strive, fr. certus determined, decided, +
    ME. stile, style, fr. OF. style, stile, fr. L. stilus,
    stylus a stake, style, manner of writing, mode of
    expression)

    The employment of alternating groups of performers,
similar or dissimilar in size and organization, vocal and/or
instrumental, is the 18th-century concertato style. The
term was introduced by 17th-century Italian composers, although its importance to Protestant church music began with
Heinrich Schütz (1585-1672) who was influenced by the motet
and madrigal principles of Giovani Gabrieli (1557-1612). In
Schütz's sacred concertato, "O Herr, hilf" (MM, 135f.), the
use of the instruments with the voices interchangeably in
imitative concertato style along with the sectional structure
which begins with a brief sinfonia mark the trend for further
concertato development. Andreas Hammerschmidt (1612-
1675) incorporated extensive use of the concertato style, particularly involving the solo voice against the ensemble, in
his Musicalische Gespräche über die Evangelia, 1655 (61
pieces of Kirchenmusik for the Sundays and festivals of the
*Christian Year). These composers together with Tunder,
Krieger, Ahle and Buxtehude developed the concertato style
of the Baroque era into a multisectional structure with instrumental ritornelli which led to the recitative and aria
format of the cantata.
    A similar concertato style is also present in the

anthems of Henry Purcell (1663-1717) by means of alternating solo and tutti ensembles with instrumental *ritornelli.

After many years of neglect the concertato style has been revived, especially in 20th-century German choral music (see the choral works of Distler (1908-1942), Pepping (b. 1901) and Zimmermann (b. 1930).

Bukofzer, Manfred. Music in the Baroque Era. New York: W. W. Norton, 1947.

Wienandt, Elwyn A. Choral Music of the Church. New York: The Free Press, 1965.

CONFESSION (OF., fr. L. confessio)

(1) The prayer of penitence on the part of the officiant and communicant which usually occurs sometime during a liturgical office is referred to as the Confession or Confession of Sins. Its historical pre-Reformation basis is the Roman Confiteor. When the first Prayer Book (1549) was published, the Anglican office of *Holy Communion incorporated this act after the consecration of the elements. However, since the 1552 revision, the Confession has remained in its present place. A Confession of Sins also prefixes the office of *Morning Prayer and Evening Prayer (*Vespers). According to the present Anglican rubrics all communicants are to say the Confession together. The composition of the Confession itself bears the influence of the old Latin form and the long form in Hermann's Consultation (1548). In the Lutheran eucharistic order the Confession follows the *invocation providing the conclusion to the introductory office.

(2) For Confession of Faith see *Credo.

Reed, Luther D. The Lutheran Liturgy. Philadelphia: Muhlenberg Press, 1947.

CONGREGATIONAL SINGING (OF. congregacion, fr. L. congregatio + *singing)

The use of vernacular singing by the assembly of the faithful in public worship is termed congregational singing (in German, Gemeindegesang). Though the main emphasis on congregational singing appeared with the Reformation, it was by no means a new development. During the early centuries of the Christian church any music which was used

was relatively simple and sung by the congregation. While
the Greek Church, at the Council of Laodicea (367), ruled
against congregational singing as a corruptive influence,
Ambrose (333?-397), Bishop of Milan, saw great benefit in
it and composed metrical hymns for congregational use.

Having seen the effectiveness of congregational singing
to unify and inspire the Hussites in their Christian beliefs,
Martin Luther (1483-1546) established the *chorale as the
people's song of the German Evangelical Lutheran Church.
At first, the singing of these chorales was in unison, but
later the organ was used in alternation with the congregational singing in the evangelical church. With the hope of
improving the inspiring strong congregational singing Lukas
Osiander (1534-1604) published Funfzig geistliche Lieder (for
four voices set in such a way that the whole congregation
can join in them, 1586), the first known publication to attempt to unite the choir and congregation in hymn singing.
This work lifted the melody from the tenor to the soprano
in a move toward instrumental support of congregational
singing.

In the Reformed Church, congregational singing was
limited to the unison singing of the metrical psalms (see
*Psalmody, metrical). As the Merbecke Booke of Common
Praier Noted (1550) made no provisions for congregational
singing and the singing of metrical psalms were unauthorized
in worship, the Anglican Church would appear to have been
void of congregational singing. This would have been the
case, except that by 1560 the practice of singing the metrical psalms congregationally before or after the service
proper became quite common in many parishes (Etherington,
106, 107).

After the Thirty Years' War with the emphasis on
organ building came the publishing of several organ books
for accompanying choir and congregational singing. Among
the earliest and more satisfying ones was Samuel Scheidt's
(1587-1654) Tabulaturbuch (1650), a work containing 112
settings of 100 melodies. Soon after this period the choir
was replaced entirely by the organ as the leader of congregational singing in the German Evangelical Church. Eventually the gradual diminishing of congregational singing came
about. For it was during the Pietistic Era (1680-1750) that
the ostentatious practices of the organists who delighted in
elaborate ornamentation rather than congregational praise
made hymn singing almost impossible (see *Zwischenspiel).
However, the importance which had been placed on congregational singing prior to this time can be seen reflected in
the treatment of the German chorales and psalm tunes in
the larger choral and instrumental forms through 1750.

Following this period and with the banishment of larger sacred musical forms along with the choral emphasis in the churches, congregational singing began to regain its esteemed position as the characteristic music of Protestant worship in Germany, though few new chorales were written.

In England, on the other hand, the 18th century witnessed the introduction of "hymns of human composure" into the congregational singing among the Nonconformists, as evidenced by Isaac Watts (1674-1748).

The struggling young nation across the ocean, America, found little time for developing a singing tradition. Thus, from around 1680 through the mid-18th century, the practice of *lining-out occurred among the New England congregations. This lengthy procedure for the congregational singing of the psalms soon reduced the repertoire in most churches to fewer than ten tunes (Curwen 110, 111). It also brought about the disintegration of congregational singing through the individuality of each singer's own embellishments. The reversal of this trend was a product of the *singing schools, which also led to the harmonized congregational singing among non-liturgical churches toward the end of the 18th and the beginning of the 19th century.

In England during the 1700's the Wesleyan revival movement must be accredited in part for the increased interest in congregational singing through their livelier tunes. This interest soon was followed by the Congregationalists, Baptists and even the Scottish Presbyterians. A similar interest in congregational singing was brought about in the Anglican church in the mid-19th century by the *Oxford Movement. Many of the hymns, both original and translations, that resulted from this movement have become standard repertoire for current congregational singing (Etherington, 182).

Causing less enthusiasm among Lutheran congregations world-wide from the late 18th century through the 19th was the singing of the chorales in a slow, equal-rhythmed manner. This bland execution of the once highly rhythmic congregational praise, not easily corrected, was due to the confusion aroused by the many differing rhythmic versions published for the same chorale. Only as each church group began to provide "authorized" hymnals in the 20th century did a standardization of rhythmic versions appear within the respective regions. Thus, enthusiastic congregational singing once again became the desired result.

Among 20th-century evangelical American congregations, singing has varied greatly but for the most part has been passive. In an attempt to stimulate enthusiastic congregational singing with understanding, the Hymn Society of America has promoted the idea of *hymn festivals and *hymn services. Several denominations have instituted the hymn-of-the-month or hymn-of-the-week approach to knowledgeable singing. A further aid has been the *graded choir program with a portion of its emphasis being on *hymnody.

Blume, Friedrich. Geschichte der evangelische Kirchen-
    musik. Kassel: Bärenreiter, 1965.
Curwen, J. Spencer. Studies in Worship Music. First
    Series. London: J. Curwen and Sons, 1888.
Etherington, Charles L. Protestant Worship Music. New
    York: Holt, Rinehart and Winston, 1962.
Fischer, Martin and Christa Müller. Gemeindesingen.
    München: Kaiser-Verlag, n. d.
Schmidt, Ferdinand. "Gemeindegesang and Orgel," MK,
    12:121-129, May-June, 1940.

CONJOINT SINGING (OF. conjoindre, fr. L. conjungere,
    -junctum, fr. con with + jungere to join, + *singing)

    The singing of psalms or hymns from a book or from the lips of a *precentor congregationally in service in 17th-century England was termed conjoint singing. This type of singing was forbidden by the Society of Friends in the mid-17th century.

CONTRAFACTUM (ML.)

    A song in which the original secular text has been replaced by a new sacred text, the melody remaining basically unchanged is known as a contrafactum (plural, contrafacta). Though this process did not originate with the Reformation, it did play a vital role in the provision of *chorales for the German *hymns of Luther and his followers. In the true contrafacta, the new sacred texts were very closely related to the secular ones; as "O Welt ich muss dich lassen" from "Innsbruch ich muss dich lassen" (CH, 79). This practice resulted from the fact that during the early Reformation, texts were being written at a faster pace than were new tunes.

Blume, Friedrich. Geschichte die evangelische Kirchen-
    musik. Kassel: Bärenreiter-Verlag, 1965.
Duerksen, Rosella R. "Anabaptist Hymnody of the Sixteenth

Century." Unpublished D.S.M. dissertation, Union
Theological Seminary, New York, 1955.
Hennig, K.   Die geistliche Kontrafactum im Jahrhundert der
Reformation.   N.p., n.p., 1909.

CREDO   (L. I believe)

The term, Credo, generally refers to the Nicene
Creed (I believe in one God ...) which is said or sung after
the *Gospel at *Holy Communion.   It is a fixed element in
liturgical work.   However, the term may also imply other
creeds, as the Apostles' or Anthanasian creeds.
The Nicene Creed originated from the modification of
the baptismal confessions of the Church of Jerusalem according to the doctrines of the Council of Nicaea (325).   Out
of the old Roman baptismal affirmation came the Apostles'
Creed, first cited in an early form by Marcellus of Ancyra
in 341.
Traditionally, the Apostles' Creed held its prominent
position in the daily hours of prayer; while the Nicene Creed
is used most commonly in the Eucharist.   The Anthanasian
Creed, "Quicumque vult salvus esse" is used particularly
during the office hours on Trinity Sunday.
Although the Creed appeared in the first Prayer Book
(1549), it was not said or sung congregationally in the Anglican Church until 1552.   Luther, in his Deutsche Messe
(1529), prepared a versification of the Nicene Creed to be
sung by the congregation ("Wir glauben all an einen Gott,
Schöpfer").
When settings of the Credo have appeared in oratorio-
type masses they are customarily divided into numerous sections of differing musical treatment (see J. S. Bach's B
Minor Mass).

Babcock, F. J.   The History of Creeds.   New York: Macmillan, 1930.
Reindell, Walter.   "Das Credo."   Kirchenchordienst, 5:66-
69, July-August, 1939.
Sigl, M.   Zur Geschichte des Ordinarium Missae in der
deutscher Choralüberlieferung.   2 vols.   Regensburg:
Pustet, 1911.

DEACONING   (fr. ME. deken, fr. OE. diacon, fr. LL.

diaconus, fr. Gr. diakonos a servant or minister,
of uncert. origin)

The English term for *lining-out is deaconing, so
called because it was the task of the deacon in the 18th-cen-
tury cathedrals to line-out the psalms for the congregation.

DECANI

The Anglican tradition of placing the choir on both
sides of the chancel for the performance of antiphonal *anthems, services and chantings, yielded the decani choir, the
choir on the south side or deacon's side. The other side
was called the *cantoris.

DE PROFUNDIS (L. out of the depths)

The penitential psalm, Psalm 130, which begins "Out
of the depths have I cried unto Thee" is called the De profundis. Along with the other penitential psalms (6, 32, 51,
102 and 143) in ancient and medieval times it was used during
periods of penitence. In the *Book of Common Prayer the
psalm is appointed for Ash Wednesday and for use as a
proper psalm for *Morning Prayer and Evening Prayer (*Vespers). The De profundis has enjoyed settings by composers
such as Orlando Lassus (1532-1594), Andrea Gabrieli (c.
1520-1586), Wolfgang Mozart (1756-1791), and Arthur Honegger (1892-1955).

Procter, Francis and W. H. Frere. A New History to the
    Book of Common Prayer. London: Macmillan, 1955.

DESCANT (Of. & L; ONF. descant, OF. deschant--F. F.
    dechant--, fr. ML. discantus, fr. L. dis apart from
    + cantus singing, melody, fr. canere to sing)

The added part or countermelody sung above the
melody of a congregational *hymn or some other well-known
church melody by a few treble voices while the main body of
singers present the principal tune is called a descant. This
rather contemporary variation to *congregational singing
harkens back to the 14th-century practice of English descant
in which the plainsong melody in the middle part was decora-
ted by the extempore descanting of individual singers above
or below it. (Cf. *Fauxbourdon.)

DEUS MISEREATUR   (L.)

"God be merciful to us, and bless us" (Psalm 67) is
the alternative to the *canticle, *Nunc dimittis, in the Anglican office of Evening Prayer (*Vespers). It was added to
the service in the 1552 revision of the *Book of Common
Prayer.

Procter, Francis and W. H. Frere. A New History to the
   Book of Common Prayer. London: Macmillan, 1955.

DEUTSCHE MESSE   (G. German Mass)

The evangelical revision of the Roman Mass by Martin
Luther in 1525 with the exclusive use of the German language, designed for maximum participation by the people, is
the Deutsche Messe.
The idea for a German mass originated from the desire of some of the followers of Luther's reformation movement to make a more complete break with Rome than provided in the *Formula Missae and to institute a total vernacular service. To this legalism Luther objected vehe-
mently, as he felt that each evangelical center should have
the freedom to devise its own liturgy. At the same time,
less satisfying attempts of all-German masses were being
made (from as early as 1522) causing great confusion. A
major concern for artistic integrity in adapting the speech
rhythm of the German language to music caused Luther to
wait until 1525 to approach this task. In this year Luther
enlisted the assistance of Johann Walther and Conrad Rupff,
both having served as *Kapellmeister of the Duke of Saxony,
for arranging the music of the German mass. The first
all-German service resulting from these efforts was held
on October 29, 1525 in Wittenberg. It appeared in print
during the early months of 1526.
The resulting order of the Sunday Service proceeded
thusly:

A German psalm or hymn
The Kyrie eleison (three-fold)
Gloria in excelsis (the inclusion is assumed from
   Luther's reverence of this text in the liturgy and
   later evidence)
Collect (intoned)
Epistle (intoned)
A German hymn (as the Gradual)
The Gospel (intoned)

The Nicene Creed (sung as a chorale--"Wir glauben all
   an einen Gott")
The sermon
The Lord's Prayer (paraphrased)
Word of Institution
Consecration of the bread and administration
The German Sanctus ("Jesajai dem Propheten das
   Geschah")
Consecration of the wine and administration
The German Agnus Dei ("Christe, du Lamm Gottes")
The collect
The Aaronic Benediction

It must be remembered that the above order was suggested by Luther, but not dogmatically insisted upon. In
fact, in the preface to his Deutsche Messe und Ordnung des
Gottesdiensts (1526), Luther emphatically stated that this
order of service should not be made a rigid law. This attitude of flexibility can still be seen in the liturgy of the
Lutheran Church today.

Regarding the music of the service, four sources are
evident: (1) the changing was Luther's adaptation of original
plain-chant from the Latin to coincide with and complement
the German language. Based on the Gregorian tones, Luther's tones are considered more melodious. The chorales
which might be substituted or sung as indicated originated
musically from (2) medieval German hymns or (3) secular
melodies, or (4) were originally composed for this use.

The effect of the Deutsche Messe as developed by
Luther, Walther and Rupff was felt strongly as a moral
force on German national life and music. Among its major
influences was the provision for the expression of the chorale, the popular church song of the Lutheran reformation.
Being designed primarily for the uneducated people, the
German mass promoted congregational participation while
retaining as much as possible of the historic order.

Eisenburger, C. F.   "The Origin, Development and Practical Application of the Deutsche Messe, 1526, as Compiled by Martin Luther." Unpublished M.A. thesis,
   Ohio State University, Columbus, Ohio, 1960.
Leupold, Ulrich S. (ed.) "Liturgy and Hymns" in vol. 53
   of Luther's Works, ed. by Helmut T. Lehman.   Philadelphia: Fortress Press, 1965. Pp. 53-90.
Smend, Julius. Die evangelische deutsche Messe bis zur
   Luthers deutsche Messe. Göttingen: n.p., 1896.

DIALOGUE (ME. dialogue, fr. OF. dialoge, F. dialogue, fr. L. dialogus, fr. Gr. dialogos, fr. dialegesthai to converse, fr. dia through + legein to speak)

The 17th-century composition similar in nature to *concertato style, being a conversation between two musical parts--two solo voices, solo and chorus, etc.--is termed dialogue. Its occurrence is quite common in the Baroque *cantata, *oratorio and *passion.

Andreas Hammerschmidt (1612-1675), somewhat following the concertato style of Schütz's Symphoniae Sacrae (1629), wrote a wide variety of musical compositions of this type for differing vocal and instrumental arrangements. Several of these are contained in his "Dialogi oder Gespräche einer glauben Seele mit Gott, Part I" (Dialogue or conversations between a believing soul and God, DTOe, XVI), a collection of 20 pieces for two or three voices and trio sonata. The dialogue treatment of Hammerschmidt's was expanded into an entirely new fashion by Johann Rudolphe Ahle (1625-1673), who renders the Isaiah 63:1-3 text for two choruses, one asking the question while the second answering, in dialogue: "Wer ist der, so von Edom kommet?" ("Who is he, who cometh from Edom?" DdT, V:76-82). The work closes with a chorale verse in a manner similar to that of Bach's cantatas. Among the surviving works of Johann Philipp Krieger (1649-1725) are found dialogues also. "Sage mir, Schönster, wo soll ich dich finden?" ("Tell me, beautiful women, where shall I find thee?" DdT, LIII-LIV:291-308) is a setting from the Song of Solomon for soprano and alto soloists and trio sonata, the solo passages being quite extensive. Traces of the dialogue found their way into the cantata, as witnessed in the Bach cantata "Ich hatte viel Bekümmernis" ("My spirit was in heaviness," BGA, V:1) where the soprano (the soul) sings in dialogue with the bass (Jesus).

The use of dialogue has been particularly effective in the settings of the passion. Karl Heinrich Graun (1704-1759) and Georg Philipp Telemann (1681-1767) both using the text by Karl Wilhelm Ramler (1725-1798) incorporated dialogue in their oratorios, Der Tod Jesu.

Hudemann, H. Du protestantische Dialagkomposition im 17. Jahrhundert. Freiburg, n.p., 1941.
Johnson, John P. "An Analysis and Edition of Selected Choral Works of Johann Rudolph Ahle." Unpublished D.M.A. dissertation, The Southern Baptist Theological Seminary, Louisville, Kentucky, 1968.

Richter, Julius. "Die geistlichen Dialoge von Rudolph Ahle
     (1648)," MMG, 12:63-68, 71-73, 1880.
Smallman, Basil. "Endor Revisited: English Biblical Dia-
     logues of the Seventeenth Century," ML, 46:137-145,
     January, 1965.

DIRECTOR OF MUSIC (AF. directour, F. directeur one
     who guides + *music)

     (1) The person, employed by the church full or part-
time or on a voluntary basis, who is responsible for the
music ministry of the church--the choirs and *congregational
singing primarily--is termed the director of music. Because of the limited amount of time and/or training, the
director of music may coordinate a more limited church
music program than the *minister of music. However, this
will vary with the individual situation and the persons involved. (Cf. *Graded choir program; *Cantor; *Choirmaster;
*Kapellmeister and *Precentor.)

     (2) In the United Methodist Church the distinction be-
tween the "director of church music" and the "minister of
church music" is that the latter must be ordained, both being
full-time employees of the church.

DOMCHOR (G.)

     The term descriptive of the choir in either the Prot-
estant or Catholic German cathedral (Dom) is Domchor.

DOMINUS VOBISCUM (L.)

     "The Lord be with you" is the *salutation which, with
its *response ("and with thy spirit"), frequently occurs in
liturgical services. The origin of this salutation can be
traced to the similar Hebrew use of the word "Emmanuel"
(God with us) as found in Ruth 2:4. In its expanded way the
Dominus vobiscum was employed by the early Christian bish-
ops as they entered the church. Soon it found liturgical
placement as an introduction to specific prayers and the
*preface. In the Lutheran and Anglican office hours and
eucharistic services this salutation precedes the collects.
The Lutheran service of Holy Communion also employs it as
the first *versicle and response of the *preface.

Reed, Luther D. The Lutheran Liturgy. Philadelphia:
    Muhlenberg Press, 1947.

DOXOLOGY (ML. doxologia, fr. Gr. doxologia, fr. doxolo-
    gos praising, giving glory, fr. doxa glory, praise +
    legein to speak)

       An ascription of praise addressed to the Trinity is a
doxology. The term may refer to the *ter sanctus and *alleluia, but more especially to the *Gloria in excelsis (the
greater doxology) and the *Gloria Patri (the lesser doxology).
The practice of singing a doxology (usually the Gloria Patri)
at the conclusion of the Hebrew psalms led to metrical versions of this doxology, which eventually transferred to
*hymns. One such metrical paraphrase which has gained
great popularity is Thomas Ken's (1631-1711) "Praise God
from whom all blessings flow." This versification together
with the tune "Old Hundredth" is commonly called by many
persons "The Doxology." This entity, used as an ascription
of praise at the commencement of a service of worship, at
the presentation of the offering, or at the end, came into
this usage and title during the mid-19th century.

Julian, John. A Dictionary of Hymnology. New York:
    Dover Publications, 1957. Pp. 308-310.
Werner, Eric. The Doxology in Synagogue and Church: A
    Liturgico-Musical Study. Cincinnati, n.p., 1946.

DWIGHT'S WATTS

       The affectionate name for the Connecticut Associa-
tion's approved American revision of Isaac Watts' The
Psalms of David by Timothy Dwight (1752-1817) was "Dwight's
Watts." The title page reads, "The Psalms of David ... by
I. Watts, D.D. A new edition, in which the Psalms, omit-
ted by Dr. Watts, are versified, local passages are altered,
and a number of Psalms are versified anew. By Timothy
Dwight, D.D., President of Yale College. At the request of
The General Association of Connecticut. To the Psalms is
added a Selection of Hymns: Hartford: printed by Hudson &
Goodwin. 1801."
       To the 150 psalms was added an appendix of 263
hymns of which 168 were by Watts and 95 by other persons.
It was readily received in the Connecticut churches where it
reigned for over thirty years. In 1833 Dr. Leonard Bacon

issued his Additional Hymns which were to be bound with
"Dwight's Watts." Eventually, Dr. Dwight's collection was
superseded by the Connecticut Association's Psalms and
Hymns (1845).

Benson, Louis F. The English Hymn: Its Development and
Use. Richmond, Va.: John Knox Press, 1962.

EASTERTIDE

The season of the *Christian Year commencing with
*Vespers on the eve of Easter and ending with *Vespers on
the eve of Pentecost, 50 days later, is called Eastertide.
Each Sunday in Eastertide bears a specific name and meaning: Easter I is Low Sunday or Quasi modo; Easter II
Misericorda Domini; Easter III Jubilate Deo; Easter IV Cantate Domino; and Easter V Vocem jocunditatis.

Wetzler, Robert and Helen Huntington. Seasons and Symbols:
A Handbook on the Church Year. Minneapolis: Augsburg Publishing House, 1962.

ECCLESIASTICAL MODES (F. and L.; F. ecclesiastique,
fr. L. ecclesiasticus fr. Gr. ekklesiastikos, fr.
ekklesia an assembly of citizens called out by the
crier, also the church, fr. ekkletos called out, fr.
ekklelein to call out, fr. ek out + kalein to call, +
F. mode, fr. L. modus a measure, manner, form)

The characteristic organization of medieval *plainsong into a system of eight scales is referred to as the
ecclesiastical modes. The modes (cf. *psalm-tones) are of
four main classes: Dorian, Phrygian, Lydian and Mixoly-
dian; each capable of being either authentic or plagal ("hypo").
The range of each mode is an octave and is comprised of
two tetrachords.

	mode	range	*final	dominant
Dorian	I	D-D	D	A
Hypodorian	II	A-A	D	F
Phrygian	III	E-E	E	C
Hypophrygian	IV	B-B	E	A
Lydian	V	F-F	F	C

	mode	range	*final	dominant
Hypolydian	VI	C-C	F	A
Mixolydian	VII	G-G	G	D
Hypomixolydian	VIII	D-D	G	C

Other modes commonly employed in music developing in the 17th century are the Aeolian (A-A, natural minor) and Ionian (C-C, major), from which arose the major-minor tonality. Occasionally used in music, especially that of folk character, are the pentatonic (five-tone) and gypsy scales.

Andrews, F. S. "Medieval Modal Theory." Unpublished Ph.D. dissertation, Cornell University, Ithaca, New York, 1935.

Daniêlo, Alain. Introduction to the Study of Musical Scales. London: The India Society, 1943.

Werner, Eric. The Origin of the Eight Modes of Music. Cincinnati: n.p., 1948.

EDITIONS, HISTORICAL

Important musical manuscripts gathered and presented in readily accessible volume(s) to the musical student and performer are here considered historical editions. In the following list of historical editions of import to Protestant church music, each entry, arranged alphabetically, includes a brief description of content. For a more comprehensive explanation see A. H. Heyer, Historical Sets, Collected Editions and Monuments of Music: A Guide to their Contents (rev., 1969). Omitted from this list are the complete works (or Ausgaben) of specific composers and geographic memorial editions

1. Antiqua Chorbuch, 2 vols., Ed. Helmut Mönkemeyer. Mainz, B. Schotts Söhne, 1951-1952. (Choral music from the Reformation through J. S. Bach.)
2. Cathedral Music, 4 vols., ed. Samuel Arnold. London, D'Almaine and Company, 1790; reprinted by Edward Francis Rimbault, 1843. (A collection of English anthems and service music of the Elizabethan, Tudor and Restoration periods.)
3. Cathedral Music, 3 vols., ed. William Boyce. London, 1760-1779; later eds. 1788, 1844, 1849, and 1894. (A collection of English anthems and service music from the 16th through 18th centuries.
4. Chor-Archiv, 25 vols. to date, various eds. Kassel, Bärenreiter, 19??- . (Continental choral music

(plus two Purcell works in German) from the 15th
to 17th centuries.)

5. Das Chorwerk, 110 vols. to date, ed. Friedrich Blume
   and Kurt Gudewill. Berlin, G. Kallmeyer, 1929-
   (Contains representative types of vocal music from
   the 15th to the 18th centuries.)

6. Early English Church Music, 5 vols. to date, ed. Frank
   Llewellyn Harrison. London, Stainer and Bell,
   1963- . (15th- through 17th-century English church
   music of the choral tradition.)

7. Harmonia Sacra, 3 vols., ed. John Page. London, 1800.
   (A collection of anthems selected for cathedral and
   parochial churches from composers of the 16th through
   18th centuries. A supplement to Boyce (3) and Arnold
   (2).

8. Kirchenmusik der Darmstädter Meister des Barock, 6
   vols. to date, ed. F. Noack and E. Noack. Berlin,
   C. Merseberger, 1955- .

9. Masterpieces of Organ Music, 73 vols. to date, ed.
   Norman Hennefield. New York, Liturgical Music
   Press, 1944- . (Basically organ music of the Pro-
   testant Baroque era.)

10. Musica Sacra, 18 vols., various eds. Berlin, Bote and
    Bock, 1839-1896. (A collection of religious music
    of the 16th through 19th centuries, many works of
    which were used by the Berlin Domchor.)

11. Musikdrücke aus den Jahren 1538 bis 1545 in praktischer
    Neuausgabe, 3 vols. of 12 proposed, ed. by Georg
    Rhaw. Kassel, Bärenreiter, 1955- . (Liturgical
    music of the early Lutheran Reformation.)

12. Plainsong and Mediaeval Music Society, various eds.
    London, 1890- . (Publications are not issued as a
    set and are unnumbered.) (Various historical works
    of interest to Roman and Anglican use. A complete
    listing through 1959 is contained in Septuagesima,
    1959, by Dom A. Hughes.)

13. The Treasury of English Church Music, 5 vols., ed.
    Gerald H. Knight and William L. Reed. London,
    Blandford Press, 1965. (A history of anthems and
    service music of the English church from 1100-1965.)

14. Tudor Church Music, 10 vols. and supplement, eds.
    P. C. Buck, A. Ramsbotham, E. H. Fellows, P. R.
    Terry, S. T. Warner. London, Oxford University
    Press, 1922-1929, 1948. (A collection of the anthems
    and service music of the Tudor church musicians.)

EJACULATORY HYMN   (L. ejaculatus, past part. of ejacu-
lari to throw out, fr. e out + jaculari to throw, fr.
jaculum javelin, dart, fr. jacere to throw + *hymn)

The spontaneous song of an excited member of the
throng during the preaching at a 19th-century *camp meeting
which was taken up by the entire gathering was termed an
ejaculatory hymn. These improvised, highly emotional songs
generally consisted of rough paraphrases of biblical passages
intermingled with everyday language and refrains including
many hallelujahs. Very often this ecstatic singing would dis-
solve the preaching and climax in a type of religious dancing.

Jackson, George Pullen. White and Negro Spirituals: Their
Life Span and Kinship. New York: J. H. Augustin
Publisher, 1943.

ELECTRONIC ORGAN

The generic term for musical keyboard instruments
whose tones are produced by an electronic means, simulating
in some fashion the tone of the pipe organ, is electronic
organ. Basically, there are four types of generators power-
ing mid-20th-century electronic organs: (1) the electromag-
netic: small, motor-driven rotary generators that produce
alternating current at frequencies corresponding to those of
the tempered scale (Hammond); (2) the electrostatic: vibrating metal reeds that produce alternating voltage of speci-
fied pitches when electrified (Wurlitzer); (3) the photoelectric:
through the use of "picture plates" and photo-electric cells a
signal voltage is selected and produced which assimilates the
copy of the installed "optical recording" (Kimball); and (4)
the electronic: vacuum tubes or transistor oscillators provide the signals which produce the tone (Allen, Baldwin,
Conn, Rodgers, Saville, etc.).
Within these four generator systems there are two
basic designs: the locked generator system and the independent generating system. The locked system uses only
12 generators for the basic chromatic octave, each note on
the organ being derived from these 12 by means of frequency
division. The independent system uses individual oscillators
for each note.

Barnes, William Harrison. The Contemporary Organ. 8th
ed. Glen Rock, N.J.: J. Fischer & Brothers, 1964.
Pp. 347-362.

Dorf, Richard H. Electronic Musical Instruments. New
York: Radiofile, 1958.
Eby, Richard L. Electronic Organs. Wheaton, Ill.: Van
Kampen Press, 1953.
Irwin, Stevens. Dictionary of Electronic Organ Stops. New
York: G. Schirmer, 1968.

EPISTLE (ME. fr. OF. epistle, epistre, fr. L. epistola,
fr. Gr. epistolé, fr. epistellein to send to, fr. epi
upon, to + stellein to send)

The portion of Scripture usually taken from one of
the New Testament apostolic letters said or sung in Sunday
services of communion is the epistle or "apostle" (the latter
term was used in early service books). Other materials occasionally chosen are from the Acts and Revelation. The
epistle traditionally has appeared in Anglican and Lutheran
worship.

Müller, Karl and W. Blankenburg (eds.). Leiturgia, Handbuch des evangelischen Gottesdienstes. 4 vols. to
date. Kassel: J. Stauda, 1954- .

EPISTLE SONATA (*epistle + It. & L. sonare to sound)

The instrumental piece designed for performance
either before or after the reading of the *epistle became
known as the epistle sonata. This 17th- and 18th-century
practice provided the stimulus for several composers, including Mozart (1759-1791), whose 17 Epistle Sonatas for
organ and chamber orchestra were written for the Salzburg
Cathedral.

Tangeman, R. S. "Mozart's 17 Epistle Sonatas," MQ, 32:
588-601, October, 1946.

ESTE'S PSALTER

"The Whole Booke of Psalmes with their wonted
Tunes, as they are sung in Churches, composed into foure
parts: ... Imprinted at London by Thomas Est, ... 1592":
this book is commonly called the Este's Psalter, edited by
Thomas Este (d. 1609). It carries the distinction of being
the first collection of psalms with tunes which bore their

own proper names. It is also among the first psalters to be printed in score rather than as *part-books. Two successive editions appeared in 1594 and 1604. Included in the list of composers were Richard Allison (fl. 1600), John Dowland (1563-1626), John Farmer (fl. 1600) and Giles Farnaby (d. 1640).

Rimbault, Edward (ed.). The Whole Book of Psalms. London: Musical Antiquarian Society, 1844. (An historical reprint of the Este's Psalter with a critical introduction.)

ET INCARNATUS EST (L.)

"And was incarnate" is a section of the *Credo or Nicene Creed which usually is set apart by a contrasting musical idea in concert settings of the liturgy.

ET IN TERRA PAX (L.)

"And on earth peace" is the second phrase of the *Gloria in excelsis, being the response of the choir and congregation to the intonation of the officiant, "Glory be to God on high. "

EUCHARIST (ME. eukarist, fr. MF. eucariste, fr. LL. eucharistria, fr. Gr. Eucharist, giving of thanks, fr. eucharistos grateful)

The title derived from our Lord's "giving of thanks" at the Last Supper (Mark 14:23) and applied to the observance of this meal is the Eucharist. One of the earliest uses of it as a title appeared in the German Church Order of Nordlingen (1525) being an alternative to the Lord's Supper. (See also *Communion service; *Lord's Supper.)

Clarke, W. K. Lowthe and Charles Harris. Liturgy and Worship: A Companion to the Prayer Books of the Anglican Communion. New York: Macmillan, 1932.

EVANGELIST (OF. evangeliste, fr. LL. evangelista, fr. Gr. euangelistes)

In *passion music, the narrative role of one of the four gospel accounts (Matthew, Mark, Luke or John) in relating the events in the life of Jesus Christ is termed the evangelist or *narrator. In the early 17th century this role was usually plainsong (Schütz's St. Luke's Passion), its sole purpose being to clarify the story by filling the gaps between the various sections.

Around the time of G. P. Telemann (1681-1767) the function of the evangelist ceases as the various soloists acquire the narrative role through their *recitatives. (Cf. *Historicus.)

Smallman, Basil. The Background of Passion Music. Naperville, Ill.: SCM Book Club, 1957.

EVANGELISTIC MUSIC   (ME. evangele, fr. OF. evangile,
      fr. LL. evangelium, fr. Gr. evangelion good news,
      fr. evangelos bringing good news + *music)

[Contents: (general); Historical perspective; (bibliography).] Evangelistic music is that used to express and create a religious sensitivity in which the proclamation of the Christian message is enhanced in its ability to bring persons into living fellowship with the Saviour, or to awaken souls from spiritual death into a new life.

Characteristically, evangelistic music is more testimonial than instructional, and personal rather than collective. It emphasizes the now and today and the importance of the commitment to Christ. Its emotional content is comparatively high. Evangelistic music may be instrumental or vocal or both. If instrumental, it will be based on a tune that readily will recall a familiar gospel text. (Cf. *Gospel song.)

Historical Perspective

Throughout the history of the Christian Church, everywhere the Gospel has been presented, music has usually accompanied it. Among the first evangelists were the disciples and apostles. According to Paul's exhortations (Colossians 3:16), singing must have been an important part of his ministry. Hymns were used to "evangelize" in the contest between the Arians and Athanosians in the fourth century, as evidenced in the hymns of Niceta of Remesiana (c.335 to c. 414). The 13th-century evangelist Francis of Assisi likewise incorporated music in his work as he and his followers sang laudi spirituale while campaigning for peace, repentance and forgiveness among all men everywhere.

The followers of Martin Luther and the Anabaptists both knew the power of music in propagating their doctrines. Through these various Reformation strains religious music returned to the people being used as a means of instruction and as a way of getting the Word of God into the hands of the people. All this led eventually to the 17th-century pietistic movement, the roots of present-day evangelism. Among these evangelists were August Hermann Francke (who influenced John Wesley and Graf von Zinzendorf), Philipp Jakob Spener and Theodor Untereyck (who influenced Joachim Neander); many of these persons were associated with church music, especially *hymnody.

In the 18th century Gerhard Tersteegen was among the foremost evangelists of pietism in western Germany. His closing song of dedication, "Thine shall be all my heart and life," rings with evangelistic fervor. The missionary and evangelistic movement of the Moravian Brethren, the Unitas Fratrum, was motivated by the piety and theological strength of Count Zinzendorf. His main message was the cross and reconciliation as seen in his hymn, "Jesus Thy blood and righteousness." In Württemburg, a poetically gifted evangelist by the name of Philipp Hiller wrote more than a thousand songs, many of which are published in his Geistliche Liederschatzlein (Small Treasury of Spiritual Songs). As seen in all eras of evangelism, the pietistic revival movement produced new musical expressions of salvation, repentance, forgiveness, faith and assurance; songs of testimony, praise and petition. These songs became "evangelists," spreading the message of salvation or strengthening the believer's faith. They were a vital force. In America, through the preaching of evangelist Johnathan Edwards, the grace of God was proclaimed with renewed emphasis. Feeling a need for a more personal music than the metrical psalms, Edwards introduced the hymns of Isaac Watts. The story of English *hymnody recounts much of the story of evangelism in 18th-century England through the efforts of George Whitefield, John and Charles Wesley, and others. The songs of this movement were songs of experience, testimony and confession, a kind of religious tutor. The basic message was to replace religious sentimentalism with a gospel of personal challenge.

A new wave of evangelism rolled over America in the early 19th century with the *camp meeting revivals, started by McGready in Logan County, Kentucky. With these meetings, designed to reach the frontiersman with a personal message of salvation, singing was an important ingredient.

The songs were simple and often spontaneous, packed with emotion, being among the forerunners of the *gospel song. At the same time in Germany a revival movement was being led by Johann Karl Philipp Spitta, who published his first collection of songs in 1833--Psalter und Harfe (Psalter and Harp). His hymns received wide acceptance because of their depth of feeling and direct simplicity. The campaigns of Charles G. Finney, both in England and America, were aimed at reaching the "man of the street." To accomplish this, an associate, the Rev. Joshua Leavitt, compiled a hymnal using secular tunes with secular texts, in quodlibet fashion.

From the mid-19th century to World War I, the norm was for each evangelist to have his own musician-Moody-Sankey, Whittle-Bliss, Torrey-Alexander, Sunday-Rodeheaver. Through their meetings, new gospel songs were presented and propagated. By means of bulletins, tracts and other publications new texts were placed into the hands of the public. Millions of Sankey's own gospel song books were sold. A vast emphasis on world-wide evangelism resulted from Moody's revivals in England and America. Evangelists, likewise, came to America from England bringing their songs as well--e.g., William Booth and Gipsy Smith. With Alexander and Rodeheaver, massive choirs and orchestral instruments were introduced into evangelistic music. Their singing and playing along with the soloists soon began to replace the congregational participation. Yet, it was Rodeheaver who introduced a livelier type of gospel song, a type which led to the gospel refrain or chorus of future decades. All of this, along with the Sunday school movement, provided an abundance of song materials in a popular vein, readily grasped by the listener and effective in the evangelistic effort.

In the mid-20th century the use of music in evangelism is exemplified in the crusades of the Billy Graham Association and in the various programs broadcast over radio and television. The use of soloists, choirs and instrumentalists has carried the musical portion of these evangelistic efforts. With this has come some new expressions of Christian testimony from contemporary songwriters and arrangers who have been influenced by the secular music of the mass-media and theater. As a result the role of the congregation has become a passive one of listening and looking-on with limited participation. Yet, as seen in the Graham crusades, this type of "big show" styled musical evangelism and its "special" music is apparently effective in fulfilling its purpose.

Downey, James C. "The Music of American Revivalism."

Unpublished Ph.D. dissertation, Tulane University, New Orleans, Louisiana, 1968.

Downey, James C. "Revivalism, the Gospel Songs and Social Reform," Ethnomusicology, 9:115-125, May, 1964.

McKissick, Marvin Leo. "A Study of the Function of Music in the Major Religious Revivals on America Since 1875." Unpublished M.M. thesis, University of Southern California, Berkeley, 1957.

McLoughlin, Wm. C. Modern Revivalism. New York: Ronald Press, 1959.

Renfro, Robert Chase. "A Historical Survey of Revival Music in America." Unpublished M.S.M. thesis, The Southern Baptist Theological Seminary, Louisville, Kentucky, 1956.

Scharpff, Paulus. History of Evangelism. Grand Rapids, Mich.: Eerdman Publishers, 1964.

EVENING PRAYER see VESPERS

FALSOBORDONE (see *fauxbourdon)

The 16th-century Italian style of conveying a text through simple four-part harmonizations of psalm tunes or other liturgical *recitatives is called Falsobordone (cf. *Fauxbourdon). This practice was used in alternation with plainsong. The concept most probably became known to Heinrich Schütz (1585-1672) during his Italian studies as it appears in the instrumental accompaniment to the Evangelist's recitatives of his Historia der Auferstehung Jesu Christ (1623).

Trumble, Ernest. "The Countratenors of Fauxbourdon," JAMS, 8:71-2, 1955.

FA-SO-LA

The system of solmization used in England and America during the 17th and 18th centuries in which the six Guidonian syllables were reduced to four was called the fa-so-la system. It originated in Elizabethan England, around the time of Shakespeare, entering America through the New England settlements. With the singing school movement the fa-so-la moved South and West.

Although the basic shapes of the fa-so-la system are attributed to Andrew Law (1749-1821), the revised shapes of William Little and William Smith (1754?-1821) became the accepted form.

ᗺ ᑭ ᑭ ᗅ
fa sol la mi

Scale: fa sol la fa sol la mi
In rural southern America (Appalachia) remnants of this system still exist.

This system of solmization and notation was promoted by many influential books in America's musical history: John Wyeth's (1770-1858) Repository of Sacred Music (1810), William Walker's (1809-1875) The Southern Harmony and B. F. White's (1800-1879) The Sacred Harp (1844).

From 1832 on, an attempt was made by Jesse B. Aiken of Philadelphia which gradually expanded the four-shaped system into a seven-shaped one, merging with the Continental system of solmization.

Chase, Gilbert. America's Music: from the Pilgrims to the Present. Rev. 2d ed. New York: McGraw-Hill, 1966. Chapter 10.

Jackson, George Pullen. White Spirituals in the Southern Uplands. Chapel Hill: University of North Carolina Press, 1933.

Marrocco, W. Thomas. "The Notation in American Sacred Music Collections," AMI, 35:136-42, 1964.

Seeger, Charles. "Contrapuntal Style in the Three-Voiced Shaped-Note Hymns." MQ, 26:483-93, October 1940.

FAUXBOURDON (F., fr. L. falsus past part. of fallere to deceive + OF., fr. ML. burdo drone)

The particular method of harmonizing a cantus firmus in which the principal melody ideally is placed in the lowest voice with the harmony of successive $\frac{6}{3}$ chords added in the upper voices is called fauxbourdon or fa-burden. In its strictest 15th-century meaning, fauxbourdon defined a two-part piece moving in sixths and octaves with an unwritten, but implied, third part supplying a fourth below the treble, the cantus firmus being in the lower part. However, its original meaning may have indicated only the contratenor or the tenor part alone. Whatever the origin of the term, about which there is great conjecture, fauxbourdon was definitely related to a restricted style of composition for liturgical

music, generally based on a preexisting liturgical melody
(cf. *Plainsong).

Bukofzer contends that fauxbourdon was for instrumental rather than choral performance in the beginning, the cantus firmus being the upper voice, the fauxbourdon being the
lower voice a sixth below the cantus except at cadences and
the contratenor improvising a fourth below the cantus. However, this style, originating on the Continent rather than
England, is seen in the Missa Sancti Jacobi of Dufay (c. 1400-
1474), definitely intended to be sung. He likewise has employed fauxbourdon in several verses of his Magnificat sexti
toni.

During the 16th and 17th centuries the *tenor of the
metrical psalm tune or similar melodic part received the
name fauxbourdon in England. The 18th century continued
to confuse the term by calling any parallel $\frac{6}{3}$ harmonic progressions fauxbourdon. (More precisely this is designated
sixth chord style.)

In current English usage, fauxbourdon is a style of
20th-century *hymnody in which the *hymn tune is placed in
the tenor with the soprano becoming a secondary melody,
the bass either remaining the same or varying (cf. *Descant). (See also *Falsobordone.)

Besseler, Heinrich. Bourdon und Fauxbourdon, Studien zum
    Ursprung der niederlandrischen Musik. Leipzig: Breit-
    kopf and Härtel, 1950.
Bukofzer, Manfred. "Fauxbourdon Revisited," MQ, 38:22-
    47, January, 1952.
_____. Geschichte des englischen Diskants und des Faux-
    bourdons. Strassburg: Heitz and Co., 1936.
Trumble, E. Fauxbourdon; an Historical Survey. Vol. I.
    Brooklyn: Institute of Mediaeval Music, 1959.
Wallin, N. Zur Deutung des Begriffes Faburden-Fauxbour-
    don. Kongressbericht Bamberg, 1953. Kassel:
    Bärenreiter, 1954.

FERIAL (fr. L. feria festive day)

(1) The service of a day which is not a feast day is
referred to as ferial. (This is a meaning opposite to that
of the original Latin word.) In current usage the opposite
to ferial is festal or festival day.

(2) The term ferial, however, may refer to the

simple harmonized settings of the responses at the Anglican
services of *Morning Prayer and Evening Prayer (*Vespers).

FIGURALITER   (OF., fr. L. figura; akin to L. fingere to
        form, shape, feign)

In the 15th through the 16th centuries the more complex method of setting the chant or psalm tune to musical
materials similar in style to the *motet form was called
figuraliter. As opposed to choraliter, figuraliter was basically an unaccompanied, polyphonic style of setting religious
songs. Needless to say, it was rendered by the choir rather
than the congregation. In its 15th-century beginnings the
figuraliter settings of *chorales, *hymns or *psalms were
sung in alternatum with the choraliter of the congregation.
However, by the 16th century the practice was so abused
that congregational singing was almost completely silenced.

FIGURED BASS   see   THOROUGH-BASS

FIGURED CHORALE

A type of organ *chorale prelude in which a characteristic motive is consistently present in one or more of the
contrapuntal voices, encircling the *chorale cantus, is called
a Figured Chorale (in German, figurierter choral).   Illustrative of this compositional technique are many of the settings
contained in the Orgelbüchlein of J. S. Bach (1685-1750),
e.g., "Alle Menschen müssen sterben" (BWV, 643).

FINAL   (OF., fr. LL. finalis, fr. L. finis limit, boundary,
        end)

The principal note of each of the *ecclesiastical
modes in *plainsong and the concluding note of a *psalm-
tone is the final. It, along with the dominant, will deter-
mine the mode and classification, whether "authentic" or
"plagal" (see *Ecclesiastical modes).

FLEXA   (L. flexum, fr. flectere to bend)

The flexa is an inflection, a lowering of the voice, at

the breathing point in *chant or *psalm-tone. The rules
governing the flexa in psalmody are: (1) when the recitation
is on do or fa the flexa is a third (do-la or fa-re); (2) in
*collects it is always a half-step (do-ti); and (3) in all other
tones it is a whole step (la-sol).

FOLK SONG (OE. folc; akin to D. volk, OS. & OHG. folk,
    G. volk, ON. folk, & prob. to L. plebs, Gr. plethos
    multitude + *song)

    The vocal repertory of a community, generally of
anonymous origin and transmitted orally, being rarely written, is folk song. This is in contradistinction to the art
music of the trained composer which most often is written.
    Within the history of Protestant church music the folk
song has occupied an important role. Briefly, it is seen as
a basis of the Reformation *chorale through the technique of
*contrafactum as well as through the ancestry of songs from
groups as the flagellants. Folk song is the foundation of the
religious carol as well. In 19th-century America the folk song
most influencing congregational praise was the *spiritual, both
Negro and white. Through the efforts of R. Vaughan Williams
(1872-1958) and Percy Dearmer (1867-1936) the early English
folk songs were recovered and incorporated into hymnals for
use as *hymn tunes (e.g., by Forrest Green). For current
use of popular folk songs in Protestant church music see
*Pop, Gospel.

Gilchrist, Anne G. "The Folk Element in Early Revival
    Hymns and Tunes," JeF-S, 8:61-95, 1927-31.
Jackson, George Pullen. White Spirituals in the Southern
    Uplands. Chapel Hill: University of North Carolina
    Press, 1933.
Junk, Klaus. "Religiöse Lieder--Religiöse Songs," MK,
    28:69-73, March-April, 1958.
Kettering, E. L. "Sacred Folksongs of the Southern Appa-
    lachians." Unpublished M.S.M. thesis, Union Theo-
    logical Seminary, New York, 1933.
Lovelace, Austin C. "Early Sacred Folk Music in America."
    The Hymn, 3:10-14, January, 1952; 3:56-63, April,
    1952.
Lowens, Irving. "John Wyeth's Repository of Sacred Music,
    Part Second: A Northern Precursor of Southern Folk
    Hymnody," JAMS, 5:114-131, Spring, 1953.
Pearce, Charles W. "English Sacred Folk Song in the West
    Gallery Period (circa 1695-1820)," PRMA, 48, 1921.

Wiora, Walter. "The Origins of German Spiritual Folk
   Songs: Comparative Methods in a Historical Study,"
   Ethnomusicology, 8:1-13, January, 1963.

FORMULA MISSAE   (L. dim of forma form, model + LL.
   missa, fr. mittere, missum to send, dismiss)

   The evangelical revision of the Latin mass as enunci-
ated by Martin Luther in 1523 is commonly referred to as
the Formula Missae, an abbreviation of the published account,
entitled Formula Missae et Communionis pro Ecclesia Wit-
tembergensi. It was the reply of Luther to the repeated requests of his friend, Nicolaus Hausmann, pastor of the
Marienkirche at Zwickau.
   The Formula Missae, considered to be Luther's
greatest liturgical writing and his greatest contribution to
general liturgical reform, was intended for local use. His
basic concern was not a new liturgical language or service
for the people, as it was in his *Deutsche Messe, but rather
he sought an objective criticism of a historic and vital institution. This it did while serving to check the marked tendency toward looseness and a complete break with the past.
   Taking the local use, probably the Augustinian missal,
Luther prepared his reconstruction of the service without
going further afield. Luther's objections centered around
the lengthy and secretive canon which followed the *Sanctus,
also the effusive *introits, *graduals, and *prefaces. Re-
jecting the medieval corruptions, and ideas of obligation,
sacrifice and good works, while still seeking to preserve the
historic order and much material of the mass, Luther greatly
stressed the principle of freedom.
   The service is in Latin except for the sermon and a
few hymns. The resulting order of service was:

          Introit (or a psalm)
          Kyrie (ninefold)
          Gloria in excelsis (may be omitted)
          Collect (only one)
          Epistle (read)
          Gradual (only one of two verse lengths)
      Hymn (preferably in the vernacular, may alternate
             Sundays with Latin)
          Sequence (only Nativity and Pentecost)
          Gospel
          Nicene Creed (sung or said)
          The sermon (may precede introit)

The Order of the Communion Office
  Salutation
  Sursum corda
  Vere dignum
  Verba (sung, read aloud or silently)
  Sanctus
Hymn
  Elevation (during Benedictus qui venit)
  Lord's Prayer
  The Pax
  Agnus Dei (permissive)
Hymn
  Communio (permissive)
  Collect
  Salutation
  Benedicamus (with alleluia)
  Benediction

After Hausmann's further prodding, Luther commissioned Paul Speratus to translate it into German. This became the authorized German version of the document.

The influence of the Formulae Missae lives on in the Lutheran liturgy today in America as stated in the preface to the Common Service Book with Hymnal (1918).

Strodach, P. S. (ed.). Works of Martin Luther. Vol. VI. Philadelphia: Muhlenberg Press, 1932.

FOUNDERY COLLECTION

The first Methodist hymnal with tunes, compiled by John Wesley (1703-1791), was known as the Foundery Collection (1742). Its proper title was "A Collection of Tunes, set to music, as they are commonly sung at the Foundery." Its name, the Foundery Collection, was due to its use at the converted cannon foundery at Moorfields where Charles and John Wesley preached. The tunes included were from German *chorales, psalm tunes, adaptations of popular songs and other unknown sources.

Lightwood, James T. The Music of the Methodist Hymn-Book. London: Epworth Press, 1938.

FREE ACCOMPANIMENT (ME. fre, freo, fr. OE. frēo, freoh, frī + F. accomplissement, fr. accomplis)

The supportive instrumental voice parts to a *hymn
tune or other choral music which are independent of the
vocal harmonization, yet related to the tune, are termed
free accompaniment or free harmonization. Free *organ
accompaniments often have been improvised by competent
musicians; however, several composed collections of such
have been published. This method has provided another
means of varying and, it is hoped, stimulating *congregational singing of hymns, being a 19th- and 20th-century relative of *fauxbourdon.

Lovelace, Austin C. The Organist and Hymn Playing. New
    York: Abingdon Press, 1962.
Noble, T. Tertius. Free Organ Accompaniments to One
    Hundred Well-Known Hymn Tunes. New York: J.
    Fischer and Brothers, 1946.

FRENCH PSALTER see PSALMODY, METRICAL (Geo-
    graphical developments--The Continent); PSALTERS

FUGING TUNE   (fr. fuging psalm tune)

The 18th-century term for the English and American
settings of psalm and hymn tunes which contain points of
imitation is fuging tune. More specifically, the typical
fuging tune consists of an ABB structure, beginning with a
homophonic section of a phrase or more which reaches a
definite cadence. The second section makes a fresh start
with each individual voice entering in succession in an imitative or "fuging" fashion. This latter section is generally
repeated.
    Historically the fuging tune is related to the Continen-
tal fugue solely through the common ancestral nomenclature,
fuga, and the imitative structure. Its real background is in
the 16th- and 17th-century English fuging psalm tune which
was the short-lived wedding of metrical psalmody and contrapuntal technique. Antecedents of this are found among the
imitative psalm tunes of the *Este's Psalter (1593) and the
"tunes in report" (see *Reports) of the Scottish psalters
(1633-1635). Exactly by whom or when the first English fuging
psalm tunes were printed has not yet been determined; however, it was likely around the turn of the 18th century that
one of the itinerant singing masters published such. Though
welcomed in the rural areas, the fuging tune was met by
opposition in urban settlements.

The American-styled fuging tune made its appearance
in Connecticut in the early 1780's whence it spread throughout New England.   This was preceded by the first American
publication of English fuging psalm tunes by James Lyon
(1735-1794) in his *Urania (1762).   Among the early composers of this form were Daniel Read (1757-1836), Jacob
French (1754-?), Timothy Swan (1758-1852) and Supply Belcher (1751-1836).   The height of this American fuging tune
was achieved through the work of William Billings (1746-
1800), whose writings have become recognized as the most
important of America's first indigenous musicians (see MA,
98-102).   Through the singing school movement the fuging
tune moved throughout New England and into the frontier
settlements.
          Isaac B. Woodbury (1819-1858), in his The Dulcimer
(1850), indicated that the fuging tunes were beginning to
wane in popularity before 1800.   This decline was due in
part to the work of Andrew Law (1749-1821), Elias Mann
(1750-1825) and Lowell Mason (1792-1872) as well as to the
ruling of the Methodist Episcopal Church against its use in
congregational singing.
          Vestiges of the fuging tune have survived among the
Sacred Harp Singers, primarily in the Appalachian region.
Its influences can be seen in the Charles Ives' (1874-1954)
bitonal treatment of Psalm 67 and in Ross Lee Finney's
(b. 1906) Variations, Fugueing and Rondo (1943).

Lowens, Irving.   "The Origins of the American Fuging
          Tune, " JAMS, 6:43-52, Winter, 1953.
Marrocco, W. Thomas and Harold Gleason.   Music in
          America: An Anthology from the Landing of the Pil-
          grims to the Close of the Civil War.   1620-1865. New
          York: W. W. Norton, 1964.
Metcalf, Frank J.   American Writers and Compilers of
          Sacred Music.   New York: Abingdon Press, 1925.
"Old Harp Singing. "   Folkway Record and Service Corpora-
          tion, New York, FP56.
Pierce, Edwin Hall.   "The Rise and Fall of the 'Fugue-
          Tune' in America, " MQ, 16:214-228, April, 1930.

FULL ANTHEM (OE., akin to L. plere to fill, Gr. plethein
          to become full, plethos multitude + *anthem)

          An anthem which employs no vocal solo sections is
termed a full anthem.   This 16th-century term became

firmly rooted in English church music as a distinction from the *verse anthem.   (See *Anthem.)

Wienandt, Elwyn A. and Percy M. Young. The Anthem in England and America. New York: The Free Press, 1970.

FULL SERVICE   (*full + *service)

The musical setting of the Anglican services of *Morning Prayer, *communion and Evening Prayer (*Vespers), in a related, continuous musical manner, all parts being in the same key, is known as a full service. Unlike the *anthem where "full" refers to the use of the entire choir without solos, here "full" describes the number of sections in the setting of the service. Full services may be either "short" or "great," referring to the style of composition. The "short service" is one that is set in a prevailing syllabic, homophonic style, whereas "great service" implies the use of polyphony and more melismatic writing.

The sections which usually composed the full service which agree with the *Book of Common Prayer are the *Venite, *Te Deum (or *Benedicite) and Benedictus Dominus (or *Jubilate) from the morning service; the *Kyrie (Response to the Commandments or the ninefold Greek Kyrie), Nicene Creed and less frequently the Gloria from the communion service; and the *Magnificat (or *Cantate Domino) and *Nunc dimittis (or *Deus misereatur) from the evening service. By the late 19th century, under the influence of the *Oxford Movement, the communion service gained greater importance than did the divine offices (*Canonical Hours); thus, the other traditional parts--the *Sanctus, *Benedictus (qui venit) and *Agnus Dei--gradually were included in the musical settings of the full service.

In the composing of a full service it has been common practice to have all sections in the same key. Thus, the custom of referring to service compositions by composer and key was established (e.g., "Boyce in C" and "Wesley in E").

Stevens, Denis. Tudor Church Music. London: Faber and Faber, 1961.
Whittaker, W. Gillies. "Byrd's Great Service," MQ, 23: 474-490, October, 1941.

FUNERAL MUSIC (OF., fr. ML. funeralis funeral)

Music which is offered at the burial or memorial service of the dead in Protestant churches may be termed funeral music. However, high Anglo-Catholic centers may refer to it as a *requiem.

In both Lutheran and Anglican churches there is no absolute prescribed order which insists on specific musical sections. Thus, throughout history there have been degrees of variation in the musical settings for Protestant funeral services.

In the Lutheran church, the concept of "rest in the Lord" having been retained from the Roman use, the traditional order at the church funeral service began with a *chorale, continued with a sermon and concluded with the Trauerlied (funeral *cantata). Included in the Trauerlied beside certain cantatas of J. S. Bach (1685-1750) are Heinrich Schütz's (1585-1672) Musikalisches Exequien and Johannes Brahms' (1833-1897) Ein deutsches Requiem (Op. 45).

Under the influence of the Reformation, the Anglican office of the dead in the Book of Common Prayer (1549) retained only the name dirge from the medieval office and selected three passages from various offices: from Vespers, "I heard a voice from heaven"; from Matins, "I know that my Redeemer liveth"; and from Lauds, "I am the Resurrection and the Life." The earliest extant setting of the burial services is Thomas Morley's (1557-1603?) work which was sung at the funeral of George II. However, its popularity was superseded by the setting by William Croft (1687-1727). This latter setting incorporates Purcell's (1659-1695) anthem, "Thou knowest, Lord, the secrets of our heart." The following is a list of the musical sections of Croft's Service (1724):

Before the lesson:
1. "I am the Resurrection and the Life."
2. "I know that my Redeemer liveth."
3. "We brought nothing into this world."
4. "I said I will take heed unto my ways."

After the lesson:
1. "Man that is born of a woman."
2. "In the midst of life we are in death."
3. Purcell's "Thou knowest, Lord."
4. "I heard a voice from heaven saying."

As illustrated by the short Requiem (1915) by Walford Davies (1869-1941), Anglican Church musicians are at liberty to compose any form of memorial service without reference to the Book of Common Prayer. Davies' example includes a setting of the Salvator Mundi ("O Saviour of the World"), an

Anglican chant for Psalm 130 ("Out of the deep have I called unto thee")--the Requiem aeternam replacing the Gloria Patri--and even a setting of John Lydgate's poem, "Tarry no longer toward thine heritage."

In non-liturgical Protestant churches, no set music is prescribed but several denominations have prepared booklets which present their ideas and suggestions of music considered appropriate for the occasion.

Robertson, Alec. Requiem: Music of Mourning and Consolation. New York: Praeger, 1967.

GATHERING-NOTE (ME. gaderen, fr. OE. gaderian, gadrian; akin to D. gaderen to collect, G. gatte husband, MHG. gate, also companion, Goth. gadiliggs a sister's son, OE. gaed fellowship, gador, geador together + OF., fr. L. nota a mark, sign)

The origin of the gathering-note involves the practice of *lining-out, an English and Scottish practice in which, following the dictation of one phrase of a psalm or *hymn tune, the first note sung by the assembly was elongated to permit all to enter before proceeding. This lengthening of the first note of each line became so accepted that publishers of psalm tunes printed these tunes with the elongations not only at the beginning but also at the end of the phrase for the sake of balance.

Curwen, J. Spencer. Studies in Worship Music. First Series. London: J. Curwen & Sons, 1888. Pp. 287ff.

GEISSLERLIEDER (G.)

The 14th-century religious folk song of the Geissler (German flagellants) sung in penitential procession are known as Geisslerlieder. Formally, this religious music of the people anticipated the Lutheran *chorale. The chief manuscript of this body of music is the "Chronikon" of Hugo Spechtshart von Reutlingen (c.1285-c.1360). (Cf. *Lauda and *Leise.)

Hübner, Arthur. Die deutschen Geisslerlieder. Berlin: W. de Grayter, 1931.

Müller-Blattau, Josef. "Die deutschen Geisslerlieder, " ZM,
17:6ff. , 1935.
Reese, Gustav. Music in the Middle Ages. New York.
W. W. Norton, 1954. Pp. 238-240.
Runge, Paul. Die Lieder und Melodien der Geissler des
Jahres 1349. Leipzig, n. p. 1900.

GEISTLICHE LIEDER   (G.)

The Geistliche Lieder auffs new gebessert (Wittenberg, 1529) is an important Reformation *hymnal edited by
Martin Luther (1483-1546) and published by Joseph Klug (one
of the four Wittenberg printers of Reformation literature).
This volume, containing 28 *hymns by Luther himself and
26 by other authors and selected by Luther especially for
this collection, is sometimes called the Klug Gesangbuch.

Luther, Martin. Das Klug'sche Gesangbuch, 1533, ed. by
Konrad Ameln. Kassel: Bärenreiter, 1954 (facsimile
reprint).
Winterfeld, Carl von. Martin Luther's deutsche geistliche
Lieder. Hildesheim: Olms, 1966 (1840).

GENEVAN PSALTER see PSALMODY, METRICAL (The
Continent); PSALTERS

GESANGBUCH see HYMNAL

GLORIA IN EXCELSIS (L.)

"Glory be to God on high" (known as the "greater
doxology") is the ancient hymn which had its simple beginnings in Luke 2:14 and in the Liturgy of St. James. Its
development and expansion can be traced through a fourth-
century Greek hymn and a later Latin translation, both used
during the Christmas season. Martin Luther (1483-1546)
retained the traditional placement of the Gloria, following
the *Kyrie eleison, in his *Formula Missae, but omitted it
in his *Deutsche Messe. However, succeeding Lutheran
liturgies retained it, if only in its German congregational
versification as Luther's "All' Ehr und Preis soll Gottes
sein" or Decius' "Allein Gott in der Höh sei Ehr. " The
latter chorale has been the inspiration for many organ com-

positions as J. S. Bach's (1685-1750) trio setting (BWV, 676), F. W. Zachow (1663-1712), J. G. Walther (1684-1748), Johann Pachelbel (1653-1706) and others. The English form of the Gloria occupied the traditional position in the 1549 Prayer Book. However, it was transferred to its present position at the end of the service in 1552.

When the Gloria occurs in musical settings of the mass it is often subdivided with each section receiving a distinct musical idea (see, e.g., J. S. Bach, Mass in B Minor, BGA, VI).

Jungmann, J. A.   The Mass of the Roman Rite.   New York: Benziger, 1959.   Pp. 231-240.
Reed, Luther D.   The Lutheran Liturgy.   Philadelphia: Muhlenberg Press, 1947.
Weil, A.   "Etwas über das Gloria Temp. pasch. und das Lied, 'Allein Gott in der Höh sei Ehr'," in: Gregorius-Blatt III, 1878.

GLORIA PATRI (L.)

The giving of praise to the Trinity sung at the end of a *psalm or *canticle is called the Gloria Patri, or "lesser doxology." It began as a Western addition to the Jewish psalms in an attempt to Christianize them.

With the Arian heresy which denied the eternity of the Son, the Gloria Patri read "Glory be to the Father in the Son, and to the Holy Ghost." However, the orthodox group reinstated the original worship and added the final clause, "as it was in the beginning...." This doxology traditionally is omitted during Holy Week, as it is in the requiem where it is replaced with the Requiem aeternam.

The Gloria Patri reads: "Glory be to the Father: and to the Son and to the Holy Ghost; as it was in the beginning, is now, and ever shall be, world without end. Amen."

Grote, Gottfried.   "Zum 'Gloria Patri'," Kirchenchordienst, 5:5-7, 1939.
Reed, Luther D.   The Lutheran Liturgy.   Philadelphia: Muhlenberg Press, 1947.

GOLDEN SEQUENCE

The hymn, "Veni, Sancte Spiritus," from medieval times is called the "Golden Sequence." It was employed as the sequence for Whitsuntide in the Roman Missal (1568-70). Its earliest possible date is around the 13th century, the most probable author being Pope Innocent III.

In its translation by Martin Moller, "Heil'ger Geist, du Tröster mein" (1584), the Golden Sequence has entered the Protestant church through its use as a hymn for Whitsuntide.

Duffield, Samuel W. The Later Hymn-Writers and Their Hymns. New York: Funk and Wagnalls, 1889. Chapter 15.

GOSPEL (ME., go(d)spel, fr. OE. godspel, fr. god good + OE. spell tidings--trans. of LL. evangelism)

The passage of Scripture read during a service of worship from one of the four Biblical Gospels is referred to as the Gospel. Traditionally, it has held an honored position in the service as witnessed by the standing of the congregation for the reading of this lesson, especially since they have been seated for the Old Testament and epistle lessons. Its honor is also seen in the framing of the Gospel with sung responses. Following the announcement of the Gospel the response, "Glory (or thanks) be to thee, O Lord," appears in the Lutheran service but is omitted from the Anglican in the Prayer Book (1552). In response to the Gospel, "Praise be to thee, O Christ" is sung in the Lutheran and the Episcopal services, as it has been in the Scottish Anglican service since 1637.

The prescribed order of the Gospels in the *Book of Common Prayer bears strong signs of the influence of the Sarum Missal.

Reed, Luther D. The Lutheran Liturgy. Philadelphia: Muhlenburg Press, 1947. Pp. 298-300.

GOSPEL POP see POP, GOSPEL

GOSPEL SONG (*gospel + *song)

[Contents: (general); Gospel in song; Antecedents of the gospel song; The 19th-century gospel song; Late 19th- and 20th-century developments; (bibliography).] By definition, a gospel song (in German, Heilslied) is a simple harmonized tune in popular style combined with a religious text of an emotional and personal character in which, rather than God, the individual (and /or the individual religious experience) is usually the center. The text, primarily concerned with the conversion experience, life after death and personal companionship with Jesus, is usually subjective in nature, developing a single thought instead of a line of thought. However, after 1870 the gospel song developed in many directions, including objective praise, teaching and theology. This primary thought usually finds its foremost expression in the repetitive refrain, which binds together the stanzas in a closely-knit unity. Thus, the form is mainly the verse-refrain pattern of the *spiritual. The melodic, harmonic and rhythmic style is often associated with the style of secular music, often drawing attention to itself and away from the text.

Gospel in Song

The musical expression of a personal religious experience, the singing of the good news of Christ, is as old as Christianity itself. The Apostle Paul records the singing of the gospel by the early Christians (Ephesians 5:19). From the eighth century, John Mason Neale drew the hymn of Christ's compassion by Stephen the Sabite, "Art thou weary, art thou languid." Further in hymnody, the gospel is seen in the hymns of the Moravian Brethren and Isaac Watts, to mention a few. Many of Charles Wesley's hymns were used in the Wesleyan revival during the 1700's, leading many persons to Christian commitment. Thus, throughout the history of Christian song the singing of the gospel is everywhere present, not being relegated to any particular type of song.

Antecedents of the Gospel Song

Definitely a revival hymn book, the Olney Hymns (1799) by John Newton (1725-1807) and William Cowper (1731-1800) is one of the popular forerunners of the gospel song book in England and America, particularly among Baptists. Of its 348 hymns, many contained the individual religious expression and emotion which was to become associated with the gospel song.

In America, where the gospel song really began and flourished as a phenomenon of the 19th-century revivalism, three chief influences are seen. (1) The folk-hymnody of the camp meeting shows a definite relation to the gospel song through its simplicity and freshness of text and tune. (2) The

spiritual of both the Negro and white American is reflected
in the gospel song as reported by Dr. George Pullen Jackson. (3) In the Sunday school songs of the early 19th century the simplicity and popular design and immediate appeal
created especially for children is seen carried over in the
gospel song.

The *camp meeting song was one of the many types
of religious expression which originated in the American
frontier country south and west of Pennsylvania among the
pioneer settlers, the real impetus coming from Jonathan
Edwards and the Great Awakening. Its simplicity and straight-
forwardness reflected the life of these believers. These
folk-hymns mirrored somewhat the texts of Watts and other
hymn writers or simply expressed a personal religious experience or Bible story in ballad style. The real impetus
for the camp meeting and its resulting music came from the
Rev. James McGready, who began a movement in 1800 in
Logan County, Kentucky, which quickly spread throughout the
frontier and even to the East. This great evangelistic movement, shared by Presbyterians, Methodists and Baptists,
promoted several types of easily learned songs: the verse-
refrain, much repetition, antiphonal, the call and response
and the one line refrain. Since books were scarce and the
people were often illiterate there were few song books at
first. The songs were composed on the spot and passed on
by oral tradition. Thus, the same tunes appeared in many
localities with different versions, at times very highly ornamented as the people sang freely. Among the early collections of this popular revival folk song was Jeremiah Ingall's
(1764-1838) The Christian Harmony (1805). Twenty years
later Lewis Skidmore published The Collection of the Latest
Social and Camp Meeting Hymns and Spiritual Songs (1825),
a Baptist collection. Some widely used hymns sung to simple folk-tunes were "Jesus, my all, to heaven is gone"
(Cennick), "Alas and did my Saviour bleed" (Watts), "Stop,
poor sinner, stop and think" (Newton) and "There is a foun-
tain filled with blood" (Cowper).

From these camp meetings with their hyperemotional
atmosphere another form of song developed, the religious
spiritual or spiritual folk song. The text of this song-type
was simplified to decrease the need of memory work on the
part of the participants; thus, repetitive passages arose.
Often the verse or main text was presented by the solo
singer or leader, the group responding with the simple refrain. Around the first decade of the 19th century, small,
oblong tune books began appearing. Many of them incorporated the four shaped-note system of solmization promoted by

Andrew Law (1748-1821) in his Musical Primer (1803). Among the outstanding collections of this nature were the Repository of Sacred Music (1810) by John Wyeth (1770-1858), Southern Harmony (1835) by William Walker (1809-1875), and The Sacred Harp by B. F. White (1800-1879). From 1832 on, an attempt was made toward a more conventional seven shapes for solmization. This is evident in Jessie B. Aiken's Christian Minstrel (1854).

Among the early "professional" evangelists to use a music director was Charles G. Finney (1792-1875). His director, Thomas Hastings (1787-1872), was one of the first to begin the use of choirs in the revival services. This new emphasis prompted Joshua Leavitt to edit his hymnal, Christian Lyre (1832).

With the growing denominational emphasis the fervor of the camp meeting deteriorated. In its place came the Sunday school movement. By 1824 the American Sunday School Union was founded with the expressed purpose of evangelizing new territories through the establishment of new Sunday schools. Since the music which it inherited (the camp meeting folk hymnody and that of the singing schools) proved to be inappropriate for its clientele, mainly children and youth, a flood of new songs with cheerful verse and "catchy" tunes appeared. These early Sunday school songs were written and compiled by George F. Root, William Bradbury and Robert Lowry, men associated with the early development of the gospel song. The basic principle was to produce a song which children could learn and sing easily.

Among the major contributors to Sunday school songs was Philip P. Bliss (1838-1876), who published many collections of this type of song--The Charm (1871), The Joy (1872) and Sunshine for Sunday School (1873). It was under Dwight L. Moody's influence that Bliss decided to make evangelistic music his vocation.

The 19th-Century Gospel Song

The evangelistic movement and its hymnody, the gospel song, had its immediate roots in the interdenominational Young Men's Christian Association, founded in 1844 in London and 1851 in Boston. Through its revival services and prayer meetings a series of hymnals developed, the first being Union Prayer Meeting Hymns (1858).

Following the Civil War, a Y.M.C.A. evangelist, D. L. Moody, recruited the services of Ira D. Sankey as musician in 1870, a relation lasting until Moody's death in 1899. Sankey's voice, which was not perfect though plentiful in volume, purity and richness, was not the key to his effectiveness but rather it was his sincerity of purpose. It was the Moody-Sankey revivals that gave birth to the term "gospel hymn" or "gospel song," though a collection of songs in 1821 used the term Gospel Melodies. The 1873 Moody-Sankey revivals in England brought the gospel song into vogue. The songs followed the major melodies of the Civil War songs rather than the waning major-minor melodies of the *fuging tunes. There harmonies were purposefully simple being designed for unison or four-part singing.

Preparation in England for Sankey's first evangelistic songs is seen in the solo-singing of Richard Weaver at his meetings in the 1850's. Giving birth to the Salvation Army, the tent meetings of William Booth and his publications, The Christian Mission Hymn Book and The Salvation Soldier's Hymn Book (the late 1860's) containing an abundance of gospel songs and American Sunday School songs, also prepared the way. Using Philip Phillip's Hallowed Songs Sankey introduced solo singing and the popular gospel song for congregational singing to Great Britain. Everywhere he went he broke down barriers, moving the people with his songs, his singing and playing.

At the same time in America P. P. Bliss, following Sankey's example, associated himself with an evangelist, D. W. Whittle, and produced a small collection called Gospel Songs (1874). The following year Bliss and Sankey jointly produced Gospel Hymns and Sacred Songs, the first in a series of six, widely accepted and dearly loved hymnals. The popularity of this music is testified to by the publisher, Biglow and Main, who published the "Gospel Hymn" series of Sankey, Bliss, McGranahan and Stebbins, selling over 50 million copies of the Sankey variety alone by 1900. When the influence of this one series is recognized and when all the other song books are considered, it is realized that the gospel song has the distinction of being America's unique contribution to Christian praise, being true religious folk music of the people as the songs of Dan Emmett and Stephen Foster are in the secular realm. The gospel song of Sankey and his immediate followers was responsible for revitalizing congregational singing which had been declining through the decades.

As was the case with "The Ninety and Nine," Ira D. Sankey and many other gospel song writers wrote their songs and tunes in a spontaneous manner for a specific meeting and occasion. These songs were kept simple since the people had to grasp them on the first hearing. For this reason and because a definite decision of personal commitment to God was the purpose of the meeting, this music was charged with emotion to move the people's hearts. In a day when public school music was in its infancy, civic orchestras were few, and broadcasting and recordings unknown, it is readily seen why this type of religious song had to be simple in design. Since people from all denominations and educational backgrounds attended these mass meetings, the music had to be within the immediate grasp of all because many would never return for a second impression.

Representative gospel songs by early song writers are "Sweet hour of prayer" by William B. Bradbury (1816-1868), "Come to the Saviour" by George Root (1820-1895), "Shall we gather at the river?" by Robert Lowry (1826-1894), "Out of the shadow-land" by Ira D. Sankey (1840-1908), "Shall you? Shall I?" by James McGranahan (1840-1907), "Ye must be born again" by George C. Stebbins (1846-1945), "Pass me not" by William C. Doane (1832-1915), "The beautiful land" by Phillip Phillips (1834-1895) and "Wonderful words of life" by P. P. Bliss. Many of the early gospel song writers would use hymns, adding a refrain as they wrote their simple tunes.

Among the later 19th-century writers of gospel song texts were Edward Mote (1797-1874) ("The Solid Rock"), Lydia Baxter (1808-1874) ("Take the name of Jesus with you"), Fanny Crosby (1820-1915) ("Pass me not, o gentle Saviour"), Annie S. Hawks (1835-1918) ("I need Thee every hour"), Joseph Scriven (1820-1886) ("What a Friend we have in Jesus"), Will L. Thompson (1847-1919) ("Softly and Tenderly"), and Katherine Hankey (1834-1911) ("I love to tell the story").

Late 19th- and 20th-Century Developments

Following the Moody-Sankey movement other men began turning toward professional evangelism and pairing themselves with singers. This line of teams includes names like Charles McCallon Alexander (1867-1920) and J. W. Chapman, Homer Rodeheaver (1880-1955) and Billy Sunday, and D. B. Towner (1850-1919) and R. A. Torrey. Charles Alexander had a reputation for being a master song-leader and revival choir director more than a composer of gospel songs. Through his enthusiastic manner, he promoted the use of these songs. D. B. Towner, composer of "Trust and obey," exerted a wide influence with the gospel song upon the nation, serving as head of the music department of Moody Bible Institute for 26 years. Through his association with Billy Sunday and his publication of evangelistic song books, Homer Rodeheaver

promoted the gospel song. His most famous composition is
"Brighten the corner where you are." Rodeheaver, like
Alexander, conducted himself more as a master of cere-
monies or leader of community singing than did Sankey. His
revival campaigns introduced the use of massed choirs and
orchestral instruments, still prevalent in the Graham Crusades. Rodeheaver was also known for his use of trombone
playing during these meetings.

The thrust of H. A. Rodeheaver's work through com-
piling and publishing evangelistic materials brought to the
public the compositions of Charles H. Gabriel (1856-1932),
B. D. Ackley (1872-1958), Haldor Lillenas (b.1885), and
A. H. Ackley (1887-1960). The style of Gabriel was a more
rhythmic one showing the influence of the western frontier.
His more prominent gospel songs are "He lifted me" and
"Since Jesus came into my heart." Ackley, pianist for Billy
Sunday, is remembered for "I am coming home" and "If your
heart keeps right." Lillenas wrote "Jesus will walk with
me."

As the sale of the gospel song publications increased,
opportunists sought to profit from them. However, since
World War II and the Billy Sunday services, a lack of inspiration, both in leadership and composition, is seen in the
gospel song. A further waning of this style of Christian
praise has resulted from the passive listening involvement
of the general public brought about by radio, phonograph and
television. In this spectator milieu the gospel song has become the property of soloists and the gospel male quartets.
Publishing and promoting this popular, highly rhythmic style
of music used by these singers was Stamps-Baxter Music
Company of Dallas, Texas. Composing much of what they
published the style of Virgil O. Stamps and J. R. Baxter,
Jr. is seen in "Launch out on the sea of God's love" and
"Sail on."

One of the outstanding mid-20th-century gospel song
writers of the church is B. B. McKinney (1886-1952).
Among his well-known gospel songs are "I am satisfied with
Jesus" and "Have faith in God." Other writers of notes are
Beatrice Bixler ("I am not worthy"), Norman Clayton (b.1903)
("Now I belong to Jesus"), Merrill Dunlop (b.1905) ("My sins
are blotted out, I know"), Wendell Loveless (b.1892) ("My
Almighty Lord"), and George Schuler (b.1882) ("Make me a
blessing").

In the 1960's the gospel song has been used in the
crusades of Billy Graham. A continual reflection of the
passive involvement of the congregation is seen in the fact
that the Graham team provides most of the music through

soloists and massive choirs. Compared with the early gospel song books with about 300 songs, the New York Graham
Crusade Song Book (1957) contained only 71 songs, six of
which were written after 1930. Of these six, four consisted
only of refrains or choruses. Thus, it would appear that
the gospel song is waning in its involvement of the congregation through singing, that the impetus for new gospel songs
is not powerful, and that the general public singing gospel
songs has become more illiterate resulting in the production
of gospel refrains instead of hymns or hymn-type stanzas
with refrains.

One exception to the above statement is the works
of John W. Peterson. The creative melodic style of this
composer is seen in much of his writing. Among his most
prominent songs is "It took a miracle." But, even here,
his songs are designed primarily for solo and choir presentation. (Cf. *Evangelistic music and *"Pop," Gospel.)

Downey, James C. "The Gospel Hymns, 1875-1930.) Un-
    published M.A. thesis, University of Southern Missis-
    sippi, Hattisburg, 1963.
_____. "Revivalism, the Gospel Songs and Social Re-
    forms," Ethnomusicology, 9:115-125, May, 1964.
Gold, Charles E. "A Study of the Gospel Song." Unpub-
    lished M.M. thesis, University of Southern California,
    Los Angeles, 1953.
Jackson, George Pullen. White and Negro Spirituals: Their
    Life Span and Kinship. New York: J. J. Augustin
    Publisher, 1943.
Kerr, Phil. Music in Evangelism and Stories of Famous
    Christian Songs. Glendale, Cal.: Gospel Music Pub-
    lishers, 1939.
Pierce, Edwin H. "'Gospel Hymns' and their Tunes," MQ,
    26:355-64, July, 1940.
Reynolds, William Jenson. "Sources for College Teachers
    of Christian Hymnody." Unpublished Ed.D. disserta-
    tion, George Peabody College for Teachers, Nashville,
    Tennessee, 1961.
Rodeheaver, Homer Alan. Hymnal Handbook for Standard
    Hymns and Gospel Songs; A Collection of Stories and
    Information about Hymns, Gospel Songs and Their
    Writers. Chicago: Rodeheaver Music Publishers,
    1931.
Sankey, Ira D. My Life and the Story of the Gospel Hymns.
    Philadelphia: Sunday School Times Company, 1907.
Tallmadge, William H. "The Responsorial and Antiphonal
    Practice in the Gospel Song," Ethnomusicology, 12:
    219-238, May, 1967.

GRADED CHOIR PROGRAM   (fr. L. <u>gradus</u> step, pace,
   grade + *choir + F. <u>programme</u>, fr. LL. <u>programma</u>
   a public proclamation, manifesto, fr. Gr. <u>programma</u>,
   fr. <u>prographein</u> to write before or in public, fr. <u>pro</u>
   before + <u>graphein</u> to write)

   The organization and direction of choirs at the various
age levels within a church, an aspect of church music education, is the graded choir program (also called multiple
choir program).   The term was coined by Hines Sims of the
Music Department of the Southern Baptist Sunday School
Board in 1946.   The four basic divisions of the graded choir
program are:

   Adult division (post-high school on) - ages 19-on
   Youth division (grades 7-12)   - ages 13-18
   Children's division (grades 1-6)   - ages 6-12
   Pre-school division   - ages 4-5

   Historically, the graded choir program is rooted in
Jewish temple worship.   In I Chronicles an account of the
grading of the music ministry of David is given: Levites
of ages 30 or above were the singers and instrumentalists
(15:16, 23-25), their sons (ages 20-30) were the "appren-
tices" (23:24) and the children were trained in "the songs
of the Lord" for future service (25:6, 7).   The training of
child (particularly boy) singers and male choristers in the
Christian church can be traced back to Pope Sylvester (314-
335), but received a strong impetus from the <u>Schola Can-
torum</u> of Pope Gregory (sixth century).   This movement continued into the Reformation in the Lutheran choir-school
(e.g., St. Thomasschule at Leipzig, conducted at one time
by J. S. Bach).   In England the choir schools of the various
cathedrals (Westminster Abbey and St. Paul's Cathedral) provided a major influence on the establishing of similar institutions in 19th-century America.
   From the all-male choir school movement came a
new type of church-related choral activity, a choir for boys
and girls.   Around the turn of the 20th century, the multiple
choir program developed in the church, augmenting the sole
adult choir.   In an attempt to provide opportunities for all
interested persons and to provide a continuity to the music
ministry, by the mid-20th century choirs appeared for all
the various age groups in the church, the constituency of the
specific church regulating the amount of division necessary.
A major contributor to the philosophy and practice of the
graded choir program has been the Music Department of the
Sunday School Board of the Southern Baptist Convention with
its graded publications, book and periodicals.

Kettring, Donald D. Steps Toward a Singing Church. Phila-
delphia: The Westminster Press, 1948.
Williams, Loren R. Graded Choir Handbook: Nashville:
Convention Press, 1958.
Wilson, John F. An Introduction to Church Music. Chicago:
Moody Press, 1965.

GRADUAL (ML. graduale fr. gradualis, fr. gradus step)

The musical composition for soloist, congregation or
choir, the words of which usually being appointed for the
day, which is sung following the *epistle in the service of
worship is termed the gradual. During the festive seasons
it is combined with the *alleluia.
Historically, the gradual reflects the custom of
singing a psalm between the Old Testament and epistle
lections. It was so named because the singers did not
ascend to the top step of the reading pulpit until the
gospel, but stood at another of the steps (gradus). The
Old Testament lesson being suspended in the fifth century,
the gradual took its place following the epistle along with
the alleluia.
The *Book of Common Prayer (1549) omitted the
gradual as did all succeeding revisions except the American
version, which prescribed a *hymn or *anthem at this point.
Thus, this name has been applied to the hymn sung following
the epistle. In the United Lutheran Church of America the
term is used for the psalm sung at this point in worship, the
texts of which are printed for each holy day according to historic series. It was at this point in the service the cantatas
of Bach and other composers were generally sung.

Brodde, Otto and Christa Müller. Das Graduallied. Mün-
chen: Kasser-Verlag, 1954.
Reed, Luther. The Lutheran Liturgy. Philadelphia: Muhlenberg Press, 1947.
Schoeberlein, Ludwig. Schatz des liturgischen Chor- und
Gemeindegesangs nebst den Altarweisen in der deutschen
evangelischen Kirche. 2 vols. in 3. Göttingen: Vandenhoeck, 1865-72.

GYMANFU GANU (W.)

All-day assemblies or festivals for hymn singing and
devotional speaking among the Welsh peoples which originated

in the mid-19th century were called <u>gymanfu</u> ganu. The
singing, which included *hymns, *anthems, oratorio choruses and new *canticles, was done in parts and often with
syllables. Among the early pioneers of these local singing
assemblies were John Williams (1740-1834), Morgan Llechyd
(1751-1844), and John Ellis (1760-1834). As these lovers of
singing immigrated to the "New World" they brought their
love for song with them. This has culminated in the establishment of the National American and Canadian Gymanfu
Ganu Association which meets annually. In localities where
there are concentrations of Welsh peoples, local <u>gymanfu</u>
<u>ganu</u> festivals are held.

Crossley-Holland, Peter (ed.). <u>Music in Wales</u>. London:
    Hinrichsen Edition, 1948.
Merkert, Tilde. "The Gymanfu Ganu," <u>The Church Musician</u>,
    20:4-7, July, 1969.

HALLELUJAH   see ALLELUIA

HANDBELLS (fr. OE. <u>hand</u>, <u>hond</u>; akin to D., G. & Sw.
    <u>hand</u>, OHG <u>hant</u>, Dan. <u>haand</u>, ON. <u>hond</u>, Goth.
    <u>handus</u> + AS. <u>belle</u>, akin to MLG. <u>belle</u>, D. <u>bel</u>,
    and AS. <u>bellan</u> to bellow)

    A series of chromatically or diatonically tuned bells
to which handles have been attached to allow individual
ringing are handbells. This is in contradistinction to the
fixed bell which is played by a series of pulleys and levers.
(Cf. *Carillon and *Change-ringing.) Currently, the handles
of handbells are of leather or wood, the bells themselves
being an alloy of copper and tin. The clappers are tipped
with leather or wood, sometimes covered with felt strips.
The clapper is controlled from free singing by a set of
springs attached to the staple. Usually a complete set of
handbells comprises five chromatic octaves or 61 bells from
c to c^5, however, a practical set may consist of only two
octaves.
    The earliest bells were crudely fashioned out of clay
or wood. Here the history of the handbell is similar to that
of the carillon. It is, in fact, from the carillonic practice
of "change-ringing" in 16th- and 17th-century England that
the handbell as we know it today developed. Since many of

the rings took hours, the towers being cold and the bells too
heavy to be pulled by rope (and producing quite a distressing
sound to the public when used for practicing), handbells were
found more expedient and comfortable for the practice ses-
sions in the heated choir room or local tavern.

By the 18th century, large sets of handbells were
being cast and used for tune ringing by village ringers much
like carolers at festive occasions as Christmas and May Day.
Ringing bands flourished in England during the 19th century
to the extent of playing symphonic scores in concert and
competing in contests.

In the mid-20th century, Margaret Shurcliff is credited
with organizing one of the first American handbell organizations, the Beacon Hill Ringers of Boston. In 1954, the American Guild of English Handbell Ringers was organized. Since
then handbell ringing has become a fast growing art, especially among music programs in local churches.

Grew, Eva Mary. "With the Bell-Ringers," ML, 11:289-94,
    July, 1930.
Parry, Scott B. The Story of Handbells. Boston: Whitte-
    more Associates, 1957.
Tufts, Nancy Poore. The Art of Handbell Ringing. New
    York: Abingdon Press, 1961.
Watson, Doris. The Handbell Choir: A Manual for Church,
    School and Community Group. New York: H. W.
    Gray, 1959.

"HANGER" NOTES (ME. hangen, hongien, fr. OE. hangian;
    akin to OS. hangon, D. hangen, G. hangen, ON.
    hanga, Goth. hahan to hang, to leave in doubt, &
    perh. to L. cunctari to delay, Skr. sankate he hesi-
    tates, + OF., fr. L. nota a mark, sign for Gr.
    gnota)

In 16th-century English church music when English
psalm texts were being fitted to music intended for Latin
texts, the added tones which could be inserted in the unison
*plainsong chanting where the words required it, were called
"hanger" notes.

Arnold, J. N. Plainsong Accompaniment. London: Oxford
    University Press, 1927.
Marshall, Parry Denison. "Plainsong in English: An His-
    torical and Analytical Survey." Unpublished S.M.D.
    dissertation, Union Theological Seminary, New York,
    1964.

HARLEIAN COLLECTION

The six weighty volumes of *services and *anthems by English Restoration composers originally collected and compiled by Thomas Tudway (c.1650-1726) for Lord Edward Harley, is known as the Harleian Collection. Compiled in 1724, the work contains 18 of Tudway's compositions. The manuscript is now housed in the British Museum (BM Harl. MSS. 7337-42).

Fellowes, Edmund H. English Cathedral Music. London: Methuen and Company, Ltd., 1946.

HARMONIUM (NL.)

A keyboard instrument whose tone is produced by a current of air, which is produced by a pair of pedal-operated bellows, setting in vibration thin metal tongues or reeds is a harmonium, American organ or reed organ. The harmonium, as used in the churches and meeting places of 19th- and early 20th-century America and England, was the primary work of the Estey Organ Company (1856) and the Mason and Hamlin Company (1861). It was used in place of the pipe organ among smaller congregations.

Curwen, John Spencer. Studies in Worship Music, First Series. London: J. Curwen and Sons, 1888. Pp. 220-226.

HEILSLIED see GOSPEL SONG

HISTORICUS (L. belonging to history)

The term given to the character (possibly several solo voices) who conveyed the Biblical story and the dramatic idea of the early 17th-century *oratorios was historicus. This character, who related the story as it appeared in the Biblical account, was also called the testo. (See, for example, the oratorios of Carissimi.) In *passions, this singer was called the *evangelist.

Smallman, Basil. The Background of Passion Music. Naperville, Ill.: SCM Book Club, 1957.
Wienandt, Elwyn A. Choral Music of the Church. New York: The Free Press, 1965.

HISTORY OF PROTESTANT CHURCH MUSIC

[This entry is devoted to a survey of the developments of the musical forms, movements and events in the Protestant church from the Reformation to the present, with cross-references to relevant articles elsewhere in this work. Contents: 1517-1600; 1600-1750; 1750-1900; 1900 to the present; (bibliography:) General histories; American histories; German histories.]

1517-1600

Historians have placed the beginning of the Reformation with the nailing of the 95 theses to the door of Wittenberg cathedral (1517) by Martin Luther (1483-1546). This proclamation set in motion a spiritual awakening which has become a major heritage of the Protestant church. As a portion of his concern to involve the people in the church, Luther sought the use of the vernacular. His Deutsche Bibel, *Deutsche Messe (1526) and vernacular *hymns were the outgrowth. These texts, together with their tunes, were collected in chorale books, the first of which was the *Achtliederbuch (1524). Supplying the background for the vernacular *chorales were the pre-Reformation *Leisen, *contrafactum, laudi spirituali (*lauda), and *carols.

From the Reformed Church, under the leadership of John Calvin (1509-1564), came the belief that the psalms were the only worthy songs of the Christian; thus, Calvin's first collection of metrical psalms came into existence, Aulcuns pseaulmes et cantiques mys en chant, 1539 (see *Psalmody, metrical and *psalters). This led to the eventual compilation of the Genevan Psalter (1562) by Marot and de Bèze. Its influence along with the *Souterliederkens (1540) and Sternhold and Hopkin's *Old Version (1562) has been readily felt throughout Protestantism.

Under the direction of Archbishop Cranmer (1489-1556) the Church of England arrived at its own liturgy as set forth in the *Book of Common Prayer (1549). To provide a musical setting for the new services John Merbecke (d. 1585) composed settings of the English liturgy to *plainsong and issued it in the Booke of Common Praier Noted, 1550. These melodies were then harmonized by Tallis, Byrd, and others while maintaining the plainsong rhythm. This gave rise to the late 16th-century harmonized chanting known in history as *Anglican chant. Aside from the chanted services, composers set the non-variable portions of the *communion service and offices of *Morning Prayer and

Evening Prayer (*Vespers) chorally. Considered to be the
first was John Hay's setting (1565). Others of this period
were by Christopher Tye (c.1500-1573) and John Taverner
(1495-1545).
    Also during the Reformation era the forms of the
*motet, *anthem and *passion were developed. The motet
found expression in the psalm motets of Claude Goudimel
(fl.1564) as well as in the chorale motets by George Rhaw
(1488-1548), Ludwig Senfl (c.1488-1548) and Johann Walther
(1496-1570). It was the motet form which influenced the
early *anthems, *passions and *cantatas of the 17th and 18th
centuries. Credited to Christopher Tye, "father of the anthem," has been the establishing of the motet-anthem as a
form, differing from the polyphonic Latin motet mainly in
its use of the vernacular text. Following in the line of anthem and service composers of this period were Thomas
Tallis (1505-1585), Richard Farrant (d.1580), Orlando Gibbons (1583-1625) and William Byrd (1543-1623). With regard
to the passion settings, a descendant of the medieval *liturgical music-drama, Luther's friend and co-laborer, Johann
Walther, produced one of the first Reformation settings of
the St. Matthew account (c.1550), incorporating Luther's
vernacular New Testament. Others to create passion settings
during this era were Antonio Scandello (1517-1580), Melchior
Vulpius (1560?-1615) and William Byrd.

1600-1750

    With the commencement of the monodic style around
1600, music moved into a new era, known as the Baroque.
During this period many of the pinnacles in the history of
Protestant church music were achieved, frequently associated
with the musical genius of Johann Sebastian Bach (1685-1750).
The two primary products of the nuove musiche style relevant to Protestantism were the *oratorio and the *cantata.
Akin to the opera, the oratorio began in Italy and is exemplified in the work of Emilio del Cavalieri (c.1550-1602).
However, making use of the more fully developed recitative
and aria were the larger-scaled oratorios of Giacomo Carissimi (1605-1674) and Alessandro Scarlatti (1660-1725).
Bringing the oratorio into the German Reformation were the
Historiae of Heinrich Schütz (1582-1672). With the oratorios
of Johann Sebastiani and Johann Theile the chorale became
fused into the form. By the beginning of the 17th century
the passion and oratorio became wedded into the passion-
oratorio, climaxing in the Bach St. John Passion. Meanwhile, in England the oratorio itself was being fully developed

by George Frideric Handel, the masterful oratorio composer.

While the interest in the oratorio waned somewhat in Germany after the death of Schütz, the development of the cantata, particularly with its use of the chorale, became a major emphasis. This was cultivated by Franz Tunder (1614-1667), Johann P. Krieger (1651-1735) and Johann Kuhnau (1660-1722) and climaxed in the work of J. S. Bach.

Regarding the musical development of the Church of England, little activity remained following the deaths of Byrd, Gibbons and Bull in the first quarter of the 17th century. Not until the Restoration in 1660 did English music raise to new expressive heights. The most significant musical form of this period in England was the *verse-anthem. The virtuoso of this form was Henry Purcell (c.1659-1695) whose influence is seen in the anthems of Maurice Green (1695-1755) and G. F. Handel. As with the development of the anthem, so it was with the services of the Anglican church. Composers such as Blow and Boyce began writing *full services and *canticles in verse form.

It was during this period that two important metrical psalters were printed: the *Bay Psalm Book (1640) in America and the Tate and Brady or *New Version (1696), in England. These were the last major psalters to be so widely accepted before the advent of the English *hymn by the "father of English hymnody," Isaac Watts (1674-1748). With the hymn came a new style of congregational tune, more flowing than the tunes of the metrical psalms, and more harmonically daring. By the end of the Baroque period, the seeds of the evangelistic hymn, associated with the Wesley revivals, were sown.

Instrumentally, aside from the use of *orchestral instruments with the cantatas and larger choral works, a major interest in composition for the organ marked church music of the Baroque era. Men connected with the North German School of organ composition were J. P. Sweelinck (1562-1621), Samuel Scheidt (1587-1654) and Heinrich Scheidemann (c.1596-1663); in central Germany, Johann Pachelbel (1653-1706) and Georg Böhm (1661-1733); and in the south, Georg Muffat (1653-1704). Other German masters later in this period were Dietrich Buxtehude (1637-1707), J. G. Walther (1684-1748) and J. S. Bach. The principle forms were the preludes, toccatas, fantasies and fugues and a large variety of types of *chorale preludes for use in conjunction with the worship service. Shaping the organ tone of the late-Baroque era were the principal organ builders, Arp Schnitger and Gottfried Silbermann.

Among the newly founded colonies of America, music played a subdued role for the most part in frontier and colonial life. Because of social limitations, *congregational singing was limited to tunes amenable to *"lining-out." By the early 18th century attempts were being made to remedy this situation through the organization of singing schools and the publication of instruction books, such as John Tufts' An Introduction to the Singing of Psalm Tunes (1721). In contrast to the above, however, were the practices of the Moravian settlers who, in 1742, organized a society for the singing of church music, marking the beginning of an important facet, though limited in scope, of American church music.

1750-1900

Following the death of J. S. Bach and G. F. Handel in the mid-18th century and with the ascendency of the orchestra and opera, church music within Protestantism lost much of its attraction for the creative musical minds of the day, a condition typical for the major portion of the organized church.

In 1759 the first known composition by a native American was written. This marked the beginning of a new musical development, American music. While it is true that the European influence on late 18th-century American music lived on in the musical practices of the Moravians and the works of their composers--such as John Frederick Peter (b. 1764), a most enthusiastic promoter of American church music-- William Billings (1748-1800), of Boston, initiated a more native style of composition for church singing. This is illustrated in the *"fuging tunes" of his New England Psalm-singer, 1770. The popularity of similarly styled tune books in colonial America is readily attested to by the nearly 300 tune books published before 1810, a majority of which contained "fuging tunes." Other composers of church music contemporary with Billings were Samuel Holyoke (1762-1820), Daniel Read (1757-1836), Supply Belcher (1751-1830) and Jacob French (1754-?).

Protestant church music in England during the last half of the 18th century produced the evangelistic hymn associated with John and Charles Wesley. It was through their Methodist revival movement that the common people of England discovered the particular genius of hymns, though the Church of England retained its metrical psalms. Other writers influenced by this movement were E. Perronet and J. Cennick. The tunes which accompanied these hymns were youthful in spirit with minimal harmony, encouraging part-singing.

The revival spirit was also felt in America. For, in the frontier settlements around the turn of the 19th century, the *camp meeting phenomenon appeared. From these gatherings, together with the influence of the tune books from the *singing schools, developed the *"fa-so-la" shaped note and the *seven-shaped notation traditions and the folk hymns originating therein. Examples of these frontier tune books were The Sacred Harmony (1844) and Southern Harmony (1845). Alongside these was developing the music of the captive Negroes, the spirituals, a genuine aspect of American hymnody.

Meanwhile, the works of J. S. Bach were being rediscovered in Europe through the efforts of Felix Mendelssohn (1809-1847) who conducted the St. Matthew Passion in 1829, the first performance of this work of Bach's since his death. This accompanied the continued interest in the oratorio among such 19th-century English composers as Arthur Sullivan (1842-1900), Charles Stanford (1852-1924), Hubert Parry (1848-1918), and Edward Elgar (1857-1934).

In English hymnody, the outstanding influence of the established church began in the 1833 Tractarian influence called the *Oxford Movement. Among the important contributions of its leaders (J. Newman, J. M. Neale and C. Winkworth) were the vast translations of Greek, Latin and German hymns into English, the prolific original hymnography, and the compilation of the outstanding Hymns Ancient and Modern (1860-1861).

On the other hand, late 19th-century American church music came under the influence of the revival meetings and under the song master, Ira D. Sankey (1840-1908) the *gospel song became the expression of the evangelistic arm of Protestantism. This influential music was to continue its expression into the mid-20th century (see *Evangelistic music).

Another phenomenon of mid-19th- and early 20th-century Protestant church music was the elimination of the volunteer choir, replacing it with the *quartet choir of salaried professional soloists. These choirs fostered the singing of verse-anthems, German cantatas and similar styled works by such composers as H. R. Shelly (1858-1947) and Dudley Buck (1839-1909).

1900 to the Present

One major concern of the Protestant church in the 20th century has been two-fold: the revitalization of congre-

gational singing and an awakened consciousness of worship
through the use of hymns as a basis for choral and instrumental music. To this has been added the concern for a
relevant and youthful expression in the last half of the century. Considering first the aspect of congregational hymnody,
a wealth of denominational and non-denominational *hymnals
have been produced during this century, exhibiting not only
the hymnic heritage of a particular denominational group but
also the historical tradition of Christian songs through the
ages (an influence of the Oxford Movement). Further encouragement has been received through such organizations as
the Hymn Society of America and its encouragement of hymn
singing through the *hymn festival movement.

Along side of the hymnic consideration has been the
revival and evangelistic crusade emphasis. Leadership for
this century came from Charles M. Alexander (1867-1920),
the originator of the gospel chorus and initiator of the use
of the piano in church music, and from Homer Rodeheaver
(1880-1955). Through this period the gospel song has continued and adapted itself to new conditions under the influence
of mass communications as seen in some of the songs of
John W. Peterson.

From the choral standpoint, the use of volunteer
choirs has replaced almost completely the era of the quartet choir. As large numbers of churches have been organized during this century and as each congregation has desired a choir to participate in their worship service, the
20th-century anthem has emerged. Because of the limited
resources of most congregations, simply written choral
music, most often with accompaniment, has been composed
for anthems, often the texts and/or the tunes being taken
from hymns (see *Hymn-anthem). With the advent of the
*graded choir program (or multiple choir program) in the
mid-20th century, a need for anthems designed for use with
children's choirs and multiple choirs was created.

Regarding 20th-century church music in England, one
of the leaders has been Ralph Vaughan Williams (1872-1958).
Under the influence of the work in folk music as a hymnic
resource by Cecil Sharp (1859-1924), Vaughan Williams made
extensive use of folk music in his editing of The English
Hymnal and in much of his choral and instrumental composition. Other eminent musicians of contemporary English
church music include Gustav Holst (1874-1934), William Walton (b.1902) and Benjamin Britten (b.1913). Through the
works of Britten, the religious music of England has achieved
a new historical climax, works such as The Burning Fiery
Furnace, War Requiem, Noye's Fludde and Festival Te Deum.

The position of German church music at the turn of the century was one of subservience to concert music. However, a new era of evangelische Kirchenmusik initiated by Max Reger (1873-1916) and Karl Straube (1873-1950) was brought to the forefront with the "festival of German church music" (1937) in Berlin. Here was revealed that the new music (Stravinsky, Hindemith, Schoenberg) and new church music (Pepping, Distler, David) had common ancestry: a detachment from the Romantic era of the 19th century, a break with functional harmony, a freedom of rhythm and melody, and a return to ostinato principles in place of the classic developmental forms. These ideas are embodied in the works of such composers as Ernst Pepping (b. 1901), Hugo Distler (1918-1942), J. N. David (b. 1895) and Joseph Ahrens (b. 1902). Formal emphasis has yielded the restoration of the passion, chorale motet and cantata among choral music and the various types of chorale preludes in organ literature.

The new trends in Protestant church music from 1950 to 1970 have been as varied as contemporary music itself. From the concert settings as the Knut Nystedt's (b. 1915) Praise to God (1968), incorporating the avant garde, to the rock musical, A Man Dies (1961) by E. Marvin and E. Hooper all facets of both concert and popular musical composition have experienced expression within the church (see, e.g., *Pop, Gospel). Jazz had its beginnings in Protestant worship through Edgar Summerlin's Liturgical Jazz (1959) and has had a further spokesman in Heinz Werner Zimmerman (b. 1931). The influence of the Broadway musical was adapted to the worship service by Geoffrey Beaumont (1904-1970) and the *Twentieth Century Church Light Music Group. The influence of the folk-musical came with Bob Oldenberg's Good News in 1967, and with other revues as the Nystrom and McKeever New Directions (1968). Even the use of electronic music has entered the church as exemplified in R. Felciano's Anthem for Pentecost Sunday (1967) for mixed chorus and electronic tape.

General Histories

Arnold, Corliss Richard. Organ Literature: A Comprehensive Survey. Metuchen, N.J.: Scarecrow Press, 1973.
Dickinson, Edward. Music in the History of the Western Church. New York: Haskell House, 1969 (1902).
Douglas, Winfred. Church Music in History and Practice. New York: Scribner's, 1937.
Routley, Erik. The Church and Music. London: Gerald Duckworth, 1967 (1950).

_____. Twentieth Century Church Music. London: Herbert Jenkins, 1964.

American Histories

Ellinwood, Leonard. The History of American Church Music. New York: Da Capo Press, 1968 (1953).
Hooper, William Lloyd. Church Music in Transition. Nashville: Broadman, 1963.
Stevenson, Robert M. Protestant Church Music in America. New York: W. W. Norton, 1966.

English Histories

Bumpus, John S. A History of English Cathedral Music, 1549-1889. 2 vols. London: T. Werner Laurie, 1908.
Curwen, John S. Studies in Worship Music. 2d series. London: J. Curwen & Sons, 1880, 1885.
Fellowes, Edmund H. English Cathedral Music from Edward VI to Edward VII. London: Methuen, 1969.
Le Huray, Peter. Music and the Reformation in England, 1549-1660. London: Herbert Jenkins, 1967.
Stevens, Denis. Tudor Church Music. London: Faber and Faber, 1961.

German Histories

Blume, Friedrich. Die evangelische Kirchenmusik. Vol. of Handbuch der Musikwissenschaft, Potsdam: Akademische Verlagsgesellschaft Athenaion, 1931.
_____. Geschichte der evangelische Kirchenmusik. Kassel: Bärenreiter, 1965.
Moser, H. J. Die evangelische Kirchenmusik in Deutschland. Berlin: C. Merseburger, 1954.
Müller, K. F. Die Musik des evangelischen Gottesdienstes. Vol. IV, Leiturgia: Handbuch des evangelischen Gottesdienstes. Kassel: Stauda, 1960.

HOSANNA (H.)

The Hebrew word of praise or greeting used by the throng at Jesus' triumphal entry into Jerusalem (Mark 11: 9f.) and incorporated into the *Sanctus and the *Benedictus is the hosanna (or osanna). Found in the Lutheran services it has been omitted from the Anglican Eucharist since the Prayer Book of 1552.

Reed, Luther D. The Lutheran Liturgy. Philadelphia:
    Muhlenberg Press, 1947.

HUGUENOT PSALTER see PSALMODY, METRICAL (Geo-
    graphical developments--The Continent); PSALTERS

HYMN (L. hymnus, fr. Gr. hymnos hymn)

    Defined as a lyrical composition expressive of genu-
ine religious feeling, the hymn is designed to be used in
corporate worship of God. Originally, the term referred to
songs in honor of Apollo. (For the history of the hymn see
*Hymnody.)
    The formal structure of the hymn is multi-stanzaic,
each *stanza being an arrangement of the same number of
*verses in their respective meters. A *refrain, dependent
on the text for its meaning, may conclude each stanza, but
rarely will a *chorus be employed. (See also *Hymnal;
*Hymn-anthem; *Hymn-festival; *Hymn meter; *Hymnody;
*Hymnography; *Hymnology; *Hymn rehearsal; *Hymn ser-
vice; *Hymns ancient and modern; *Hymn tune.)

Pirner, Reuben G. "The Nature and Function of the Hymn
    in Christian Worship," Church Music, 1966. 1[sic]:
    1-5, 1966.
Price, Carl Fowler. What Is a Hymn? Papers of the
    Hymn Society, No. 6. New York: The Hymn Society
    of America, 1937.

HYMNAL

    A collection of hymns, with or without set tunes,
bound within one cover is termed a hymnal or hymnbook
(in German, Gesangbuch). Among the earliest hymnals published in the vernacular and in sympathy with Reformation
ideals, were two by the Bohemian Brethren, one in 1501
and the other in 1505. The long line of Lutheran hymnals
or chorale books began the *Achtliederbuch of 1523 and continues; the hymnals of the Calvinists began with the Strasburg
Psalter of 1539.
    Although hymnals are presently thought of along de-
nominational or church lines, they were also designed for
personal use in private devotion. (See also *chorale;
*Hymnody; *Hymn tune; *Psalmody, metrical; and *Psalters.)

Mahrenholz, Christhard. Das Evangelische Kirchengesang-
buch; Ein Bericht über seine Vorgeschichte. Kassel:
Bärenreiter, 1950.
Sydnor, James Rawlings. The Hymns and Congregational
Singing. Richmond, Va.: John Knox Press, 1960.
Chapter 7.
Torhorst, Von Arnold. "Absonderliches und Ergötzliches
aus alten Gesangbuchern," Der Kirchenchor, 11:53-58,
May-June, 1951.

HYMN-ANTHEM

(1) Taking much the same place as the *chorale
preludes do in the organist's repertoire, the hymn-anthem
is essentially a *hymn tune set with varied organ parts,
varied choral treatment, *descant, fa-burden (see fauxbourdon), and any other composer's device that will turn three
or more stanzas of the same tune into an attractive anthem.
Its use of an existing tune in a partita (*chorale partita)
fashion offers variations and musical comment.

Arising in America and England around the turn of
the 20th century, the hymn-anthem has provided a means
for making known good tunes that congregations do not have
in their ordinary repertory. Among the functional composers of this form are Gustav Holst (1874-1934) and Healey
Willan (1880-1968).

(2) Developing from the *evangelistic music of the
late 19th century, associated with Ira D. Sankey (1840-1908)
and James McGranahan (1840-1907) are the "two-page anthems" included in various revival hymnals, also referred
to as hymn-anthems. Among the first collections to include
these "two-page anthems" was The Gospel Choir (1885) by
Sankey and McGranahan. This music has continued to exist
in the 20th century through its inclusion in the back section
of hymnals like The Broadman (1940), Nos. 468-478. As
example of such an anthem is McGranahan's "Hallelujah for
the Cross."

Wienandt, Elweyn and Robert Young. The Anthem in England and America. New York: The Free Press, 1970.

HYMN FESTIVAL   (*hymn + OF. fr. L. festivus festive, gay)

A planned service of worship, centered around a theme

in which hymns are used as the major vehicle of communication in a large gathering such as a church or community is termed a hymn festival. (Cf. *Hymn service.) The introduction of hymn singing festivals during the 1920's has been a notable contribution of the Hymn Society of America. The hymn singing festival, however, had its predecessor in the *Gymanfu Ganu, a mid-19th-century singing festival among the Welsh folk. Unlike the traditional "hymn-sing" where the selection of hymns is a random one, the hymn festival is a thoughtful arrangement of hymns to achieve a worshipful experience.

The hymn festival movement in America has in the past half-century helped to produce a greater understanding and appreciation of hymns in corporate and private worship as well as to alert the congregation into enthusiastic singing of the spiritual truths contained in the hymns. Through the community and interdenominational hymn festival an appreciation of Christian brotherhood has been fostered also.

McAll, Reginald L. The Hymn Festival Movement in America. Papers of the Hymn Society, No. 26. New York: The Hymn Society of America, 1951.

HYMN METER (*hymn + ME. metre, fr. OF. metre, fr. L. metrum, fr. Gr. metron)

The syllabic rhythms of each *verse of poetry within a *hymn is the hymn meter. The particular meter is generally indicated by a numerical statement or an accepted formula indication for the number of syllables in each verse of a *stanza. The more common meters are indicated:

Short Meter	(S.M.)	66.86	(6.6.8.6)
Long Meter	(L.M.)	88.88	(8.8.8.8)
Common Meter	(C.M.)	86.86	(8.6.8.6)

All other meters are indicated by numerals. The doubling of any of the above meters is indicated by "D." Each may be extended by a *refrain or *"alleluias."

A complete statement of the meter of a hymn also includes the position of the first poetic accent. The four fundamental patterns of accent are:

Iambic	first syllable unstressed
Trochaic	first syllable stressed
Anapaestic	first two syllables unstressed
Dactylic	two unstressed syllables following a stressed.

Lovelace, Austin C. The Anatomy of Hymnody. New York:
Abingdon Press, 1965.

HYMNODY (Gr. hymnoidia, fr. hymnos hymn + oide a
song, a singing)

[Contents: (general); Early Christian hymnody; German hymnody; English hymnody; American hymnody; 20th-
century hymnody; (bibliography:) General; Early; German;
English; American; 20th-century; Hymnal companions.] The
body of religious poetry in metrical form, i.e., hymns,
suitable for corporate singing in the worship of God, is
called hymnody (in German, das Hymnersingen or der Hymen-
gesang). It is among the several modes adopted by the
Christian church to translate her doctrines and beliefs and
her Bible into the language of music.
     At the foundation of Christian hymnody is the Hebrew
Psalter, the Old Testament "Book of Psalms." It not only
served the Jewish peoples for their worship, but it was also
the hymnbook of the early Christian Church. In the Gospel
account of the Last Supper, Jesus and the Twelve sang a
hymn from the psalter, perhaps a portion of the Great Hallel,
Psalms 113-118. This was the traditional hymn for the
Feast of the Passover (Patrick, 17). The Apostle Paul
makes mention of singing and the singing of "psalms, hymns
and spiritual song" several times in his epistles (Ephesians
5:18, 19); Colossians 3:16; I Corinthians 14:15). This plus
historical accounts from the first centuries indicate that
many of these songs were the Psalms. Soon, however, the
new church began to feel its freedom and desired to express
itself. Among the first forms are the songs surrounding the
nativity as recorded in Luke's Gospel. Three of these, the
*Magnificat, *Benedictus and the *Nunc dimittis are the evan-
gelical canticles familiar to Anglican and Lutheran services.
Other songs embedded in various portions of the New Testament show two major purposes: doctrinal or liturgical (I
Timothy 3:16 and Revelation 2:17) and doxological (Revelation
15:3-4).

Early Christian Hymnody--East and West

     From the early days of persecution, four hymns of
the Church have survived. Two show the influence of the
seraphic song from Isaiah--the Trisagion ("Holy God, Holy
and mighty, holy and immortal, have mercy upon us"), and
the Ter sanctus ("Holy, holy, holy, Lord God of hosts").

Another, a brief doxology based on Psalm 65:1 is the Te decet laus ("To Thee belongeth praise, to Thee belongeth laud, to Thee belongeth glory, Father, Son and Holy Spirit, for ever and ever. Amen.") The fourth is an expansion of the angel's song at the Nativity, the Gloria in excelsis ("Glory be to God on High"). Also belonging to this period is the Greek hymn for candlelighting, the Epiluchnion or Latin Lucernariun ("O gladsome Light"--translated by R. Bridges; CH, 72) (Frost, 4).

While the early church was hammering out its creedal statements, one of the greatest hymnic creeds took shape in the *Te Deum laudamus ("We praise Thee, O God: we acknowledge Thee to be the Lord"). This Latin doxological statement of faith is commonly ascribed to Niceta, Bishop of Remesiana in Dacia (b.c.410).

The first hymnwriter known to us by name is Clement of Alexandria (c.170-c.215), a Gnostic. This Greek scholar is the author of "A hymn to the Savior" (paraphrased, "Shepherd of eager youth"--H. M. Dexter) (Patrick, 29). Written shortly before A.D. 300 the so-called Oxyrhynchos hymn (named from its inclusion in the manuscript of the Oxyrhynchos Papyri) is a unique Hellenistic-Jewish synthesis of praise to God. Its major importance is the fact that it constitutes the oldest manuscript of the early Church containing a text accompanied by musical notation (Patrick, 30). Another early Greek hymnographer is Syrenius of Crete (c.375-414?), whose "Lord Jesus, think on me" (translated by A. Chatfield) is a genuine expression of Christian feeling. From one of the earliest liturgies, the Liturgy of St. James (5th century) comes the Cherubic Hymn, "Let all mortal flesh keep silence" (translated by G. Moultrie; CH, 55).

At the pinnacle of Greek Christian hymnody (seventh to ninth centuries) are three eminent poets. St. John of Damascus (eighth century), one of the Fathers of the Greek Church and among the names of Mar Saba, has two hymns in common use today, both translated by John Mason Neale-- "The Day of resurrection!" (CH, 100) and "Come ye faithful, raise the strain" (CH, 26). St. John's nephew, Stephen the Sabite (c.725-815), also lived at Mar Saba where he penned "Art thou weary, art thou languid" (translated by Neale). Joseph the Hymnographer (fl.840-883) is probably the most prolific of Greek hymnwriters--"Let us now our voices raise" (Neale). From this time on Greek hymnody declined.

The Church in the West is said to have been introduced to hymns of Hilary of Poitiers (c.310-368). However, the popularizer of hymnody in the West is Ambrose of Milan (340-397), a statesman, scholar and poet. Ambrose, in

trying to battle the Arian controversy, wrote a number of
"battle hymns." Thought to be of this type is "The eternal
gifts of Christ the King" (translated by Neale; CH, 103i).
Often called the "Latin Watts," Aurelius Clemens Prudentius
(348-413) ranks high as a hymnographer, as seen in his
great hymn, "Of the Father's love begotten" (Neale; CH, 88).
A contemporary of Pope Gregory I (c. 540-604) was Venantius
Honorius Clementianus Fortunatus (c. 530-609). From the
number of his hymns to survive two are well-known. His
great processional hymn, "Vexilla regis prodeunt" ("The
royal banners forward go"; CH, 108), and "Salva, festa dies"
("Welcome happy morning"; CH, 114) are preserved in the
translations of Neale and J. Ellerton, respectively. It was
during this period of Latin hymnody that the hymn abandoned
its old classic metrical concept of quantity and adopted rather
the popular rhythmic form of natural word accent.

Turning to the Middle Ages, the most creative hymnic
compositions were coming from within the cloistered life of
the monasteries, which had become the refuge for the scholars. From this world of seclusion comes an early eighth-
century Ascension hymn, "Hymnum cananuis gloriae" ("A
hymn of glory let us sing"--translated by B. Webb: CH, 1),
by the noted English priest and poet Venerable Bede (673-
735). A most noble figure in the whole monastic line is
Bernard of Clairvaux (1090-1153). Attributed to Bernard,
though of uncertain authorship, is the medieval hymn to
Jesus entitled "Jesu dulcis memoria" ("Jesus, Thou joy of
loving hearts"--R. Palmer; CH, 53). From the 12th century, Bernard of Cluny poured his sorrow over the corrupt
world of his day into the satire, "De contemptu mundi" ("On
Contempt for the World"). The genius of Dr. Neale reveals
a section of this work in the translation, "Jerusalem the
golden" (CH, 85). Also translated by Neale is the hymn,
"O that their joy and their glory must be" (CH, 85), a hymn
by the noted medieval philosopher and theologian, Peter
Abelard (1079-1142). The hymns of this period, like the
liturgy, were the sole property of the clergy and trained
choirs. Singing was done for, not by the congregation, as
it would remain until the Reformation.

Within monastic life there were many opportunities
for poets to display their skills. Due to an elaborate organization of services (Canonical Hours) a need arose for a great
cycle of hymns known as "office hymns." Specific hymns
were also provided for the different seasons of the liturgical
year as well as for feast days. Within each monastery
there usually were several hymns for each occasion. Thus,
the body of Latin hymnody at that time must have been vast.

From the monastery of St. Gall, a new type of hymn developed called the sequence. It is from this tradition that the famous ninth-century Latin hymn, "Gloria, laus, et honor" ("All glory, laud, and honor"--Neale; CH, 6) was written. Due to the enormous increase of these additions to the liturgy and to their excessive use, the Council of Trent (1570) abolished all but four of them. A fifth one, the Stabat Mater ("At the cross her station keeping"--R. Mant; CH, 13) by Jacopone de Todi (1230-1306), was permitted in 1727 (Patrick, 62).

As the 13th century began, the task of saving the world from its dreadful condition of life was far removed from monastic thinking. Thus, leaving the secluded life within monastic walls, Francis of Assisi (1182-1226) turned toward the people and their poverty. The simplicity and sincerity of his life are carried through the ages in his "Canticle of the Sun" ("All creatures of our God and King"-- translated by W. Draper). While Francis and his Franciscan followers presented their simple Gospel, Thomas Aquinas (c. 1227-1274) and other Dominicans sought to fight heresies from within the church. Among the Communion hymns of this great theologian is "O Saving Victim, opening wide"-- Neale; CH, 80).

Other Latin hymns of this later period are--"O sons and daughters, let us sing, " by Jean Tisserand (d. 1494)-- Neale, tr. (CH, 81); "Good Christian men rejoice"--Neale, tr.; "O Sacred head now wounded"--J. W. Alexander, tr. (CH, 791); "The strife is o'er, the battle done"--F. Pott, tr. (CH, 110); and "O come all ye faithful, " by John Francis Wade (c. 1710-1786)--translated by F. Oakeley (CH, 69).

German Hymnody

(For the German hymn tune see *Chorale.)
With the origin and growth of the schola cantorum from the reign of Pope Gregory I, the "liturgy" of the laity declined into a passive state of seeing and listening, rather than the Sitz im Leben of the Latin hymnody which developed during the fifth and sixth centuries. Against this ideology Martin Luther promoted the doctrine of the priesthood of all believers, returning to the congregation the right and responsibility to be the primary carrier of liturgical action through the hymn.

Preparing the way for the Reformation were the 13th-century controversies between the German rulers and the papacy, which resulted in numerous vernacular hymns, as "Christ ist erstanden" ("Christ is arisen"--translated by W.

Buszin; CH, 17) and "Nun bitten wir den heiligen Geist"
("Now thank we Holy Ghost"). From the 13th- and 14th-cen-
tury flagellants a forerunner of the Lutheran hymn is seen
in the *Geisslerlieder. During the 15th century a strong
movement toward the use of the vernacular in the church
appeared, as seen in the decree of the Synod of Schwerin in
1492. Likewise, an important predecessor was the mixed
song, partly Latin and partly Greek, as "In dulci jubilo"
("Good Christian men rejoice").

The followers of John Huss, the Bohemian Brethren
(later called Moravians) were the first Protestants to incorporate congregational singing into their worship, publishing
the first Protestant hymnbooks in 1501 and 1505. Under the
leadership of Count Zinzendorf, the Moravians strengthened
their fellowship and set themselves to the task of evangelizing the world. Their impact is widely felt in hymnody,
not only through their own hymns but also through their influence on the lives of Luther, the Wesleys and James Montgomery (Hostetler, xv-xvi).

Martin Luther (1483-1546), seeing an urgent need in
the new church for vernacular singing by the people, encouraged German poets to compose hymns to be sung during
the mass. Following his example, poets and musicians like
J. Walther, Torgau, Justus Jonan, J. Klug and Valentin
Babst compiled an abundance of hymnals, the first of which
being the Achtliederbuch in 1524. That same year, Luther
and J. Walther published the Geistlich Gesangbüchlein in
Wittenberg. From this time to the end of Luther's life
nearly a hundred such hymnals were produced among all the
areas of the Reformation. The sources of Luther's hymns
were five: the psalter, paraphrases from other portions of
Scripture, transcriptions of Latin office hymns and antiphons,
pre-Reformation Leisen recast, and original hymns of which
last are, for example, "Ein' feste Burg ist unser Gott" ("A
mighty fortress is our God"; CH, 2) and "Wir glauben all in
einen Gott" ("We all believe in one true God"; CH, 113).

Other hymnists of Luther's day are Paul Speratus
(1484-1551), Justus Jonas (1493-1555) and Lazarus Spengler
(1479-1534). Active in North Germany was Nikolaus Decius
(c.1485-1546) whose hymns for the Ordinary of the Mass
were quite popular--"Allein Gott in der hoh sei ehr" ("All
glory be to God on high"; CH, 5) and "O Lam Gottes"
("Lamb of God, pure and holy"). The spirit of these hymns
breathes a universal spirit of boldness and faith in the great
work of salvation not one of individual reflection and confession.

Following the signing of the Formula of Concord in

1577, much of the vigor of subsequent hymnody vanished.
However, two men merit mention for their productivity.
Nikolaus Selnecker (1528-1592) shows childlike simplicity in
"Erhalt uns, Herr, bei deinen Wort" ("Lord, keep us steadfast in Thy Word"; (CH, 63). Known as the king of chorales,
"Wachet auf, ruft uns die Stimme" ("Wake, awake, for night
is flying"; CH, 112) by Philipp Nicolai (1556-1608) is also
from this period.
     In the next period of German hymnody (1618-1675) a
new style of poetry and character of hymn is seen developing. The sorrows of the Thirty Years' War (1618-1648) and
the new activity in the realm of poetry combined the true
faith, hope and trust in God with a sincere folklike and biblical manifestation. This new poetic style was both rhythmically and poetically more suave and clean, and theologically more personal. The founder of this new style, the
Silesian school of poets, was Martin Opitz (1597-1639). However, the first to adopt these new poetic rules in his hymn-
writing was Johann Heermann (1585-1647)--"Herzliebster,
Jesu" ("Ah, holy Jesus"; CH, 44). Known especially for the
hymn often called the "German Te Deum, " "Nun danket alle
Gott" ("Now thank we all our God"; CH, 68), is Martin
Rinkart (1568-1649). It is a fine expression of personal
thanksgiving from this period.
     Other Silesian poets are Heinrich Held (1620-1659),
Matthaeus Lowenstern (1594-1648), and Johann M. Meyfart
(1590-1642).
     Beginning with Paul Gerhardt (1607-1676) the individ-
ualistic hymn appears. Among his finest hymns is "Wer
nur den lieben Gott lässt walten" ("If God Himself be for
me"; CH, 44). Following this tendency is Johann Franck
(1618-1677) whose "Jesu, meine Freude" ("Jesus, priceless
treasure"; CH, 51) reflects an intense personal religious con-
viction.
     In his efforts to counteract the "dead orthodoxy" de-
veloping in the Reformed Church, and to revive a vital
Christianity, Philipp J. Spener (1635-1705) led what is called
the Pietistic Movement (1675-1750). Though many fine hymns
resulted from this revival, the real contribution was the
Gesangbuch (1704) edited by Johann Freylinghausen (1670-
1739). The warmth of feeling expressed by the German
hymnody contained therein has had a great effect on English
hymnody through John Wesley (Patrick, 83). Included in this
period are Count Ludwig von Zinzendorf (1700-1760), founder
of the Moravian Brethren, who wrote over 2000 hymns, and
Joachim Neander (1650-1680), one of the greatest hymnists of

the Reformation Church, who is remembered most for his
"Lobe den Herren, den machtigen König" ("Praise to the
Lord, the Almighty"; CH, 92).

Reacting to the pietism of this time were Benjamin
Schmolch (1672-1737)--"Mein Jesu, wie du wilst" ("My Jesus,
as Thou wilt") and Erdmann Neumeister (1671-1756)--"Sinners
Jesus will receive." This is the age of the musical master,
Johann Sebastian Bach.

Because of the pietistic lack of intellectual strength
and the coming of the Age of Reason (c. 1750-1850) the church
underwent some very grave trials. The lack of artistic productivity was everywhere present in the lack of musical compositions and texts for use in the German church. One rather
theologically apologetical hymn worth of note is Christian
Furchtegott Gellert's (1715-1769) "Jesus lives! The Victory's
won." On the other hand, the Lutheran church in the Scan-
dinavian countries produced several fine hymns during this
time. Of note are "Built on the Rock, the Church doth
stand" by Nicolai F. S. Grundtvig (1783-1872) and "We worship Thee, almighty Lord" by Johann Olaf Wallin (1779-1839)
(Patrick, 85).

English Hymnody

The second main movement of church song in the
Reformation came from the influence of John Calvin and the
Reformed Church. The basic form of congregational praise
for the Reformed Church was the metrical psalm (see
*Psalmody, metrical). However, as early as 1556, versi-
fications of other Biblical passages and prayers appeared in
England. In 1561 an attempt at recognizing the old Latin
church hymnody is seen in the inclusion of the "Veni Creator
Spiritus" (Benson, 37).

It was due to the growing dissatisfaction with both the
content and literary form of the metrical psalms among
English-speaking churches that the modern practice of singing
hymns began. Benson suggests three evolutionary lines link-
ing the metrical psalm to the hymn in the early 17th century.
(1) An effort was made to improve the literary character of
the authorized psalters. (2) An effort to create a greater
relevance of the Scriptural text to the present day worship-
pers was in process. (3) The principle of Scriptural paraphrase extended to cover the evangelical hymns and other
Biblical passages (Benson, 46-55).

In the years preceding the Restoration, the first industrious attempt at supplementing metrical psalmody with
Christian hymns for congregational use was George Wither's

(1588-1667) <u>Hymns and Songs of the Church</u> (1623). Despite
its unfortunate circumstances it is of note because it included
hymn tunes by Orlando Gibbons. The first author to see his
hymns used in the church was John Cosin (1594-1672) whose
excellent version of the Latin "Veni, Creator Spiritus"
("Come, Holy Ghost, our souls inspire") is still in use today. Another important figure is George Herbert (1593-
1632) whose every hymn radiated a sense of finest artistry.

The change of atmosphere brought about by the Restoration (1660) provided for the decline of psalmody and the
increase of hymnody. Among these early hymnists, forerunners of Isaac Watts, are Thomas Ken (1631-1711) ("All
praise to Thee, my God, this night," CH, 10), John Bunyan
(1628-1688) ("He who would valiant be," CH, 39, from <u>The
Pilgrim's Progress</u>), and Joseph Addison (1672-1719) ("The
spacious firmament on high," CH, 109).

Two names of import for introducing hymnsinging into
English churches are John Playford (1623-1686) and Richard
Baxter (1615-1691). John Playford's <u>The whole Book of
Psalms: with the usual Hymns and Spiritual Songs ...</u> (1677)
was very influential among the re-established Church. Richard
Baxter's work was mainly among the Presbyterians.

At the ebb of psalmody and its deplorable state at the
end of the 17th century appeared a man of great spirit and
fertile resources. Isaac Watts (1674-1748), taking his cue
from Dr. John Patrick, published <u>The Psalms of David imitated in the language of the New Testament ...</u> in 1719.
From these Christianized psalms came the first great missionary hymn, "Jesus shall reign where'er the sun" (CH,
52), and one of the most majestic hymns in the English language, "Our God, our Help in ages past" (CH, 90). The
next logical step from Christianized Psalms was hymns of
human composition. Watt's hymns, like "When I survey the
wondrous cross" (CH, 115), are only a portion of his legacy,
for through them he forever showed all hymnwriters what a
congregational hymn should be; thus, justifying his title, "the
real founder of English hymnody" (Patrick, 123).

Carrying the torch lit by Watts were Simon Browne
(1680-1732) and Philip Doddridge (1702-1751), writer of "O
God of Bethel, by Whose hand" (CH, 74).

Amidst what has often been called a period of moral
decay came the Wesleys, John and Charles. Both were
trained in the singing of psalms, being the sons of a rector.
John Wesley (1703-1791), on his missionary voyage to America, came under the influence of German pietist hymnody
through the Moravian emigrants on board ship. Though little
else was accomplished on this mission, Wesley introduced

hymns to America, and published the first hymnbook on the
continent, Collection of Psalms and Hymns (1737), in Charleston, South Carolina.

Returning to London in 1738, John and his brother,
Charles, came under the Moravian influence of Peter Böhler
and experienced a definite conversion. The result of this experience brought about their evangelizing campaigns. Charles
Wesley (1757-1834) set about writing. From his pen, about
6500 hymns have come into existence, many of them being
journalistic material. Two of his more remembered hymns
are "O for a thousand tongues to sing" (CH, 71) and "Christ
the Lord is risen today." It was through Charles Wesley
that two new kinds of hymnody were brought into existence:
the hymn of Christian experience and the evangelistic hymn.

John Wesley, though a hymnist in his own right, contributed greatly to hymnody through his translations.

Under the influence of the Wesleyan movement other
preachers and workers began writing hymns. Edward Perronet (1726-1792) wrote "All hail the power of Jesus' name!"
(CH, 7) and John Cennick (1718-1755) shares authorship with
Charles Wesley for "Lo! He comes, with clouds descending"
(CH, 58). A strong division between the Calvinistic theology
and the Armenian doctrines caused the revival movement to
run in two channels. Representative of the Calvinistic line
is Augustus Montague Toplady (1740-1778), who wrote the
beloved "Rock of Ages, cleft for me."

Also from the Calvinistic thought is the Olney Hymns
(1779), a collection written by William Cowper (1731-1800)
and John Newton (1725-1807), used by the Low Church party
in the Established Church of England. From this hymnbook
Cowper's "God moves in a mysterious way" (CH, 36) and
Newton's "Glorious things of Thee are spoken" (CH, 35) have
come to our hymnals today (Bailey, 121-122).

Carrying this Calvinistic fragment to Wales, the revivals of George Whitefield had a great influence in the
forming of the Calvinistic Methodists. Being fine singers
the Welsh people were eager to express this spirit in song.
Their chief spokesman was William Williams (1717-1791) who
wrote 800 hymns, the best-known being "Guide me, O Thou
great Jehovah" (CH, 37). Though the Welsh hymns are of
good quality, it is their hymntunes, an expression of their
fine singing tradition, which is their main contribution to
modern hymnody.

Representative of the dissenting group of Baptists
come two hymnic expressions. The one is by John Fawcett
(1739-1817), "Blest be the tie that binds," and the other is
the anonymous "How firm a foundation, ye saints of the

Lord" (CH, 42) from John Rippon's (1751-1836) <u>A Selection</u> <u>of Psalms and Hymn Tunes</u> (1791).

With the turn of the century a new age of intellectual revival spread throughout Western Europe. It was marked by an awakening of interest in the past and a wonder toward the realities of life. Under the influence of the writings of Sir Walter Scott, all of this was guised in an essence of romance. It was during this movement that the hymn gained new strength as "literary" poetry, a true lyric expression of emotion in elegant form (Patrick, 142). Representative of this new style are the hymns of Reginald Heber (1783-1826). "Brightest and best are the sons of the morning" (CH, 15) is one of Heber's earliest hymns written for use on Epiphany; thus, revealing the efforts of the day toward revitalizing the Christian Year. Written for Trinity Sunday is Heber's "Holy, holy, holy, Lord God Almighty" (CH, 41). Thomas Kelly (1769-1854) likewise wrote hymns for the Christian Year, "Look, ye saints, the sight is glorious" being for the second Sunday of Advent.

Realizing the vast treasury of hymnic materials in the Breviaries of the Middle Ages, a surge of energy began to manifest itself in translations of these Latin hymns. Among these translators are Isaac William (1802-1865), John Chandler (1806-1876), Bishop Mant (1776-1848) and John Henry Newman (1801-1890). However, the two outstanding translators of Latin and Greek hymns are John Mason Neale (1818-1866) and Edward Caswall (1814-1878). The major translator of German hymns is Catherine Winkworth (1827-1878).

In response to the worldliness of the clergy, church hostility toward reform, and the church's privileged position in society, John Keble, with his sermon, "National Apostacy," set in motion the *Oxford Movement (July 14, 1833) (Bailey, 189-190). Seeking to show the Church's divine origin and destiny, many persons started producing tracts; thus, the name "Tractarians." The close affinity of the members of the Oxford Movement to the Roman Church is seen not only in the title of Anglo-Catholic and in their High Church order, but also in the fact that many individuals actually turned to Catholicism. Among these was John Henry Newman whose hymn, "Lead, kindly light," is universally loved, Frederick William Faber (1814-1863)--"Faith of our fathers, living still," and Matthew Bridges (1800-1894)--"Crown Him with many crowns" (CH, 28).

Among the greatest contributions of the Oxford Movement was the final compilation of the hymnal to supersede the old versions of the psalter. This book, *Hymns Ancient and Modern (1861), illustrates the contributions of the major eras of hymnody (Latin and Greek hymns included) and the use of hymns for the Christian Year. Although the Oxford Movement was a powerful force in the 19th century, the remainder of English hymnody in the Victorian era is divided into High Church, Broad Church and the Evangelical School.

With the introduction of hymnody into the Anglican Church by the Dissenters and Evangelicals, High Churchmen were very reluctant to incorporate them into the service. However, the prejudice melted away when the older Latin and Greek hymn translations placed the hymn in catholic use. Sir Henry Williams Baker (1821-1877), known for his reconciling chairmanship of Hymns Ancient and Modern, produced fine hymns, as "The King of Love my Shepherd is" (CH, 106), for the High Church. Other contributors to this collection are William Chatterton Dix (1837-1898) ("As with gladness men of old," CH, 12), William Walsham How (1823-1897) ("For all the saints who from their labors rest," CH, 32), Cecil Frances Alexander (1823-1859) ("All things bright and beautiful"), and John S. B. Monsell (1811-1875) ("Fight the good fight with all thy might," CH, 31). The quality of texts and tunes represented by the High Church as evidenced by their publication of Hymns Ancient and Modern has shown a more durable character and has influenced succeeding hymnbooks.

The Broad Church gained its impetus from Frederick Maurice who opposed the "backward" look of the Tractarians and sought to instill within the church an involvement in society--"Christian humanitarianism" (Patrick, 156). Few hymnwriters have expressed this thought. Yet, representing the Broad Church are Charles Kingsley (1819-1875) ("From Thee all skill and science flow") and Dean Stanley (1815-1881) ("The Lord is come!").

Probably the most productive of hymns during this century was the Evangelical School. Many of its personal pietistic hymns are among the beloved hymns of congregations today. Prominent among these writers are women. Charlotte Elliot (1789-1871) wrote the classic "Just as I am without one plea." Frances Ridley Havergal (1839-1879), writing hymns of Christian commitment, penned "Take my life and let it be consecrated Lord to Thee." In a similar vein, Elizabeth Clephane (1830-1869) expressed "Beneath the Cross of Jesus." Second only to Watts and Wesley, James Montgomery (1771-1854) has more hymns in popular use today than any other hymnwriter. Two of his finest are the messianic hymn, "Hail to the Lord's Anointed" (CH, 38) and the Christmas hymn, "Angels from the realms of glory" (CH,

11). An important New Testament scholar, Dean Henry Alford (1810-1871) wrote hymns of joyful worship--"Come, ye
thankful people, come." "Go, labor on: spend and be
spent" is by the Presbyterian Horatius Bonar (1809-1889),
who serves as one of the main contributors for this sector
of Christian hymnody.

American Hymnody

As with England, so the English colonies in America
began their congregational praise with the singing of metrical psalms (see *Psalmody, metrical). On the other hand,
the Moravian and Mennonite colonies, particularly in Pennsylvania, brought with them a heritage of Lutheran hymnody.
The Mennonite hymnbook brought to this country, Das Ausbund: Das ist Etliche schöne christliche Lieder (1583), is
still in use among the Amish of Pennsylvania, making it the
oldest continuously used hymnal in America. Among the
first German hymnals published in America was Das kleine
Davidische Psalterspiel der Kinde Zions (1744), a collection
of hymns with bold allegories and sentimental style.
An outstanding early 18th-century immigrant musician
was Johannes Kelpius (1663-1708), a pietist, who with four
others, left a manuscript book of 70 pages containing 12
German hymns with melodies. This collection, never published, represents the first hymns written in the North
American colonies (Foote, 129). However, it was the Moravian settlements that created many of the earliest hymns in
America. For them, the singing of praise accompanied all
that they did. Through their strong missionary vision, they
published a Harmony of the Gospels (1763) and a hymnal in
the language of the Delaware Indians (Foote, 140).
It was not until the "Great Awakening" (1739-1741) by
George Whitefield that a more vital and evangelical type of
congregational song was desired in the English speaking colonies. John Wesley's first English hymnbook printed in
America, Collection of Psalms and Hymns (1737), furthered
the cause even more. However, the beginning of a distinctive American hymnody came with Dr. Timothy Dwight's
(1752-1817) revision of Isaac Watts' psalms and hymns for
American life. From "Dwight's Watts" comes the lyrical
version of Psalm 137, "I love Thy kingdom, Lord" (CH, 43).
Other Presbyterian hymnwriters of this time are J. W.
Alexander (1804-1859), George Duffield (1818-1888) ("Stand
up! stand up for Jesus"), and William Cullen Bryant (1794-
1878) ("Look from the sphere of endless day," CH, 60).
Gifted Episcopalians of this era are George Washington Doane

(1799-1859) ("Softly now the light of day") and Arthur Cleveland Coxe (1818-1896) ("O where are kings and empires now," CH, 86).

Remembered for his poems from which hymns have been extracted is John Greenleaf Whittier (1807-1897), a Quaker. "Dear Lord and Father of mankind" (CH, 29) and "Immortal Love, forever full" (CH, 46) exemplify his literary genius.

Among the Unitarians of this era are the eminent poets--Emerson, Longfellow, Holmes and Lowell. Their reaction to the rigidity of Calvinism is seen in the striving for a more humanitarian concept of God and a kindlier life. Reflecting these thoughts are Oliver Wendell Holmes' (1809-1894) "Lord of all being, throned afar" (CH, 64), Samuel Longfellow's (1819-1892) "Now on land and sea descending" and Samuel Johnson's (1822-1882) "City of God, how broad and far" (CH, 20) (Patrick, 168-170).

Ray Palmer (1808-1887) and Leonard Bacon (1802-1881) represent Congregational hymnody in 19th-century America. The beloved "My faith looks up to Thee," by Palmer, and "O God, beneath thy guiding hand," by Bacon, reflect an evangelistic and personal quality.

It was during this century that the zeal of evangelism and missionary outreach was championed. With this movement especially through the influence of the Moody-Sankey revivals the phenomenon of the gospel song developed (see *Gospel song).

In the latter half of the 19th century a new theology and a renewed interest of the church in society emerged. This social gospel, as it has been called, provided the fuel for many heated debates and upheavals in the hierarchy of many denominations. Hymnwriters who were spokesmen of this movement are Phillips Brooks (1835-1893) ("O little town of Bethlehem"), Sidney Lanier (1842-1881) ("Into the woods my Master went"), Maltbie Davenport Babcock (1858-1901) ("This is my Father's world") and Henry van Dyke (1852-1933) ("Joyful, joyful we adore Thee"). Further reaction to the injustices caused by the Civil War and the industrial revolution caused Washington Gladden (1838-1918) to write "O Master, let me walk with Thee" (CH, 77) and Frank Mason North to pen "Where cross the crowded ways of life" (CH, 116).

20th-Century Hymnody

Within the 20th century a combination of the main roots of hymnody have begun to be wedded together through

the scholarly editing of many fine hymns, designed both for
denominational and non-denominational use. Representative
of these hymnals are: the revised edition of Hymns Ancient
and Modern (1904), The English Hymnal with Tunes (1906),
Robert Bridges' Yattendon Hymnal (1899), Congregational
Praise (1953), The Hymnal 1940, and the National Council
of the Churches of Christ's modest collection, Christian
Hymns (1963). The influence of the Oxford Movement is
clearly seen in each of these collections.

The influence of the social gospel also carried into
the hymnody of the 20th century. This is seen in Jay T.
Stocking's (1870-1936) "O Master-Workman of the race" and
F. M. North's hymn of the city, "Not only where God's free
winds blow." "Eternal God, whose power upholds," a hymn
of brotherhood by H. H. Tweedy (1868-1953), was awarded
honors by the Hymn Society of America in 1929 (Foote, 313-
316).

Seeking to influence the knowledge, use and production of hymns and tunes, the Hymn Society of America was
founded in 1922. Thirteen years later its English counterpart, The Hymn Society of Great Britain and Ireland, was
formed. Through promotional work and industrious laborings
of these societies the cause of fine hymnody has been championed.

For the dedication of Riverside Church in New York
City in 1930, Harry Emerson Fosdick (1878-1969) wrote the
noble "God of grace and God of glory." For the Second
Assembly of the World Council of Churches in 1954, Georgia
Harkness (b. 1891) wrote "Hope of the world, Thou Christ of
great compassion." Thus, it is seen that some 20th-century
hymnody is created for special occasions.

Another source for inspiring new hymnic expressions
beside the contests of the Hymn Societies are the hymn
searches by various denominations, especially as they prepare new hymnals and observe different historical landmarks.
For example, the Church Music Department of the Southern
Baptist Sunday School Board sponsors a biannual hymn compe-
tition.

In the evangelical tradition the 19th-century *gospel
song has continued and flourished in the early 20th century
over and above the evangelical hymn.

Following the mid-20th century the church in England,
Germany and America has felt the strong, vital surge of
youth. In a time which cries for relevance, the church has
seen an attempt to incorporate modern "pop" influences into
its life and congregational praise. Much of what is being

done is musical, i.e. hymntunes; however, Weinberger (London) publishes Twenty-seven Twentieth Century Hymns, a collection of new texts and tunes by members of the Twentieth Century Church Light Music Group. Also from England has come a fine attempt to transform religious poetry for popular singing, as seen in Sydney Carter's "I danced in the morning when the world was begun." A German contribution in Jazz hymnody is Paul Stein's paraphrase of Psalm 103, "Lobe den Herren, meine Seele." The International Jazz Festival (1962) in Washington, D.C. also presented some new texts for congregational praise in its worship service. Although it may not be a major force in Christian hymnody for the present, jazz and "pop" hymnody are an expression of a vital and youthful segment of the Christian church in this day and time.

General

Bailey, Albert E. The Gospel in Hymns. New York: Scribner's, 1950.

Julian, John. A Dictionary of Hymnology. London: John Murray, 1892.

Patrick, Millar. The Story of the Church's Song. Richmond: John Knox Press, 1962.

Early Hymnody--East and West

Daniel, Herm. Adalbert. Thesaurus Hymnologicus. Lipsiae [Leipzig]: Sumptibus J. T. Loeschke, 1855.

Duffield, Samuel Willoughby. The Latin Hymn-writers and Their Hymns. New York: Funk and Wagnalls, 1889.

Messenger, Ruth Ellis. The Medieval Latin Hymn. Washington, D.C.: Capital Press, 1953.

Wellesz, Egon. A History of Byzantine Music and Hymnography. London: Oxford University Press, 1949.

Werner, Eric. The Sacred Bridge: The Interdependence of Liturgy and Music in Synagogue and Church during the First Millennium. New York: Columbia University Press, 1959.

German Hymnody

Fischer, Albert Friedrich Wilhelm. Kirchenlieder-Lexicon. Gotha: Friedrich Undreas Perthes, 1878.

von Fallensleben, Hoffmann. Geschichte des Kirchenliedes bis auf Luthers Zeit. Hildesheim: Georg Olms, 1965.

Koch, Eduard Emil. Geschichte des Kirchenlieds und Kirchengesangs. 8 vols. Stuttgart: Chr. Belser'che Verlagshandlung, 1866.

Leupold, Ulrich S. Luther's Works. Vol. 53. Philadelphia: Fortress Press, 1965.

Nelle, Wilhelm. Geschichte des deutschen evangelischen Kirchenlieder. 4th ed. Hildesheim: Georg Olms, 1962.

Riedel, John. The Lutheran Chorale: Its Basic Tradition. St. Louis: Concordia Publishing House, 1968.

Wackernagel, Philipp. Das deutsche Kirchenlied von ältesten Zeit bis zu Anfang des XVIII. Jahrhunderts. 5 vols. Leipzig: B. G. Teuber, 1867.

English Hymnody

Benson, Louis. The English Hymn: Its Development and Use in Worship. Richmond, Va.: John Knox Press, 1962.

Duffield, S. W. English Hymns: Their Authors and History. New York: Funk and Wagnalls, 1886.

American Hymnody

Foote, Henry Wilder. Three Centuries of American Hymnody. Cambridge, Mass.: Harvard University Press, 1940.

Ninde, Edward S. The Story of the American Hymn. New York: Abingdon Press, 1921.

20th-Century Hymnody

Hagen, Rochus A. M. "Texte des Jazz in der Kirche," MK, 38:26-31, January-February, 1968.

Routley, Erik. Hymns Today and Tomorrow. New York: Abingdon Press, 1964.

Hymnal Companions

Buck, Emory Stevens (ed.). Companion to the Hymnal (United Methodist Church). New York: Abingdon Press, 1970.

Dearmer, Percy. Songs of Praise Discussed. London: Oxford University Press, 1933.

Ellinwood, Leonard (ed.). The Hymnal 1940 Companion (Episcopal Church). New York: The Church Pension Fund, 1951.

Frost, Maurice (ed.). Historical Companion to Hymns Ancient and Modern. London: William Clowes, 1962.

Haessler, Aremin. The Story of Our Hymns (Evangelical and Reformed Church). St. Louis: Eden Publishing House, 1952.

Hostetler, Lester. Handbook to the Mennonite Hymnary.
Newton, Kan.: General Conference of the Mennoninte
Church of North America Board of Publications, 1949.
Mahrenholz, Christhand, and O. Sohngen. Handbuch zum
evangelischen Kirchengesangbuch. 3 vols. Göttingen:
Vandenhoeck and Ruprecht, 1965.
Martin, Hugh (ed.). The Baptist Hymn Book Companion.
London: Psalms and Hymns Trust, 1962.
Parry, K. L. and Erik Routley. Companion to Congrega-
tional Praise. London: Independent Press, 1953.
Reynolds, William Jensen. Hymns of Our Faith (Southern
Baptist Church). Nashville: Broadman Press, 1964.

HYMNOGRAPHY

The actual writing of hymns, i.e. the texts, is
called hymnography. (Cf. *Hymnody.)

HYMNOLOGY

The science of systematic study of *hymnody from
the historical, theological, topical and musical aspects, i.e.
the sum total of hymnic materials is hymnology.

Lovelace, Austin C. The Anatomy of Hymnody. New York:
Abingdon Press, 1965.

HYMN REHEARSAL (*hymn, + ME. rehercen, rehersen,
fr. OF. rehercier to harrow over again, to repeat,
fr. re- re- + hercier to harrow, fr. herce harrow)

A practice period when a congregation is instructed
in the singing of a *hymn or hymns is a hymn rehearsal.
This is a technique which may be employed to renew interest
in hymn singing as well as to familiarize the singers with
new tunes and texts and their meanings.

Lovelace, Austin C. and William C. Rice. Music and Worship in the Church. New York: Abingdon Press,
1960. Chapter 10.

HYMN SERVICE (*hymn + ME., service, servise, fr. OF.
servise, service, fr. L. servitum)

A service centered around a theme which is mainly conveyed through the singing of hymns among a small group or congregation is termed a hymn service. During such services the congregation does most of the singing rather than the choir. This has been a 20th-century technique in an attempt to revitalize the meaningful use of hymns and congregational singing in worship. (Cf. *Hymn festival.)

HYMNS ANCIENT AND MODERN

The English hymnal, an out-growth of the *Oxford Movement, edited under the direction of Sir Henry Baker and published in 1860/61 is entitled Hymns Ancient and Modern.
The idea for a hymnal which would include both new and old texts and music, from the earliest Latin hymnody to the present developments in hymnody, began its embryonic stage in the autumn of 1858. By January 1859, a formal planning meeting was held at which more than 200 clergy were in attendance with the purpose of organizing for the task at hand. Following much labor and several experimental editions, the complete book, Hymns Ancient and Modern (so entitled by William Henry Monk, musical coadjutor) appeared in 1860/61. About one-half of this first edition was comprised of hymnic translation from Latin hymnody, German chorales, and other languages.
Fifteen years later (1875) the revised edition appeared which included a thorough appraisal and re-editing of most of the materials. This hymnal has come through several other major revisions, the latest being in 1950. In 1962, the revision of the Historical Companion to Hymns Ancient and Modern appeared as a continuation of Bishop Frere's valuable scholarship in its original edition (1909).

Clarke, W. K. Lowther. A Hundred Years of Hymns Ancient and Modern. London: William Clowes, 1960.
Frost, Maurice. Historical Companion to Hymns Ancient and Modern. London: William Clowes, 1962.
Sceats, Godfrey. "English Hymnal and Hymns A. & M.," ML, 32:235-46, July, 1951.

HYMN TUNE   (Gr. hymnos hymn + ME. tun, tune tone)

[Contents: (general); The chorale and psalm tune; The Restoration tunes (1685-1738); The Evangelical period

(1738-1801); The 19th century; The 20th century; The American scene; (bibliography).] The melody which is associated with the metrical verse of the congregational *hymn is the hymn tune. It is generally supported by a harmonization in four-parts. A melody which has become associated to a fixed text is called a "proper tune," as opposed to the interchanging of various texts and tunes of the same meter, i.e. "common tunes." The distinction of the differing tunes from each other through the procedure of names can be traced back to tabernacle services and the Jewish musical leaders, the Levites (cf. Psalm 22, "according to the Hind of the Dawn"). Throughout the early centuries of the Christian Church the sequences sung to the alleluia-jubilus likewise served as proper names.

The Chorale and Psalm Tune

With the restored interest in the congregational song by Martin Luther (1483-1546) there came about not only a need for new texts but also desire for singable melodies to carry the poetry. The German Lutheran solution was the *chorale. Its lines were, at first, simple and folk-like, having originated in the secular and spiritual songs of various medieval groups and sects. These melodies often ranged the compass of a tenth, beginning to adhere to the then new major and minor tonalities. Highly rhythmic, these tunes also bore the shape of the bar-form. (For further information see *Chorale.)

From the Genevan tradition of the Reformed church came the psalm tune. Their strict design reflected the influence of the staunch leader of the Genevan Church, John Calvin (1509-1564). The modal harmonies, the more conservative rhythms and the dominating a b a b c c b[1] form characterized the early psalm tunes. Though Calvin endorsed unison congregational singing in the church, some of the early psalters--e.g., Bourgeois' Cinquante Pseaulmes (1547) and Goudimel's Psalter (1565)--contained four-part harmonizations, probably for home use (Routley, 30).

Characteristic of many of the tunes of Louis Bourgeois (1510-156?), the father of the modern hymn tune, are the matching first and last lines, more natural word accents and the use of the mediant triad at the beginning of phrases. The striking note of these tunes has been Bourgeois' ability to produce such admirable congregational tunes of universal appeal. His tune to the Nunc dimittis (CH, 72) is an example of his employment of a popular tune (a similarity to the chorale).

The psalm tune of English and Scottish psalmody during the period from 1562-1677 is almost exclusively in common meter of the "fourteeners" (8.6.8.6) and its double. One of the oldest common-meter tunes is Thomas Tallis' (c.1505-1585) "Tallis's Ordinal" (CH, 86), published in 1561 (Routley, 43). With the increasing of common-meter tunes came the interchangeability of these tunes for any psalm (or hymn) in this particular meter, and thus the "common tune" which was firmly established in the Scottish Psalter (Hart) of 1615. This practice also gave rise to the identification of tunes by names, first employed by Thomas Este (d.1609) in his psalter (1592) and systematically approached in the Ravenscroft Psalter (1621) the definitive English psalter until after the Restoration. As for the tunes themselves, they remained in the tenor with few exceptions. Representative tunes of this period of psalmody, which encompasses also the Playford (1671) and Scottish psalters (1615 & 1635), are "London New" (CH, 36), "Winchester Old" (CH, 117), "Dundee" (CH, 74) and "York" (CH, 107). The three outstanding composers of these times were Thomas Tallis, Orlando Gibbons and Henry Lawes (1596-1662).

Beside "common tunes" and *"proper tunes" a third type of tune existed called "tunes in reports." These are basically in the common-meter pattern with an elongated imitative fughetta-style third phrase, or the entire tune is set contrapuntally. The earliest known tune of this kind is "Bon Accord" from the Aberdeen Psalter of 1625 (Routley, 48). (For further information see *Psalmody, metrical.)

The Restoration Tunes (1685-1738)

With the restoration of the English monarchy in 1660 and the emerging of the homophonic elements of music, new tunes began to appear. These tunes, unlike the prior period, are beginning to appear signed. Among the Restoration tune composers are Benjamin Rogers (1614-1698) with his Hymns Eucharistrais; the celebrated Jeremiah Clark (1659-1707) "St. Magnus" (CH, 105) and the flowing "Bishopthorpe" and the first example of a modulation in a hymn tune, "Bromley"; William Croft (1678-1727) with his psalm-like "St. Anne" (CH, 90); and John Bishop (1665-1737) with his dance-like setting for Psalm 122, "Chichester."

Of the more outstanding psalters and tune collections of this period one must include Green's Psalmody (1715), W. Anchors' A Choice Collection of Psalm-Tunes (1721?) and W. Tans'ur's A Compleat Melody; or the Harmony of Sion (1735). It is the tunes of this period which have pro-

vided the link from the staid metrical psalm tune to the
flowing dance-like tunes of the Evangelical Period.

The Evangelical Period (1738-1801)

The 18th century saw a time of religious consciousness to fight off the moral ills and religious apathy in England. This becomes evident in the revival movements of
John Whitefield, John Cennick and Charles and John Wesley.
This evangelical revival movement realized the importance
and the validity of simple, melodic music as a vehicle to
carry the salvation messages to the individual man. Thus,
exuberant melody became the natural expression for the individual's ecstatic responses as common in the Wesleyan
movement. Bearing the influences of the old psalm tune
and the Handelian style the first Wesleyan tune book, the
*Foundery Collection (1742), came into being with 40 tunes.
It contained the first anglicized version of "Winchester New."
The style of these tunes was typically rhythmic for youthful
spirit with minimal harmony (V-I primarily) for amiable
part-singing, and simple and repetitive melodic lines. On
the other hand, from these Wesleyan collections have come
some classic tunes as Felice de Giardini's (1716-1796)
"Trinity" ("Moscow," CH, 23), Franz Joseph Haydn's "Austria"
(CH, 35), and Meyer Lyon's (1751-1797) "Leoni" (CH, 104).
Aside from the Wesleyan tunes, the strong interest
in psalm tunes continued throughout this post-Restoration
period. However, it was not without the metrical influence
and melodic freedom of the Methodist idiom, employing
triple time more frequently. Representative of this are
Thomas Haweis' (1734-1820) "Richmond" (CH, 20), and John
Hatton's (d. 1793) "Duke Street" (CH, 52).
Meanwhile, in Scotland the "great eclipse" of Scottish
psalmody was in process with limited psalm tunes, most of
which were in common meter. By the end of the 18th century, a revival of the psalm tune style occurred, the influence of Wesleyan tunes was felt, as well as the musically
extended anthem-like tunes (Routley, 100).

The 19th Century

At the outset of the 19th century the English churches
possessed two rich storehouses of music, the 18th-century
psalm tunes and the Methodist tunes. From the beginning
of this period, Edward Miller's The Psalms of David (1790)
and Sacred Music (1802) provided the present version of
"Rockingham" (CH, 115) and the first printing of "Austria"

as a hymn tune. In search for new tunes, adopters turned
to the instrumental classics, both opera and oratorio. Men
involved in this were William Gardiner (1770-1853) and H.
J. Garenlett (1805-1876). The merits of these arrangements
have been a matter of great debate.

Three events of the 19th century have influenced hymnody and the hymn tune greatly in England. In 1821, the
final authorization of hymns in the worship of the Church of
England was given by Archbishop Harcourt; in 1833, the
beginning of the Oxford Movement occurred through John
Keble's sermon, "National Apostasy"; and in 1861, the first
musical edition of *Hymns Ancient and Modern was published.

Through the work of Hymns Ancient and Modern not
only was an appreciation for the hymns of the past a major
contribution, but also the wedding of certain hymns to particular tunes was regarded as important. The joining of
William H. Monk's (1823-1889) "Eventide" (CH, 3) to "Abide
with me," and John B. Dykes' (1823-1876) "Nicea" (CH, 41)
to "Holy, Holy, Holy" are only two examples of a long list
of tunes and hymns originally mated in Hymns Ancient and
Modern which have remained indissoluble for more than a
century.

From this era of Victorian composers which includes
John B. Dykes, Sir Arthur Sullivan (1841-1900), S. S. Wesley (1810-76), W. H. Monk (1821-89), Sir Fredrick Ouseley
(1825-89) and Joseph Barnby (1838-96) came tunes with which
most mid-20th-century American churchgoers are familiar.
"St. Agnes," "St. Gertrude," "Aurelia," "Just As I Am"
and "Diademata" readily come to mind. Characteristics of
these tunes are the repeated note melodies, the stagnant
bass lines and mild rhythms of romanticism.

In opposition to the principles of the Oxford Movement stands the revival spirit of the Moody-Sankey era with
its *gospel song tunes. The Sankey tunes bore simple melodies with choruses, supported only by basic harmonies (I,
IV, V), and lacked contrapuntal interest. Their attractiveness lay in the memorable rhythmic motives (see *gospel
song).

The 20th Century (1890 to the Present)

Into the 20th century came not only the influence of
Hymns Ancient and Modern, but also the Revival and the
Victorian hymn tunes, the latter being disowned by musi-
cians. Thus, Sir Hubert Parry (1848-1949), Sir Charles
Stanford (1852-1924), Basil Harwood (1859-1949) and Sir
Walford Davies (1869-1941) sought unsuccessfully to redeem

the hymn tune. The primary leaders to succeed in this effort were Ralph Vaughan Williams (1872-1958), Percy Dearmer (1867-1936), Robert Bridges (1844-1930), and G. R. Woodward (1848-1934), compilers of the English Hymnal (1906). It should be noted that this hymnal introduced to hymnody a number of English folk songs such as "King's Lynn" (CH, 75), while presenting new, dynamic rhythmic tunes as "Sine Nomine" (CH, 32) and "Antiphon" (CH, 56). Also derived from folk songs are many tunes of Welsh hymnody. Representative in many hymnals are Joseph Parry's (1841-1903) "Aberystwyth" (CH, 50), William Owen's (1814-1893) "Bryn Calfaria" (CH, 61), and John Hughes' (1873-1932) "Cwm Rhondda."

More current on the English scene have been the hymn tunes by the *Twentieth Century Church Light Music Group to a "pop" rhythm, harmony and melody. Malcolm Williamson's (b.1931) "Jesus, Lover of My Soul" is an example of the popular love ballad of the Broadway show during the 50's. Geoffrey Beaumont's (1904-1970) "Now Thank We All Our God," from the Twentieth Century Folk Mass has found its way into several denominational hymnals during the late 60's.

The American Scene

The outstanding hymn tune from early American life is Oliver Holden's (1765-1844) "Coronation" (CH, 7), the oldest American hymn tune in common use today. However, it is from *camp meetings that much of American hymn tunes, the folk-songs of the people, arose. The famous "Amazing Grace," "Wondrous Love" and "Foundation" (CH, 42) represent a few in common usage today which were found in the Sacred Harp (1844). Other tunes from American life are found among the spirituals as "Let Us Break Bread Together" (Communion Spiritual) and "Were You There." From early 20th-century America and the more academic composers came such tunes as Graham George's (b.1912) "The King's Majesty" (CH, 95) and C. Winfred Douglas' (1867-1944) "St. Dunstan's" (CH, 39).

Among the mid-20th-century hymn tune composers are Lloyd Pfautsch, Robert Powell, Leo Sowerby, Katherine Davis and Austin Lovelace (Burke, 50).

Since the hymn tune is the folk song of the church-- the hymn tune composer being, therefore, the composer of folk sings--it remains to be seen what the hymn tunes of the later 20th century will be in the light of the contemporary, commercial folksong. (Cf. *Pop, Gospel.)

Burke, Emory Stevens (ed.). Companion to the Hymnal.
    New York: Abingdon Press, 1970.
Frost, Maurice. English and Scottish Psalm and Hymn-
    Tunes. London: S.P.C.K., 1953.
_____. Historical Companion to Hymns Ancient and
    Modern. London: William Clowes, 1962.
McCutchan, Robert Guy. Hymn Tune Names: Their Sources
    and Significance. New York: Abingdon Press, 1957.
Pratt, Waldo S. The Music of the French Psalter. New
    York: Columbia University Press, 1939.
Routley, Erik. The Music of Christian Hymnody. London:
    Independent Press, 1957.
_____. Hymn Tunes: An Historic Outline. (Study Notes,
    No. 5.) Croyden, Surrey, Eng.: R.S.C.M., 1959.
Truio, Bishop of. "The Rhythm of Metrical Psalm Tunes,"
    ML, 9:29-33, January, 1928.
Zahn, J. Die Melodien der deutschen evangelischen Kirchen-
    lieder aus den Quellen geschöpft und mitgeteilt. 6 vols.
    Hildescheim: Olms, 1963. Reprint.

ICTUS (L., fr. icere, ictum to strike)

In the rhythm of *plainsong the ictus is the demarca-
tion which indicates the commencement of the basic duple or
triple grouping fundamental to the rendering of *chant. It is
not a "bar-line" accent but simply a performance aid instituted by the Monks of Solesmes as they sought to reinstate the
rhythmic flow of authentic Gregorian chanting.

Liber Usualis. Boston: McLaughlin and Reilly, 1950.
    Pp. xxvi-xxxv.

INCEPTIO (L. fr. incipere to begin, fr. in in + capere to
    take)

The first part of the melodic formula used in the
chanting of the psalms to *psalm-tones or *plainsong is the
inceptio or initium. (Cf. *Intonation).

IN MEDIO CHORI (It.)

In medio chori is a musical term employed by Tudor

church musicians whose meaning has been somewhat uncertain to musicologists and liturgists. Edmund H. Fellows has given a most probable solution when he suggests that a small group of solo singers from the cathedral choir was placed outside the choir-stalls in the center of the chancel nearer to the congregation--that is in medio chori. However, it is pointed out that a larger body of singers than the usual complement of a cathedral choir would be needed. It is not to be confused with the terms *verse, *full, *decani, or *cantoris.

    Works containing this term are Weelkes' Service No. 5, John Holm's Evening Canticles and John Mundy's Evening Services.

Fellowes, Edmund H. English Cathedral Music. London: Methuen and Company, Ltd., 1946.

INTERLUDE (ME. enterlude, fr. ML. interludium, fr. L. inter between + ludus play)

    An instrumental passage, usually for organ and often extemporaneous, which is interpolated between *verses or *stanzas of a *hymn or *canticle is called an interlude (cf. *Zwischenspiel). In the 18th century, when "lining-out" was in vogue in England, even in churches with organs where that practice was not necessary, the *hymn tune remained broken into fragments by interludes. Though most interludes during the 18th century were improvised, one of the earliest printed collections of such music was Daniel Purcells's (1660-1717) The Psalms Set Full for the Organ or Harpsichord ... as also with their Interludes of Great Variety (1718). During the 19th century extemporaneous improvisation degenerated and required the printing of interludes in order to maintain the practice. Illustrative of a collection of interludes for between stanzas was William Gresham's Psalmody Improvised (c.1797).

    With the 20th century and a new emphasis on *congregational singing the use of interludes between verses has disappeared almost entirely; however, the practice of interludes between stanzas, particularly prior to the final stanza of a hymn, is used in various locations.

    Also termed interludes are the musical offerings, usually organ, between various portions of the service in evangelical churches in America.

INTERMEDIATE CHOIR   (ML. intermediatus, fr. L. inter-
    medius, fr. inter between + medius middle, +
    *choir)

A choral organization for youth, ages 13 through 16
or grades seven through nine, or the choral organization for
the younger aged youth is the intermediate choir or junior
high choir. Within the *graded choir program of each church
the age group will fluctuate because of various extra-musical
factors. Basically, this is the choir which deals with the
problems of the changing voice and the emerging adolescent.
(Cf. *Youth choir.)

Bobbitt, Paul. The Intermediate Choir Leadership Manual.
    Nashville: Convention Press, 1967.
Lovelace, Austin C. The Youth Choir. New York: Abingdon
    Press, 1964.
Luck, James T. "A Study Relating to the Boy's Changing
    Voice in Intermediate Church Choirs of the Southern
    Baptist Convention." Unpublished Ed.D. dissertation,
    Florida State University, Tallahassee, 1957.
McKenzie, Duncan. Training the Boy's Changing Voice.
    New Brunswick, N.J.: Rutgers University Press, 1956.

INTONATION (fr. ML. intonatus, fr. intonare, intonatum,
    fr. in in + L. tonus tone)

(1) The short introductory phrase of a *chant or
*psalm-tone is called the intonation. It is sung by the
cantor alone in the first stanza, but in subsequent stanzas
by the choir.

(2) The organ composition used to introduce a chant
to be sung by the choir or congregation is also called the
intonation.

Nolte, Ewald V. "The Magnificat Fugues of Johann Pachel-
    bel: Alternatum or Intonation?" JAMS, 9:19-24,
    Winter, 1957.
Ritter, A. W. Zur Geschichte des Orgelspiels in 14-18.
    Jahrhunderts. Leipzig: M. Schmitz, 1884.

INTONING (ML. intonare, intonatum, fr. in in + L. tonus tone)

The act of singing prayers and *versicles in an in-

flected manner by the minister during the liturgy is called
intoning. Among the liturgical churches of Europe and England, intoning is a common practice, being akin to Catholic
tradition. However, it is not foreign to certain Lutheran
and Episcopal congregations in America. (CF. *Psalm-
tone.)

INTROIT (F. introit, fr. L. introitus, fr. introire to go
      into, to enter, fr. intro within + ire to go)

   (1) The entrance song at the eucharistic service
which is sung chorally and is proper to the day is termed
the introit. In its present form the introit begins with an
*antiphon, followed by the *psalm (a representative verse or
verses) and the *Gloria Patri, and may be concluded with
the singing of the antiphon again. When the introits are
derived entirely from the psalms they are called "regular";
however, when other scriptural passages are incorporated
they are "irregular."
   It is traditionally accepted that the introit originated
in the West from the early fifth-century practice by Pope
Celestine (d. 432) of the double choir singing antiphonally
an entire psalm appropriate to the thought of the service as
the clergy entered from the sacristy to the altar. Pope
Gregory the Great was responsible for providing the abbre-
viated form in current use. With the Reformation, the
practice was continued in the Lutheran rites (Luther preferring the use of the entire psalm), but it was eliminated
in the Anglican *Book of Common Prayer (1552).
   In the Anglican church, the term is often applied to
the *hymn or *anthem which opens the service. Thus, the
first hymn of the communion service may be called the introit hymn. In a similar sense, the short anthem sung at
the beginning of the service in free churches also is called
an introit.

   (2) The introductory prayer of a worship service
addressed to God and spoken by the minister is called an
introit. (Cf. *call to worship and *invocation.)

Brodde, Otto. "Der Introitus im lutherischen Gottesdienst,"
      MK, 29:175-185, July-August, 1959.
_____. "Der Introituslied," MK, 30:190-194, July-
      August, 1960.
Reed, Luther D. The Lutheran Liturgy. Philadelphia:
      Muhlenberg Press, 1947. Pp. 261-266.

Reindell, Walter. "Der Introitus," Kirchenchordienst, 8:42-
        44, May-June, 1942.
Schrems, T. Die Geschichte des gregorianische Gesang in
        den protestantischen Gottesdiensten. Freiburg, Switz.:
        n.p., 1930.

INVITATION HYMN   (F., fr. L. invitatio to invite + *hymn)

        The religious song offered by the congregation of
believers seeking a positive acceptance of the non-believer
to God's gift of salvation is termed the invitation hymn in
evangelical Protestant churches. This *hymn usually is
sung at the conclusion of the sermon, following a spoken
invitation. It may also be designated hymn of consecration,
commitment or dedication. (Cf. *evangelistic music.)

Wilson, John F. An Introduction to Church Music. Chicago:
        Moody Press, 1965.

INVITATORY   (L. invitatorium)

        The antiphon or refrain sung before the *Venite (the
Invitatory Psalm) and repeated in part, or entirely after
each verse of the psalm in the office of *Morning Prayer
is referred to as the Invitatory. It may be seasonal to permit the psalmody to partake of the spirit of a particular occasion. Its purpose is to invite the worshipper to join in
the following psalmody.
        Although it was omitted from the 1549 Prayer Book,
it has retained its important position since its inclusion in
1552. Both the Lutheran and Anglican churches employ
*Anglican chant with its use.

Procter, Francis and W. H. Frere (eds.). A New History
        of the Book of Common Prayer. New York: Mac-
        millan, 1955.

INVOCATION   (OF. fr. L. invocatio fr. invocaro, fr. in-
        in, + vocare to call)

        The prayer or "calling upon" God at the commence-
ment of the worship service is termed the invocation. It is
a vestige of the Roman church where the priest invoked the
presence of the Trinity in private devotion before the mass

or other services. At the time of the Reformation the invocation was retained by Luther and made into a public congregational act. However, the Anglican Church eliminated it
from the service. The invocation, as placed in the Lutheran
liturgy may be intoned or spoken.

Reed, Luther D. The Lutheran Liturgy. Philadelphia:
     Muhlenberg Press, 1947.

JAZZ   see "POP," GOSPEL

JUBILATE (L. imper. of jubilare to shout for joy)

     "O be joyful in the Lord, all ye lands" (Psalm 100)
is an alternative to the Gospel *canticle, *Benedictus, after
the second lesson in the Anglican office of *Morning Prayer.
It was added to the service in the 1552 revision of the *Book
of Common Prayer. Musical settings of the Jubilate are
found in Anglican Services by various composers (Byrd, Purcell, and Handel), as well as individual works in anthem
form by other composers.

Procter, Francis and W. H. Frere (eds.). A New History
     of the Book of Common Prayer. New York: Mac-
     millan, 1955.

JUNIOR CHOIR (L. compar. of juveni young + *choir)

     The basic singing organization within the church for
boys and girls between the ages of nine and 12 (or grades
three to six) is the junior choir (cf. *Youth choir). Though
the history of children's choirs can be traced from early
Jewish worship, the history of the junior choir for both
girls and boys within the church is a 20th century phenomenon unique to American Protestantism (see *Graded choir
program). In 1906, Elizabeth Van Fleet Vosseller of Flem-
ington, New Jersey, organized what is thought to be one of
the first junior choirs. It was composed of boys and girls
from the church school for the express purpose of providing
singers in the future for the adult choir of that Methodist
Episcopal Church. Through her two books (see the bibliography) the early foundations of the junior choir movement can
be studied.

With the growing interest in junior choirs around the mid-20th century, the Chorister's Guild (1949) was founded by Ruth Jacobs for the purpose of helping church musicians of any denomination establish and maintain a children's choir ministry. This, along with the emphasis of the Baptist, Methodist and Presbyterian denominations, firmly established the junior choir as an agent for musical and Christian education within the church. Considered to be the first children's choir collection to be published by a denominational press was Anthems for the Junior Choir (1944) by Westminster Press. Since that time, extensive publications of anthems, cantatas, musical dramas and hymnals have become readily available.

Ingram, Madeline D. Organizing and Directing Children's
     Choirs. New York: Abingdon Press, 1959.
Jacobs, Ruth. The Children's Choir. Vol. I. Rock Island,
     Ill.: Augustana Press, 1958.
Sample, Mable Warkentin. Leading Children's Choirs.
     Nashville: Broadman Press, 1966.
Tufts, Nancy Poore. The Children's Choir. Vol. II.
     Philadelphia: Fortress Press, 1965.
Vosseller, Elizabeth Van Fleet. Junior Choirs: More
     Helps and Suggestions. N.p.: Democrat Printing
     Office, 1939.
_____ . The Use of a Children's Choir in the Church.
     Its Methods and Practical Value. New York: H. W.
     Gray, 1907.

JUNIOR HIGH CHOIR   see   INTERMEDIATE CHOIR

KANTIONAL (G., fr. L. cantionale fr. cantio a song)

     (1) The late 16th- and early 17th-century style of composition associated with the *chorale which involved a simple four-part homophonic harmonization of the chorale-melody in the soprano was called Kantional style. This style, designed for congregational use, off-set the imitative, polyphonic, tenor-dominated 16th-century choral motet.

     (2) Kantional may also refer to a collection of simple, homophonic settings of chorales and other service music for the German Protestant church. An early example of these

hymnbooks is Johann Hermann Schein's (1586-1630) Kantional
--or Cantionae oder Gesangbuch Augsburgischer--published
in 1627 at Leipzig.

Reckziegel, W. Das Cantional von Johann Hermann Schein;
  seine geschichtlichen Grundlagen. Vol. V, Berliner
  Studien zur Musikwissenschaft. Berlin: Mersenberger,
  1963.
Reidel, Johannes. The Lutheran Chorale: Its Basic Traditions. Minneapolis: Augsburg Publishing House, 1967.
  Pp. 56-69.

KANTOREI (G.)

        The term used by the early reformers for the choral
and orchestral institutions performing polyphonic musical
forms during the 16th and early 17th centuries is the Kantorei. These organizations existed during the mid-15th century, prior to the Reformation, in the princely courts of
Germany and Flanders, performing music in the predominantly Netherlands style. Thus, it was only for Luther to
emphasize their continuation that they were brought into the
activities of the Reformation. The first Kantorei of the
Reformation was established in Torgau by Johann Walther
(1496-1570) in 1529. Through his efforts and those of the
Wittenburg music printer, George Rhaw (1488-1548), the
Kantorei was united with the church, becoming the institution
for musical training of the townspeople. Rhaw's publications
for the Kantorei during the 1520's numbered 778 compositions, about 550 of which were liturgical motets of the Netherlands style. The Protestant cantor became the composer, a
practice begun in J. Walther and continued through J. S.
Bach. Yet, along side these Protestant German works the
Catholic Netherland liturgical compositions (Josquin des Près,
Heinrich Isaac, Ludwig Senfl) were used.
        The Kantorei, usually consisting of citizens of the
villages organized for artistic singing in public worship
preferably accompanied by instruments, reached their height
during the late 16th century, remaining until the Thirty Years'
War. After the war, attempts to reorganize it reached limited success, but were further stymied with the emergence of
the new Italian style as illustrated in the life and works of
Heinrich Schütz (1588-1672).

Bornefeld, Helmut. "Was ist eine Kantorei?" Der Kirchenchor, 11:51-53, May-June 1951.

Ehmann, Wilhelm. "Changes in Choral Singing in Europe
     Today, " in: Cantors at the Crossroads, ed. Johannes
     Riedel. St. Louis: Concordia Publishing House, 1967.
     Pp. 193-200.
Schrade, Leo. "The Choral Music of the Kantorei, " in:
     Musical Heritage of the Church, ed. Theodore Hoelty-
     Nickel. St. Louis: Concordia Publishing House, 1959.
     Vol. V., pp. 128-139.

KAPELL MEISTER (G.)

     Literally, "the chapel master" (cf. *Choirmaster),
this individual is the director of the musicians (vocal and
instrumental) who serve the church (e.g., J. S. Bach at
Leipzig). (Cf. *Director of music and *Minister of music.)

KIRCHEN- (G. church)

     When used to modify other nouns the following trans-
lations may be presumed:

     Kirchenjahr--church year.
     Kirchenkantata--church cantata.
     Kirchenlied or Kirchengesang--church song: when
          Protestant, a *chorale, Catholic, a German hymn
          (as opposed to Latin hymn).
     Kirchenmusik--church music.
     Kirchensonate--church sonata (sonata da chiesa).
     Kirchenton--church mode.

KYRIE ELEISON (LL., fr. Gr. kyrie eleeson)

     Developing from the first section of the ordinary of
the *mass, the Kyrie eleison ("Lord, have mercy") is the
sacrificial prayer of intercession following the *introit in
the Lutheran service. The origin of this simple litany-type
petition is early Christian; however, its inclusion in Western
liturgy cannot be traced prior to the fourth century. During
the Middle Ages the Kyrie bore a penitential interpretation.
Such an interpretation is seen in the complex settings by the
great composers: Bach (B Minor Mass), Mozart, Gounod
and others. The Lutheran Church of America has sought to
reinstate the original tone of this act of worship. The Anglican Prayer Book (1552) and the successive revisions have
incorporated the Kyrie uniquely as a response to each com-

mandment of the Decalogue, with the tenth commandment
answered by "Vouchsafe to write it in our hearts by Thy
Spirit." Aside from choral settings by numerous composers,
this element of the service is generally sung to *chant.

"Die einstimmige Weisen Satze." Vol. I, Handbuch der
    deutschen evangelischen Kirchenmusik. Göttingen:
    Verlag von Danderhoed and Ruprecht, 1941.
Jungmann, J. A. The Mass of the Roman Rite. New York:
    Benziger, 1950. Vol. I, pp. 333f.
Müller, Karl Ferdinand (ed.). Leiturgia, Handbuch des
    evangelischen Gottesdienstes. Kassel: Johann Staude,
    1952. Vol. II, pp. 14f.

LAST SUPPER see LORD'S SUPPER

LAUDA (IT. for one of laudi spirituali)

    The non-liturgical *hymns of devotion and praise sung
by the flagellant bands in Italy principally from the 13th to
the mid-19th centuries are known as laudi spirituali. Among
the most famous of these is the "Canticle of the Sun" by St.
Francis of Assisi (1182-1226). In form the lauda is divided
into three parts: a ripresa (refrain), a middle section
(stanza--of two piedi and a volta) and a final ripresa (refrain). These "hymns," often popularized Gospel stories,
were sometimes acted in procession or in the oratorium of
the chapel. Thus, the germ for the early *oratorios of
Peri and Caccini can be seen in these religious folk songs
from the 13th century. (Cf. *Geisslerlieder).

Dent, E. J. "The Laudi Spirituali in the XVIth and XVIIth
    Centuries," PRMA, 43, 1917.
Reese, Gustav. Music in the Middle Ages. New York:
    W. W. Norton, 1940. Pp. 237-238.

LECTION (L. lectio, fro. legere, lectum to read)

    The readings or *lessons from the Bible, appointed
for the services of worship of the *Christian Year, are
called lections. (Cf. *Epistle; *Gospel; *Lesson.) Luther,
in his *Formula Missae (1523), suggested the epistle be
chanted to the 8th tone and the Gospel to the 6th tone.

Blume, Friedrich. Geschichte der evangelischen Kirchen-
     musik. Kassel: Bärenreiter, 1965.

LEISE (G.)

     The medieval congregational hymn in the German lan-
guage which concluded with the words *Kyrie eleison was
known as a Leise. It developed as a type of hymnody from
the *mass (though never a part of the mass), in a folk nature
similar to the sequence, serving as a congregational response
to the Kyrie. Gradually it was lengthened into poems with
the Kyrie or a similar petition inserted at various points.
     Two types of Leisen have been found. The first, be-
cause of its complexity, is called ceremonial-liturgical,
having been created and sung by the clergy ("Media vita in
morte sumus"). The second type was the popular Leise,
simple in construction, easily remembered, and created by
the people. Martin Luther (1483-1546) chose from both types
in developing the *chorale.
     Among the oldest extant Leisen are "Nun bitte wir den
heiligen Geist," "In Gottes Namen fahren wir," and "Christ
ist erstanden."

Riedel, Johannes. "Leisen Formulae: Their Polyphonic
     Settings in the Renaissance and Reformation." Un-
     published Ph.D. dissertation, University of Southern
     California, Los Angeles, 1953.
     _____. "Vocal Leisen Settings in the Baroque Era," in:
     The Musical Heritage of the Lutheran Church, ed.
     Theodore Hoelty-Nickel. St. Louis: Concordia Pub-
     lishing House, 1959. Vol. V.

LESSON (ME. lessoun, fr. OF. leçon lesson, reading, fr.
     L. lectio a reading, fr. legere to read, collect)

     In the broadest concept, any passage of Scripture
read or chanted during an office or service of worship is
termed a lesson. However, in a more narrow sense, the
Lutheran liturgy refers only to the Old Testament reading
as the lesson. Thus, the Lutheran church has three readings from Scripture at *communion--the *lesson, the *epistle
and the *Gospel--whereas the Anglican church employs only
the latter two. During the Hours of Prayer readings are
usually representative of both Testaments.
     Historically, the reading of Scripture at gatherings of

the faithful among the early Christians relates to the regular
readings from the Law and Prophets during the synagogue
service. As the Christian church matured, readings from
the epistles and gospels were added and the Old Testament
readings were reduced to one. This threefold lesson, maintained by Ambrosian and Mozarabic liturgy, was reduced to
two by the Roman church, eliminating the Old Testament
reading. (Cf. *Pericopes.)

Müller, Karl Ferdinand (ed.). Leiturgia, Handbuch des
    evangelischen Gottesdienstes. Kassel: Johann Straude,
    1954. Vols. VIII and IX.
Procter, Francis and W. H. Frere. A New History of the
    Book of Common Prayer. New York: Macmillan,
    1955. Pp. 465-466.
Reed, Luther D. The Lutheran Liturgy. Philadelphia:
    Muhlenberg Press, 1947. Pp. 292-293.

LINING-OUT   (fr. F. ligne line, fr. L. linea)

       A practice, prevalent from the 17th century up to the
beginning of the 19th century in England, Scotland and New
England, in which each phrase or pair of phrases of a metrical *psalm or *hymn was given out (read or sung) by the
*precentor, parish clerk or some other official before being
sung by the congregation, is lining-out (or *"deaconing").
This dictational procedure, originating in England and Scotland and later practiced in America, was applied to the English psalm- and hymn-tunes which generally consisted of
short, easily remembered phrases. As these tunes became
dissected the first note of each phrase was elongated to permit the "gathering in" of all the voices before the phrase
proceeded. (See *Gathering-note.) The practice of lining-
out came into existence where many of the congregation were
unable to read and where books were limited; thus, singing-
by-rote became the most convenient means of maintaining
congregational praise. It should be mentioned that lining-out
was not the practice of the first settlers in the New England
colonies, but rather one that was introduced from England
later, becoming a general practice around 1750. History
records that lining-out was begun in the Plymouth Church on
October 9, 1681; and for about sixty years this church and
others like it in New England reduced their tune repertoire
to not more than ten tunes, later five or six.
       As the urban culture of Boston began to dominate all
of New England, lining-out, being abolished in some Boston

churches as early as 1699, disappeared from this region,
taking refuge in the frontier settlements. In the movement
to the frontier the procedure of lining-out found an influential role. The call-and-response pattern of the *camp
meeting songs as well as that of the *spiritual shows great
similarity to this 18th-century tradition, even to the point of
assimilation of the one by the other.

   Lining-out was finally abandoned by most religious
bodies after bitter opposition in the mid-19th century, with
only isolated vestiges of it remaining.

Chase, Gilbert. America's Music: From the Pilgrims to
     the Present. 2d ed. New York: McGraw-Hill, 1966.
     Chapter 2.
Tallmadge, William H. "Dr. Watts and Mahalia Jackson--
     The Development, Decline, and Survival of a Folk
     Style in America," Ethnomusicology, 5:95-99, May,
     1960.

LITANY (ME. letanie, fr. OF. letanie, fr. LL. litania,
     fr. Gr. litaneia to pray, fr. L. litare to make
     sacrifice)

   A responsive prayer consisting of a series of biddings
and petitions, though all moods of worship may be expressed,
led by the officiant with each article followed by a brief
fixed response of the people, is a litany. It is one of the
most archaic forms of common worship, being found in pagan and tribal rituals. Because of its simple and obvious
device of repetition, it has been a means for securing the
attention and united involvement of the congregation. Being
among the first steps toward liturgy, the development can
be traced from the probable litany-manner of reciting the
*psalms in early Christian worship. The litany entered the
Roman church chiefly as processional prayers, which later
developed into prayers for the saints. With the coming of
the Reformation, the value of the litany was seen by Martin
Luther, who in 1529 wrote the "Great Litany," a work bearing Augustinian influences but containing new petitions. This
litany, along with those of the Eastern Orthodox and medieval
Roman churches, strongly influenced the litany of the *Book
of Common Prayer (1549). This litany, written by Archbishop Cranmer, is the oldest segment of the Prayer Book,
having been issued by King Henry VIII in 1544. This first
vernacular service of the Church of England was noted and
sung in procession. Traditionally, it is used in the Anglican

Church after *Morning Prayers on Sundays, Wednesdays and Fridays, and on Sundays properly preceding the *communion service.

Analytically, the Anglican litany consists of five parts, with all but the first invocation being addressed directly to God. The first invocation, directed to the Trinity, is a combination of praise and penitence. The second and third sections deal with the deprecations--the deliverance from evil, and the obsecrations--the entreaties recalling God's redemptive work on man's behalf. Part four, the largest portion of the litany, contains the suffrages and the Lord's Prayer (*Pater Noster). The concluding section maintains the strong medieval influence for use in time of war with its special penitential intercession. However, at the discretion of the minister the fifth part may be omitted by passing to the final prayers.

In the Lutheran *Vespers the litany is appointed for use in place of the *Magnificat on occasion. John Wesley's abridged version of the Book of Common Prayer for Methodist congregations included the litany. The influence of this form of common prayer is also seen among the Moravian congregations who regularly incorporate the "Litany of the Life, Passion and Death of Jesus Christ" and the "Church Litany" into their worship. They, along with the *Oxford Movement, are responsible for the production of litany hymns (see Hymnal 1940, 229-234). The effectiveness of litanies for congregational prayers has been seen by the non-liturgical churches as well, as can be witnessed by the inclusion of litanies on special occasions and for special needs (e.g., "Litany for the Starving").

From a musical standpoint the early litanies were sung to plainsong formulae. Martin Luther, for both his Latin and German litanies, provided musical settings for use with double choirs. However, when two choirs were impossible the pastor sang or spoke the petition and the choir and congregation responded. Luther's melody for the German text, being universally accepted among Lutherans, was first adapted to the English text in the Choral Service Book (1901) by Archer and Reed.

The Prayer Book and Litany of Cranmer (1544) was first set musically by John Merbecke (c.1510-c.1585) in his monumental work, The Booke of Common Praier Noted (1550). The plainsong version which accompanied the 1544 choral responses was set in four and five parts by Thomas Tallis (c.1505-1585) and other Tudor composers.

Bond, LeRoy Miller. "The Litany As a Form of Worship."

Unpublished master's thesis, Philadelphia, Lutheran
Theological Seminary, 1947.
Hunt, J. Eric. Cranmer's First Litany, 1544, and Merbecke's Book of Common Prayer Noted, 1550. London: S.P.C.K., 1939.
Reed, Luther. The Lutheran Liturgy. Philadelphia: Muhlenberg Press, 1947. Chapter 30.

"LITTLE LENT"

The period of the three Sundays prior to Lent in the
*Christian Year is sometimes referred to as "Little Lent"
or "Pre-Lent." It contains the "-gesima" Sundays: Septuagesima, Sexagesima and Quinquagesima.

Wetzler, Robert and Helen Huntington. Seasons and Symbols:
A Handbook on the Church Year. Minneapolis: Augsburg Publishing House, 1962.

LITURGICAL BOOKS

The following is a partial listing of important liturgical books in English, both historic and current, arranged
alphabetically by denomination.

Anglican--Protestant Episcopal

Altar Service of the Protestant Episcopal Church. Oxford
Edition. New York: Oxford University Press, n.d.
The Anglican Church of Canada. The Book of Common
Prayer and Administration of the Sacrament.... To-
ronto: Anglican Book Center, 1962.
Book of Common Prayer ... Protestant Episcopal Church in
the United States of America. Milwaukee: Morehouse
Pub. Co., 1929.
Book of Common Prayer: with the additions and the devia-
tions proposed in 1928. London: Oxford University
Press, 1928.
Buchanan, Colin O. (ed.). Modern Anglican Liturgies 1958-
1968. London: Oxford University Press, 1968.
The Canadian Book of Occasional Offices. Toronto: Angli-
can Church of Canada, 1964.
Clay, William K. (ed.). Liturgical Services: Liturgies and
Occasional forms of prayers set forth in the reign of
Queen Elizabeth. N.p.: n.p., 1847 (reprint).

Ketley, Joseph (ed.). Two Liturgies: A.D. 1549 and A.D.
      1557. New York: Johnson Reprint (1844).

Baptist

Hiscox, Edward T. Star Book for Ministers. Valley Forge,
      Pa.: Judson Press, 1968.
Hobbs, James R. Pastor's Manual. Nashville: Broadman
      Press, 1940.
Skoglund, John. Manual of Worship. Valley Forge, Pa.:
      Judson Press, 1968.

Congregational

Congregational Christian Churches in the United States,
      General Council. Book of Worship for Free Churches.
      New York: Oxford University Press, 1948.

Disciples of Christ

Osborn, G. Edwin (ed.). Christian Worship, a Service
      Book. St. Louis: Bethany Press, 1953.

Episcopal see Anglican

Lutheran

Altar Service Book, authorized version. Philadelphia: For-
      tress Press, 1960.
Doberstein, John W. Minister's Prayer Book. Philadel-
      phia: Fortress Press, n.d.
Strodach, Paul Z. (ed.). Oremus. Minneapolis: Augsburg
      Publishing House, 1966.

Methodist

The Methodist Church. The Book of Worship for Church
      and Home. Nashville: Methodist Publishing House,
      1965.

Non-Denominational

McCabe, Joseph E. Service Book for Ministers. New
      York: McGraw-Hill, 1961.
Morrison, James Dalton (ed.). Minister's Service Book
      for Pulpit and Parish Use. New York: Willett, Clark,
      1937.
Payne, Ernest A., Stephen F. Winward and James W. Cox
      (compilers). Minister's Worship Manual. New York:
      World, 1969.

Presbyterian

Book of Common Worship. Philadelphia: Board of Christian
      Education of the Presbyterian Church in the United
      States of America, 1946.
Church of Scotland, General Assembly. Book of Common
      Order of the Church of Scotland. London: Oxford
      University Press, n.d.
McLauchlan, T. (ed.). The Book of Common Order: Com-
      monly called John Knox's Liturgy. Edinburgh: Edmon-
      ston and Douglas, 1878.

Protestant Episcopal see Anglican

LITURGICAL MUSIC-DRAMA

In its strictest sense, liturgical music-drama refers
to the presentation of Biblical stories through music and
action within the church during the medieval times (10th
through 13th centuries) by the clergy. This is in distinction
to the mystery plays of the laity from the same period which
were performed outside the church. The two further differ
in that the liturgical music dramas were sung in Latin with
little instrumental assistance, whereas the mystery plays
were in the vernacular and freely accompanied by the professional instrumentalists of the day. However, to enlarge
the meaning of liturgical music-drama to include the post-
medieval enactments, it may be said that liturgical music-
drama is any musical presentation of a Biblical story with
action.
The medieval liturgical music-drama was a development of the Germanic and French lands of the 10th through
13th centuries. It originated from the *introit tropes of the
Easter Mass which were sung antiphonally to depict the dialogue between the Angel and the searching Marys (see Quem
queritis trope of the Introit "Resurrexi," GMB, 5). Other
plays developed around the Christmas story and other Biblical accounts, as the Conversation of Paul, the Last Judgment and Daniel. Sung primarily by the clergies and choirboys, the text was entirely sung to monophonic Gregorian
style lines, some incidental use of antiphons and canticles
being permitted. Since the dramas were most often performed after *Matins on the various feast days, they frequently concluded with the singing of the *Te Deum laudamus.
With the emergence of the Renaissance (14th-16th
centuries) the liturgical drama moved from the church to the

village square and evolved into the mystery plays. Its Latin
texts became that of the vernacular and instruments were
used more freely, along with dance. This led to the creation of the opera and *oratorio.

In modern times music-drama has remained largely
outside the church; however, Benjamin Britten (b.1913) has
created several music-dramas based on the mystery plays
suitable for liturgical use. Such a work is his Noye's Fludde,
Op. 59 (1958) which takes the character of the medieval Chester
miracle plays and presents it in a similar style musically for
the church congregation. Similarly the three parables for church
performance by Britten--Curlew River, Op. 71 (1964), The
Burning Fiery Furnace, Op. 77 (1966) and The Prodigal Son,
Op. 81 (1968)--have presented religious stories in the manner
reminiscent of the medieval liturgical music-drama.

With the advent of children's choirs and the *graded
choir program other composers and publishers are entering
into church music-drama in the mid-20th century. Bob
Burrough's David (1969) for *junior choir and soloists recounts the childhood of David from the shepherd boy to the
conqueror of the Philistine giant in five scenes.

Hotze, Alphonse John. "Medieval Liturgical Drama, the
    Origin and Religiosity." Unpublished Ph.D. disserta-
    tion, University of Missouri, Columbia, 1956.
Riedel, Johannes. "The Liturgical Play," JCM, 5:2-4+,
    March, 1963.
Smolden, William. "Liturgical Drama," in: New Oxford
    History of Music. Vol. II. Ed. by Dom Anselm
    Hughes. London: Oxford University Press, 1954.
_____. "The Music of the Medieval Church Drama,"
    MQ, 48:476-497, July 1962.
Young, Karl. The Drama of the Medieval Church. Oxford,
    Eng.: Clarendon Press, 1933.

LITURGY (F. liturgie, fr. ML. liturgia, fr. Gr. leitourgia
    a public service, the public service of God, public
    worship, fr. leitos, leitos belonging to the people,
    public + the root of ergon work)

In a general sense any officially authorized form of
public worship of the Christian church is termed liturgy.
More specifically, it may denote the eucharistic services of
the Anglican and Lutheran churches. The term was introduced in the 17th century to mean the order of public worship of God, with subsequent implications from the Old

Testament temple worship. (For the services of other denominations see *worship services; also see *mass, *communion service, *Anglican chant and *liturgical books.)

Lohfink, Wilhelm. "Bibel und Liturgie," KM, 7:243-248, September-October, 1935.
Poole, J. W. "Liturgical Perspectives," ECM, 1966:3-15, 1966.
Procter, Francis and W. H. Frere. A New History of the Book of Common Prayer. New York: Macmillan, 1955.
Reed, Luther D. The Lutheran Liturgy. Philadelphia: Muhlenberg Press, 1947.
Ritter, K. B. Die Liturgie als Lebensform der Kirche. Krassel: Bärenreiter, 1947.

LORD'S PRAYER see PATER NOSTER (see also VATER UNSER)

LORD'S SUPPER

The commemoration of the meal taken by Jesus and his disciples the night in which he was betrayed is the Lord's Supper (in German, heilige Abendmahl), a term based on I Corinthians 11:20. (See *Eucharist; *Communion Service; *Full Service; *Mass.)

Freeman, Elmer S. The Lord's Supper in Protestantism. New York: Macmillan, 1945.

MACARONIC VERSE (It. maccheronico, F. macaronique mixed + *verse)

The type of verse, common to the early *carols and *chorales, in which lines of Latin were interspersed with those of the vernacular, is known as macaronic verse. These lines are not necessarily Latin quotations, but simply Latin versifications of the vernacular text (e.g., "In dulci jubilo").

MAGNIFICAT (L. it magnifies)

The Gospel *canticle from the Roman office of *Vespers,

commonly referred to as the "Song of Mary" (Luke 1:46-55), is the Magnificat. It occurs as the first canticle in the office of *Evening Prayer (*Vespers), with the possible alternatives of the Cantate Domino or Bonum est confiteri. In the Lutheran order of Vespers the Magnificat is prescribed to be sung following the sermon during festal seasons.

The Magnificat has been sung in the Western liturgical office of Vespers since the sixth century. Since the Reformation it has been sung generally to chant settings on the tonus Peregrinus (pilgrim tone) when done congregationally. However, the text has inspired many choral settings of the canticle replacing congregational use. Among some of the earlier Reformation settings are the two Magnificats by H. L. Hassler (1564-1612), the even verses only; Magnificats "a4" and "a5" by Thomas Tallis (c.1505-1585) in initiative style and even verses only; Johann Hahnel's (c.1490-?) Christmas Magnificat in the 5th Mode, even verses, using the Latin cantus firmus with popular Christmas songs; and the Magnificat in the 5th Tone by Michael Praetorius (1560-1629) using carols with the Latin cantus firmus as well. Other German settings include Sixt Dietrich (c.1492-1548), Melchior Vulpius (c.1560-1615), Johannes Crüger (1598-1663), and J. S. Bach (1685-1750). Two contemporary Magnificats of note are one by Alan Hovhaness (1958) for soli, chorus and orchestra, and the Festival Magnificat (1963) by Daniel Pinkham.

Organ chorale settings of the Magnificat have been written by composers as Samuel Scheidt, Johann Pachelbel, J. S. Bach and others.

"My soul doth magnify the Lord, and my spirit hath rejoiced in God my Saviour. For he hath regarded the low estate of his handmaiden. For behold from henceforth all generations shall call me blessed. For he that is mighty hath done to me great things; and holy is his Name.

"And his mercy is on them that fear him from generation to generation. He hath shewed strength with his arm; he hath scattered the proud in the imagination of their hearts. He hath put down the mighty from their seats, and exalted them of low degree. He hath filled the hungry with good things; and the rich he hath sent empty away. He hath holpen his servant Israel, in remembrance of his mercy; as he spake to our fathers, to Abraham and to his seed for ever" [BCP].

Illing, C-H. Zur Technik der Magnificat-Komposition des 16. Jahrunderts. Wolfenbüttel: Kallmeyer, 1936.

Kulp, Johannes. "Das Magnificat und das Nunc Dimittis,"
MK, 7:271-277, November-December, 1935.

MAROT-BÈZE PSALTER

"Pseaumes de David mis en rime francaise par
Clement Marot & Théodore de Bèze ... " (1562): The
above title denotes the book known both as the Huguenot
Psalter and the Marot-Bèze Psalter. It is one of the monumental *psalters of this period along with the English, Genevan and Scottish ones. The translation was the work of
Clement Marot (c. 1497-1544) and Théodore de Bèze (1519-
1605) who skillfully wrote the Latin psalms in exceptional
poetic form. Its significance is also in the breadth of circulation and influence, having been published in at least 115
editions before 1685, over a century after its inception.
(See *Psalmody, metrical (The Continent); and *Psalters.)

Douen, O. Clement Marot et le psautier huguenot. 2 vols.
     Paris: L'Imprimerie Nationale, 1878.
Hugenottenpsalter von Marot und Beza mit Sätzen von Claude
     Goudimel. Eds. P. Pidoux and K. Ameln. Kassel:
     Bärenheiter, 1935 (facsimile Reprint of 1565 ed.).
Pidoux, Pierre. Le psautier huguenot du XVIe siècle. 3
     vols. Kassel: Bärenreiter, 1960-.
Pratt, Waldo Selden. The Music of the French Psalter.
     New York: Columbia University Press, 1939.
Teuber, Ulrich. "Notes sur la rédaction musical du Psau-
     tier Genevois (1542-1562), " AM, 4:113-128, 1956.

MASS (ME. masse, messe, fr. AS. maesse, fr. LL.
     missa, fr. mittere, missum to send, dismiss; fr.
     Ite missa est the mass is ended)

     The musical items of the *communion service, the
celebration of the *Lord's Supper, compose the mass. Generally speaking, this consists of the choral settings of the
*ordinary as assimilated into the worship service of the Lu-
theran Reformation from the Roman Catholic tradition (see
Luther's *Formulae Missae and *Deutsche Messe). In the
Anglican tradition the choral sections of the communion
service originally included only the Kyrie and the Creed, the
Gloria, Sanctus and Agnus Dei being added in the mid-19th
century. Though the Anglican Eucharist may be called a
mass, it is usually referred to as Holy Communion. In

Sweden all Sunday services are called "High Mass" (Hög-mässa) whether the Eucharist is observed or not, the actual celebration being termed "communion mass."

(Regarding musical settings of the Protestant mass, in the Anglican tradition see *Full service and *Communion service; for the Lutheran Mass see *Deutsche Messe and *Formulae Missae.)

Clarke, W. K. Lowther and Charles Harris. Liturgy and Worship: A Companion to the Prayer Books of the Anglican Communion. London: S.P.C.K., 1932.

Fellerer, Karl Gustav. Die Messe. Dortmund: Cruwell, 1951.

Nichols, James Hastings. Corporate Worship in the Reformed Tradition. Philadelphia: Westminster Press, 1968.

Reed, Luther. The Lutheran Liturgy. Philadelphia: Muhlenberg Press, 1947.

Ritter, Karl Bernhard. Die eucharistische Freier. Kassel: Strauda, 1961.

Schild, Emil. Geschichte der protestantischen Messenkomposition im 17. und 18. Jahrhunderts. Wuppertal-Elberfeld: F. W. Kohler, 1934.

Schmidt-Görg, Joseph. History of the Mass. Vol. XXX, Anthology of Music, trans. Robert Kobben. Cologne: Arno Volk Verlag, 1968.

Schulze, Willi. "Die mehrstimmige Messe im frühprotestantischen Gottesdienst." Unpublished dissertation, University of Kiel, Wolfenbüttel, 1940.

Wagner, Peter. Geschichte des Messe bis 1600. Wiesbaden: Breitkopf und Härtel, 1963.

MATINS (OF., fr. L. matutinus of the morning)

The historical name for the *Morning Prayer office of the *Canonical Hours in the Roman and Lutheran rites is Matins. Outside of the Eucharist it is probably the most ancient public service of the church. Originally a continuation of the all-night vigils preceding festivals, it became the richest of all offices in materials and variety within the monastic tradition. Luther simplified and continued its usage in the church schools on weekdays and for the congregation on Sundays and feast days. Its significant quality is praise, with prayers for strength and guidance for the day. (Cf. *Morning Prayer; see also *canticle.)

Order of Matins (Lutheran)

The Versicles
  "O Lord, open thou my lips" (Psalm 51:15)
  "Make haste, O God, to deliver me" (Psalm 70:1)
  Gloria Patri
The Invitatory "O come, let us worship the Lord"
Venite exultemus (Psalm 95)
Office hymn
The psalm and Gloria Patri
The lesson and response
Responsory or hymn
Sermon
Canticle (Te Deum laudamus or Benedictus--the latter
      for Advent and Lent)
The Prayer
  Prayers
  Kyrie eleison
  The Lord's Prayer
  The Salutation
  The Oremus
  The Collect for the Day
The Collect for Grace
Benedicamus
Benediction (II Corinthians 13:14)

Mauder, Albert, ed. Evangelisches Tagzeitenbuch. Kassel:
    Strauda, 1967.
Reed, Luther. The Lutheran Liturgy. Philadelphia: Muh-
    lenberg Press, 1947. Pp. 388-427.

MEDIATION (fr. L. mediatio, fr. mediare to be in the
    middle)

    The inflection of the monotonic recitation of a *plain-
song melody which occurs at the end of the half-verse of
the *psalm is the mediation. Unlike the corresponding portion of an Anglican chant, the number of notes in the mediation of plainsong varies with the *ecclesiastical mode or
*psalm-tone. The mediation may be abridged or have some
notes omitted if the verbal structure of the psalm verse
requires it.

MEDIUS (NL., fr. L. medius middle)

    The third- or middle voice-part of a three-part setting

of a 17th-century psalm tune is the medius, the other parts
being the cantus and bassus. The term is used in Playford's (1623-1686) Whole Book of Psalms (1677; 3-part rev.
of 1671 ed.). Each vocal line is contained on its own staff.

MELODEONS   (fr. ME. melodie, fr. OF. melodie, fr. LL.
    melodia, fr. Gr. melōidia a singing, choral song, fr.
    melōidos musical, melodious, fr. melos song, tune)

The zither-like instrument of five strings invented by
Johann Petzmayer of Munich in 1823 is the melodeon. Its
five strings are tuned to permit both viola and violin pitches
when bowed. This instrument, along with the *psalmodicon,
was used by the Swedish Lutheran congregations in America
prior to the use of organs.

Besseraboff, Nicholas. Ancient European Musical Instru-
    ments. Cambridge, Mass.: Harvard University Press,
    1941. P. 320.

METER   see   HYMN METER

MINISTER OF MUSIC   (ME. ministre, fr. OF. ministre, fr.
    L. minister + *music)

The person who combines the tasks of ministry and
music leadership is often called the minister of music and
is often ordained to the ministry with music as the tool of
his calling. This role includes the gathering of the people,
the teaching of them and the caring for them through a
musical dimension within the total redemptive-creative activity of the church.
This term, "minister of music," is relatively recent
to church music having appeared around the mid-20th century among evangelical Protestant churches in America. A
real impetus toward its use came from the Southern Baptist
Convention with its establishment of the Department of Church
Music (1941) as a part of the Sunday School Board and its
implementation of Schools of Church Music in the various
seminaries.
Unlike the *director of music, the minister of music
is involved with more than simply choral and instrumental
ensembles and leading the *congregational singing. He is
concerned with the total congregation, what the needs are of

the congregation as individuals, and what music will best
meet these needs and effect a desired response. Through
his choice and use of music he is involved in the process
of instilling theological concepts as well as a devotional
vocabulary. His ability to know his congregation and individual attitudes, to identify with these and to provide the
catalyst for a feeling of community in the proclamation of
Christian truth through music comprise the discipline and
limits of his musical work.

The antiquity of Jewish worship yields evidence about
the minister of music through the Levites, the musical
leaders of temple worship (I Chronicles 16:4-5). Resulting
from the establishment of the synagogue, the musical leadership role became that of the *cantor. The medieval Christian church likewise adopted the role of the cantor for its
musical leadership, as did the Lutheran Reformation movement. The Church of England, on the other hand, employed
its chief musician as *choirmaster (G. *Kapellmeister) or
organist-choirmaster. This term came over to America
where it has retained a prominent place, as well as being
modified to choir director. As the church music program
has expanded in the evangelical churches of 20th-century
America, the responsible leader has come to be known as
the director of music. This latter term has become tempered in the mid-20th century by the changing concept and
training for the leadership of music in the church, which
has more and more come to see the music director as an
ordained minister of music, an outgrowth of the multiple
ministries of the church.

July, Marvin T. The Multiple Staff Ministry. New York:
    Abingdon Press, 1969. Chapter 8.
Routley, Erik. Music Leadership in the Church. New
    York: Abingdon Press, 1966.
Sims, John N. "The Musician as Minister," The Review
    and Expositor, 63:84-94, Winter, 1966.

MISERERE   (L.)

The opening psalm of the Anglican Penitential Office
specifically ordered for use on Ash Wednesday is the
Miserere (Psalm 51): "Have mercy upon me, O God."

Procter, Francis and W. H. Frere. A New History of the
    Book of Common Prayer. London: Macmillan, 1955.

MISSA CANTATA (L.)

A choral communion service in the Anglican tradition may be denoted by the term, missa cantata, or sung *mass. The term reflects its Roman Church extraction where it also implied a choral service with one officiant.

MISSA DE ANGELIS (L.)

A unison setting of the congregational parts of the ordinary of the mass in the *plainsong style, but of major tonality, is called Missa de angelis. Though it has been largely used among Roman Catholic churches, settings adapted for English words have been used to some extent at choral *communion services in the Church of England.

MISSIONS, MUSIC IN

The use of music for the propagation of the gospel in African, Asian and Latin American cultures, a product of the 19th- and 20th-century missionary efforts of the Christian Church, may be considered music in missions or more specifically, music in foreing missions.

According to available information the first recorded use of music in Christian missions was by William Carey, missionary to India, who composed a hymn in Bengali about 1798. This hymn, translated "The Penitent's Prayer and Resolve," was in meter and sung to the tune, "Helmsley" (Stevenson, 746). Wherever missionaries went, they took their hymns with them. These hymns they sought to translate as quickly as possible. Among the earliest *hymnals resulting from the 19th-century missionary movement were a Bengali hymnal (India) prepared by Baptists in 1810, a Chinese hymnal prepared by Dr. Morrison in 1818, and a small Madagascan hymnal in 1828. A rather comprehensive and accessible history of hymnody in foreign missions during the 19th century is presented by W. R. Stevenson in Julian's A Dictionary of Hymnology.

Among the challenges of incorporating music into the missionary movement have been the assimilation of the role of music within the specific cultures as well as an understanding of the musical idioms and language native to each group. Whereas the use of indigenous musical idioms has been readily accepted by African converts, both in liturgical music and hymns (Weman, 153), within the Christian congre-

gations of Japan the use of classical Japanese music is of-
fensive (Saito, 72). Thus, as the missionaries have worked
with the various ethnic societies around the world they have
had to take care in translating or seeking to create hymns
and other religious musical expressions for their converts,
as music has been a readily accepted means of presenting
the gospel.

During the mid-20th century much work in Protestant
church music has been accomplished in the Orient. Both in
China (through the efforts of Bliss Wiant and others) and in
the Philippines, and somewhat in Japan, these have been a
blending of East and West in Christian musical expression,
a type of "hybridizing." The principle of the native music,
but not the exact melodies, are being applied to Western
forms, thus forming a new and unique expression. This has
provided for the retention of national spirit within the native
church (Espina, 286). A further development in Protestant
music in this region has been the establishment of the oratorio chorus, a result of the mission schools and their
choirs. It has been through the oratorio societies that Protestant church music has made itself felt in the communities,
especially since most performances of these large choral
works have been presented before capacity audiences. In
Japan, where Protestant church music seems to have come
into its own, a hymn society (The Japanese Hymn Society
of the United Church of Christ in Japan) and a center for
training in sacred music (the Christian Music Center, 1963)
have been established.

Turning to Africa, the work of Henry Weman in South
Africa (1956) has illustrated the ready acceptance of Protestant church music which employs native musical materials.
Thus, it has become the music missionary's task in this
culture to guide the African Christian to understand and
develop his own musical expression of Christian beliefs
(Weman, 188-189). Through the mission schools and the
organization of the All-African Church Society this aim is
being supported.

Since 1950, the advent of the missionary specifically
appointed by a mission board with musical responsibilities
has arrived. The first missionaries so appointed by the
Southern Baptist mission board were Donald Orr and his wife
in 1951, to Colombia, South America. Another later 20th-
century development has been the organized tour of musical
groups to various mission fields. Also the use of sacred
concerts by Christian musicians has provided opportunities
to present the Christian message to vast audiences in the
concert halls and auditoriums around the world. This, combined with the potential of radio, television and film in mass

communication, has made the use of music in missions indispensible and invaluable.

Espina, A. Beaunoni. "Music in the Philippines and the Development of Sacred Music There." Unpublished D.S.M. dissertation, Union Theological Seminary, New York, 1961.

Saito, Eva. "A General Survey of Church Music in Japan Today." Unpublished M.S.M. thesis, Union Theological Seminary, New York, 1963.

Stevenson, W. R. "Missions, Foreign," in: A Dictionary of Hymnology, ed. John Julian. New York: Dover, 1957.

Weman, Henry. African Music and the Church in Africa. Uppsala: A. B. Lundquistska Bokhandeln, 1960.

MORNING PRAYER (ME. morning, morwening after evening + ME. preire, fr. OF. preire, fr. VL. precaria, fr. L. precarius got by prayer, fr. precari to pray)

The morning office of the Church of England, sometimes known as *Matins, is a combination of Matins, Lauds and Prime of the Roman Catholic rite (cf. *Canonical Hours). The two *canticles (the Te Deum laudamus and the Benedictus) received their alternatives in 1552.

Order of Morning Prayer (Anglican)

I.   Introduction and Preparation
        Opening Sentences (vary with the season)
        Exhortation (a call to confession)
        A General Confession
        The Declaration of Absolution
II. The Office Proper
        The Lord's Prayer
        Versicles "O Lord, open thou our lips" (Psalm 51:15); also "O God, make speed to save us" (Psalm 70:1)
        Gloria Patri
        Invitatory Antiphons
        Venite, exultemus Domino (Psalm 95)
        The Psalms and Gloria Patri
        First Lesson
        Hymn
        Canticle Te Deum laudamus; Benedictus es, Domino; or Benedicite, omnia, opera Domine
        Second Lesson

Hymn
Canticle Benedictus or Jubilate Deo
III. Suffrages and Collects
The Creed
The Prayers
The Salutation
The Lord's Prayer
The Versicles (Psalm 85:7 & 51:10-11)
Collect for the Day
A Collect for Peace
A Collect for Grace
Litany (optional)
Prayers of General Intercession
A General Thanksgiving
A Prayer of St. Chrysostom
The Grace (II Corinthians 13:14)

Proctor, Francis and W. H. Frere. A New History of the
Book of Common Prayer. London: Macmillan, 1955.

MOTET (F., dim. of mot word)

A musical composition, being a multivoiced setting of
a psalm verse(s) or other Biblical text, generally in a polyphonic style, is a motet. This broad, general definition
speaks basically of the 15th-century motet which involved
close imitative counterpoint over a cantus firmus (Johannes
Okeghem, c.1430-c.1495). The motet of this time involved
settings of Latin texts. Its influence on the *anthem readily
can be seen in that the early anthems and motets of the
Reformation in England differed only in texts: the former
in the vernacular, the latter in Latin. It was the motet
which through its union with the *chorale in the *chorale
motet prepared the way for the Baroque *cantata. Claude
Goudimel (1510-1572) also made extensive use of the motet
in his psalm motets based on the Genevan Psalter cantus
firmi. (For the main history of the influence of the motet
in Protestant church music see *Anthem; *Cantata; *Chorale
motet.)

Bukofzer, Manfred. "The First Motet with English Words,"
ML, 17:225-33, July, 1936.
Kerman, Joseph. "Byrd's Motets: Chronology and Canon,"
JAMS, 14:359-382, Summer, 1961.
Lawry, Eleanor McCheaney. "The Psalm Motets of Claude
Goudimel." Unpublished Ph.D. dissertation, New York

University, Graduate School of Arts and Sciences, New
York, 1954.
Seaich, John E. "Leichtentritt's History of the Motet: A
Study and Translation (Chapters 7-15)." Unpublished
Ph.D. dissertation, University of Utah, Salt Lake City,
1958.

MOTET-ANTHEM see ANTHEM

MULTIPLE CHOIR PROGRAM see GRADED CHOIR
PROGRAM

MUSICA DEO SACRA (L.)

     Subtitled "Musick dedicated to the Honor and Service
of God, and to the Use of Cathedral and other Churches of
England" is the Musica Deo Sacra. This collection of church
music by Thomas Tomkins (1575?-1656) was gathered and
published by his son, Nathaniel, in 1668. It is contained in
five volumes after the tradition of the *part-book; four volumes of the various voice-parts and one pars organica (or-
gan-part). The contents include five services (TCM, VIII),
five settings of *canticles, one set of *preces and *responses,
antiphonal settings of two psalms, 41 *verse-anthems, 29
*full anthems, six anthems for men's voices, 19 anthems for
three-part mixed voices, and five metrical psalms (25 verse-
anthems in EECM, V & IX).

Cavanaugh, Robert W. "The Anthems in Musica Deo Sacra
     by Thomas Tomkins." Unpublished Ph.D. dissertation,
     University of Michigan, Lansing, 1953.
Rose, Bernard (ed.). Thomas Tomkins: Music Deo Sacra
     II, Vol. IX, Early English Church Music, London:
     Stainer and Bell, 1963.

MUSICIANERS see MUSICKERS

MUSICKERS

     Members of the *Old Church Gallery Minstrels were
called musickers or musicianers, whether they played an
instrument or sang.

MUSIC THERAPY (OF. musique, fr. L. musica, fr. Gr.
mousike any art over which the Muses presided, fr.
mousikos belonging to the Muses or fine arts, fr.
Mousa Muse + NL. therapia, fr. G. therapia)

    The use of music as an agent for the prevention of
illness, the alleviation of disease or the helpmate of physical
or mental health may be considered music therapy. The
history of music as therapy is almost as old as time itself
with evidences being found in ancient Egyptian and Persian
cultures. The classic Biblical example, often used as a
basis for therapy in church music, is the account in I Samuel
16:14-23 of the singing and playing of David to sooth the rav-
aged spirit of King Saul. The ancient Greeks and Romans,
Plato, Xenocrates and Pythagoras, also saw music as a
therapeutic agent. The history of music therapy to the present century is recorded elsewhere, [e.g. Gaston and Podolsky]
and the interested reader is encouraged to seek this information. It is the concern here of the use of music as therapy
within the Protestant church.
    Since music is considered as an essential and neces-
sary function of man, having influenced his behavior and
conditions for thousands of years, it becomes essential to
look at the music ministry within the Protestant church as
a potentially therapeutic agent. Such an attitude must have
been realized on the part of Martin Luther when he placed
the emphasis on the *congregational singing of his followers.
For, through the group singing of *hymns a spirit of community is achieved which tends to alleviate painful aloneness.
Besides this spirit of closeness, music when properly used
can be the means for focusing the worshipper's mind on communion with God. Furthermore, a familiar hymn may be a
source of inner strength in one's daily routine through its
simple and direct voicing of a person's innermost thoughts.
    Within the structured music ministry of the local
church the organizational and educational aspects contribute
to the feeling of community through participation in the various choral and instrumental ensembles. Through these,
music permits personal feelings to be expressed and aids in
the merger of these feelings within the group. Some such
feelings to be expressed include the proclamation of truth,
the reiteration of history, the affirmation of faith, and the
consecration of self. To achieve this the *minister of music
must enlarge the vision of the Christian ministry to include
the whole person in his particular cultural context, in the
name of Christ.
    Considering a possible outreach of the music ministry

in the Protestant church, through guidance and communication with local institutions (as mental hospitals, Veteran's Administration Hospitals, convalescent homes, penal institutions, etc.) the various ensembles, particularly youth and adult, have provided concerts and led in worship services. More skilled persons in the church music ministry have volunteered their time to teach individual handicapped or exceptional persons under therapeutic treatment. A minister of music, extending his own outreach, has the potential to coordinate an institutional music ministry (as a choir at a penal institution) and that of his local congregation. The possibilities are limitless. The area of music therapy in church music is in its infancy and open to intelligent, creative and understanding approaches. The rewards are redemptive to both participants, patient and volunteer.

Gaston, E. Thayer. Music in Therapy. New York: Macmillan, 1968.
Podolsky, Edward (ed.). Music Therapy. New York: Philosophical Press, 1954.
Sims, John N. "The Therapeutic Dimension of Music Ministry," The Church Musician, 29:4-5, August, 1968; 29:8-9, September, 1968; 29:12-14, October, 1968.

MUSIKANDAKT   (Sw. Music-worship)

     A presentation, similar to the German *Abendmusik, yet apart from the liturgical services, which combines the emphasis of music and worship in the churches of Sweden is designated Musikandakt. These recital-services consist of about a half-hour of music focused on a definite idea followed by a brief period of worship, including a hymn, lesson and prayer.

NACHSPIEL   see   POSTLUDE

NARRATOR   (fr. L. narratus, fr. narrare to narrate, prob. for gnarare, fr. gnarus knowing)

     The singer, who in *cantatas, *oratorios and *passions (occasionally operas) gives the exposition of the dramatic idea usually in *recitative, is called the narrator, testo or

*historicus. In the passion settings he may be called Evan-
gelista or Chronista. After the reign of the Baroque oratorio, the duties of the narrator were dissolved and absorbed
by the various other soloists.

Wienandt, Elwyn A. Choral Music of the Church. New
      York: The Free Press, 1965.

NEGRO SPIRITUAL see SPIRITUAL

NEUME (F. fr. ML. neuma a group of notes sung to a
      final syllable as long as the breath lasts, fr. Gr.
      pneuma breath)

      In the notation of *plainsong, the notes which can indi-
cate one or more tones are called neumes. This term appeared in the 11th century and has been used from then on
to specify the written signs of Gregorian notation. However,
neume notation was familiar in Rome as early as the seventh
century according to the Venerable Bede.

Apel, Willi. The Notation of Polyphonic Music (900-1600).
      Cambridge, Mass.: The Medieval Academy of
      America. 1945.
Parrish, Carl. The Notation of Medieval Music. New
      York: W. W. Norton, 1957.
Tack, Franz. Gregorian Chant. Köln: Arno Volk Verlag,
      1960. Pp. 8-12.

NEW VERSION

      The affectionate name for the second authorized met-
rical *psalter in England, the Tate and Brady, was the New
Version (1696). (See *Psalmody, metrical (England); and
*Psalters.)

NOËL (fr. L. natalis birthday)

      A Medieval *hymn or *canticle of French origin
(c.16th century), composed and performed in honor of the
nativity of the Christ-child, is called a noël. The predecessor of the English ballad *carol (also see *ballad), the
noël developed from a kind of popular song associated with

the narrative troubadour ballads, the popular entertainment
of medieval France.

Poulaille, H. La Grande et Belle Bible des Noëls anciens
 ... du XIIe au XVIe siècle. Paris: A. Michel, 1950.

NUNC DIMITTIS (L. nunc now + dimittis thou lettest
  depart)

  The Gospel *canticle from the office of *compline
commonly referred to as the "Song of Simeon" (Luke 2:29-
32), is the Nunc dimittis. It occurs as the second canticle
in the office of Evening Prayer (*Vespers), with the possible alternatives of the Deus misereatur of "Benedic, anima
mea." Although it was not included in Luther's original
order for *Vespers the Nunc dimittis was included as an
alternate for the *Magnificat in other early German liturgies
of the 16th century (Nürnberg, 1525, and Strasbourg, 1525).
  The Nunc dimittis also appeared in Jean Calvin's
Strasbourg French "Order of Communion" (1540) to be sung
in meter after the post-communion collect. However, this
was omitted in his Genevan order (1542), though its use
was probably continued.
  Although Anglican chant settings are normally employed, anthem settings do exist for chorus and/or soloists.

 "Lord, now lettest thou thy servant depart in peace,
 according to thy word; For mine eyes have seen thy
 salvation, which thou hast prepared before the face of
 all people; A light to lighten the Gentiles, and the
 glory of thy people Israel."

Fornacon, Siegfried. "Ein reformiertes Nunc Dimittis,"
 MK, 22:61-66, March-April, 1952.
Kulp, Johannes. "Das Magnificat und das Nunc Dimittis,"
 MK, 7:271-277, November-December, 1935.
Reed, Luther D. The Lutheran Liturgy. Philadelphia:
 Muhlenberg Press, 1947.

OCCASIONAL MUSIC (OF., fr. L. occasio, fr., occidere,
  occasum, to fall down, fr. ob down + cadere to fall,
  + *music)

  The English term for music (chorale in particular)

written for a specific historical event (such as thanksgiving
for a victory at battle, funeral of royalty or coronation) is
occasional music. Representative anthems of this are: John
Blow (1649-1708), "Let my prayer come up" (TECM, 3:68),
for the coronation of William and Mary (1689); William Croft
(1678-1727), "The souls of the righteous," for the funeral of
Queen Anne (1714); and C. H. Hubert Parry (1848-1918), "I
was glad," for the coronation of Edward VII (1902).

Fellowes, Edmund H. English Cathedral Music. London:
    Methuen, 1946.

OFFERTORY (L. offertorium)

Originally, a procession of the faithful bringing their
food and gifts for the clergy and the poor to be dedicated to
God, the offertory has come to mean different things among
different religious groups. In the Anglican church the offertory is the time for presenting the alms collected and the
placing of the eucharistic elements on the Holy Table. During this time sentences (offertory sentences) may be read or
a *hymn or *anthem may be sung. Among the Lutheran
congregations the verses of the psalms or other variable
*offertory sentences sung following the offering and before
the general prayer in the *Eucharist are considered the offertory. However, during the mid-19th century, among the
non-liturgical congregations the meaning of the offertory developed into the music (hymn, anthem or instrumental work)
performed during the collection of monetary gifts.

Procter, Francis and H. W. Frere. A New History of the
    Book of Common Prayer. London: Macmillan, 1955.
    Pp. 497-482.
Reed, Luther D. The Lutheran Liturgy. Philadelphia:
    Muhlenberg Press, 1947. Pp. 310-312.

OFFERTORY SENTENCES (*offertory)

The collection of passages of Scripture (generally
from the Book of Psalms) appointed to be said during the
gathering of the alms and the presentation of the Eucharist
elements in the service of *communion is called the offertory sentences. These passages were set to music as offertory anthems by many Victorian composers.

Michell, G. A. Landmarks in Liturgy. London: Darton,
    Longman and Todd, 1961. Pp. 41-75.

OFFICE (OF., fr. L. officium, prob. fr. opus work +
    facere to do)

In its most inclusive meaning, any prescribed order
or form of worship for a religious observance of the church
is an office. Historically, the term more specifically has
denoted the eight daily office hours (*Canonical Hours or
divine offices) of the Roman Catholic Church, the *Opus Dei.
However, from the Reformation it has also been applied to
the morning and evening prayer services of the Anglican and
Lutheran churches, as well as certain portions of the order
of worship (e.g., Office of the Word, Office of Communion,
etc.). (See also *Morning Prayer; *Matins; *Vespers;
*Deutsche Messe; and *Full service.)

OFFICE HYMN (*office + *hymn)

A hymn appointed for use during one of the *Canonical Hours is the office hymn. Its heritage lies in the wealth
of Latin hymns written for the various Roman office hours.
Although they are not appointed for use in the Anglican
Morning and Evening Prayer Services, according to the
*Book of Common Prayer, many of the Latin hymns have
been translated and employed in the churches, particularly
following the first lesson at Evening Prayer (*Vespers).
In the Lutheran liturgy the term, office hymn, appears separating the *Venite from the other *psalms in
*Matins. At *Vespers, the term does not occur as German
hymns were supplied in place of the Latin office hymns.

Dearmer, Percy (ed.). The English Hymnal. London: Ox-
    ford University Press, 1933. (Pp. 985f contain office
    hymns.)
Knaresborough, Bishop of. "Where Should the Office Hymn
    Be Put?" ECM, 31:69-70, October, 1961.

OLD CHURCH GALLERY MINSTRELS

In accordance with the Order of Council (1644) from
the House of Lords, which removed all organs, art works
and liturgical garb from the Church of England, instrumental

music and virtually all choral music was dealt the deathly
blow of silence and destruction in the religious life of England. Thus, when Charles II began his reign in 1660 permitting the use of music (including instrumental accompaniment) in worship, volunteer musicians of some proficiency
in nearly every village banded together in the rear gallery
of the local churches to provide the music for the worship
service. They became known as the Old Church Gallery
Minstrels. These Restoration music makers, called "musicianers" or *"musickers", flourished from 1660 to 1860 in
the village churches of England.
      The membership in the Old Church Gallery Minstrels
varied from parish to parish. Normally it consisted of three
to eight (occasionally a dozen or more) voluntary players and
an SATB choir of men, women and children. Often the membership within a village band would represent proud family
histories of several generations.
      Regarding the instrumentation of the Gallery musi-
cians, great variation existed. A few of the representative
instruments included the flute, clarinet, bass-viol, bassoon,
violin, trombone, oboe, serpent, flageolet, ophicleide, cor-
nopean, fife, Kent-bugle, French horn, pitch-pipe, triangle,
barrel organ and reed organ. The musical literature was
primarily that of the *Old and New Versions, but no hymnbooks. (See *Psalmody, metrical (England).) One early
instruction book influencing the performance of these minstrels was John Playford's Introduction to Music (1664) with
"Rules and Directions for Singing the Psalms."

Hardy, Thomas. Under the Greenwood Tree. (A fiction
      about the old Mellstock Quire). London: Chatto and
      Windus, 1868.
MacDermott, K. H. The Old Church Gallery Minstrels.
      London: S.P.C.K., 1948.

OLD VERSION

      The affectionate name for the first authorized metrical
*psalter in England, also called the Sternhold and Hopkins
Psalter, was the Old Version (1562). (See *Psalmody, metrical (England); and *Psalters.)

OPUS DEI (L.)

      The continuous and orderly singing of the liturgical

services of the church which traditionally is the primary duty
of members of a contemplative religious community, and the
principal responsibility of the clergy attached to it is the
Opus Dei or Work of God.   The tradition of the Opus Dei
was continued after the Reformation in the Anglican Cathedral system.   (See *Canonical Hours.)

ORATORIO (It. orig., place of prayer, fr. LL. oratorium;
        so called from musical services in the oratory of St.
        Philip Neri in Rome)

        [Contents: (general); Early history; Italy; Germany;
England; France; America; (bibliography).]   The oratorio is
a musical art form with an extended libretto of a religious
or contemplative character for chorus, solo voices, orchestra and/or organ, independent of, or at least separable from
the liturgy.   It may be performed in the concert hall or
church, being without scenery, costume or action.   In the
oratorio the chorus has greater emphasis placed on it than
in the opera.   It lacks the quick dialogue of opera, but frequently incorporates a narrator (testo, or *historicus) to
introduce the personalities and prepare the mental image.
Compositions of a similar character, such as the *mass,
*passion, and *requiem, which are based on a scriptural or
liturgical text, are usually not considered in this category.
However, there are passion oratorios whose texts incorporate the passion story rather loosely.   Basically, length
distinguished the oratorio from the *cantata; the former
being more extended and of a continuous nature.

Early History

        The preparatory foundations for the oratorio were
made by early types of dramatic music, the *liturgical
dramas of the late Middle Ages and the mysteries of the
14th and 15th centuries.   However, the history of oratorio,
per se, began in the mid-16th century under the leadership
of Saint Philip Neri (1515-95), one of the greatest spiritual
leaders of the Renaissance.   In Rome, he inaugurated a
special order called the "Oratorians" (Oratoriani), which
persons congregated in the oratory (chapel) of the Church
of San Girolamo della Carita for regular services of a popular character--much like those of the Salvation Army.   These
services included scripture readings, sermons and the singing of hymns of religious praise and devotion, laudi spirituali.
A special type of *laudi were the dialogue-laudi, i.e., re-

ligious poems in the form of a dialogue between God and the
Soul, Heaven and Hell, etc. These were performed by different singers or, more accurately--considering their polyphonic style--by different groups of singers who might have
dressed according to the characters they represented. It is
from these presentations (called rappresentazione, storia,
esempio, misterio) that the oratorio properly developed.
Palestrina as well as other famous 16th-century composers
is reputed to have written music for such occasions. With
these performances in Rome, commonly called oratorios, it
was not long before all of Europe received it under the title
Drama Sacra per Musica (Sacred Drama of Music).

Italy

        Around the same time that Jacopo Peri (1561-1633)
and Giulio Caccini (1546-1618) were seeking to develop a
new style of dramatic music (early opera) in Florence,
Emilio del Cavalieri (c.1550-1602) attempted the same in
Rome. From this came his sacred drama, La Rappresentazione del Anima e del Corpo (Representation of the Soul
and of the Body, February 1600, CdMI, X), which was
written in the newly invented stile rappresentativo. First
performed at the Oratory of S. Maria in Vallincella (Rome),
one of Neri's oratories, it is generally considered the
earliest example of oratorio ever presented in public.
(Some writers claim it as "sacred opera" because of its
costuming, ballets, and elaborate staging--see, e.g., GD,
II, 127.) The general character of the music permits no
distinction between recitative and aria. The next recorded
attempt with oratorio in Italy was Giovoni Francesco Anerio's
(1567-1620) Teatro Armonico Spirituali (The Harmonious
Spiritual Theater, 1619) in which a refined madrigal style
is adopted for the choral portions, alternating with monody
for the solo parts within which the use of a narrator is already found.
        In 1622, Vittorio Loreto (early 17th century) set to
music his Saint Ignatius Loyola of which neither poetry nor
music is extant. However, Erythnaeus reports of its
finest excellence and great success. Loreto wrote two other
oratorios: La Pellegrina Constante (The Constant Pilgrim,
1647), and Il Sagrifizio d'Abramo (The Sacrifice of Abraham,
1648).
        Other oratorios of this period included Michelangelo
Cappelini's (17th century) Il Lamento di S. Maria Vergine
(Lament of St. Mary the Virgin, 1627); S. Alessio (1632)
and Daniel (AMI, V), both by Stefano Landi (c.1590-1655);

and <u>Erminia sul Giordano</u> (Erminia on the Jordan, 1637), by
Michel Angelo Rossi (c.1600-c.1660).   For these early compositions only the words are extant.

Greatly celebrated in its day was Domenico Mazzoc-
chi's (1592-1665) <u>Querimonia di S. Maria Maddalena</u> (Lamentation of St. Mary Magdalena, c.1640). This work is important not only for its refinement of expression, but also
as an example of <u>oratorio</u> vulgare--i.e., an oratorio in the
vernacular, not in Latin. He also wrote <u>Il Martirio dei SS.</u>
<u>Abbundio ed Abbundanzio</u> (The Martydom of Saints Abbundio
and Abbundanzio, 1631), performed in Rome. Yet his fame
rests mainly upon the <u>Querimonia ...</u>, which when performed by Vittorio Loreto, Buonaventura or Marcantonio,
reportedly drew tears from all who heard it.

As the oratorio settled into the 17th century it entered
a new phase--that of recognition as an art form. This was
due mainly to the work of Giacomo Carissimi (c.1605-1674),
the first composer of the monodic school to instill the new
style with a degree of dignity and pathos. In his <u>Jeptha,</u>
<u>Judicium Solomonis</u> (Judgment of Solomon), <u>Jonas, Abraham</u>
<u>et Isaac</u>, and <u>Extremum</u> Judicium (Last Judgment--CdMi, V,
Dt, II) one finds the first oratorios created which according
to their extension and diversity, their realistic and powerful
choruses and vital recitatives and arias, deserve this name.
It was at this time that the extravagant scenery and costuming began to decline in importance and the poetry was
modified to incorporate the personage of the *historicus
(testo). This person was assigned the narrative passages
interpolated between the clauses of the dialogue for the purpose of intelligent continuity in the absence of scenic action,
an idea undoubtedly influenced from the liturgical presentations of the passions during Holy Week. After Carissimi's
creative example, this practice was soon adopted throughout
Italy and Germany.

Following Carrissimi in the field of oratorio were
Antonio Draghi (1635-1700), who composed more than forty
oratorios; Alessandro Stradella (1645-1682), with his oratorio <u>S. Giovanni Battista</u> (St. John the Baptist, 1675) and
<u>Susanni</u> (1681); and Alessandro Scarlatti (1659-1725) who
wrote a large number of oratorios of which 18 are preserved
with the music. Among these are his <u>I Dolori di Maria</u>
<u>Sempre Virgine</u> (The Sorrows of Mary Ever Virgin, 1693),
<u>Passio secundum Ioannen</u> (St. John Passion, c.1680), <u>Il</u>
<u>Martirio di S. Teodoria</u> (The Martyrdom of St. Theodoria,
1685) and <u>La Concezzione della Beata Virgine</u> (The Conception of the Blessed Virgin, 1703). His craftsmanship shows
great breadth of style and dignity of manner achieved through

his contrapuntal skill. It was he who gave the aria the definite structure which it retained for more than a century --the da capo form of a first or principal strain, a second contrasting section and a return to the original material.

Representative of the Roman-Venetian tradition are the oratorios of Antonio Lotti (1667-1740) and Antonio Caldara (1670-1736). Their compositions presented a more reserved style, combining noble dignity with slightly sentimental pathos. On the other hand, the oratorios of the Neapolitan school were marked by virtuosity and vocal display, thus moving the form away from its ideal. Identified with the Neapolitan school are the eight extant oratorios of Leonardo Leo (1694-1744), including La Morte de Abele (The Death of Abel, 1732) and Il Trionfo della Castita di S. Alessio (The Triumph of the Chastity of St. Alessio, 1713?); the 14 by Johann Adolph Hasse (1699-1783), which include La Conversione di S. Agostino (The Conversion of St. Augustine, 1750, DdT, XX); and Nicola Jomelli's (1714-1774) La Passione di Gesu Cristo (The Passion of Jesus Christ, 1749, CdMi, XV).

Germany

While it is true that the oratorio had its birth in Italy alongside the opera, as it declined in importance relative to the opera, its religious liturgical music met the spirit of the passion music in Germany. Whereas the Italian oratorio as a whole stressed the importance of recreation, all other oratorios laid more importance on the religious materials.

The real link between Italy and Germany in the oratorio is Heinrich Schütz (1582-1672), who studied with Giovanni Gabrieli (1557-1612) and Claudio Monteverdi (1567-1643) and assimilated a great measure of their techniques. His works, including Historia der Auferstehung Jesu Christi (The Story of the Resurrection of Jesus Christ, 1673), Historia von der ... Geburt ... Jesus Christi (Christmas Oratorio, 1664), Die sieben Wörte Jesu Christi am Kreuz (The Seven Words of Jesus Christ on the Cross, c.1645) and the four passions (one according to each evangelist), are hailed as the first real fruits of German music. In these works, Schütz has one uppermost thought, i.e., to faithfully represent the subject matter in all its solemnity. Thus, his balanced arched form and extensive use of musical symbolism displace any hint of staging and thought of attractiveness.

Upon the death of Schütz, the last remnants of plainsong as a basis for inspiration gave way to the indigenous product, the hymn or chorale. In 1672, Johann Sebastiani (1622-1683) produced a passion-oratorio (DdT, XVII) at Königsberg, as did Thomas Selle (1599-1663) (Cw, XXVI) and Johann Theile (1646-1724) (DdT, XVII), which belong to the category of the passion. From this time until that of J. S. Bach, composers showed a preference to the smaller form of the cantata. Disregarding his passions, Johann Sebastian Bach (1685-1750) wrote two oratorios--Weihnachts-Oratorium (Christmas Oratorio, 1733-1734) and Öster-Oratorium (Easter Oratorio, 1736?). The Christmas Oratorio, Bach's own title, is in reality a collection of six separate cantatas written for six separate holy days, from Christmas through Epiphany; however, the Easter Oratorio is more like the Schütz model, not being based on a chorale or hymn. Following J. S. Bach, a mixture of oratorio forms occurred --Johann Ernst Eberlin's (1702-1762) Der blutschwitzende Jesus (The Bleeding Jesus, 1755, DTOe, XXVIII:i); the intensely dramatic Der Tag des Gerichts (The Day of Judgment, 1761, DdT, XXVIII) of Georg Philipp Telemann (1681-1767); and Die Kindheit Jesu (The Childhood of Jesus, 1773) and Die Auferweckung des Lazarus (The Raising of Lazarus, 1773, DdT, LVI) of Johann Christoph Friedrich Bach (1732-1795). This period of development in the history of the oratorio came to a close with the truly fine works of Carl Philipp Emanuel Bach (1712-1788) as seen in his Die Israeliten in der Wüste (The Israelites in the Desert, 1775) and Die Auferstehung und Himmelfährt Jesu (The Resurrection and Ascension of Jesus, 1787). In C.P.E. Bach, there is a unique eclecticism, a looking backward to the work of his father and a foresight of the vocal handling and orchestration of Haydn.

Next in importance are the works of Joseph Haydn (1732-1809). His Il Ritorno di Tobias (The Return of Tobias, 1775) and the deeply moving Die sieben Wörte am Kreuz (The Seven Words on the Cross, 1797), originally a string quartet) mark a new era in oratorio writing, the former often claimed to be the finest example of this form in the 18th century. Later Haydn wrote two more oratorios, Die Schöpfung (The Creation, 1797) and Die Jahreszeiten (The Seasons, 1801). One might question the "sacredness" of the latter, though it is descriptive of God's handiwork, nature. This seems to be one of the last instances in history that the term oratorio is used this loosely, for the modern idea of the oratorio as a non-liturgical work of religious character has become firmly established. Coming early in Ludwig van Beethoven's (1770-1827) life, the difficult Christus am Olberg (Christ on the Mount of Olives, op.

85) was his only use of this form, though he contemplated
another one later in life, to be entitled Die Höllenfahrt des
Erlösers (The Descent into Hell of our Savior).

During the first half of the 19th century, Germany
was passing through a period of oratorio worship, similar
to that of England. Lesser artistic works were met with
tremendous popular success--Ludwig Spohr's (1784-1859)
Das jüngste Gericht (The Last Judgment, 1811/1812),
Friedrich Schneider's (1786-1853) Das Weltgericht (Judgment
of the World, 1830), and Karl Loewe's (1796-1869) Hieb
(Job, 1848). It was Felix Mendelssohn (1809-1847) who
captured the spotlight in the last half of the 19th century.
His Paulus (St. Paul, 1836) and Elias (Elijah, 1846), with
their romantically colored Bach/Handel style, have earned
their place in oratorio literature.

After Mendelssohn several composers ventured into
the field of oratorio. Among some of these attempts are
included Liebesmahl der Apostel (Love-feast of the Apostles,
1844) by Richard Wagner (1813-1883); Die Legende von der
heiligen Elisabeth (The Legend of St. Elizabeth, 1863) and
Christus (1866), by the Hungarian Franz Liszt (1811-1886);
and St. Ludmila (1866), by the Bohemian Antonin Dvořák
(1841-1904).

Representative of the 20th-century oratorio are Paul
Hindemith's (1895-1963) Das Unaufhörliche (The Incessant,
1931), and Herman Reutter's (b.1900) Der grösse Kalender
(The Great Calendar, 1933), and Georg Schuman's (1866-
1952) Ruth (1909).

England

The oratorio, little known in England before Handel,
became a national institution with his skilled craftsmanship.
George Frideric Handel (as he styled his name in England)
(1685-1759) turned to this field of composition when his
operatic attempts proved dissatisfactory. And England was
awaiting such an art-form. From his early La Resurrezione
(The Resurrection, 1708) to his greater works--Israel in
Egypt (1738), Messiah (1741), Samson (1741), Judas Macca-
baeus (1746) and Jephtha (1751)--Handel reigned supreme.
Originally his oratorios were designed mainly for performance
during Lent, when British law forbade the presentation of
theatrical works.

Greatly overshadowed by the Handelian model were
other composers of these Lenten oratorios such as John
Christopher Smith (1712-1795), who composed Paradise Lost
(1758); Charles John Stanley (1712-1786), who wrote Jephtha

(1757), Zimri (1760), and The Fall of Egypt (1774); William
Boyce (c.1710-1779), David's Lamentation (1736); and Thomas
Arne (1710-1778), who wrote Abel (1744) and Judith (1764).
Upon the death of Arne in 1778, the English oratorio as an
art form became mired in the depths of works of indifferent
quality produced on demand to meet the appetites of the in-
satiable, oratorio-loving public.
    Following more than a century of this mediocrity a
notable revival of the English oratorio occurred. Representative of this renewed interest are Sir Arthur Sullivan's
(1842-1900) Light of the World (1873); Sir Hurbert Parry's
(1848-1918) Judith (1888), Job (1892) and King Saul (1894);
Sir Alexander Mackenzie's (1847-1935) The Rose of Sharon
(1884); and Sir Charles Stanford's (1852-1924) Eden (1891).
In the 20th century one discovers the works of Sir Edward
Elgar (1857-1934)--e.g., Dream of Gerontius (1900), The
Apostles (1903), and The Kingdom (1906); Walford Davies'
(1869-1941) Everyman (1904); William Walton's (b.1902)
Belshazzar's Feast (1931); and Robin Milford's (b.1903) The
Prophet in the Land (1929/30) and The Pilgrim's Progress
(1931/32). The oratorios of Martin Shaw (1875-1958) have
continued this traditional form in his Easter (1930), The
Rock (1934) and The Redeemer (1945) while Michael Tippett's
(b.1905) A Child of Our Times (1944), which incorporates
spirituals, stretches the form somewhat.

France
‾‾‾‾‾

    The oratorio in France had uncertain growth, but
bore strong marks of its Italian model. Relatively obscured
by the great Lully, Marc-Antoine Charpentier (1634-1704), a
pupil of Carissimi, produced the first major oratorios in
France--Histoires Sacrées (Sacred Histories), Judicium Solo-
monis (Judgment of Solomon), Filius Prodigius (Prodigal Son),
and Le Reniement de St. Pierre (The Denial of St. Peter),
all being in Latin.
    About a century and a half later the form was rein-
stated by Hector Berlioz (1803-1869) in his oratorio L'En-
fance du Christ (The Childhood of Christ, 1854). This work
was followed by César Franck's (1822-1890) Les Béatitudes
(The Beatitudes, 1879) and Rebecca (1881); neither of which
has retained a major role in oratorio history.
    Representative of a different type of oratorio, the
salon oratorio, are the works of Gounod, Massenet and
Saint-Saëns. Jules Massenet's (1842-1912) approach was
quite Parisian, as seen in his Marie Magdeleine (1873) and
Eve (1875). The approaches of Charles Gounod (1818-1893)

in La Redemption (1881) and Mors et Vita (Death and Life,
1884), and Camille Saint-Saëns (1835-1921), particularly in
Le Deluge (The Flood, 1876) and the Promised Land (1913),
were more in line with the English taste.

In the 20th century the outstanding representative of
oratorio is Arthur Honegger's (1892-1955) Le Roi David (King
David, 1923), a work which is eclectic in style, incorporating
Hebrew melodies, the polyphony of J. S. Bach, and even
jazz. However, preceding him was Gabriel Pierne (1863-
1937), whose La Croisade des Enfants (The Crusade of the
Children, 1905) and Les Enfants à Bethlehem (The Children
of Bethlehem, 1907) call on vast resources of children's
voices.

America

The first oratorio to be created in America came al-
most a century after the founding of the nation.   John
Knowles Paine (1839-1906), dean of the Harvard University
School of Music, wrote Saint Peter in 1873.   Others soon
followed his example.   Among them were two immigrants,
Max Vogrich (1852-1916), who composed The Captivity (1884),
and Humphrey Stewart (1856-1937), who wrote The Nativity
(1888).   Of major importance are the oratorios of Horatio
Parker (1863-1919); his Hora Novissima (Cometh Earth's
Latest Hour, 1894) shows fine craftsmanship and good cho-
ral writing, as does The Legend of St. Christopher (1898).

In the 20th century, the oratorio has not been fostered
so much by composers as by conductors, who have been re-
viving and reproducing already existing works.   However,
Leo Sowerby (1895-1968) has written three--e.g., The
Vision of Sir Launfal (1926).   More recent interest has come
from Ronald Nelson, What Is Man? (1965), and David Brubeck, Light in the Wilderness (1968).

Burkholder, Samuel Ray.   "The Oratorio: Its Development
        Since the Time of Mendelssohn." Unpublished Mus. D.
        dissertation, Northwestern University, Evanston, Illi-
        noise, 1938.
Patterson, Annie W.   The Story of Oratorio.   London:
        Walter Scott Pub. Co., 1902.
Schering, A.   Geschichte des Oratorium.   Leipzig: Breit-
        kopf and Härtel, 1911.
Upton, George.   The Standard Oratorio.   Chicago: A. C.
        McClurg, 1888.
Wienandt, Elwyn A.   Choral Music of the Church.   New
        York: The Free Press, 1965.

ORCHESTRAL INSTRUMENTS (L., fr. Gr. orchestra, orig.,
the place for the chorus of dancers, fr. orcheisthai
to dance, + OF. instrument, estrument, fr. L. in-
strumentum, fr. instruere to construct, equip)

The mechanical devices which produce musical sound
and commonly are included in a large performing ensemble,
known in the 18th through the present as the orchestra, are
orchestral instruments. These may be classified into three
categories: stringed instruments, wind instruments and percussion instruments. The wind instruments may be divided
further into woodwind and brass instruments (see *Brass
choirs).

Historically, the use of instruments in the worship of
God is readily traced to the Jewish temple services and is
verified by their specific mention in the Book of Psalms.
However, during the first ten centuries of the history of the
Christian church, the use of instruments in worship for all
practical consideration was non-existent. By the 14th and
15th centuries, the use of instruments other than the organ
appeared as accompaniment to vocal compositions in the
church. With the coming of the Reformation in Germany,
at a time when the concertato style of the Gabrielis was
exerting an influence, various types of instruments were incorporated into worship services through polyphonic hymn
arrangements. The works of Michael Praetorius (1517-1621)
clearly favored the use of instruments in worship as he discussed his concerti in book three of his Syntagma Musicum.
By the mid-17th century, instrumental music had generally
become equal to vocal music. This is seen in the cantatas
of J. S. Bach (1685-1750) and in the oratorios of G. F.
Handel (1685-1759). Instrumental interludes in the services,
between the *Epistle and the *Gospel, were so accepted that
by the early 18th century the "epistle sonata" and the sonata
da chiesa had attracted such composers as Dittersdorf (1759-
1799) and W. A. Mozart (1756-1791).

While the 18th and 19th centuries generally saw the
movement of music, including instrumental music, away
from the church, it must be noticed that the Moravian Brethren maintained a strong tradition of instruments in worship
through this period. As they emigrated to America they
quickly established their musical heritage with a trombone
choir in 1744, a tradition still current. It was from this
beginning that they developed the first symphony orchestra
in this country, performing Haydn's Creation in 1810 (the
American premiere) in Bethlehem, Pennsylvania.

A late 19th-century development in the use of instru-

ments in Protestant church music was the formation of the
first Salvation Army Band in 1873. Through the use of wind
and percussion instruments the Salvation Army has attracted
many people to its cause.

Incorporation of the various orchestral instruments
into the worship services and Christian education programs
of the Protestant church has become more commonplace in the
mid-20th century. Particularly common has been the use of
brass and woodwinds with choirs and with congregational
singing. However, instrumental ensemble music may be
provided in place of the organ *voluntaries. (Also see *Old
Church Gallery Minstrels.)

Boeringer, James. "Praise the Lord with Everything," JCM,
    12:2-4, February, 1970; 12:6-8, March, 1970; 12:2-5,
    May, 1970; 12:6-8, June, 1970; 12:11-13, July-August,
    1970; 12;12-14, October, 1970.
Friedemann, Lilli. "Instrumentalpflage in der Kirche,"
    MK, 28:205-208, September-October, 1958.
Gelineau, Joseph. Voices and Instruments in Christian Wor-
    ship. Collegeville, Minn.: The Liturgical Press,
    1964.
Mansfield, Orlando A. "Some Anomalies in Orchestral Ac-
    companiments to Church Music," MQ, 2:199-209,
    April, 1916.
Pirner, Reuben G. "Instruments in Christian Worship,"
    Church Music, 70.1[sic]:3, 1970.
Torbian, Hellen. The Instrumental Ensemble in the Church.
    New York: Abingdon Press, 1963.

ORDINARY (L. ordinarius, fr. ordo, ordinis order)

    The non-variable portions of the *mass compose the
*ordinary, in contradistinction to the variable ones known as
the *proper. Included in the ordinary are the *Kyrie eleison,
*Gloria in excelsis, *Credo, *Sanctus, *Benedictus qui venit
and *Agnus Dei. (Also see *Communion service.)

Reindell, Walter. "Das 'Ordinarium'," Kirchenchordienst,
    1:6-13, January-February, 1935.

OREMUS (L.)

    The brief salutation, invitation or bidding often sung
before liturgical prayers is called the oremus. In its sim-

plest form it may be, "Let us pray." In the Eastern Rite
the imperative "Pray" is employed; while the Byzantine form
is "In peace let us pray to the Lord." Historically, the
oremus served as an invitation to private prayer with which
specific requests were coupled (similar to "guided prayers").
Thus, this bidding originally introduced a period of silent
prayer with the *collect serving as a brief conclusion to
these prayers.

In the *Book of Common Prayer the oremus maintains
two functions: to mark the change from versicles and responses to prayers of the collect-type and to mark the beginning of the prayer-sections of the services.

Reed, Luther D. The Lutheran Liturgy. Philadelphia:
    Muhlenberg Press, 1947. Pp. 423-424.

ORGAN (OF. & L.; OF. organe, fr. L. organum, fr. Gr.
    organon)

A keyboard instrument whose tone is produced by a
vibrating column of air within the given pipework is a pipe
organ. This instrument may contain one or more keyboards
connected mechanically (i.e., with tracker action), pneu-
matically, electrically or electro-pneumatically to one or
more sets (ranks) of pipes, the pipework being positioned on
a windchest which channels the air to the selected pipes.

From its legendary ancestry of the "Syrinx" (pan-
pipes) through the hydraulos (Ktesibios, c. 250 B.C.) and the
early pneumatic organs (c. A.D. 120), the organ developed
into the crude mechanical instrument at the Winchester Cathedral (c. 950) whose exceedingly powerful sound came from
its supposed 400 pipes controlled by two keyboards of 20
"keys" each and 26 bellows. By the time of the Reformation
the organs of Germany had become firmly established in the
churches. These instruments were quite advanced, having
two or more manuals, individually controlled registers and
an independent pedal division.

The use of the organ during the first century of the
Reformation remained similar to that of the Roman Catholic
tradition, that of alternatum. The congregation and organ
would alternate in the presentation of stanzas or portions of
the service. The organ also became important in the introduction of most sung portions of the service, establishing the
key or tonal center. However, it did not accompany the
singing by choir, congregation or cantor as the choral polyphony of the day did not adapt to instrumental accompaniment
by the organ.

During the 17th century the organ was used to accompany the congregational and choral singing since the
*cantus firmus of the *chorale was lifted from the tenor to
the top voice part. One of the earliest evidences of this
practice was Johann Hermann Schein's (1586-1630) Cantional
(1627), which included a figured bass accompaniment to the
four- to six-part chorale settings. A similar occurrence
appeared in the hymnbooks of Hans Leo Hassler (1564-1612)
and Michael Praetorius (1560-1629). However, claimed to
be the first chorale book specifically designed and used to
accompany *congregational singing was Samuel Scheidt's
(1587-1654) Tabulatur-buch 100 geistlicher Lieder und
Psalmen D. Martini Lutheri und anderer gottseligen Manner.
Thus, the movement by composers and organists of the Reformed tradition to develop organ composition in new directions through the arrangement of chorale melodies (see
*Chorale prelude) occurred, a development culminating in
the chorale compositions of J. S. Bach (1685-1750). Although the organ was permitted to accompany congregational
singing by the mid-17th century, it still provided introductions and interludes to the hymns and chants.

While the above practice developed on the Continent,
in 17th-century England and Scotland the advent of Puritanism
was silencing choral singing and organ music in the church.
This devastating movement against the organ was felt in
English churches for the next two centuries. However, with
the Restoration a few organs appeared in the larger cathedrals, providing a thread of organ tradition in English church
music.

By the 18th century the services of the Lutheran
churches on the Continent traditionally were begun with an
organ prelude; the instrument was also used to accompany
congregational singing and the choral music (motets and cantatas). With the accompanying of the congregational hymns
came the insertion of organ *interludes between *stanzas
(see *Zwischenspiel), a practice which by the early 19th
century grew to interluding between *verses.

The influence of the 17th-century Puritan organ purge
remained alive in the 19th-century organ controversies within
the churches of England and Scotland, though the organ was
clearly gaining ground. By the mid-19th century Congre-
gationalist, Presbyterian and Anglican churches were in-
stalling organs.

Organs were known to have existed in churches in
America as early as 1703. Their use in services was similar to that of the European congregations. With the coming
of the 19th century the "American organ" or reed organ was

developed by Mason and Hamlin. This instrument provided
the organ accompaniment to services in the small churches
of America and was exported as well to England for similar
use (see *Harmonium).
    In the 20th century, a renewed interest in organ music
for the church has appeared. Composers such as Ernst Pepping (b. 1901), Helmut Walcha (b. 1907), Ralph Vaughan Williams
(1872-1958), Healey Willan (1880-1968) and Leo Sowerby
(1895-1967) have provided compositions suitable for organ
voluntaries for before and after services. T. Tertius Noble
(1867-1953), David N. Johnson (b. 1922) and others have aided
organists by providing free harmonizations (see *Free accompaniment) and introductions to hymns for accompanying congregational singing. 20th-century technology has also produced the electronic organ, which has provided an assimilated
organ tone and made it available at a minimal cost to many
churches. Thus, with the exception of few Protestant denominations the organ has become the "church tone" of 20th-
century church music.

Arnold, Corliss Richard. Organ Literature: A Comprehen-
    sive Survey. Metuchen, N.J.: Scarecrow Press, 1973.
Bibliotheca Organologica. Vols. I-IX of XIII. Hilversum,
    1962 (facsimile reprints of older works about organ
    building and performance).
Bruinsma, Henry A. "The Organ Controversy in the Nether-
    lands Reformation to 1600," JAMS, 6:205-212, Summer,
    1954.
Frotscher, G. Geschichte des Orgelspiels und der Orgel-
    kompositionen. 2 vols. Berlin: Merseburger, 1959.
Haupt, R. Die Orgel in evangelischen Kultraum in Ges-
    chichte und Gegenwart. Vol. II, Orgelwissenschaftliche
    Arbeits- und Musikgemunschaft. Hillerse: Rudolf
    Haupt, 1954.
Liemohn, Edwin. The Organ and Choir in Protestant Wor-
    ship. Philadelphia: Fortress Press, 1968.
Sumner, William Leslie. The Organ: Its Evolution, Princi-
    ples of Construction and Use. London: Macdonald,
    1962.

ORGAN CHORALE   see   CHORALE PRELUDE

OXFORD MOVEMENT (OE. oxnaford, lit., oxen ford,
    whence ML. Oxonia + OF. --F. mouvement--fr. F.
    mouvoir, fr. L. movere)

The 19th-century religious movement of the Church of England which was greatly responsible for a deepening of spiritual growth was the Oxford Movement. Its commencement is dated July 14, 1833, with the delivery of John Keble's (1792-1866) sermon, "National Apostacy," at St. Mary's Church, Oxford. The distinctive characteristics of the Oxford Movement were its profound interest in the preservation and incorporation of the sacred traditions from the early Christian church of the first five centuries; its conception of the church as a divine, holy, catholic society; its objectivity toward accomplishing human salvation; and its reverence of sacramental and liturgical worship. Beside Keble, some of the outstanding leaders of the movement were John H. Newman (1801-1890), Hurrell Froude (1803-1836), Edward B. Pusey (1800-1882) and Isaac Williams (1802-1865).

The attempt of the Oxford Movement to revitalize the role of the church in a changing society was manifested in many ways, none the least of which were the multifarious tracts (thus, the name "Tractarians"). Its impact on Protestant church music has been felt in the heritage of hymns written, translated and compiled by the scholarly members of this movement, in the appreciation and incorporation of art and music in the church service, and in the reverence for the organization of the *Christian Year.

Among the hymnographers of the Oxford Movement are John Newman, "Lead, kindly light"; Frederick Faber (1814-1863), "Faith of our fathers"; and Matthew Bridges (1800-1894), "Crown him with many crowns." The inclusion of many Latin and Greek hymns in current hymnals is a result of members of the Oxford group such as Edward Caswell (1814-1878), "Jesus the very thought of thee," and John Mason Neale (1818-1866), "Of the Father's love begotten." However, one of its major hymnological contributions was the compilation of the hymnal, *Hymns Ancient and Modern, and the coordinated historical companion.

Over and above its contributions to hymnody the Oxford Movement brought about the appreciation of a high quality in church music, particularly choral. During this time the training of surpliced choirs was reintroduced as were the daily services.

Benson, Louis F. The English Hymn: Its Development and Use. Richmond, Va.: John Knox Press, 1962. Chapter 10.
Davies, Horton. Worship and Theology in England, 1690-1850. Vol. III. Princeton, N.J.: Princeton University Press, 1961. Chapter 10.

Ollard, S. L.   A Short History of the Oxford Movement.
   London: A. R. Mowbray, 1915.

PARAPHRASES (F., fr. L. paraphrasis, fr. Gr. paraphrasis, fr. paraphrazien to say the same thing in
   other words, fr. para beside + phrazien to speak)

   The metrical versions of Scriptural passages other
than the psalms are called paraphrases. From the very
beginning of the metrical paraphrasing of the psalms (see
*Psalmody, metrical), paraphrases of the canticles also ap-
peared (included in Calvin's Genevan Psalter). Likewise,
paraphrases appeared in the English Psalter (*Old Version)
and the *Scottish Psalter (1635). From this book on into
the 18th century, great controversy was experienced in the
Church of Scotland over paraphrases of Scripture. One of
the better known collections of this period was Patrick
Symson's (1556-1618) Spiritual Songs or Holy Poems (1685).
   The English movement toward paraphrases was exemplified in the work of William Barton (c.1603-1678) whose
Six Centuries of Selected Hymns and Spiritual Songs Collected
Out of the Holy Bible (1688) was a mixture of English prose
translations, handled in the freedom of metrical paraphrase
technique. This led to the development of the *hymns of
human composure by the father of English *hymnody, Issac
Watts (1674-1748).

Maclagan, Douglas J.   The Scottish Paraphrase. Edinburgh:
   Andrew Elliott, 1889.
Patrick, Millar.   Four Centuries of Scottish Psalmody.
   London: Oxford University Press, 1949.

PARODY MASS (F. or L.; parodie, fr. L. parodia, fr.
   Gr. parōidia, fr. para beside + ōide a song, +
   *mass)

   The musical setting of the ordinary of the *mass in
which a portion of the musical content or its entirety is drawn
from existing, often secular material is called a parody
mass. Primarily a Latin mass, it made inroads into the
early German Reformation through the deutsche Messen
which set the Ordinariumslieder in the form of the *chorale
motet. An early example of this can be found in Michael
Praetorius' (1571-1621) Polyhymnia Caduceatrix, 1619.

Lockwood, Lewis. "On 'Parody' as Term and Concept in
16th Century Music," in: Aspects of Medieval and
Renaissance Music, ed. Jan LaRue. New York: W.
W. Norton, 1966.

PARS (L. pars, partis a part)

A section of a *motet, *anthem or work of Lutheran
Kirchenmusik was referred to as pars or partes during the
late 15th and 16th centuries. Usually each pars within a
given work was of a contrasting style to the adjacent one.

PART-BOOK

A manuscript of the 15th or 16th century in which is
contained the music for an individual voice part of a polyphonic composition, instead of all the parts under one cover
as in the practice in present day octavos, is called a part-
book (in German, Stimmbuch). This practice, common
during the English Restoration Period, required a full complement of part-books--a cantus (discantus or superius);
altus; tenor and bassus (Bassis)--for performance. (Cf.
*choir-book.)

Apel, Willi. The Notation of Polyphonic Music 900-1600.
5th ed. Cambridge, Mass.: Medieval Academy of
America, 1961.
Ford, Wyn K. "An English Liturgical Partbook of the 17th
Century," JAMS, 13:144-160, Spring, 1961.

PARTES see PARS

PASSION (MUSIC)

[Contents: (general); The choral or plainsong passion;
Polyphonic passion; The motet passion; The oratorio passion
(17th century); The passion oratorio (19th century to the
present); (bibliography).] A musical setting of the text from
one of the Gospel accounts relating the events in the last
week of the life of Christ is known as a passion, or passion
music (in German, Passionmusik). Similar to the *oratorio,
the passion is an outgrowth of the medieval mystery plays
whose purpose was to enact the Gospel narratives, making

the stories intelligible to the people (cf. *Liturgical music-drama). As time progressed some plainsong doubtless was absorbed into the dramatic presentation, as music tends to do in every type of dramatic presentation, thus providing an important link with the passion.

The Choral or Plainsong Passion

Another source of passion music lies within the ecclesiastical custom of reciting in church the passion narratives in a dramatic way during Holy Week. Although this practice can be traced to the fourth century it was during the eighth century that one discovers a priest reciting the passion narrative from one Gospel with only the words of Christ being given out in traditional plainsong. The method became more elaborate through the centuries with a single voice transmitting all portions of the text using different ranges of the voices to convey different participants in the story: Christ received the lowest register, the evangelist the middle and the remaining characters (the synagoga) the highest. By the 15th century these clergy took part--the deacon, a tenor as narrator or evangelist; the priest, a bass, as Christ; and the sub-deacon, an alto as the disciples and the crowd (*turba). This practice, known as the choral passion or plainsong passion, continued through the Middle Ages with the four gospels being recited thusly on four days of Holy Week: St. Matthew's on Palm Sunday, St. Mark's on Tuesday, St. Luke's on Wednesday and St. John's on Good Friday.

Polyphonic Passion

The earliest attempts at polyphonic settings of the passion date from the mid-15th century in England. Two have survived in manuscript form in the British Museum (MS, Egerton 3307). Both the setting according to St. Matthew and the one according to St. Luke were written for the royal chapel of St. George, Windsor. They are both harmonized, three-voice settings of the "other speakers" and the turba, but not of the narrator or Christ. Thus, the interweaving of polyphonic settings among the plainsong in the dramatic passion achieved an increased dramatic effect over the plainsong setting of the choral passion. A four-part setting in the form of the St. George's Chapel Passions dating around 1500 is accredited to Richard Davy (fl. 1491-1506). The extant fragments of this work were reconstructed and completed by Sir Richard Terry and performed at Westminster Cathedral in 1921.

Whereas the French Calvinists eliminated the passion altogether from their Reformed liturgy, the German Lutheran followers maintained and adapted it, retaining the plainsong. Johann Walther (1496-1570), Luther's friend, adapted the dramatic passion to the Lutheran liturgy with a setting of the Matthew narrative (c.1550), representing an early association of Luther's vernacular (German) New Testament with ancient plainsong formulas. The evangelist, a tenor, departs from tradition by adopting a uniform cadence for Christ (bass) and the turba (DATB). Walther's Passion enjoyed wide usage, being performed as late as 1806. In performance practice the sermon usually separated Jesus' desertion by the disciples from His leaving the trial for crucifixion by a silent pause for the Lord's Prayer following the words, "Jesus yielded up the ghost."

About forty years later Antonio Scandello (1517-1580) wrote a St. John Passion for the court at Dresden blending the characteristics of the scenic and motet passion. Conventional plainsong remained solely for the evangelist, while all other parts received from two- to four-part harmony. However, the turba sentences were set in five parts (D_1D_2ATB).

Other notable composers of German texts were Jakob Neiland (1542-1577), Thomas Mencken (1550-1620), Bartholomäus Gesius (1555?-1613/14), Melchior Vulpius (1560?-1615), Samuel Besler (1574-1625), Otto Siegfried Harnisch (d.1630). Composers of Latin texts were Claude de Sermisy (d.1562), Francisco Guenero (1528-1599), Orlando Lassus (1532-1594), Tomás Luís Victoria (c.1535/40-1611), William Byrd (1543-1623), Jakob Reiner (1560?-1609), and Giovanni Matteo Asola (d.1609).

The Motet Passion

With the advancement of musical composition, the passion incorporated the more elaborate style in its entirety and became known in the 16th century as the motet passion. Basically this type of passion was an a cappella, polyphonic setting of the whole text, based on the plainsong cantus. An early setting of the St. Matthew Passion (actually a combination of all four gospels), traditionally misattributed to Jakob Obrecht (d.1505) and later verified as belonging to Antoine de Longueval (fl.1509-1552), seems to have been a model for this type of passion. Divided into three sections, the narrative and turba were usually set in four parts (DATB) and the words of Christ, Peter and Judas in two parts. A printed edition of this passion appeared in Wittenberg in 1538. It enjoyed wide popularity and influence. With this passion

being the first to mosaic all the Gospel accounts, it should
be noted that Longueval's solution to traditional announcement of the source in the <u>Exordium</u> was the simultaneous
naming of all sources:

"Passio Domini nostri Jesu Christi secundum $\begin{cases} \text{Johannem.} \\ \text{Lucam.} \\ \text{Matthaeum.} \\ \text{Marcum.''} \end{cases}$

It was this practice of incorporating all the Gospel narra-
tives which led eventually to settings of the Seven Last
Words. Other composers of motet passions include Johannes
Galliculus (c.1520-1550), who was the first German com-
poser to compose a Latin passion, Ludwig Daser (d.1589),
Jacobus Gallus (1550-1590), Vincenzo Ruffo (b.1554), Jacob
Regnart (1540-1600), Bartholomäus Gesius (1555?-1613/14)
and Orlando Lassus (1530 or 1532-1594).

The passion, being quickly assimilated into the Lutheran service, found its first expression in the vernacular
as a German motet passion in 1568 through Joachim von
Burgk's (Moller or Müller) (1541?-1610?/16?) Die deutsche
<u>Passion, das ist, die Historia des Leidens unsers Herrn</u>
<u>Jhesu Christi, nach dem Evangelisten S. Johannes in Figural</u>
<u>Gesang</u>. Other writers of German motet passions were Jo-
hannes Steurlin (1576), Johann Machold (1593), Johannes
Heroldt (1594), LeonHard Lechner (1594) and Christoph De-
mantius (1631).

During the period of transition from the choral and
motet passion to the oratorio passion several significant
works should be mentioned. One, belonging to the family
of motet passions is Ambrosius Beber's (fl.1610-1620) <u>Das</u>
<u>Leiden Unsers Herrn Jesu Christ nach dem Heiligen Evan-</u>
<u>gelisten Marco</u> (CW, LXVI). It is noted that the characters
are so arranged vocally as to portray their common action--
those who harm Christ by word (Peter, Judas and the
Sponge-bearer) being set AT; those who harm Christ by
deed (Judas, High Priest and Pilate) being ATB. The evangelist is portrayed in plainsong style similar to that used by
Heinrich Schütz some years later in his passion settings.

Important to the church music of Hamburg around the
mid-17th century was the composer, Thomas Selle (1599-
1663), whose <u>Passion nach dem Evangelisten Johannes</u> (CW,
XXVI) of 1643 was conceived in three sections. Whereas
Beber characterized his participants by various vocal arrangements, Selle used soloists, each accompanied by a
continuo and a unique instrumental grouping. The choir
(SATB) is used at the conclusion of each section (<u>intermedio</u>)
as a choral reflection in elaborate motet form.

Heinrich Schütz (1585-1672), often referred to as the

father of German music in the Baroque period, showed a
return to the long tradition of choral passions in his three
settings--according to St. Matthew, St. John and St. Luke
(1665-1666), the St. Mark Passion being a spurious work.
These passions consciously conceived in simplicity bear the
following characteristics: an absence of instrumental writing;
strict adherence to the Biblical text with the exception of the
exordium and conclusio; the limitation of all individual roles
to unaccompanied solo singing--a lyrical style for all but the
evangelist, who sang a kind of plainsong; imitative counterpoint. Thus, unlike his other choral works which were
most creative and innovative in compositional techniques,
Schütz turned back to a style untainted by secular associa-
tions to convey a deeply religious mood.

The Oratorio Passion (17th Century)

On the other hand, Heinrich Schütz was among the
first composers to break the traditions of setting the passion
story exclusively from one Gospel. In his Die Sieben Wörte
Jesu Christi am Kreuz (The Seven Words of Jesus Christ on
the Cross, c.1645), taken from all the Gospels. Schütz incorporated the Venetian influence of unspecified instruments,
using them both for accompaniment and for the two identical
symphoniae which frame the main body of the text. The
introitus, (exordium) and conclusio are short reflective introductory and final choruses a5 based on chorale texts. The
handling of the characters in the drama is most inventive,
being a combination of styles integrated into a unified whole.
The words of Jesus are set for tenor solo with a trio sonata
accompaniment; whereas, all other characters are accompanied solely by continuo. The evangelist part is not limited
to one voice, but to several different ones as well as to a
quartet of voices. Through the symmetry, restraint and inti-
mate nature of his treatment, Schütz has provided a most
reverent composition for Holy Week.
In the 1660's, with the first performance of Johann
Sebastiani's (1622-1683) Passion According to St. Matthew
(DdT, XVII, 1-103), evidences of opera and oratorio influences become clearly visible in passion composition. Beside his unique assignment of different instrumental accompaniments to each leading character, Sebastiani included reflective chorale stanzas for accompanied solo voice in order
that the congregation might experience a deep devotional
awakening. This added contemplative aspect was influential
in the passions of J. S. Bach. Also foreshadowing Bach
was Sebastiani's treatment of the words of Jesus with trio

sonata accompaniment. The turba sections incorporated
SATTB chorus with full instrumental accompaniment. However, it was through the treatment of the chorale verses in
arioso style that this work was truly an oratorio passion
(Wienandt, 302-303).

The St. Matthew Passion (CW, LXXVIII-LXXIX) by
Friedrich Funcke (1642-1699) moved this form closer to the
oratorio since it not only included reflective solos, choruses
and chorales but also brief sinfonia sections for strings. It
should be noted that the old style remained in the plainsong-
styled recitatives which were supported by figured bass.
Other composers of oratorio passions during this period, influencing future passion composition, were Johann Theile
(1646-1724), Johannes Georg Kühnhausen (fl. 1700), Augustin
Pfleger (fl. 1670) and Johann Kuhnau (1660-1722).

The Passion Oratorio (18th Century to the Present)

　　　By the early and mid-18th century, the influences of
the Italian opera had permeated the oratorio and passion
forms to such an extent that they became labeled as "sacred
opera." In 1704 the passion completely broke its ties with
the Biblical narrative with the rhymed libretto of Christian
Friedrich Hunold-Menantes, Der blütige und sterbende Jesus
(The Bleeding and Dying Jesus) set by Reinhard Keiser
(1674-1739). This work, containing no chorales, was composed in three cantatas of "soliloquia": the "Lamentations
of Mary Magdalene"; the "Tears of Peter"; and the "Love-
song of Zion's Daughter." Its final section served as an
inspiration for Brockes, Picander and Bach. Though not
well received by the clergy, this libretto found imitators in
Johann Ulrich König, Johann Georg Seebach and Johann
Philipp Kafer, to mention a few.

　　　Of great popularity in its day was the dramatic, operatic libretto by the Hamburg senator Barthold Heinrich
Brockes (1680-1747), Der für die Sunden der Welt gemärtere
und sterbende Jesus (Jesus Tormented and Dying for the Sins
of the World, 1712), which enjoyed setting by such composers as Keiser, Telemann, Mattheson and Handel. Handel's
setting of Brockes' passion in 1717 reveals a greater maturity
in German sacred music and restraint in the adaptation of
Italian styles than does his earlier St. John Passion (1703).
The arias are intensely passionate, but yet the grandiose
gestures of opera are restrained to only a few climactic
moments.

　　　Georg Philipp Telemann (1681-1767), wrote 44 settings
of the passion many of which contained popular operatic de-

vices. These included a setting of Brockes' passion, a
three-part passion, Blissful Reflections upon the Sufferings
and Death of Our Lord, and his St. John Passion (1741).
     Also relying on Brockes' passion text, Johann Sebas-
tian Bach (1685-1750) wrote his St. John Passion (BGA, XII)
(finished in Leipzig, 1723). This marks a return, in part,
to the Biblical account with the St. John narrative being used
for the recitatives and short turba choruses, together with
masterful blend of Brockes' poetry reflecting through the
arias and large choruses and Lutheran chorales. The St.
John Passion marks the decline of the Hamburg operatic
passion in northern Germany.
     Bach's other extant passion, the St. Matthew Passion
(BGA, IV, 1729) incorporated the text, Über den leidenden
Jesus, by Picander (Christian Friedrich Henrici) with the
evangelist's account. This is the larger and more lyrical
of the two passions, introducing a non-Biblical figure "the
daughter of Zion." The musical forces require a double
chorus in eight parts, two orchestras and a boys' choir.
Through his ingenious blending of non-Biblical lyrics and
Biblical narrative into a congruous whole, Bach has indeed
restored the genuine spirit of the passion, elevating it to
new heights. Only a portion of the St. Mark Passion remains in the Trauer-Ode of 1727. All claims of other passions by Bach have been disproven.
     The liturgical order for the performing of Bach's
passions on Good Friday at *Vespers in Leipzig was as
follows:

     Chorale: Da Jesus an den Kreuze stand
     Part I of the Passion
     Chorale: O Lamm Gottes unschuldig
     Chorale: Herr Jesus Christ, dich zu uns wend
     Sermon
     Part II of the Passion
     Motet: Ecce quonodo moritur justus--Gallus
     Passion collect (intoned)
     Chorale: Nun danket alle Gott
     Blessing

Following the death of J. S. Bach the passion was treated
mainly in *cantata or *oratorio form. Johann Ernest Bach
(1722-1777) wrote the Passionoratorium (DdT, XLVIII);
C.P.E. Bach wrote two passions for Hamburg use (1787,
1788).
     Other passion music of import following the height of
its development in the Baroque era include settings of the
seven (Last) words, Stabat Mater and passion cantatas and

oratorios. A partial listing of works includes K. H. Graun's Der Tod Jesu (1755), Haydn's Die sieben Wörte am Kreuz (1785), Beethoven's Christ am Ölberge (1803), Ludwig Spohr's Des Heilands letzte Stunden (1835), John Stainer's Crucifixion (1887), and Arthur Sommervell's The Passion of Christ (1914).

With the 20th-century Bach revival, renewed interest has been kindled in the true spirit of the passion. Evidence of this revival are the Motet-Passion (1927) of Kurt Thomas, the Choral-Passion (1933) of Hugo Distler, the Passionbericht des Matthäus (1949-1950) by Ernst Pepping, and Passionsbericht des Matthäus (1948) by Hans Friedrich Micheelsen. The first two are truly in the style of Heinrich Schültz, being polyphonic settings with soloists, chorus and the use of chorales. The latter settings are for chorus a2-a10 with no soloists, as they are motet passions. Micheelsen has also written two other passions, according to St. John and St. Mark. In the character of the oratorio passion with multi-choruses, soloists and orchestra is the austere sounding Passion According to St. Luke (1965) by Krzysztof Penderecki (b.1933).

Adams, H. M.   "Passion Music Before 1724," ML, 7:258-264, July, 1926.
Braun, Werner.   Die mitteldeutsche Choralpassion im 18. Jahrundert.   Berlin: Evangelische Verlagsanstalt, 1960.
Epstein, Peter.   "Zur Geschichte der deutschen Choralpassion," Jahrbuch der Musikbibliotek Peters, 36: 35-50, 1930.
Geck, Martin.   Die Wiederentdeckung der Mattäuspassion im 19. Jahrhundert.   Regensburg: Bosse, 1967.
Gerber, R.   "Die deutsche Passion vor Luther bis Bach," Luther Jahrbuch, 13:131f., 1931.
Lott, Walter.   "Zur Geschichte der Passionskomposition von 1650-1800," AMW, 3:285-320, 1921.
Smallman, Basil.   The Background of Passion Music.   Naperville, Ill.: SCM Book Club, 1957.

PASSIONTIDE (OF., fr. LL. passio, fr. pati, passus to suffer + ME. tide, tid, fr. OE. tid time)

The season of the *Christian Year commencing with Ash Monday and ending on Easter eve is called Passiontide or Lent.

Brodde, Otto. "Die Begehung der Passionszeit," Kirchen-
    chordienst, 9:25-30, March-April, 1949.
Wetzler, Robert and Helen Huntington. Seasons and Sym-
    bols: A Handbook on the Church Year. Minneapolis:
    Augsburg Publishing House, 1962.

PATER NOSTER (L. pater father + noster our)

The Pater Noster refers to the "Prayer of Our Lord"
(Matthew 6:9-13) as included in most liturgies in connection
with the *Eucharist. It often follows the canon or prayer
of consecration. Although this prayer is frequently recited
by all the people, the Lutheran service calls upon the minister to sing or say the prayer through "but deliver us from
evil." At this point the choir and congregation respond with
the assigned fourth-century liturgical doxology, "For thine
is the kingdom...." The Anglican Prayer Book (1662) calls
upon the priest and people to sing the Pater Noster after the
communion. It also appears in the daily services of prayer.
        In Free Churches the Lord's Prayer (as it is called)
is usually spoken unless it is used as the text of an anthem
being sung by the *choir (e.g., Flor Peeters' "Lord's
Prayer"). (See also *Vater Unser.)

PAX, THE (L. pacis; akin to L. pacere, paciscere,
        pacisci to make an agreement)

"The peace of the Lord be with you alway" is the
short *benediction which follows the Lord's Prayer (*Pater
Noster) and precedes the *Agnus Dei in some eucharistic
observances. It is a surviving fragment of two practices
of the early church--the solemn blessing of the people, as
found in the Eastern and Gallican churches, and the Kiss of
Peace, a mark of fellowship and unity found in all early
liturgies at the very beginning of the Mass of the Faithful.
Luther held it in high esteem as a blessing and absolution.
He called it "the voice of the gospel announcing the forgiveness of sins ... the only and most worthy preparation for
the Lord's Table" (Reed, 366). Some recent prayer books
of the Anglican communion have restored The Pax, dropped
in 1552. All emphasize its ancient meaning in the words,
"Ye who ... are in love and charity with your neighbors
... draw near." The Scottish Liturgy (1929) adds the words,
"Brethren, let us love one another, for love is of God."

Reed, Luther D. The Lutheran Liturgy. Philadelphia:
    Muhlenberg Press, 1947. Pp. 365-368.

PERICOPES (LL., fr. Gr. perikope, fr. peri around +
    koptein to cut)

        The term for readings from the Holy Scripture, and
more specifically the traditional system of *Epistles and
*Gospels for the services of the *Christian Year is peri-
copes. (Cf. *Lesson.)

Reed, Luther D. The Lutheran Liturgy. Philadelphia:
    Muhlenberg Press, 1947.

PERIODICALS OF PROTESTANT CHURCH MUSIC

        [Contents: Historical background; General church
music; Graded choir program; Hymnology and liturgy; Instrumental.]

Historical Background

        Among the earliest known periodicals of Protestant
church music are the English monthly The Parish Choir
[or Church Music Book] (London: Society for Promoting
Church Music, 1846-1851); The Tonic Sol-Fa Reporter (London: Curwen, 1851-1920); Choir, and Musical Record (London, 1863-1787--superseded by Saturday Musical and Review, then The Choir, 1879-1880); and Musician, Organist
and Choirmaster (London, 1866-1870). In America the first
periodicals of this nature known are the Church's Musical
Visitor (Cincinnati, 1871-1888) and Parish Choir (Medford,
Mass., 1874-1919).
        There follows a selected list of periodicals related
to Protestant church music primarily issued during the 20th
century. This listing is alphabetically arranged within categories.

General Church Music

    All-Africa Church Music Association Journal (Salisbury,
    Rhodesia, 1963-). Buzz (of the Music Gospel Outreach,
    London, 1966-). The Choral and Organ Guide (Mt.
    Vernon, New York, 1947-). The Choir (Westminster,
    Eng., 1910-1934). The Choir and Musical Journal (Lon-
    don, 1934-). Choir Guide (New York, 1947-1952).
    Der Chor (Frankfort am Main, 1949-). The Chorister

(London, 1935-1940). Church Music (Philadelphia, 1905-1909). Church Music (St. Louis, 1966-). The Church Musician (Nashville, 1950-). The Church Times (London, 1863-?). English Church Music (Croydon, Surrey, Eng., 1930-). Evangelische Kirchenmusik in Baden, Hessen und Pfalz (Heidelberg, 1924-1959). Evangelische Musik-Zeitung (Bern, 1907-). Expression (Chester Springs, Pa., 1969-). Gottesdienst und Kirchenmusik (Munich, 1951-). Journal of Church Music (Philadelphia, 1959-). Kirchenchor (Dayton, Ohio, 1897-1930). Der Kirchenchor (Kassel-Wilhelmshöhe, West Germany, 1929-). Der Kirchenmusik (Langensalza, 1919-1921). Der Kirchenmusiker (Berlin, 1950-). KMT /KSF (Vagnharad, Sweden, 1967-). Kyrkosangforbundet (Uppsala, Sweden, 1926-1966). Monatsschrift für Gottesdienst und kirchliche Kunst (Göttingen, 1895-1941). Music Ministry (Nashville, 1959-1968). Music Ministry (Nashville, 1969-). Musical Salvationist (London, 1890-). The Musician (in the interest of Salvation Army musicians, New York, 1941-). The Musician of the Salvation Army (London, 1938-). Musik und Gottesdienst (Zürich, 1947-). Musik und Kirche (Kassel-Wilhelmshöhe, Germany, 1928-). The Nonconformist Musical Journal (London, 1888-1934). Promoting Church Music (Croydon, Surrey, Eng., 1963-). Response, in Worship, Music and the Arts (St. Paul, Minn., 1959-). The Sacred Musician (South Pasadena, Cal., 1932-1934). Sursum Corda (Minneapolis, 1939-1955). Tidskrift för kyrkomusic och svenskt gudstjänstliv (Lund, Sweden, 1926-1941).

Graded Choir Program

The Children's Music Leader (Nashville, 1966-1970). Choral Overtones (Nashville, 1970-). Choral Tones (Nashville, 1970-). Choristers Guild Letters (Dallas, 1919-). The Junior Musician (Nashville, 1963-1970). Music for Primaries (Nashville, 1965-1970). The Music Leader (Nashville, 1970-). Music Makers (Nashville, 1970-). Opus One (Nashville, 1970-). Opus Two (Nashville, 1970-). Young Musicians (Nashville, 1970-). The Youth Musician (Nashville, 1963-1970).

Hymnology and Liturgy

Boletín del Círculo Himno Evangélico (Chile, 1956-). The Hymn (New York, 1949-). Hymn Lovers' Magazine (Los Angeles, 1947-). The Hymn Society of Great Britain and Ireland Bulletin (Edinburgh, 1936-). Jahrbuch für Liturgik und Hymnologie (Kassel, Germany,

1956-). Siona; Monatschrift für Liturgie und Kirchen-musik (Gütersloh, Germany, 1876-1920).

Instrumental

The American Guild of Organists Quarterly (New York, 1956-1966). The American Organist (New York, 1918-). The American Recorder (New York, 1960-). Ars Organi; Zeitschrift für das Orgelwesen (Berlin, 1951-). Bulletin (of the Guild of Carillonneurs in North America, Lawrence, Kan., 1940-). The Diapason (Chicago, 1908-). The Handbell Choir Loft (Staten Island, New York, 1958-). Music: The AGO and RCCO Magazine (New York, 1967-). The Organ (Bedfordshire, Eng., 1920-). The Ringing World (of the Central Council of Church Bell-Ringers, London, 1911-).

PER RECTO ET RETRO (L.)

An unusual type of composition used in 19th-century chant and *hymn tune writing in which one section of the composition is obtained by reading backwards all parts of the preceding section is known as per recto et retro. Dr. William Crotch (1775-1847) wrote a well-known chant in this manner, while Sir John Stainer's (1840-1901) hymn tune composed in this manner and bearing this name is incorporated in the original edition of the Church Hymnary.

McCutchan, Robert Guy. Hymn Tune Names. New York: Abingdon Press, 1957.

PIANO (It., short for pianoforte, fr. piano soft, fr. L. planus even, smooth + It. forte loud, fr. L. fortis, strong)

The stringed instrument of the percussion division whose tone is produced by key-activated hammers striking the metal strings is a piano. The credit for its invention is given to Bartolomeo Cristofori (1655-1731), a harpsichord maker, who around 1709 placed hammers instead of jacks in a harpsichord to produce gradations of dynamics; thus, the pianoforte, the "soft-loud."

Principally a domestic keyboard instrument, the piano made its way into the Protestant church very slowly. As late as the mid-19th century pianos were unknown in churches of America even for rehearsal of the church choir. Sometime

between 1850 and 1925 pianos began to appear in Protestant
churches, though organs were more fashionable. In fact,
the earliest use of the piano in revival services to accompany the singing is accredited to Charles Alexander (c.1900).
In churches whose services favor the evangelistic style,
pianos have been employed, often along with the organ.
The so-called "evangelistic piano playing" is characterized
by the pianist's underlaying the singing of hymns with an
amount of improvised accompaniment, including scale elabo-
rations, arpeggiated figures, driving bass, etc.

    With the emphasis of Christian education through the
church school, music being a valued tool of teaching, pianos
have been found almost indispensible. A further importance
of the piano has come about with the *graded choir program,
as it serves as a help-mate in the teaching of melodies,
illustrating principles and providing accompaniment.

Harkness, Robert. The Harkness Piano Method of Evange-
    listic Hymn Playing. Rev. and ed. by Sidney Cribbs.
    Kansas City, Mo.: Lillenas, 1962.
Mathis, William S. The Pianist and Church Music. New
    York: Abingdon Press, 1962.
Midkiff, Helen Trotter. The Church Pianist. Nashville:
    Convention Press, 1957.
Sumner, William Leslie. The Pianoforte. London: Mac-
    millan, 1966.

PLAINSONG (English version of L. cantus planus level
    singing)

    The 10th-century term for Gregorian chant, when it
was beginning to enter the decadent period of long, uniform
duration, is called plainsong (in French, plain chant; in
German, Gregorianischer Choral). However, in the mid-
20th century the two terms are used interchangeably. Thus,
plainsong is a non-mensural, unaccompanied melody in one
of the *ecclesiastical modes traditionally employed for the
choral singing of prose texts in the liturgical services of
the Christian church. (See also *"Hanger" notes.)

    Historically, plainsong is directly related to Jewish
and Oriental chant, particularly the former, as the early
Christian church incorporated the psalmody of the synagogue
with its musical forms and styles into its worship. However, as the liturgy developed it was the *office rather than
the *Mass which first received the abundant musical forms,
psalmody being the only music permitted in the early mass.

This practice was reversed in the Middle Ages, as witnessed by the inclusion of *antiphons in the mass by Pope Celestine I (d. 432). With the rule of Pope Gregory I (d. 604) plainsong became codified into the Roman liturgy through the Antiphonarium Gregorianum. This collection essentially has remained the standard of plainsong throughout the ages. Thus, the zenith of the art of plainsong was reached during the seventh century, to remain unchanged even as harmony came into existence.

With the coming of the Reformation, plainsong melodies were retained quite extensively throughout the Lutheran church in Germany. The 16th-century service books which contain hundreds of these melodies clearly established the historical validity of Gregorian music in the Lutheran church. The Anglican church, on the other hand, saw a decline in the use of plainsong and the evolution of the harmonized *Anglican chant. As a result of the 19th-century *Oxford Movement a revival of modern plainsong occurred in England. This renewed interest was begun by Dyce's Book of Common Prayer Noted (1843). The seriousness of this revival is found in the establishment of The Plainsong and Medieval Music Society in 1888.

The influences of plainsong upon Protestant church music are numerous. In *hymnody, with the interest in translation that the Oxford Movement brought, many Latin breviary hymns were recovered along with plainsong melodies which have enriched the *hymnals of the 20th century (see, e.g., CH, 103i--"The Eternal Gifts of Christ the King"). In the Anglican service, plainsong was the model for John Merbecke's Booke of Common Praier Noted (1550), the first musical setting of the English liturgy, and for Martin Shaw's (1875-1958) Anglican Folk Mass (ECM, V:53-56), acclaimed as the first successful congregational setting since Merbecke. The role of plainsong in the German Reformation is quite extensive when, upon examination, one discovers that the melodies of many *chorales are mensural versions of traditional plainsong with vernacular texts. In fact, a study of the *cantus firmi of J. S. Bach's (1685-1750) *chorale preludes clearly indicates an inter-relationship between chorale and plainsong.

In the 20th century the Joint Commission on Church Music of the Episcopal Church issued plainsong settings of the service in the official publication, The Chorale Service. The Lutheran Church of America likewise has provided its churches with an entire plainsong service, the Evangelical Lutheran churches of Europe having maintained such settings somewhat throughout its existence.

Apel, Willi. Gregorian Chant. Bloomington: Indiana University Press, 1958.

Arnold, J. H. Plainsong Accompaniment. London: Oxford University Press, 1927.

Conner, M. J. B. Gregorian Chant and Medieval Hymn Tunes in the Works of J. S. Bach. West Hartford, Conn.: Department of Publications, Saint Joseph College, 1957.

Higginson, J. Vincent. Revival of Gregorian Chant: Its Influence on English Hymnody. Papers of the Hymn Society, No. 15. New York: The Hymn Society of America, 1949.

Marshall, Parry Denison. "Plainsong in English: An Historical and Analytical Survey." Unpublished S.M.D. dissertation, Union Theological Seminary, New York, 1964.

Paleographie musicale. Tournay: Société de Saint-Jean l'Evangéliste, Desclée et cie, 1924-   .

Phillips, C. Henry. "The Aesthetics of Plainsong," ML, 15:128-38, April, 1934.

Pierik, Marie. The Spirit of Gregorian Chant. Boston: Bruce Humphries, 1939.

Rosenwald, Hans. "The Influence of Gregorian Chant on Protestant Hymnology of the Reformation Period," Music Teachers National Association Studies in Musical Education, History and Aesthetics. Pittsburgh, 1944. Pp. 248-254.

Tack, Franz. Gregorian Chant. Köln: Arno Volk Verlag, 1960.

Wagner, Peter. Einführung in der Gregorianische Melodien. 3 vols. Wiesbaden: Breitkopf, 1962.

         . Introduction to the Gregorian Melodies. Part I, Origin and Development of the Forms of the Liturgical Chant. London: The Plainsong and Medieval Music Society, 1907.

POINTING (ME. point, pointe, fr. OF. point a prick, dot, fr. LL. punate, fr. L. pungere, punctum to prick)

A method used to guide the singers in the fitting of the words to the melodic formulas of *Anglican chant or *plainsong by the marking of the text of the prose *psalter is called pointing.

The earliest usage of this term was in the 1662 Prayer Book where it was stated that the *psalms were pointed as they were intended to be sung or said in churches;

this, however, was simply the use of the colon to distinguish
the two phrases of the binary psalm verse. It was not until
1837, though, that any printed attempt was made available at
a method of pointing. This was Robert Janes' The Psalter
of David, Carefully marked and Pointed to enable Voices of
a Choir to keep exactly together by singing the same Syllables to the same Note.... This was an attempt to permit
non-metrical psalm singing among parish churches as was
the custom in cathedrals and collegiate chapels. Under the
inspiration for the reforming of Anglican chant through the
pamphlet by Robert Bridges, the poet laureate, many pointed
psalters came into existence. Four which were of major
consequence are The English Psalter (1925) by E. C. Bair-
stow, P. C. Buck and C. Macpherson, The Psalter Newly
Pointed (1925) by A. Ramsbotham, The Oxford Psalter (1929)
by H. F. Ley, E. S. Roper and C. Hylton Stewart, and The
Parrish Psalter (1932) by S. Nicholson.
        The basic purpose in pointing the psalms is not metri-
cal rigidity, but the aiding of singers in more natural speech
rhythm as they chant.

Brown, Ray F. The Oxford American Psalter. New York:
        Oxford University Press, 1949.
Grace, Harvey. "Some Early Anglican Pointing," Musical
        Times, 56:226-229, 1915.

"POP," GOSPEL

        The use of the popular musical idioms (the musical
styles of the mid-20th-century jazz musicians, folk singers
and rock groups) for the communication of the Christian message is here defined by the conglomerate term, Gospel "pop."
        Since the 1950's the church, in an attempt to find new
means of communication with the secular world, to seek
modern equivalents for the allegedly meaningless traditional
elements, and to develop a musical expression for the purpose of attracting converts to Christianity, has turned to the
popular idioms of folk-rock and jazz. Among the earliest
attempts was the Twentieth Century Folk Mass (1956) by
Geoffrey Beaumont (1904-1970). This popular styled Anglican
service was in the "Broadway" musical tradition. It gave
birth to the *Twentieth Century Church Light Music Group
which has fostered the continued use of this popular style in
the hymns and other music of the church.
        Making use of idiomatic jazz patterns have been litur-
gical works by several jazz musicians. In 1959 Edgar

Summerlin set a Methodist liturgy, Liturgical Jazz: A Musical Setting for an Order of Morning Prayer, for the National Convocation of Methodist Youth in Lafayette, Indiana. This was followed by Frank B. Tirro's American Jazz Mass in 1960. Other uses of jazz in the church of the 1960's have been Standroed T. Carmichael's For Heaven's Sake (1961), a musical revue; Duke Ellington's Concert of Sacred Music (1965), at Fifth Avenue Presbyterian Church, New York; and Dave Brubeck's oratorio, The Light in the Wilderness (1968). Likewise the German composer, Heinz Werner Zimmermann (b. 1930), has captured the expressive characteristics of the jazz idiom, welding it to the German chorale tradition, incorporating the *chorale, and has produced several convincing compositions for the church, including his "Psalmkonzert" (1957) and motet, "O Sing unto the Lord" (1961).

     In the popular folk music idiom of the day Good News, a Christian folk musical, was compiled and edited by Bob Oldenburg in 1967. This marked the beginning of the use of folk musicals in Christian communication. In 1968 Phillip Landgrave's Purpose was created "to guide youth in discovering a meaningful life in Christ." Other folk musicals in a popular style produced in the late 1960's include Ralph Carmichael's Tell It Like It Is (1969), and Otis Skilling's Life (1970). Predominant features of these compositions have been the driving, syncopated rhythms, the frequent use of guitars and drums, the basic unison or two-part texture (occasionally more), and the employment of spoken dialogue as a bridge between selections. From England have come several collections of popular folk songs for the positive expression of Christian truths. Edited by Peter Smith are the three collections, Faith, Folk and Clarity, Faith, Folk and Nativity and Faith, Folk and Festivity (1968-1969). The contents of these volumes illustrate the Christian life today in straightforward contemporary verse, generally set to simple verse-refrain melodies with guitar accompaniment.

     The incorporation of the driving rhythm and irregular phrases of hard rock has also come about in some Christian music of the 1960's. Among several of the contemporary dramatic and musical services employing rock have been "A Man Dies," on the passion of Christ, "The Word Is," a service for rock band, and "Rite of Reconciliation," a Christian drama incorporating a psychedelic rock group.

Gehrle, Ralph. "Martin Luther Is Alive and Well and Writing Acid Rock Hymns in the Wartburg," Church Music, 69.2[sic]:31-32, 1969.
"Die Geister, die ich rief...," Der Kirchenchor, 22:66-76, July-August, 1962.

Haag, Herbert. "Jazzgottesdienst?" MK, 32:111-114, May-
    June, 1962.
Hagen, Rochus. Jazz in der Kirche. Stuttgart: Kohlham-
    men, 1967.
Le Huray, Peter. "Popular Elements in Church Music,"
    ECM, 1967:15-24, 1967.
Miller, William Robert. The World of Pop Music and Jazz.
    St. Louis: Concordia Publishing House, 1965.
Music Educator's Journal, 56, November, 1969 (whole issue
    devoted to youth music).
Savary, Louis M. The Kingdom of Downtown. New York:
    Paulist Press Deus Books, 1967.
Wienandt, Elwyn A. "Jazz as a Christian Expression," in:
    Christian Faith and the Contemporary Arts, ed. Finley
    Eversole. New York: Abingdon Press, 1962. Pp.
    171-178.

POSTLUDE   (fr. L. postludum, fr. post after + ludere to
    play)

    The closing *voluntary of the worship service is the
postlude (in German, Nachspiel). Ideally, it is an integral
part of the service functioning as a period of reflection for
the worshipper upon the spiritual edification just received.
However, Friedrich Schleimacher (1786-1834) in his Prak-
tischen Theologie spoke of the postlude as strictly not being
a part of the service but an addition "during which the
organist often played marches." There appears to be no
liturgical precedent for the postlude through the 20th century,
though it has been a common practice since the 16th century.

Albrecht, Christoph. "Der liturgische Ort des gottesdienst-
    lichen Orgelnachspiels," MK, 34:73-78, March-April,
    1964.
Simmons, Morgan. "Afterthought on Afterpieces," Clavier,
    4:42-43, January-February, 1965.

PRAYER BOOK   see   BOOK OF COMMON PRAYER

PRAYER RESPONSE   (ME. preiere, fr. Of. preiere, fr.--
    assumed--VL. precaria, fr. L. precarius got by
    prayer, fr. precari to pray + *response)

    The choral affirmation of the pastoral prayer on behalf

of the congregation at the conclusion of its offering is the prayer response (e.g., "Hear our prayer, O Heavenly Father").

PRECENTOR (LL. praecentor, fr. praeinere to sing before, fr. prae before + canere to sing)

(1) The priest who, in a cathedral or collegiate church establishment, is responsible for the ordering of the sung services is the precentor. The first mention of this office was made in the fourth century. Later it was used in connection with John, the precentor of St. Peter's in Rome, who was sent to England to improve the psalmody.

(2) The official who, when organs were not used in the Nonconformist churches of England, was responsible for the announcing of the tune and the leading of the unaccompanied singing of *hymns and metrical psalms by the congregation is called the precentor. This form of the precentor made its way into American history through the *lining-out of Colonial times and the frontier religious gatherings.

Curwen, John Spencer. Studies in Worship Music, Second Series. London: J. Carver & Sons, 1885. Pp. 88-94.

PRECES (L.)

The term for supplications set in the form of *versicles and *responses in the rites of the Anglican Church is preces. It is often used in place of the term *suffrages. However, according to the Prayer Book, preces refers specifically to the versicle of *Morning Prayer and Evening Prayer (*Vespers), which begins "O Lord, open Thou our lips." Polyphonic settings of the preces by Tallis, Morley and others are extant.

PREFACE (L. praefatio, fr. praefari to say beforehand, fr., prae before + fari, fatus to speak)

The liturgical introduction to the communion service which precedes the Canon or Prayer of Consecration and which begins with *Dominus vobiscum and *Sursum corda is called the Preface. It is among the oldest portions of the

liturgy, being found in practically every ancient rite. Luther
included the Preface in his Latin service, but deleted it from
his German order, which emphasized homiletical features.
In the Common Service Book (1888) the Preface had made a
definite return to the Lutheran Service. From the first
Prayer Book (1549), the Anglican rite has included the
Preface.

The Preface is formed in four parts: the prefatory
sentences (Dominus vobiscum and Sursum corda), the thanksgiving ("It is truly meet ..."), the proper preface (variable),
and the ascription ("Therefore with Angels ..."). Referred
to as the "common Preface" is the thanksgiving and the ascription, which together with the prefatory sentences are invariable. The "proper Preface" which may be inserted
varies with the season.

The chanting of the Preface is by the celebrant to a
plainsong melody which leads to the *Sanctus sung by the
choir or the people.

Harford, George and Morley Stevenson. The Prayer Book
    Dictionary. London: Sir Isaac Pitman, 1912. Pp.
    559f.
Reed, Luther D. The Lutheran Liturgy. Philadelphia:
    Muhlenberg Press, 1947. Pp. 323-330.

PRELUDE (L. praeludere, praelusum, fr. prae before +
    ludere to play)

A musical composition designed to be performed as
an introduction (to a service of worship or to another composition such as a fugue or suite) is a prelude. This definition, appropriate to the history of the prelude in Protestant
church music, is not to be confused with the 19th-century
character piece for piano (e.g., Chopin, Scriabin, Debussy).
When the prelude is based on a *chorale it is known as a
*chorale prelude.

Frotscher, Georg. Geschichte des Orgelspiels und der
    Orgelkomposition. Berlin: Merseburger, 1959.
Gillespie, John. Five Centuries of Keyboard Music. Bel-
    mont, Cal.: Wadsworth Pub. Co., 1965.
Jachisch, Frederick F. "On Preludes," JCM, III:9-13,
    May, 1961.
Rietschel, G. Die Aufgabe der Orgel im protestantische
    Gottesdiensts bis im das 18. Jahrhundert. Leipzig,
    n.p., 1893.

PROCESSION (OF., fr. L. processio, fr. L. procedere to go before)

(1) A short service before a choral service of *communion or after a choral office in which two hymns are sung while the choir and ministers proceed from the chancel, around the church and back to the chancel again is known liturgically as the procession. The singing of the first hymn is to end when the choir reaches the end of the center aisle of the nave. There a station is made for the chanting of the *versicle, *response and *collect. Then the second hymn is sung while the choir returns to its position in the chancel. These processions could be either festal or penitential using the singing or chanting of *hymns, *psalms or *litanies.

(2) The orderly entrance of the choir and ministers at the beginning of a service (a "choral march" without authority or precedent) is sometimes called a procession, although it is simply a necessary movement of a body of people from one place to another.

Klein, Theodor Heinrich. Die Prozessionsgesänge der Mainzer Kirche aus dem 14. bis 18. Jahrhundert. Speyer: Deuck Verlag, der Jägerschen Buch, 1962.
Schult, William Hubert. "The Procession in Christian Worship." Unpublished M.S.M. thesis, Union Theological Seminary, New York, 1938.

PROPER (ME. propre, fr. OF. propre, fr. L. proprius)

The parts of a liturgical service which may vary according to the Sunday or a festival of the *Christian Year are the propers, as distinguished from those parts of the service which are invariable, known collectively as the *ordinary. The variable material as fitted into the fixed framework of the liturgy provides the congregation with the complete teachings of the church during the annual cycle.

As early Christian worship became more complex with weekly celebrations and annual commemorations the organization and preservation of the liturgical materials was the logical outgrowth to avoid confusion and repetition. Thus, *liturgical books were compiled to perpetuate a continuity in the readings and other variable materials of the Western liturgies. In the Western liturgy of the Roman mass the proper grew into nine parts. Each service has its own *introit, *collect, *epistle, *Gradual, *Gospel, *Offertory, secret

communio and post-communio; and the Lutheran Reformation
retained the first five and added the *lesson. In 1549, the
Anglican *Book of Common Prayer eliminated the gradual
from the first five, and likewise the *introit in 1552. Also
included within the Western liturgical propers are the proper
*Prefaces in the communion and the proper *psalms for
certain festivals.

Reed, Luther D. The Lutheran Liturgy. Philadelphia:
      Muhlenberg Press, 1947. Pp. 450-575.

PROPER TUNE   (*proper + ME. tun, tune, fr. OF. ton,
      fr. L. tonus a sound, tone, a stretching, fr. Gr.
      tonus a stretching, straining, raising of the voice,
      pitch, accent, measure or meter)

      The particular tune which traditionally is associated
with a particular *psalm or *hymn to the exclusion of any
other association is considered a proper tune. This particularly applies to the Lutheran *chorale and to the metrical *psalmody of the English Restoration.

PSALMI FESTIVALES   (L.)

      The manuscript term for the method of rendering the
psalms in Elizabethan times was psalmi festivales, after the
old Latin festal practice of singing salmi concerti. The
style is similar to modern *Anglican chant with the antiphonal structure. The main melodic material usually recurs
in every verse or two verses, the phrase varying according
to the number of words in each individual verse. Because
of the length of the psalms only the first few verses of any
Psalm were set to music, the remainder being omitted. It
is thought that these Psalm settings may have had a strong
influence on the 17th- and 18th-century development of the
Anglican chant.
      Among the composers of psalmi festivales are Tallis,
Parsons, Morley, Byrd, Gibbons, Tompkins and Hooper.
Thomas Tallis (c.1505-1585) himself wrote three sets of
psalmi, which are the earliest of their kind (see his "Wherewithal shall a young man cleanse his way?" ECM, II:8).

Fellowes, Edmund H. English Cathedral Music. London:
      Methuen, 1946.
Reese, Gustav. Music in the Renaissance. New York:
      W. W. Norton, 1954.

PSALMODICONS (*psalmody)

The 19th-century monochord introduced by Johann Dillner in 1829 for the playing of *psalms in the churches and schools of Sweden is the psalmodicon. The inventor prepared a special book of melodies for it in 1830. The Swedish church musician, Johann Olaf Wallin, is reported to have had a keen interest in the instrument. Before the organ became common in the American settlements the psalmodicon was used in Swedish Lutheran congregations. It remained popular for some forty years when it was re- placed by the *harmonium. (Cf. *Melodeons).

Baines, Anthony. European and American Musical Instru- ments. New York: The Viking Press, 1966.

PSALMODY, METRICAL (LL. psalmodia, fr. Gr. psalmodia, fr. psalmos psalm + aedein to sing)

[Contents: (definition); Early history The Continent; England; Scotland; America; Influences and present-day oc- curences; (bibliography:) General; The Continents; England; Scotland; America.] The act of singing psalms, even more specifically, the singing of the "Psalms of David," in meter is called metrical psalmody.

Early History

Psalmody throughout the centuries has referred to the "Psalms of David," the Book of Psalms of the Old Testa- ment. These were originally the songs of the children of Israel for praise, confession and instruction in their God. When the Christian church was in its infancy, the believers in Christ adopted these psalms as a major portion of their song repertoire, translated from their original Hebrew into Greek, and later into Latin. The music accompanying these songs was in the contemporary style of chant. This chant later became canonized by the Church of Rome. With the eventual break within the Roman Church brought about by the Reformation, there was a renewed interest in psalm singing by the people. And, since the music of the people was metrical music, it was only logical that the "Psalms of David," as they were translated into the language of the people, be set in the prominent meters of the music which was common to these folk. Thus, metrical psalmody was created as the leaders of the Reformation movement sought to bring the psalms to their people. The last of the 15th century and the beginning of the 16th century saw a political, social and religious unrest that needed but one strong individual to upset the status quo. That person was Martin Luther, accompanied later by John Calvin. As was true with previous minor reform movements and reawakenings so it was true then, that a type of vernacular hymnody developed to proclaim the belief and doctrine (e.g., the Italian laudi spirituali of the Franciscan movement and the hymns of the Bohemian Hussite movement). From Luther, a rich heritage of German hymnody arose; whereas metrical psalmody came from the Calvinistic line. With these developments and the invention of printing, the time was right for religious renewal.

Looking into John Calvin's philosophy of church music as he sought to establish this revitalized Christian thought, one finds him greatly distressed with the popular songs of the day. The French songs were frivolous and the German songs of the 15th century were no better. Yet, in arranging a worship for the Reformed Church he proposed to ignore the historical development of worship in the Latin Church, and to reinstate the simpler conditions of the primitive church (Benson, 23). Seeing Scriptural foundation for *congregational singing in the church, yet seeing how the *hymns of human composure" as found in the Latin breviary could embody false doctrine, he adopted the strict proposition that there could be no better songs than the inspired songs of Scripture, especially and almost exclusively the psalms. Thus, as the Calvinistic doctrine spread throughout the world, the metrical psalm which accompanied it became its characteristic song, much as the hymn did for the Lutheran movement.

The Continent

The founder and originator of metrical psalmody was not Calvin, as one might expect, but a witty poet of the court of Francis I, Clement Marot (c.1497-1544) (Terry, 2). By the end of the 15th century, a versification of the seven penetential psalms had become current in France. However, it was not until Marot's time that the translation of the psalms into vernacular verse was attempted on anything approaching an extensive scale. In 1533, this writer of comic and Greek and Latin verse turned his energies toward the Hebrew verses of David in the Book of Psalms (beginning with Psalm 6). At first Marot's poems were circulated only in court circles. But soon their popularity grew in noble and

kingly places, actually becoming the fashion of the day. At
the same time these poems with music also by Marot crept
into humble groups of Protestants as they worshipped. So
it was that in 1539 thirteen of them were printed in an altered form by Calvin in Strasburg, without Marot's knowledge or consent, under the title, Aulcuns Psealmes et Cantiques mys en chant. Strasburg 1539. This Strasburg
Psalter of 1539--or "Calvin's First Psalter, " as it is sometimes called, published with unharmonized melodies--became
the parent of all other psalters (Frere, xxxvii). Upon
learning about this publication Marot set himself to the task
of publishing 30 authentic psalm texts. This work, completed in 1542 at Paris, caused such a fury that he fled for
his life to the safety of Geneva. Whereupon, meeting Calvin, he completed a total of 50 psalms to serve as a permanent nucleus for a complete psalter (Cinquante Pseaulmes,
August 1543). The volume also contained versifications of
the Commandments, the Articles of Faith, the *Lord's
Prayer, the *Magnificat, and prayers before and after meeting
(Patrick, 16). After Marot's untimely death in 1544, progress on the complete psalter was halted until 1548, when
the young poet Théodore de Bèze (1519-1605) arrived in Geneva
and took up the work. During the next 14 years some 30
portions of the psalter were published. In 1562, the complete French Psalter (also, Genevan Psalter or Huguenot
Psalter) was finished and published. This psalter, first
adopted by the French Huguenots, was one of the earliest
Reformation manuals of popular song and the only one that
has endured practically unchanged until recent times (Pratt,
1935, 27). Its treasured importance was second only to the
Bible in the Reformed movement, a phenomenon seen in the
fact that 225 editions were printed during the first century
of its existence (exceeding a million copies). It has been
reported to have undergone extensive translation into at
least twenty languages or dialects with some 30 editions of
the Dutch version and 20 of the German. The earliest
foreign rendering was into Dutch by Datheen (1564), which
soon became the official manual of the Reformed Church in
the Netherlands. It was then translated into German by
Lobwasser (1573), becoming the source of French melodies
for many German composers. The 1592 translation into
English exerted little influence because of the rival development of the Anglo-Genevan Psalter of 1561.

Regarding the content of the French Psalter, one
finds the great freedom of versification reminiscent of 12th-
century poets. This results in iambic, trochaic and ana-
pestic meters; a copious intermixture of lines with feminine

and masculine endings; varied line lengths from four to 13
syllables; stanzas from four to 12 lines; and much variety
in the grouping of lines by means of rhyme (Pratt, 1939, 6).
Yet a certain number of lines make up a stanza which is
more or less complete in itself, with successive stanzas
being alike in structure so that a single melody could serve
for the whole of any one poem. Through both the variety of
verse and music, it is everywhere clear that the aim of the
writers of the French Psalter was to make each psalm individual and memorable. For the tunes the chief credit is due
to the editorship and originality of the composer, Louis
Bourgeois. He suffered much in his efforts to compose for
this work as he sought to make some alterations in some of
the existing tunes. In 1565, Claude Goudimel published the
French Psalter with four- and five-part motet harmonizations
intended for private use.

    The real significance of this complete French Psalter
lies in the fact that it served as the basis for three more or
less distinct lines of development (German, French and British). It is a milestone in the development of Reformed congregational expression through the character of its poetic
framework and of the music added to it. It also is a literary
phenomenon in the breadth of circulation and in its persistence of use in its entirety. Finally, it was this psalter of
these two authors, Marot and de Bèze, which played an important role in the large awakening of French popular thought
to the nature and richness of the Bible.

    Before leaving the Continent, one other psalter must
be mentioned. The first psalter of the Anglo-Genevan
Church (the Protestant English refugees who had fled the
wrath of "Bloody Mary") appeared in 1556 as the 11th section of the Genevan "Book of Common Order." This volume,
published with tunes, contained the original 44 psalm versions
of Sternhold and Hopkins (see following section, England) and
seven new ones, known to have been by William Whittingham
(1524-15??). A second edition was published in 1558 containing 62 psalms; which provided the nucleus for the complete Scottish Psalter of 1564. In 1561, with 25 fresh psalm
versions by William Kethe, the complete Anglo-Genevan
Psalter was published. Scholarship, thus far, has not provided knowledge regarding the source of the original tunes
(Patrick, 31).

England

    Turning now to England, one finds several early at-
tempts at psalm-versifications, some even before the Refor-

mation.   Bishop Aldhelm of Sherborne (d. 709) is said to
have composed a psalter.   T. Brampton printed his Seven
Penitential Psalms in 1414.   Mention is also made of a
translation of St. Jerome's Gallican Psalter into English in
the time of Henry II or Richard I.

     With Edward VI's "Act of Uniformity for the Use of
the Common Prayer in English" which authorized the first
*Book of Common Prayer (1549), and which also allowed
psalm singing, came several attempts at the versification of
the Psalms.   The Seven Penitential Psalms were again done
by Sir Thomas Wyatt in 1549, and three others were versified by Earl of Sarrey.   Miles Coverdale, under the influence
of Martin Luther, brought out 13 psalms in his Goostly
psalmes and spiritual songs....   With this edict of the king
also came England's first complete metrical psalter (1549)
by Robert Crowley (Glass, 14).   It was a monotonous version
written completely in common meter and set to harmonized
chant.

     The model for English psalters, however, was con-
ceived by Thomas Sternhold (1500-1549), Gentleman of the
Privy Chamber of King Henry VIII.   Sternhold, being a
devout and sensitive person, despised the amorous and ob-
scene songs sung in the court and by the common people.
So he set himself to the task of versifying the Psalms of
David into the popular meters so that they might be sung to
well-known British ballads.   Thus, it was that in 1549,
Thomas Sternhold published 37 of his translations.   Upon
his death, his good friend, John Hopkins (d. 1570) took up
the task of continuing the psalter.   He contributed 60 versifications before his death.   The completed metrical psalter
was published in 1562 by John Day and became known as the
Sternhold and Hopkins Psalter or the Day Psalter, and later
as the Old Version.   Most of the psalm versions were in
common meter or short meter.

     During the conception of the Sternhold and Hopkins
Psalter several other less successful attempts were made.
Among these was Certayne Psalms chosen out of the Psalter
of David and drawn forth into English Meter by Wm. Hunnes,
London, by the wydow of John Hereforde, 1550, written after
the style of Sternhold.   In 1553, Frances Seager produced 19
psalms with music in four parts arranged in one book to be
sung at once.   However, in all the music for all the psalms
there were only two tunes.

     Issued about the same time as the Sternhold and
Hopkins was The Whole Psalter, translated into English
metre, with an argument and collect to each Psalm: John
Day, London (exact date not known), written by Archbishop

Mattheus Parker while he was in exile during the reign of Queen Mary. This psalter was composed with scholarly care and was of value, not only for the metrical versions, but for the collects as well. Beside the three usual meters (S.M., L.M. and C.M.) he used stanzas of eights; and one or two curious measures; and then supplied a quaint doxology for each meter. Its lack of acceptance was probably due to the fact that the Sternhold and Hopkins received a vastly larger circulation, having been bound with the Authorized Version of the Bible.

In 1563, John Day boosted the popularity of the Sternhold and Hopkins by publishing four-part settings for the psalms, which were apparently quite successful. Because of its royal sanction and wide acceptance, the Sternhold and Hopkins was the psalter of England for nearly a century and a half.

However, the predominance of the Sternhold and Hopkins does not presume no further attempts of worth. Quite the contrary is the case. In 1592, Thomas Este came out with his own compiled psalter, The Whole Book of Psalms: with their Wanted Tunes.... This was probably the first collection of psalm tunes which bore the names of places. The tunes still remain in the tenor. However, 58 of its tunes were harmonized by outstanding English composers of that day (Macdougall, 13). Among the composers engaged for the four-part settings were John Farmer, John Dowland and Giles Farnby. One psalter which is said to show the pure Elizabethan counterpoint in perfection throughout as Richard Allison's The Psalms of David in Meter ... 1599. Here the use of instruments is encouraged, and the tunes appear in the uppermost voice.

Among many persons there was still some dissatisfaction with the Sternhold and Hopkins versions. Thus, further attempts were still being made. In 1612, Henry Ainsworth (1571-1622) published his version, The Book of Psalms Englished both in Prose and Metre with Annotations, opening the word and sentences, by conference with other scriptures (commonly called the *Ainsworth Psalter). This volume was a complete new translation in prose at the same time as the King James Version of 1611. In it each psalm is accompanied by a brief commentary of high Biblical criticism, with a metrical setting rendered along side of the prose translation. For the 15 different meters in this collection, 39 different tunes were given, the texts being set syllabically in binary rhythm almost exclusively. This volume will be referred to later with regard to its influence on American psalmody. Of importance for its inclusion of

many tunes is the *Ravenscroft Psalter of 1621. The practice of naming tunes by locality was continued. Among the
new tunes introduced were a few Genevan tunes, three German, two Dutch and one Italian. Meeting with grave hard-
ship was Thomas Hopper's curious attempt to introduce
Genevan tunes complete into England by translation in his
psalter of 1632. One great rival to the Sternhold and Hopkins was the 1632 version by George Wither, who obtained a
privilege from the King which ordered it to be bound up with
every copy of the Bible. His version contained more varied
meters than the Sternhold and Hopkins, with the tunes by
Orlando Gibbons.

However good this psalter may have been, that by
George Sandys was acclaimed by many to be the best metrical version. Around 1635 the educated Englishmen were
beginning to be repulsed by the crudeness of the Sternhold
and Hopkins. Thus, in 1638, George Sandys published a
complete psalter, A Paraphrase upon the Divine Poems,
with settings by Henry Lawes. These settings show the
great influence of the new Italian School of the day. It
seems, however, that this version was designed for private
use only.

Continuing this desire for a finer literary version,
the Committee of Peers in 1640 recommended that the meters
of the psalms should be corrected and allowed to be circulated publically. Such was the task of Francis Rous, whose
version appeared in 1641. By its third edition in 1646, the
House of Commons ordered it to be sung in all churches and
chapels within the Kingdom. However, the House of Lords
approved a rival versification by William Barton (third edition,
1646), causing a deadlock between the two Houses for authorization of a new psalter.

It seems that dissatisfaction with the Rous Psalter
caused John Milton to attempt a version in 1648. This he
translated directly from the Hebrew. The Hebrew words
were printed in the margin; and every word not in the original was printed in italics. This scholarly effort, however,
was never successful or even completed.

From Sternhold to Rous the prevailing principle of
translation was literary exactness. However, from about
1660 to the end of the century (the period following the Restoration), there was an emphasis in the direction of literary
excellence. This can be seen in the psalters of Richard
Baxter, Miles Smyth, Sir John Denham (who monotonously
used long meter) and John Patrick. The latter was probably
the most successful, though not exactly literal. It adopted a
mode of evangelical interpretation which foretastes of Isaac
Watts.

Regarded as the real turning point toward literary excellence in the translating of the psalms was the 1696 version entitled A New Version of the Psalms of David, Fitted to the Tunes Used in Churches by Nahum Tate (1652-1715) and Nicholas Brady (1659-1726), dedicated to William III. (This psalter is commonly called the Tate and Brady Psalter.) This was the culmination of at least two earlier installments. A second "corrected" edition was published in 1698. This volume contained three types of psalms: (1) psalms of an ornate character with occasional vigorous rhythm (L.M. and P.M.), (2) psalms in C.M., and (3) psalms in sweet and simple verse. Unlike the Old Version the authorship of each individual psalm in the New Version cannot be distinguished.

The next great step in the history of English metrical psalmody occurred in 1719, when Isaac Watts published The Psalms of David imitated in the language of the New Testament.... In keeping with his attitude of "Christianizing" the psalms and making David a contemporary, Dr. Watts did not include the complete psalter, for he felt there were parts that could never be sung. The renderings are more para-phrases than translations. He freely drew upon the Lutheran technique of the evangelistic interpretation of the psalms as transmitted by John Patrick's A Century of Psalms, 1679. In light of this he embodied in his verse the New Testament implications of the Lord, the apostles and the messianic psalms in the light of the life of Christ. This provided the real springboard for future English *hymnody.

From this point onward, little new is seen in any other approaches to the psalms. Sir Richard Blackmore in 1721 made an unsuccessful return to naked literalism. Two unique attempts appeared in 1765: the continuous lining of James Merrick and Christopher Smart's strongly disguised psalms with New Testament interpretation.

The 19th century brought a few additional attempts at paraphrasing the psalms. James Montgomery released his Songs of Zion in 1822 which was nearly half of the psalter. Harriet Auber's Spirit of the Psalms (1829) was a free evan-gelical interpretation. H. F. Lyte's collection by the same title (1834) was a free paraphrase or expansion of a few verses as a theme, interweaving his own thoughts and meta-phors. In 1839 John Keble introduced The Psalter; or Psalms of David in English Verse, which was an improved metrical version of the psalms adhering closely to the origi-nal Hebrew meaning. His style was very refined, with imaginative energy and lyric force, yet rather abrupt. One of the best versions was that of Archdeacon Churton, The

Cleveland Psalter (1854), written in firm, equal and melodious verse, though somewhat loosely textured and translated.

        With the development of hymns and freer meters for hymn tunes, the versification of psalms became less restricted in meter and spirit. A new freshness appeared in the later 19th century as can be seen in the words and music of The Companion Psalter (1874) by the Rev. T. R. Birks. His lyric measures are often soft and melodious; he introduces freely evangelical ideas; but they are not always the legitimate unfolding of the psalms, and sometimes the groundwork is barely perceptible. From that time on, few if any, complete new metrical psalter versions were published since the hymn seems to dominate the area of congregational praise.

Scotland

        The first evidence of work on an official psalter was in the December 1562 meeting of the General Assembly of the Church of Scotland, which authorized a sum of 200 pounds for a printer to acquire materials for printing a psalter. It was undoubtedly the Anglo-Genevan Psalter, Four Score and Seven Psalms of David (1561), revised, which served as the nucleus for the Scottish Psalter, the completion of which seems to have been under the leadership of John Knox, assisted by Robert Pont (d. 1608) and John Craig (1512-1600). By the time of its printing, 46 psalms were of Scottish authorship and the rest were English. Like the English psalters of this period, this psalter contained little of poetic interest, but projected a deep adherence to the original text. The influence of the French Psalter on this Scottish Psalter, officially accepted on December 26, 1564, is seen more in the inclusion of French tunes and in the composition of versions in French meters than in direct translations from Marot and de Bèze. More than 27 different meters are used with 105 tunes.

        In 1568 Thomas Bassandyne published an unauthorized "Psalm Booke" which had several later editions. His edition of 1575 for the first time calls the psalter The CL Psalms of David. Yet it also included Coxe's "Lord's Prayer," Whittingham's "Ten Commandments" with a responsory prayer, the first Lamentation and the Veni Creator, (Patrick, 53). Of interest for its "conclusions" is the Charteris edition of 1596. These 32 doxologies were included to suit all the meters of the psalms in this edition.

        After 1622 most of the Scottish psalters were published without music. However, in 1625 an edition was discovered which seems to be the first published with the common tunes harmonized. And, as a last dying effort, The Psalter of 1635 was published, completely harmonized (Edward Willar, editor). The tunes were divided into three types: proper tunes--tunes assigned to a particular psalm; common tunes-- tunes in common meter, placed at the beginning of the book with no words to be used with any psalm in this meter; and, psalms in reports--a short contrapuntal motet with a psalm tune as the cantus firmus (Frost, 9).

It was now time for a new psalter. Desiring a common bond and uniformity in the worship of the churches of England and Scotland in 1643, the Westminster Assembly was formed. One phase of their work was to prepare a common psalter. However, because of the battle in Parliament over the Rous and Barton Psalters, the Scottish Church finally chose to produce its own, a drastic revision of the Rous Psalter. This work was appointed to four persons: John Adamson (Psalms 1-40), Thomas Crawford (Psalms 41- 80), John Row (Psalms 81-120), and John Nevey (Psalms 121-150). These were advised also to use versions by Zachary Boyd and Sir William Mure of Rowallan, as well as The Scottish Psalter of 1564. After evaluations from the individual presbyteries were made, a final committee examined the suggestions and revised the work for issuing in 1650. On May 1, 1650, it was authorized as the only version to be used and has long been used by the Presbyterian Church of Scotland without revision. This was the product of the Scottish Committees of Assembly who selected the best elements they could find in all existing versions, including the *Bay Psalm Book, and wove them together into the version now known. This was the sole medium of church praise in Scotland until 1794, when the first hymnbook was printed in Scotland. Since The Psalter of 1650 was published without music, a collection of 12 tunes, all in common meter, was published in 1666 for use with the new psalter.

Also to be mentioned is The Gaelic Psalms, published in its complete version in 1684 by the Rev. Robert Kirk. After some debate it received the authorization of the General Assembly in 1694 for use in Gaelic-speaking congregations instead of The Psalter of 1650.

America
‾‾‾‾‾‾‾

The first of the metrical psalters to be developed, the French Psalter, was also the first to reach the shores of America, being brought over by the short-lived Huguenot ex- peditions of 1562-1565 to Florida. Here the Indians found

great delight in singing them. In other settlements along the
coast during the subsequent centuries, the French psalms
were sung by Huguenots as long as they maintained their own
separate services. However, there seems to be no evidence
that the French Psalter was ever printed in the American
colonies.

It was the 1566 Dutch translation of the French Psalter, by Datheen to the tunes of Bourgeois, which was sung
in the first church organized in New Amsterdam in 1628.
Here the Dutch and French joined together in singing their
respective languages. This Datheen translation was employed
until 1767, when, after the introduction of English preaching,
Francis Hopkinson was commissioned to adapt English words
to the traditional tunes.

In 1620, when the Pilgrims landed at Plymouth, they
brought with them the *Ainsworth Psalter of 1612. This
contained 19 Bourgeois tunes out of a total of 39. It seems
to have used without "lining-out," among the Pilgrims until
1692.

Other versions also arrived in the Colonies. The
Old Version was brought to the Jamestown settlement in
1607, using the musical setting of Thomas Este (1592). In
the Massachusetts Bay Colony (1628-1630) the *Ravenscroft
Psalter of 1621 was used. However, the Old Version soon
was felt unsatisfactory to the young, theocratic colony. So
the Puritan colonists--also seeking to emphasize their distinction from the Pilgrims, who were using the Ainsworth
Psalter--appointed a committee of New England clergy to
revise the metrical psalms. These 30 "divines," who were
more distinguished for their piety and learning than for their
poetic gifts, undertook to prepare a more literal metrical
translation of the psalms. The result of their efforts was
The Whole Book of Psalms Faithfully Translated into English
Metre, 1640, Cambridge, Massachusetts (the first book
printed in English in North America). Since virtually every
congregation in the Massachusetts Bay Colony immediately
adopted the psalter, it became known as the Bay Psalm Book,
though this title does not appear on the title page. This
1640 psalter contained no music, but it did suggest 48 psalm
tunes to be used: the common meter tunes were from the
Ravenscroft Psalter, the short meter from the Old Version,
and the long meter ones from those in common use. All in
all, the gravest limitation of the Bay Psalm Book was its
use of only six metrical schemes, thus pronouncing a virtual
death on the use of all the old Genevan tunes. In 1647 a
second edition was published. However, it was the 1651 edition and revision which is of importance. It was the work of

Henry Dunster and Richard Lyon who applied a little more
art to the original Bay Psalm Book to produce The Psalms,
Hymns and Spiritual Songs of the Old and New Testament,
faithfully translated into English metre. Soon this revision
was known as The New England Psalm Book and was used
in the churches until it finally gave way to the New Version
or to the rising popularity of Isaac Watts. Except for the
Sternhold and Hopkins, the Tate and Brady, and the Watts
versions of the psalms, no psalter in English ever achieved
greater popularity (Lowens, 26), even being printed in England and Holland. In 1698 an edition containing 13 tunes
inserted at the back of the book was published. These tunes
were in two-part harmony, bass and treble, with the music
in old diamond-shaped notes. (This is the earliest example
of music printing in the American Colonies.)

During the development of the Bay Psalm Book, John
Elliot, "the Apostle to the Indians," prepared a versification
of the Psalms for the Algonquin Indians in their language,
Wame Ketoochomae Uketoohaonqash David (1661). It was
this work that influenced the conversion of Samson Occum,
a Mohican hymn writer of the next century in America (Foote,
54).

By the middle of the 17th century, singing in the
Colonial churches of the Bay area had deteriorated greatly.
In 1664, an official ordinance prescribed the method for the
"lining-out" of psalm tunes. However, this was to be a
temporary measure; and it was hoped to be abolished in the
future when there was time for more general music education.
Thus, the psalm tune repertory became extremely small.

The education was slow in coming. It was in 1712
that the Rev. John Tufts (1688-1750) of Newbury, Massachusetts, published An Introduction to the Singing of Psalm
Tunes in a plain and Easy Method with a Collection of Tunes
in Three Parts. This was to become the earliest book of
musical instruction printed in the English colonies of North
America. With it is seen the beginnings of the revival of
singing.

By the mid-18th century the New England churches
were slowly moving away from the Bay Psalm Book. The
Rev. John Barnard (1681-1770) of Marblehead published A
New Version of the Psalms; Fitted to the Tunes Used in the
Churches with Several Hymns out of the Old and New Testament (1752) in which he abandoned the antiquated verse forms
of the Bay Psalm Book in favor of his own rather free translation into current mid-18th-century style.

The metrical psalms began to wane with the publication of James Lyon's Urania, which included psalm tunes in

both the older style and the new fuging style. As the Bay
Psalm Book was fast waning in popular use, the Rev. Thomas
Prince (1687-1758) sought to revise it.   In 1758 he published
his improved revision, which still claimed literary accuracy.
However valiant his attempt, it still failed in his purpose.
Yet it is interesting to note that Prince also included 50 other
hymns in his volume.   These claimed to be on the important
Christian subjects (42 of them were by Watts) (Foote, 157).

     According to various records one can see the impact
of Isaac Watts' Psalms and Hymns already in the Colonies,
having been accepted in some New England parishes as early
as 1773.   However, after the Revolution, it was felt that
some of Watts must be revised for the new nation.   This
task was undertaken by John Mycall in 1781 and more suc-
cessfully by Joel Barlow in 1785.   Yet the leaders of the
churches of this growing country were dissatisfied.   So the
General Assembly of the Presbyterian Church commissioned
Dr. Timothy Dwight (1752-1817) to alter Watts appropriately
and versify the omitted psalms of Watts anew.   Thus, in
1801 this adaptation was published with a number of hymns
and came to be known as Dwight's Watts (Foote, 164).   (See
*Dwight's Watts for more information.)

     These developments away from metrical psalmody
lead the way toward spiritual songs and folk hymns such as
are found in collections like The Christian Harmony and The
Sacred Harp as well as other literary American hymns.

Influences and Present-day Occurrences

     The metrical psalm has held a major place in the
history of congregational praise of the Protestant church.
Even when the hymn became accepted in Reformed churches,
the metrical psalm was still dutifully sung along with it.
Only in America does it seem that the metrical psalm was
superseded by the hymn and the *gospel song.   Although in
certain isolated Reformed congregations psalm singing remained alive, with few exceptions it has become virtually a
dead issue.

     To the strict view of Calvin which insisted on the use
of songs from the Bible, hymnology is indebted for the large
use of Scriptural versifications and paraphrases by many
hymn writers who evolved from this tradition, the main in-
novator being Isaac Watts.   As was stated earlier, the
French Psalter was responsible for awakening French thought
to the nature and richness of the Bible.   Truly, the witty
court poet, Marot, was of great importance.

     Unlike the *hymn tune and the *chorale, the psalm

tune has not been incorporated into larger church music
forms such as the *cantata, *chorale prelude, and *concertato. With the exception of Scotland, the metrical psalm
has generally declined in its cherished position in favor of
the hymn and gospel song.

However, with some of the recent anniversaries of a
few of the major psalters, the Hymn Society of America and
the Hymn Society of Great Britain as well as some of the
major denominations have sought to revive the importance
and use of psalm singing. Many of the newest hymnals are
incorporating this rich heritage of Christian psalmody. One
such example is The Methodist Hymnal (1966), whose committee claimed metrical psalmody to be one of their six
major emphases. Beside the hymnals, publishers are also
producing practical performing editions of some of the metrical psalms of the great psalters, which might be rendered
by choirs.

Though metrical psalmody has been a waning interest
in church music, with the aid of musicology and the current
interest in things historical more and more of these works
will probably be brought into common use as Christian praise.

General

Frere, Rev. W. H. Hymns Ancient and Modern: Historical
    Edition. London: William Clowes, 1909.

The Continent

Doen, Orentin. Clément Marot et le Psautier Huguenot.
    Paris: n.p., 1878.
Pratt, W. S. "The Importance of the Early French Psal-
    ters," MQ, 21, 25-32, January, 1935.
    _____. The Music of the French Psalter of 1562. New
    York: Columbia University Press, 1939.
Terry, Sir Richard (ed.). Calvin's First Psalter (1539).
    London: Ernest Benn, 1932.

England

Benson, Louis F. The English Hymn. Philadelphia: Pres-
    byterian Board of Publication, 1915.
Brooke, William T. Old English Psalmody. 3 vols. Lon-
    don: William Reeves, 1916.
Frost, Maurice. English and Scottish Psalm and Hymn
    Tunes, c.1543-1677. London: Oxford University Press,
    1953.
Glass, Henry Alexander. The Story of the Psalter. London:
    Kegan Paul, Trench, 1888.

Scotland

Livingston, Neil. The Scottish Metrical Psalter of 1635.
Glasgow: MacLure and MacDonald, 1864.
Patrick, Millar. Four Centuries of Scottish Psalmody.
London: Oxford University Press, 1949.

America

Foote, Henry Wilder. Three Centuries of American Hymnody. Cambridge, Mass.: Harvard University Press, 1940.
Haraszti, Zoltan. The Enigma of the Bay Psalm Book.
Chicago: University of Chicago Press, 1957.
Lowens, I. "The Bay Psalm Book in Seventeenth Century New England," JAMS, 8:22-29, Winter, 1955.
Macdougall, Hamilton Crawford. Early New England Psalmody. Brattleboro, Vt.: Stephen Daye Press, 1940.
Metcalf, Frank J. American Psalmody. New York: Da Capo Press, 1969.

PSALMS (ME. psalm, salm, saume, fr. OE. psalm, sealm, fr. OF. salme, psaume, fr. LL. psalmus, fr. Gr. psalmos, fr. psallein to pull, to play upon a stringed instrument, to sing to the harp)

The 19th book of the Old Testament is the Book of Psalms. This selection of Jewish songs served the early Christian church as a basis of divine praise. With the Reformation the translating of the psalms into metrical vernacular verse (see *Psalmody, metrical) became the basis for Protestant *hymnody.

Avenary, H. "Formal Structure of Psalms and Canticles in Early Jewish and Christian Chant," Musical Disciplina, 7:1-13, 1953.
Ellinwood, Leonard. "Tallis' Tunes and Tudor Psalmody," Musica Disciplina, 2:198-203, 1948.
Kelk, A. H. Singing of the Psalms and Canticles to Anglican Chant, Shorter Papers of the Church Music Society, No. 6. London: Oxford University Press, n.d.

PSALM-TONES (*psalm + L. tonus tone)

The recitation melodies used for chanting of the *psalms in the Roman, Anglican and Lutheran churches are

called psalm-tones.   There are eight regular psalm-tones,
each corresponding to one of the eight *ecclesiastical modes,
and one irregular one.   The <u>tonus peregrinus</u> or irregular
psalm-tone is so called because the recitation for the last
half-verse is a tone lower than the first half.   Each psalm-
tone may be characterized as an inflected monotonic melody,
the main tone of which is called the recitation, *reciting
tone or *tenor.   The beginning of the first phrase is the
*intonation, while the half cadence is the *mediation.   The
second phrase of the binary structured psalm-tone consists
only of a tenor and final cadence, termination.   When the
phrase between the intonation and mediation or mediation
and termination is too lengthy for one breath, a vocal inflection, called a *flexa, occurs at the breathing point.

intonation   tenor flexa   tenor

Con-ser-va-me. . . in te; + dixi. . .

mediation   tenor   termination

me-us es tu   quo-ni-am. . .me-o-rum non e-ges.

Psalm 15:1   "Conserva me Domine, quoniam speravi it te;
+ dixi Domino: Deus meus es tu.   quoniam bonorum
meorum non eges" (<u>Liber Usualis</u>, 923).

Mahrenholz, Christhard.   "Die deutsche Psalmodie," MK,
12:25-30, January-February, 1940.

PSALTERS (OE. <u>psaltere, saltere</u>, fr. L.; ME. <u>sauter</u>,
fr. OF. <u>sautier, saltier</u>, fr. L. <u>psalterium</u>, fr. Gr.
<u>psalterion</u> a stringed instrument, fr. <u>psallein</u> to play
on a stringed instrument)

The name for the collections of the Book of Psalms
translated into the vernacular, often in rhythm and meter,
is the psalter.   The vernacular prose psalms sung in the
Church of England to *Anglican chant are also collected in
psalters (cf. *Psalm-tone).
The metrical psalters have provided an anthology of

the music of the Reformed church prior to the 18th century, when the hymn emerged. The following is a partial list of some psalters of major import in the history of metrical psalmody:

1539- Aulcuns pseaulmes et cantiques mys en chant (Calvin's First Psalter; or, Strasburg Psalter)
1540- Souterliedekens (Dutch)
1562- Marot-Bèze Psalter (Huguenot or Genevan Psalter)
      Old Version (Sternhold and Hopkins or English Psalter)
1564/65- Scottish Psalter
1592- Este's Psalter
1612- Ainsworth Psalter
1621- Ravenscroft Psalter
1635- Scottish Psalter
1640- Bay Psalm Book
1671- Playford Psalter
1696- New Version (Tate and Brady)

For an historical overview of psalters and details of their composition and inter-relation, see *Psalmody, metrical.

Glass, Henry A. The Story of the Psalters (1549-1885). London: Kegan Paul, Trench, 1888.
Metcalf, E. J. American Psalmody. New York: C. F. Heartman, 1917.
Patrick, Millar. Four Centuries of Scottish Psalmody. London: Oxford University Press, 1949.
Warrington, J. Short Titles of Books Relating to and Illustrating the History and Practice of Psalmody in the United States (1620-1820). Philadelphia: n.p., 1898.
Welch, A. C. The Psalter in Life, Worship and History. Oxford, Eng.: Clarendon Press of Oxford University Press, 1926.

PULSATOR (L. a striker)

The player of the 11th-century English *organ was called a pulsator due to the manner in which he was required to depress the "keys." The "keys" were actually levers--three to five inches wide and a yard or more long-- which were attached to valves by ropes, the action often being a foot in depth. Thus, to make a pipe speak the player was required to give a thump or a strong jerk.

QUARTET CHOIR (F. quartette, fr. It. quartetto, dim. of
     quarto the fourth, fr. L. quartus the fourth + *choir)

The 19th- and 20th-century phenomenon particularly
strong in American Protestantism in which the volunteer
chorus of the church was augmented by a quartet of solo
voices (SATB) for the offering of the anthem at Sunday services is the quartet choir. Some churches went as far as
to employ only a professional quartet for all the choral
music of the church, dismissing the volunteers entirely.

The origin of the quartet choir is unclear; however,
the English *verse-anthem and the German *chorale cantata
provide a possible precedent for its existence, in that European churches had a tradition of "professional" male singers
in their choirs for the performance of such works. It can
be readily seen in the sacred music composed in America
from the mid-19th century into the 20th century that this
type of choir held a strong influence on composition. (See,
e.g., H. R. Shelley's (1858-1949) "The King of Love My
Shephere Is.") (See also *History of Protestant church
music.)

Ellinwood, Leonard. The History of American Church
     Music. New York: Morehouse-Gorham, 1953. Chap-
     ter 9.
McPhee, Edward Wallace. "The Quartet Choir in the Wor-
     ship Service." Unpublished M.S.M. thesis, Union
     Theological Seminary, New York, 1931.

QUEMPAS (L.)

The well-known medieval Latin *carol, marking the
advent of the Christ-child, which was widely accepted among
Reformation congregations is the Quempas carol. It receives
its name from its first two Latin syllables, Quem pastores
laudavere.... In its completeness there are actually three
texts.

Regarding the origin and exact date of the Quempas
no definite conclusion is available. However, the custom
of singing the Quempas at the midnight service on Christmas
Eve by groups in all four corners of the church to announce
from north, south, east and west that "Heaven's all-glorious
King is born," dates back to the Middle Ages. This expression of the "Quempas goes 'round'" has been used in
Silesia for several centuries.

The earliest extant manuscript to contain the Quempas

was discovered around 1450 in southern Bohemia. This
Hohenfurth Ms. has the first two Latin carols of the Quempas facing each other at the very beginning of the manuscript.
        Quite ignored by Martin Luther (1483-1546), the
Quempas fared sumptuously during the late 16th and 17th
centuries, having clearly been established in customary use
and was included in many notable hymnals. Part settings
appeared in the 17th century, the most famous being by
Michael Praetorius (1571-1621).

Klammer, Edward W. "The Quempas Goes 'Round'," in:
     The Musical Heritage of the Church, ed. Theodore
     Hoelty-Nickel. Vol. VI. St. Louis: Concordia Pub-
     lishing House, 1963. Pp. 55-63.

QUICUMQUE VULT (L.)

        The statement of faith known as the Athanasian Creed,
employed by Charlemagne (742-814) as a *canticle and thusly
introduced into church music, is the Quicumque vult (Whoso-
ever will be saved). Strictly speaking, it is not a canticle,
but an affirmation of faith bearing strong Trinitarian doctrine. Its authorship is unknown, but the earliest references
to it are in the writings of Bishop of Arles (503-543). It
has been appointed for use in the Anglican Church since the
first Prayer Book (1549), during the office of *Morning
Prayer of feast days, in the place of the Apostles' Creed.
The Church of England has employed the Quicumque congregationally whereas the Roman Church has used it for private
devotion prior to the service.
        When chanted, the Quicumque appears in a simple
form of the eighth Gregorian tone. (See *Ecclesiastical
modes.)

Kelly, J. N. D. The Athanasian Creed. New York: Harper
     and Row, 1965.

RAPPORTS see REPORTS

RAVENSCROFT PSALTER

        "The Whole Booke of Psalms with the Hymns Evan-

gelicall, and Songs Spirituall. Composed in 4. Parts ... by
Tho: Ravenscroft ... 1621." This title was that of the
Ravenscroft Psalter, as printed by the Company of Stationers,
London. This collection by Thomas Ravenscroft (1592?-
1635?) was the first printing of the *Old Version with *hymns
appended to it. The tunes, in four-part settings, contained
many new common meter tunes, including "Old 104th" for the
first time.

Frost, Maurice. English and Scottish Psalm and Hymn
    Tunes (c.1543-1677). London: S.P.C.K., 1953.
Havergal, Rev. W. H. (ed.). Ravenscroft's Book of Psalms.
    London: J. A. Novello, 1845 (reprint).
Mark, Jeffrey. "Thomas Ravenscroft," Musical Times,
    65:881-884, 1926.

RECITATIVE   (Fr. recitatif, G. Recitativ, It. recitativo,
    fr. L. recitare, fr. re re + citare to call, to cite)

    The declamatory portions by a single voice of an
*anthem, *cantata, *oratorio or *passion (also of opera) is
the recitative. It has been called the rhetorical element in
music, being the vehicle of rapid changes of thought and
emotion as in prose, narrative and dialogue.
    The recitative in relation to the anthem is seen in the
sectional development of this form during the Restoration
period as the *cantata-anthem began to evolve. "O Lord,
my God" (CM, II:242-247), by Pelham Humphrey (1647?-
1674), contains a brief bass recitative, illustrative of the
care taken by this composer for correct verbal accentuation
of the English language. Brief recitatives may also be found
in the solo anthems of Boyce (1710-1779), Travers (c.1703-
1758) and Greene (1695-1755).
    In the cantatas of J. S. Bach (1685-1750), recitatives are
accompanied by the *basso continuo and also the full or partial
ensemble. This is in keeping with the broadening classification of recitatives in the late Baroque era: recitativo secco
being a skeletal harmonic progression for continuo and string
group, and recitativo accompagnato being the sustained chordal
accompaniment of the continuo group. The *arioso represented an elaboration beyond the recitativo accompagnato, the
accompaniment being more florid than chordal, incorporating
the instrumental ensemble. It was not unlike the 18th-cen-
tury composers to incorporate any or all styles in any given
recitative.
    In early oratorio composition the solo style varied

between recitativo accompagnato and *arioso. The 18th-
century use of the recitative in oratorio composition paral-
leled that of the cantata. However, in the 19th century its
importance declined somewhat. When recitative did appear
in the 19th-century oratorios it was generally brief and aca-
demic--e.g., L. Spohr's (1784-1859) Der Fall Babylons and
A. Sullivan's (1842-1900) The Prodigal Son. The 20th-cen-
tury composition recitative in some cases has been replaced
by the spoken narrative, as in A. Honegger's (1892-1955)
King David.

Gerber, Rudolf. Das Passionsrezitativ bei Heinrich Schütz
    und seine stilgeschichtlichen Grundlagen. Gütersloh:
    C. Bertelsmann, 1929.
Heuss, Alfred Valentin. "Bachs Rezitativbehandlung mit
    besonderer Berucksichtigung der Passionen, " Bach-
    Jahrbuch, 1904: 82-103, 1904.
Jammers, Ewald. "Der Choral als Rezitativ, " AMW, 22:
    143-168, 1965.
Melchert, H. "Das Rezitativ der Kirchenkantaten J. S.
    Bach, " Bach-Jahrbuch, 1958:5-83, 1958.
Newmann, F. H. Die Aesthetik des Rezitativs; zur Theorie
    des Rezitative im 17. und 18. Jahrhundert. Strasburg:
    Edition P. H. Heitz, 1962.
Spitz, Charlotte. "Die Entwicklung des Stile recitativo, "
    AMW, 3:237-244, October, 1921.

RECITING TONE (fr. L. recitare, recitatum, fr. re re +
    citare to call, to cite)

    The principal note of recitation in a *psalm-tone or
*Anglican chant is the reciting tone or *tenor. Its rhythmic
value fluctuates according to the number of syllables in the
half-verse which are not included in the intonation or cadence
(*mediation or termination). Recitation tone, repercussio
and turba are other nomenclatures occasionally applied to the
reciting tone.

RECORDER (prob. fr. ME. record to warble like a bird,
    fr. L. recordari to call to mind, fr. re re + cord
    heart)

    The woodwind instrument, flute-like in tonal character,
which possesses a vertical tubular body with a head and
mouthpiece at one end, is a recorder (in German, Blockflöte).

It is sometimes called an English flute. Characteristic of
the mouthpiece is the wood block or "fipple" which channels
the player's breath through a narrow channel onto the aper-
ture and lip of the head. The vibrations set up by this
process are regulated by the eight finger holes in the tapered
body of the recorder.

Since the ancestry of the recorder harkens back to the
primitive whistle, it is impossible to date its true origin.
Its existence in the Middle Ages has not only been confirmed
by paintings and sculptures but also by one of the first references to it--in the household account of King Henry IV of
England, who bought a "fistula nomine Ricordo" in 1338.
Its popularity during the Baroque era is attested to by compositions for it by such composers as Purcell (1659-1695),
Croft (1678-1727), Handel (1685-1759) and Telemann (1681-
1767). Even J. S. Bach (1685-1750) raised it to new heights
by including it as an orchestral instrument, using it to accompany "O grief, how throbs His heavy-laden breast" in
the St. Matthew Passion (BGA, IV:1) and in at least 26 of
his cantatas.

With the rise of the modern orchestra the recorder
seemed doomed to an obscure existence. However, after
the Baroque revival at the turn of the 20th century interest
in the recorder as a chamber or house instrument was re-
awakened, particularly in Germany and Austria. This enthusiasm reached America prior to World War II, bringing
about the establishment of the American Recorder Society
in 1939.

Realizing the value of the recorder in the music ministry of the church, not only from the standpoint of involvement and teaching but also as an instrument for use in worship, some Protestant churches have instituted recorder ensembles as an activity in the *graded choir program. Publishers have even begun furnishing music for recorder ensembles as well as recorder obbligati to anthems.

Alker, Hugo. Recorder Music Bibliography. New York:
        C. F. Peters, 1966.
The American Recorder. Quarterly periodical of the
        American Recorder Society. New York, 1941-   .
Degen, Dietz. Zur Geschichte der Blockflöte in dem ger-
        manischen Ländern. Kassel: Bärenreiter-Verlag,
        1939.
Ganassi, Sylvestro. Open intitulata Fontegara (1535). New
        edition, ed. Hildemarie Peter, trans. Dorothy Swainson.
        New York: C. F. Peters, 1956.
Hunt, Edgar Hubert. The Recorder and Its Music. London:
        H. Jenkins, 1962.

Schmidt, Lloyd John. "A Practical and Historical Source-
Book for the Recorder." Unpublished Ph.D. dissertation, Northwestern University, Evanston, Illinois,
1959.

REFRAIN (OF., fr. refrainde to break, modulate restrain,
fr.--assumed--VL. refrangere, fr. L. refringere to
break off)

In *hymnody, the one or two identical lines recurring
at the end of each *stanza of a *hymn is called a refrain.
It differs from the *chorus in that the meaning of the refrain is dependent on the main text. The historical antecedents of the refrain can be seen in the singing of the early
Christian Church in antiphonal and responsorial styles. (See,
e.g., "O come, o come, Emanuel," CH, 70; and "Rejoice,
ye pure in heart," CH, 94.)

REPORTS (OF. report, or raport, fr. L. reportare to
bear or bring back, fr. re re + portare to bear or
bring)

Motet-like settings of the *psalms in meter, the
psalm tune generally allotted to the *tenor with imitative
counterpoint and elaboration in the other voices, are called
"Psalms in Reports." These settings appeared in the Scottish Psalter of 1635. "Aberfeldy" and "Bon Accord" are
illustrative of this style of psalm setting. (Cf. *Fuging
tune.)

Frost, Maurice. English and Scottish Psalm and Hymn-
Tunes. London: S.P.C.K., 1953.
Terry, Sir Richard. The Scottish Psalter of 1635. London:
Novello, 1935.

REPROACHES (F. reproche, fr.--assumed--VL. repropriare,
fr. L. re re + propriare to draw near)

A series of anthems and responses, sung antiphonally
by cantors and choir during the service of the Veneration of
the Cross on the morning of Good Friday is called the reproaches or improperia. It is composed of 12 verses and
responses representing Christ as he reproached his people
for the sufferings of the passion. Probably originating in
10th-century France, it was adopted into the Roman liturgy

during the 12th century. The reproaches in an English trans-
lation is incorporated into some Anglican Holy Week orders.
(See a setting of the reproaches by G. Palestrina (d. 1594) in
Latin.)

REQUIEM   (acc. of L. requius rest)

Differing from the Roman Catholic practice of an
entire service of prayer for the dead, that they may rest
in peace, the requiem in the German Lutheran sense denotes
a portion of the *funeral service retaining the idea of "rest
in the Lord." The two great requiems of German Protestantism are Heinrich Schütz's (1585-1672) Musikalisches
Exequiem (1636) and Johannes Brahms' (1833-1897) Ein
deutsches Requiem (1867).
    The Schütz Requiem is composed in three major
divisions. The first is a "Concerto in the form of a German Requiem" with Biblical passages and stanzas of *chorales arranged together with the *Kyrie and *Gloria. A
motet on the sermon text for Prince Heinrich's funeral,
"Lord, if I but thee may have," comprises the second division. The final division bears the Italian influence with
the Song of Simeon being countered by a separate choir
singing "Blessed are the dead."
    The six movements of the Brahms Requiem are all
settings of Scripture which are appropriate for the time of
bereavement, yet non-liturgical. The Scriptures include
passages from both Old and New Testaments as well as from
the Apocrypha. The scope and size of this work has given
Brahms an important place in the field of choral literature.
(See also *Funeral music and *Oratorio.)

Robertson, Alec. Requiem: Music of Mourning and Conso-
    lation. New York: Praeger, 1967.

RESPOND   (fr. OF. respondre, fr. L. respondere, respon-
    sum, fr. re re + spondere to promise)

A short choral statement to prayers or readings by
the priest is a respond. Usually they are sung during the
*Canonical Hour Offices to plainsong melodies.

RESPONSE   (*respond)

(1) The short sentences or petitions said or sung by

the congregation or choir in reply to the *versicle or petitions of the officiant in the Anglican or Lutheran offices are responses. These responses occur in connection with the *preces, the *suffrages, the *litany and the Decalogue, to mention a few instances. When the term, "festal responses," is used, it usually implies the five-part setting of the tenor plainsong, as for example by Thomas Tallis (c.1505-1585) in his Preces and Responses.

(2) In non-liturgical congregations the response is often a short independent choral piece sung at the conclusion of a prayer or scripture lesson (e.g., the prayer response, "Hear our prayer, O Lord").

RESPONSORY (L. responsorium)

The responsory is a type of chant characteristically sung after each lesson at *Matins in the Roman Church as a musical reply to the Scripture. With the Reformation, it was retained and altered by the Lutheran Reformers to be sung only after the last lesson at Matins and at *Vespers. The Anglican communion, because of its elaborateness of text and difficulty of translation, omitted it entirely from the Prayer Book.

Liturgically, the responsory combined appropriate verses and response from Scripture for the feasts and the seasons of *Christian Year. Designed in two parts, the responsory proper consists of a series of verses and responses. The "verse" (the second part) is so constructed that its final section may serve as the response in the responsory proper. This is followed then by the first section of the *Gloria Patri with the concluding portion of the verse once again.

During the periods of Pietism and Rationalism in Lutheran history the responsory was lost with the neglect of Matins and Vespers. However, they have been restored in a portion of Lutheran congregations, with appropriate musical settings available such as Max Reger's (1873-1916) Twenty Short Anthems or Responses and J. F. Ohl's (1850-?) The Responsories of Matin and Vespers, Set to Music.

Heschke, Richard J. "A History of the Responsory of the Divine Office." Unpublished A.Mus.D. dissertation, University of Rochester, Rochester, New York, 1965.
Procter, Francis and W. H. Frere. A New History of the Book of Common Prayer. London: Macmillan, 1955.

Reed, Luther D. The Lutheran Liturgy. Philadelphia:
    Muhlenberg Press, 1947. Pp. 401-403.

RHYTHM INSTRUMENTS   (F. & L.; F. rhythme, fr. L.
    rhythmus, fr. Gr. rhythmos measured motion,
    measure, proportion; akin to flow + OF. instrument,
    estrument, fr. L. instruments, fr. instruere to con-
    struct, equip)

    Any percussion instruments, those struck to produce
tone, are considered rhythm instruments. In a more limited
sense, this term relates solely to those instruments which
sound only one pitch and to those which are incapable of
sounding a melodic line. A typical set of rhythm instruments includes drums, rhythm sticks, triangle, sandblocks,
tambourine, tone blocks, cymbals and gong.
    While the "Kindersinfonie" (1788) of Franz Joseph
Haydn (1732-1809) is scored for rhythm instruments, the
early use of rhythm instruments by children in concert is
recorded in 1885 at Covent Garden. By the early 20th century in England and America the creative use of rhythm instruments in music education was developing into an active
part of the program (see especially the seven volumes of
Rhythmic Ensemble Band-Books for Children by Angela Diller
and Kate Stearns Page published by G. Schirmer).
    With the 20th-century work of Carl Orff (b.1895) at
the Güntherschule in Munich and his publication, Das Schul-
werk, new horizons in the rhythmic instruction of children
appeared. His creative approach to music, both rhythmic
and melodic, has provided valuable and rewarding results
with children.
    Regarding the use of rhythm instruments in Protestant
church music, their role is invaluable with the younger choirs
of the *graded choir program. In fact, music publishers are
now making available anthems which incorporate the use of
rhythm instruments.

Orff, Carl and Gunild Keetman. Music for Children, 5 vols.
    English adaptation by Doreen Hall and Arnold Walter.
    Mainz: B. Schotts Söhne, 1961.
Schmidt, Brita. "Orff-instrumentarium im Kinderchor,"
    Der Kirchenchor, 27:24-25, 1967.
Swanson, Bessie R. Music in the Education of Children.
    3rd ed. Belmont, Cal.: Wadsworth Pub. Co., 1969.

RITORNELLO   (It. dim. of ritorno return, fr. reiornare to
    return)

The 17th-century term for the instrumental interlude
in a *cantata, *aria, or solo song is ritornello. This instrumental section could occur as an introduction, between
sections or at the conclusion of these forms. Buxtehude
(1637-1707) in his "Erhalt uns, Herr bei deinen Wort" ("Lord
keep us steadfast in thy Word") incorporated the ritornello
as an interlude for trio sonata between stanzas of the *chorale. Purcell (1659-1695) also employed the instrumental
ritornelli in his *cantata-anthems as a unifying defice (e.g.,
"It is a good thing to give thanks").

Schering, A. Geschichte des Instrument--Konzert bis auf
    die Gegenwart. Leipzig: n.p., 1927.

ROCK see "POP," GOSPEL

SALUTATION (OF., fr. L. salutatio)

The Hebrew form of greeting, "The Lord be with
you," and its response, "And with thy spirit" (Ruth 2:4;
Judges 6:12 and Luke 1:28), is known as the salutation. It
entered the Christian liturgies during the first centuries as
a responsive introduction to new and different portions of
the services. In the communion service the salutation introduces the *collect, the *Preface, and the *benediction; in
*Canonical Hours it precedes the collects and prayers. (Cf.
*Sursum corda.)

Reed, Luther D. The Lutheran Liturgy. Philadelphia:
    Muhlenberg Press, 1947. Pp. 277-278.

SANCTUS (L. holy)

The solemn act of adoration said or sung as the
climax and conclusion to the *Preface at the Eucharist is
called the Sanctus. Liturgically, it balances the *Gloria in
excelsis of the ante-communion, or pre-communion portion
of the service. The text: "Holy, holy, holy, Lord God of
Sabaoth; Heaven and earth are full of they glory; Hosanna in

the highest. Blessed is he that cometh in the Name of the
Lord; Hosanna in the highest. " The origin of this early
*hymn is uncertain, for it is found in various forms among
the early liturgies. However, it is thought to have developed
in North Africa (c. A.D. 200), with the addition of the *Benedictus in the fifth century by the Syrian church. It should be
noted that the Sanctus does bear some of the influence of the
Kedushah (Sanctification) of the daily synagogue service from
Jewish rituals (Isaiah 6:2-3).

With the coming of the Reformation, Luther adopted
the Sanctus for use after the Words of Institution in his
*Formula Missae (1523). This, however, was returned to
its original place with the official Common Service (1918) of
the Lutheran Church in America. The Anglican church retained the Sanctus in its Prayer Book (1549), but omitted the
Benedictus.

Reed, Luther D. The Lutheran Liturgy. Philadelphia:
    Muhlenberg Press, 1947. Pp. 330-333.
Reindell, Walter. "Das Sanctus," Kirchenchordienst, 7:33-
    39, March-April, 1941.

SANG-SCHULE see SINGING SCHOOL

SARUM BREVIARY

    Originally the breviary (also portiforium or portius)
was a volume containing only the first words of each *psalm,
*Antiphon, etc., as indicated for the offices of the Hours of
Prayer. Prior to the 13th century in monastic life several
distinct volumes contained various materials in complete
form for the office. However, with the private observance
of the office arising in the 13th century, all individual volumes were gathered into one compact cover for the whole
office. One of the most influential books of this kind was
the Sarum Breviary of Salisbury Cathedral (39 editions from
1475 to 1544). It contained the *psalter, legend, antiphonal,
*hymnal and collector. The influence of this breviary can
be seen in the King's Primer (1545), and, according to
Louis Benson, it holds an important role in the evolution of
the English *hymn.

Wordsworth, C. and F. Procter. Breviarium ad usum
    insignis eccl. Sarum. Cambridge, Eng.: Academiae
    Cantabrigiensis, 1886.

SARUM USE

The term "use," in the Anglican Church refers to the
principles controlling cathedral life: (1) the governing principles, (2) the words and orders of services, and (3) the cere-
monial directions for conducting the services. The Sarum
Use, though traditionally ascribed to St. Osmund (Bishop
1078-1099), was truly the work of Richard le Poer (Dean
1173-1215) at Salisbury Cathedral. These principles held a
strong influence upon the writers of the first *Book of Common Prayer, as did the *Sarum Breviary upon the development of English *hymnody.

Frere, W. H. Use of Sarum. Cambridge, Eng.: n.p.,
    1901.
Harrison, F. Ll. "Music for the Sarum Rite," AM, 6:99-
    144, 1963.
Warren, Frederick E. (trans.). The Sarum Missal in Eng-
    lish, 2 vols. London: Alcuin Club Collections, 1913.

SCHOOLS OF PROTESTANT CHURCH MUSIC

The following is a listing of colleges and universities
in the United States, and then seminaries, which offer graduate degrees in church music and which are currently accredited by the American Association of Theological Schools
or the National Association of Schools of Music.

Colleges and Universities

Baylor University, Waco, Texas; Boston University, Bos-
ton, Mass.; Butler University, Jordan College of Music,
Indianapolis, Ind.; Converse College, Spartanburg, S.C.;
Florida State University, Tallahassee, Fla.; Indiana Uni-
versity, Bloomington, Ind.; New England Conservatory of
Music, Boston, Mass.; Northwestern University, Evanston,
Ill.; Ohio State University, Columbus, Ohio; George Pea-
body College for Teachers, Nashville, Tenn.; Peabody
Conservatory of Music, Baltimore, Md.; Hartt College of
Music, University of Hartford, West Hartford, Conn.;
University of Missouri in Kansas City, Kansas City, Mo.;
University of Oregon, Eugene, Ore.; University of Roches-
ter, Eastman School of Music, Rochester, N.Y.; Univer-
sity of Southern California, Los Angeles, Cal.; University
of West Virginia, Morgantown, W.Va.

Seminaries

Boston University, Boston, Mass.; Christian Theological Seminary, Indianapolis, Ind.; Garrett Theological Seminary, Evanston, Ill.; Golden Gate Baptist Theological Seminary, Mill Valley, Cal.; Hamma Divinity School, Wittenberg University, Springfield, Ohio; New Orleans Baptist Theological Seminary, New Orleans, La.; Perkins School of Theology, Southern Methodist University, Dallas, Texas; The Southern Baptist Theological Seminary, Louisville, Ky.; Southwestern Baptist Theological Seminary, Fort Worth, Texas; and Union Theological Seminary, New York, N.Y.

Hooper, William Lloyd. "The Master's Degree in Church Music in Protestant Theological Seminaries of the United States." Unpublished Ph.D. thesis, George Peabody College for Teachers, Nashville, 1966.
Proceedings of the 44th Annual Meeting, November 25 to November 27, 1968. National Association of Schools of Music. Washington, D.C.: National Association of Schools of Music.

SCOTTISH PSALTER

The two collections of the Psalms of David in meter (1564/65 and 1635) for use by the Church of Scotland are called the Scottish Psalters. (See *Psalmody, metrical (Scotland); and *Psalters.)

Frost, Maurice. English and Scottish Psalm and Hymn Tunes (c.1543-1677). London: S.P.C.K., 1953.
Livingston, Rev. Neil (ed.). The Scottish Metrical Psalter of A.D. 1635. Glasgow: Maclure and Macdonald, 1864 (reprint).
Patrick, Millar. Four Centuries of Scottish Psalmody. London: Oxford University Press, 1949.
Terry, Richard R. The Scottish Psalter of 1635. London: Novello and Co., 1935.

SERVICE (ME. service, servise, fr. OF. servise, service, fr. L. servitum)

In the broadest concept of Protestantism, any meeting of the faithful for the express purpose of divine worship is a service. However, in a more limited sense, any setting of the basic choral portions (other than the responses) of liturgical worship may be termed a service. In the Anglican tradition these services must be in agreement with the *Book of Common Prayer. (Cf. *Full service.)

Mid-20th-century experimental services have been prepared in an attempt to offer contemporary worship settings. Among these are Geoffrey Beaumont's Twentieth Century Folk Mass (1956) and Daniel Moe's Worship for Today (1968). (Cf. *"Pop," Gospel.)

SERVICE BOOK   see   LITURGICAL BOOKS

SEVEN-SHAPED NOTATION

The system of solmization invented by Jesse B. Aiken of Philadelphia about 1832 which expanded the four-shapes of the *fa-so-la system to seven, in an attempt to harmonize this method with the Continental solfeggio constitutes the seven-shaped notation. This system appeared in Aiken's Christian Minstrel (1846) and William Walker's (1809-1875) Christian Harmony.

do   re   mi   fa   sol   la   ti

Chase, Gilbert. America's Music: from the Pilgrims to the Present. New York: McGraw-Hill, 1966.
Eskew, Harry Lee. "Shape-note Hymnody in the Shenandoah Valley, 1816-1860." Unpublished Ph.D. dissertation, Tulane University, New Orleans, Louisiana, 1966.
Hooper, William Lloyd. Church Music in Transition. Nashville: Broadman Press, 1963.
Marrocco, Thomas W. "The Notation in American Sacred Music Collections," AMI, 36:136-142, 1964.
Seeger, Charles. "Contrapuntal Style in the Three-Voiced Shaped-Note Hymns," MQ, 26:483-493, October, 1940.

SINGING SCHOOL (OE. singan; akin to D. zingen, OS. & OHG. singan, G. singen, ON. syngja, Sw. sjunga, Dan. synge, Goth. siggivan, and prob. to Gr. omphē voice + ME. scole, fr. OE. scol, fr. L. schola, fr. Gr. scholē leisure, disputation, lecture, a school)

The musical institution of 18th-century America which

initially fostered improved psalm singing and later hymns, spiritual songs and anthems, is the singing school. Its history reflects back to the training of boy singers by the Roman Church, and more nearly the Sang-schules of the Scottish Church. In 1599 by an Act of Council in Scotland, Sang-schules were reestablished to teach psalter tunes rather than Gregorian tones (as well as other subjects) to the youth of various communities.

In America, the first record of a singing school is by William Byrd II, who in 1710 attended one in Virginia. Another early school was organized in 1720 by the Rev. Samuel Sewall in Boston. These schools usually met for two or three evenings a week for a number of weeks, being a social diversion as well as the kernel for the development of the church choir. Cotton Mather (1663-1728), an outstanding leader of American Puritanism, strongly encouraged the use of the singing school for the improvement of psalm singing in The Accomplished Singer (1721).

A session of the singing school would find the chairs, benches or planks arranged in a circle with the singing master in the center. Each voice part would have its own book. The material taught normally included the rules for singing and the music fundamentals of rhythm and sol-fa. Since no standard manual of instruction was employed the quality of teaching in the early singing schools widely varied according to the leader. However, two early instructional books are extant though how widely they were used is in question: The Art of Singing Psalm Tunes (1720) by John Tufts (1689-1750) and The Grounds and Rules of Music Explained (1721) by Thomas Walter (1696-1725).

The most potent force upon 18th-century American church music, the singing school contributed not only to the improvement of psalm singing, but also to the establishment of church choirs, the organization of choral societies (as the Handel and Haydn Society), and the foundation of the rural homespun hymnody of the American frontier (see *Camp meeting).

While the singing school was both urban and rural in the 18th century, as the latest European musical fashions became infused into the urban culture of early 19th-century America, this institution moved into the frontier regions where it became wedded to the *fa-so-la system.

John, Robert W. "The American Singing School Movement, 1720-1780," JAMS, 7:165-66, Spring, 1955.
Lowens, Irving. "The Singing School Movement in the United States." Report of the Eighth Congress of the

International Musicological Society. New York: Bärenreiter, 1961. Pp. 88-89.

SINGSTUNDE (G. singing lesson)

The service of praise and prayer through singing
among the German Moravian Brethren was called Singstunde.
The practice of these services was brought to America by
the German immigrants in the 18th century. Through the
Singstunde the musical proficiency of these people was maintained in a new land, otherwise quite illiterate musically.
This singing service dates back to Count N. L. von Zinzendorf who instituted the custom on Cantate Sunday in 1727.
The service began with the singing of several hymns in toto,
followed by the spontaneous singing of individual *stanzas.
The spontaneous stanzas, intoned by Zinzendorf, were readily
joined by the assembly as the people recognized the text and
tune. As these stanzas were often drawn from different
hymns, yet related thematically, the entire practice might
be referred to as a Liederpredigt (song-sermon). The in-
formality and spontaneity of the service was aided in the
traditional practice of singing without hymnals. The development of this practice was encouraged by the use of the Singstunde in the home as well as prescribed places of worship.

"A Modern 'Singstunde', " The Moravian Music Foundation
        Bulletin, 14:2, Spring, 1970.

SOCIETIES OF PROTESTANT CHURCH MUSIC

The following is a selected listing of societies related
to Protestant church music or of interest to some facet of
this field. The arrangement is alphabetical.

1. The All-African Church Music Association. Founded
in 1963, this organization is headquartered in Salisbury, Rho-
desia. Its official periodical is the All-African Church Music
Association Journal.

2. The American Guild of English Handbell Ringers
(A. G. E. H. R.). Founded in 1954 for the promotion of handbell ringing through festivals and publications, this organization produces the publication, Overtones.

3. American Guild of Organists (A. G. O.). In 1896
this organization was founded to advance the cause of worthy

religious music. It also conducts comprehensive examinations in organ playing and conducting. The official periodical is Music: The AGO and RCCO Magazine.

4. The American Recorder Society, Inc. Founded in 1939 by Suzanne Bloch, this society publishes the periodical, The American Recorder.

5. The Choristers Guild (C.G.). This interdenominational organization, founded in 1949, is dedicated to the promotion of successful children's choir programs within the churches. Its periodical is The Choristers Guild Letters.

6. The Church Music Society. This English society, founded in 1906, has as its purposes (a) promotion of the selection and performance of the music most suitable for different occasions of divine worship and for choirs of varying powers, and (b) provision for an advisory committee to the School of English Church Music.

7. Evangelischer Sängerbund. Founded by the state church of Germany in 1898, this organization espouses the encouragement of knowledge about hymns and the enthusiastic singing of them.

8. The Friends of Church Song (F.C.S.). This Swedish society, founded in 1896, promotes the improvement of church song within the congregation.

9. German Christian Singing Society. Founded by E. Gebhardt in 1879, this organization encourages the knowledge and singing of hymns.

10. The Guild of Carillonneurs in North America. Begun in 1936, this non-denominational organization serves to promote the development of proficient carillonneurs, to improve the quality of carillon music, to encourage the improvement of carillon installations and to advance the art in North America. The official periodical is the Bulletin.

11. Hymn Society of America. Founded in 1922, this organization promotes a better understanding of hymns and hymn singing through its sponsorship of hymn festivals, arranging of new hymn projects and maintaining a library in cooperation with Union Theological Seminary. Its official publications are The Hymn and Papers of the Society.

12. The Hymn Society of Great Britain and Ireland. Founded in 1936 for the promotion of knowledge about the various aspects of hymnody, this organization serves its aims through its periodical The Hymn Society of Great Britain and Ireland Bulletin.

13. Methodist Church Music Society. Begun in 1935, this group has these purposes: (a) to encourage among English Methodists a belief in the value of music as a means of worship, (b) to foster a sense of vocation among musicians, (c) to increase their musical equipment and (d) to utilize all the resources available for the purpose of making worship in Methodism more worthy. The official journal is The Choir.

14. Musical Gospel Outreach (M.G.O.). Organized in 1965, this society is designed to help link the Christian folk-rock groups of England together for overall effectiveness.

15. National Church Music Fellowship (N.C.M.F.). Begun in 1951 this society was founded to develop and promote a practical philosophy of music for the Bible-centered, evangelistic, missionary-minded church that, through the power of the Holy Spirit, will bring the most powerful and permanent spiritual results. The official periodical is Dimension.

16. National Fellowship of Methodist Musicians (Na.F.O.M.M.). Organized in 1956, this society of the United Methodist Church proposes (a) to promote the use of the best in musical culture, (b) to train persons for leadership in parishes, (c) to place persons most effectively and (d) to guide students in the selection of schools and curriculum. Its official bulletin is the Newsletter.

17. Moravian Music Foundation (M.M.F.). Founded in 1956, this organization seeks to advance early American Moravian music and complimentary music through research, publications and education.

18. Royal College of Canadian Organists (R.C.C.O.). Organized in 1909 this organization promoted the cause of worthy religious music through examinations, publications and conventions. The official publication is Music: The AGO and RCCO Magazine.

SOLO (It., lit., alone, fr. L. solus alone)

The musical art form in which a single voice, generally accompanied, conveys a text in a lyrical manner is a solo or solo art song. In relation to the church the solo has been called a paradox, for the single voice must be manipulated in such a way that it does not become the focal point of interest.

Historically, the soloist in worship harkens back to

Jewish and medieval Christian liturgies where the role of the
cantor was that of a soloist. In fact, the solo singer reached
his zenith in the *mass and *offices of the Roman Church
during the Middle Ages. In 1322 Pope John issued an edict
curbing what he thought were excessive abuses of the solo
tradition in the church. A further influence on its decline
was the rise of *congregational singing in the Reformation.
        After the decline of the 14th-century solo motet with
instrumental accompaniment, solo singing began to reappear
in the late 16th- and 17th-century English *anthems and
*services, in verse form. The Baroque era on the Conti-
nent gave rise to the solo cantata (e.g., Schütz, "Sinfonia
Sacra") and the incorporation of solos in *cantatas (e.g.,
Bach, "Christ lag in Todesbanden"). Basically these solo
passages from the cantatas and *oratorios were *arias and
*recitatives. However, individual songs were composed--
see, e.g., Bach's Schmelli Gesangbuch (1736, BGA, XXXIX:
279) and Purcell's Divine Hymns with their flowing vocal
style and continuo accompaniment.
        From the Classic and Romantic eras the art song and
oratorio arias have provided the bulk of solo literature used
in churches of the present century. Characterized somewhat
by theatrical display are the Moravian Songs of Peters (1746-
1813), the Biblical Songs of Dvořák (1841-1904) and the Weih-
nachtslieder of Cornelius (1824-1874). While originally composed for the concert hall, such songs have often been used
in the church in a meaningful expression of worship.
        The sacred solos from the late 19th century and first
half of the 20th century, during the heyday of the *quartet
choir, represent composers such as Stephan Adams (1844-
1913), Oley Speaks (1874-1948), George Chadwick (1854-1931),
Fred S. Converse (1879-1953), James MacDermid (1875-1940),
Geoffrey O'Hara (1882-1967) and Albert Hay Malotte (1895-
1964). These songs are characterized by dramatic melodies
supported by sumptuous chromatic harmonies, often in the
arpeggiated or reiterating-chordal fashion. Textually, they
vary from Biblical origin to non-Biblical or original poetry.
This period also witnessed the rise of the "inspirational
songs" whose roots are in the spiritual, country music, carol
or folk-styled song. These "inspirational songs" were often
strophic and closely akin to the *gospel song, though too difficult for congregational use.
        During the mid-20th-century period of worship, solos
in the modern harmonic idioms have appeared. The emphasis is placed on conveying the text, which is Biblically associated, rather than the singer's voice or the composer's
melodic ability. Rhythmically and harmonically there is

greater freedom. Representative of this style are "Alleluia"
by Ned Rorem (b.1917) and "Three Psalms" by Leo Sowerby
(1895-1968).

Berlinski, H., Preston Rockholt and Gertrude Tingley. "The
    Sacred Solo in Divine Worship," The NATS Bulletin,
    24:6-13, 21, October, 1967.
Coffin, Berton. "The Sacred Solo, Its Significant Com-
    posers and Trends," The NATS Bulletin, 7:2, 16,
    March-April, 1952.
Espina, Noni. Vocal Solos for Protestant Services. N.p.,
    n.p., 1965.
Gohl, Wilhelm. "Geistliche Sololieder des Barock," KM,
    11:113-120, May-June, 1939.
Homann, Hans-Elwin. "Sologesang im evangelischen Gottes-
    dienst," KM, 9:158-168, July-August, 1937.
Koopman, John. "Sacred Song: The Repertoire and Its
    Problems," The NATS Bulletin, 22:1:10-11, 15, Octo-
    ber, 1965.
_____. Selected Sacred Solos in Modern Idiom. Minne-
    apolis: Augsburg Publishing House, 1965.
Siebel, Katherine. Sacred Songs: A Guide to Repertory.
    New York: H. W. Gray, 1966.

SONG LEADER (OE. song, sang; akin to D. zang, G. sang,
    ON. söngr, Goth. saggws + ME. leden, fr. OE.
    laeden to go)

    The 19th- and 20th-century term for the person who
directs the congregation in the singing of *hymns and *gospel
songs is song leader. With the emphasis on *congregational
singing that came with the Protestant Reformation, a director
or leader of this singing traditionally has played an important
role in church music. Luther placed this duty along with
other musical responsibilities on the *cantor, for whom
schools of specialized training were set up. In the Reformed
Church and the Church of England the leadership of metrical
psalm singing was the duty of the minister, parish clerk or
*precentor.
    It was the precentor who carried the greatest influence
on the American innovation of the song leader, as the former
came to the Colonies with the early settlers. As the procedure of *lining-out was shifted from urban America to the
frontier settlements and became wedded to the *camp meeting
tradition of the Rev. James McGready, the early vestiges of
the song leader began to emerge. At this time the song

leader, who was usually the evangelist, sang mostly the "call" of the antiphonal, call-and-response styled songs.

However, with the era of "professional revivalism" (see *Evangelistic music) the function of the song leader became that of a person other than the evangelist. One of the earliest evangelist-song leader teams was Charles G. Finney (1792-1875) and Thomas Hastings (1784-1872). It was through this team that choirs began to appear and to play an active role in revivals. The mass choir, which grew in size to over 150 singers at the turn of the 20th century, provided the song leader with an aid for creating the atmosphere of spontaneous singing, even with unfamiliar songs. The musician of the Moody team, Ira D. Sankey (1840-1908) might be considered a song leader, yet it was his solo singing for which he is remembered. The real dynamic revival song leader of the early 20th century was Charles Alexander (1867-1920) who was noted for his jaunty way of handling the mass revival choirs. This tradition of the revival song leader-choir director has continued to the present, as witnessed in the crusades of Billy Graham in the person of Cliff Barrows (b.1923).

With the influence of the gospel song and the Sunday school movement on the evangelical churches in America, the revival song leader has found a place in the local church, where his duty is that of conducting the congregational singing in an enthusiastic, but meaningful manner.

Curwen, J. Spencer. Studies in Worship Music, 2nd series. London: J. Curwen and Sons, 1888.
Hooper, William Lloyd. Church Music in Transition. Nashville: Broadman Press, 1963.
Lorenz, Edmund S. Practice of Church Music. New York: Fleming H. Revell Co., 1909.

SONG OF MOSES

Deuteronomy 32:1-43, called the "Song of Moses," and sung at the placing of the Book of the Law inside the Ark of the Covenant was versified in meter and included as one of the *paraphrases in the Scottish Psalter (1635), where it was instructed to be sung to the same tune as Psalm 32 (identical to the tune of Psalm 29).

SOUTERLIEDEKENS

"Souterliedekens, een Nederlandsch Psalmboek van

1540": the first complete Dutch collection of metrical psalms with tunes was the Souterliedekens, published in Antwerp by Symon Cock. It contained 154 monophonic psalm tunes taken, in part, from Dutch folk songs, the original secular texts indicated. Many of these tunes were borrowed by the German compilers of psalter. This psalter underwent more than thirty editions.

Bruinsma, H. A. "The Souterliedekens and Its Relation to Psalmody in the Netherlands." Unpublished Ph.D. dissertation, University of Michigan, Lansing, 1949.

SPIRITUAL (fr. L. L. spiritualis, of breathing, of wind, fr. L. spiritus, spirit, breath)

The late 18th- and 19th-century religious folk songs of the American Negro and the white settlers of Appalachia comprise the body of vocal music called spirituals. Like the early Reformation chorale, they were the songs "born" from the people, constituting their "oral Bible," as it were. (The white spirituals are discussed under *Camp meeting and *Fa-so-la; the Negro spiritual is the major consideration of this entry.)
To understand the religious songs of the American Negro, one must briefly recount the history of events which led to their development. As is commonly known, the Negro was first brought to America in 1619 by Dutch merchants, who sold them into bondage. Thus, the black man was uprooted from his native African environment and forced to acclimate himself to a new land, language and way of life. With him, however, came his cultural rhythmical aptitude and religious feelings which provided the foundation for the creation of the spiritual.
As early as 1693, a group of Negroes in Boston are recorded to have ruled on the acceptable place of psalm singing in their service. This is most interesting when one realizes that the Bay Psalm Book was not printed with musical notation until 1698. In the South, however, psalm and hymn books were very limited and thus the practice of *lining-out was adopted. This practice was continued for so long a time that the slaves accepted it as a part of the psalm or hymn. When the intervention of spoken lines was finally omitted, the Negroes thought the tunes to be incomplete and thus continued the practice on their own, not only singing all common psalm tunes with accuracy, but also adding original verses.

One must remember that not all religious songs of the Negroes are spirituals, for the Negro sings the same songs that the white man sings, as well as his chanted prayers and chanted sermons. Also, it should be noted that the term, "spiritual," is not the only name by which these songs have been known. They have sometimes been called plantation songs or melodies; and in Louisiana they have been called "mellos," a corruption of melodies, from plantation melodies.

With regard to the influences upon the origins of the Negro spiritual there seem to be two conflicting attitudes among scholars: the first claims the African origins while the second seeks strong Anglo-American influences.

Turning first to the African theories as expounded by James Weldon Johnson, one finds the claims that Negro spirituals are as distinct from the folksongs of other peoples as those songs are from each other. Quite unusual is his willingness to expound the "miracle theory" of conception. It maintains that at the precise and psychic moment of time, there was blown through and fused into the vestiges of the Negroes' African music the spirit of Christianity as they came to know it through the missionaries. This argument is cogently argued by Paul F. Laubenstein in the Musical Quarterly (16:382-383), in which the similarities of the Judeo-Christian religious concepts with those of the African religions are compared.

The early Negroes in America carried over their considerable native musical traditions and talents to America; thus, the spirituals possess the fundamental characteristics of African music. They have a unique striking rhythmic quality, and show a marked similarity to some African songs in form and intervallic structure. Though based upon these primitive rhythms, the spirituals proceed in advance of African music through greater melodic development and the added harmonic element.

M. M. Fisher continues this viewpoint with a listing of internal and external evidences as to the Afro-Negro influences upon the spiritual, tracing the evolution of religious institutions of Negroes from the ancient African secret meetings, through the American "Valley" or "Wilderness" Convocations, to the Praise houses, independent Negro churches and holiness groups by means of the spiritual. This general viewpoint is shared by such contemporary scholars as Gunther Schuller, Imamu Baraka (LeRoi Jones), and Charles Keil in their studies on blues and jazz.

Contrary to this viewpoint stands the research of George Pullen Jackson and others who believe the Negro

spiritual to be of American birth, with influences from England and Holland. These men cause us to remember that it
was the Protestant Dutch and English settlers who began to
import African natives about the mid-17th century. The
singing of hymns and psalms was for a long time their chief
source of diversion, Yet, this by no means implies that the
tune of this or that Negro spiritual can be found in the Ainsworth, Sternhold and Hopkins or even New England psalters.
What is being claimed is that the musical prototype was
there, and the bewildering imagery and florid circumlocutions
of those old hymns had a direct bearing on the manner in
which the Negro converts sang of their faith and hope in the
new God they learned to worship. Thus, it was the inability
of the Negro to copy literally the "sacred music" of his
masters combined with the rich inheritance of his pagan ancestry which produced the spirituals. To this G. P. Jackson
offers his list of 114 tunes which compares white tunes and
Negro spirituals as further proof of common origin, which he
attributes to the old *camp meetings and the *gospel song.

Turning now toward historical evidences, Dena J.
Epstein sights two early references which possibly might
refer to the origin of the Negro spiritual phenomenon in 1816
and 1821. However, it is believed that a report in 1830,
discussing the Negro population of Charleston, unequivocally
documents the existence of a distinctive type of sacred song
(with an example given of what might be called a spiritual).

From the mid-1830's on, frequent reports on the distinctive religious Negro songs are found, though these reports fail to distinguish between the songs learned at mixed
religious meetings and those exclusively belonging to the
slaves.

The Evangelist, a religious weekly in New York, was
the first to have an extended article to discuss the spirituals.
The unsigned article was "Songs of the Blacks," published
October 23, 1856 (Vol. XXVII:1).

The first American Negro spiritual to appear in print
with its music is believed to be "Roll, Jordan, Roll," published by Miss Lucy McKim of Philadelphia in 1862.

On November 15, 1867, the first book of Negro songs
was published, Slave Songs of the United States. Its compilers, W. F. Allen, C. P. Ware and Lucy McKim Garrison,
claimed to have brought together 136 songs from all parts of
the South never before published.

From the Emancipation to the present, the Negro
spiritual, in its original form, style and performance, has
become concertized almost to the point of being beyond recognition. The main source of this work came from the Fisk

University Singers (founded in 1871). This group of Negro
singers concertized in most major cities both of America
and Europe, receiving ecstatic receptions. Much of the
popularity of the Negro spiritual is due to them and one of
their tireless leaders, John W. Work.

Epstein, Dena J. "Slave Music in the United States before
    1860," Notes, 20:203-205, Spring, 1963.
Jackson, George Pullen. White and Negro Spirituals. New
    York: J. J. Augustine Publisher, 1943.
Jones, LeRoi. Blues People: Negro Music in White America.
    New York: William Morrow, 1963.
Keil, Charles. Urban Blues. Chicago: University of Chi-
    cago Press, 1966.
Lomax, John A. "'Sinful Songs' of Southern Negro," MQ,
    20:177-187, April, 1934.
Schuller, Gunther. Early Jazz: Its Roots and Musical
    Development. New York: Oxford University Press,
    1968.
Washington, Joseph R., Jr. "Negro Spirituals," The Hymn,
    15:102-104, October, 1964.

STABAT MATER   (L. the mother was standing)

The non-liturgical hymn on the contemplation of the
sorrows of the Mother of Christ at the cross is called Stabat
Mater (dolorosa). This famous Latin sequence, traditionally
ascribed to Jacopone da Todi (c. 1230-1306), has been adopted
as a sequence in the Passiontide Mass of The Seven Sorrows
of the Blessed Virgin Mary in the Roman Catholic Church.
In the 18th-century translation by E. Caswall (1814-1878), it
begins, "At the Cross her station keeping, Stood the mourn-
ful Mother weeping, Close to Jesus at the last."
While Stabat Mater is of Roman origins, with good
translations provided the congregation, many of the settings
by noted composers have been offered in Protestant churches
of many denominations. A selected list of such composers
is the following: Giovanni Palestrina (1525-1594), Alessandro
Scarlatti (1660-1725), Antonio Caldara (1670-1736), Giovanni
Pergolesi (1710-1736), Gioacchino Rossini (1792-1868), Giu-
seppe Verdi (1813-1901), Antonin Dvorák (1841-1904) and
Francis Poulenc (1899-1963).

Hoffman, Jack. "The Stabat Mater." Unpublished M.S.M.
    thesis, Union Theological Seminary, New York, 1953.
Robertson, Alec. Requiem: Music of Mourning and Consola-
    tion. New York: Praeger, 1967.

STANZA

The grouping of *verses of poetry into a division is called a stanza. This term often refers to the text which accompanies the singing through of a *hymn tune one time. (See *Hymn meter and *Hymnody.)

STERNHOLD AND HOPKINS PSALTER see PSALMODY, METRICAL (England); PSALTERS

STRASBURG PSALTER see PSALMODY, METRICAL (The Continent); PSALTERS

SUCCENTOR (LL. an accompanier in singing, fr. succinere to sing, fr. sub under, after + canere to sing)

The minor canon in a cathedral to whom the authority of the *precentor is delegated and who is responsible for the direction of the choral services is the succentor. This office is found only in Old Foundation cathedrals.

SUFFRAGES (OF., fr. L. suffragium vote, political support)

Literally a prayer of intercession, the suffrages are objective, poetic forms of prayer resembling the *litany with the employment of *versicles and *responses used at services of prayer and communion among Western liturgies. The term is often used synonymously with *preces. Taken chiefly from the psalms, the suffrages recognize the importance of congregational participation in corporate prayer.
In the Lutheran church the General Suffrages are from the preces feriales of the Roman Breviary for Lauds and Vespers with certain omissions; while the suffrages for *Matins and *Vespers are from the preces feriales for Prime and Compline. A corporate part of these services which concluded Morning and Evening Prayer in Luther's Small Catechism was the *Lord's Prayer and the *Credo.
The responsive prayers of the suffrages appear in the prayer services of the Anglican Church following the Creed. These short intercessions may be chanted by the priest, to which the choir sings brief responses (see, e.g., Thomas Tallis, 1505-1585, Dorian Service--CM, I:1-42; also Hymnal 1940, nos. 601, 602).

In the Presbyterian Church of England and Wales the suffrages compose the beginning of the First Order of Service.

Reed, Luther D. The Lutheran Liturgy. Philadelphia: Muhlenberg Press, 1947. Pp. 639-651.

SURSUM CORDA (L. upward + hearts)

The salutation, "Lift up your hearts," together with the response, "We lift them up unto the Lord," at the beginning of the *preface in the Eucharist is termed the Sursum corda. This is attested by the Canons of Hippolytus (third century) but thought to date from at least the second century. It is sometimes called the *salutation.

Procter, Francis and W. H. Frere. A New History of the Book of Common Prayer. London: Macmillan, 1955.
Reed, Luther D. The Lutheran Liturgy. Philadelphia: Muhlenberg Press, 1947.

SYNAGOGA (LL., fr. Gr. synagoge a bringing together, an assembly, fr. synagein to bring together, fr. syn with + agein to lead)

Traditionally, the Synagoga encompassed the utterances of all the minor characters as well as the crowd in the *passion settings and was sung by the choir. The more distinct division, reserving the choir entirely for the utterances of the crowd, occurred in the late 16th century in the passion settings by Victoria. (Cf. *Turba.)

Smallman, Basil. The Background of Passion Music. Naperville, Ill.: SCM Book Club, 1957.

TATE AND BRADY PSALTER see PSALMODY, METRICAL (England); PSALTERS

TE DEUM LAUDAMUS (L. te acc. of tu thou + Deum acc. of Deus God + laudamus ind. 1st per. pl. we praise)

The ancient hymn of the Christian church which is

sung as a *canticle at the service of *Morning Prayer or
*Matins and also at services of special thanksgiving is the
Te Deum laudamus. In the Anglican office it is sung following the first lesson except during Advent and Lent, when
the Bendicite omnia opera is provided as an alternate. The
Lutheran service places the Te Deum following the sermon;
the *Benedictus is substituted for it during the penitential
seasons.

    The Te Deum, being one of the earliest extant Chris-
tian hymns of praise, generally is ascribed to Niceta, Bishop
of Remesiana, (c.400), though not with certainty. It properly
ends with the verse, "Make them to be numbered with thy
saints in glory everlasting." Other additions of versicles
and responses have been added from time to time.

    With the Reformation, Martin Luther translated the
Te Deum in the style of the German chorale. His translation, "Herr, Gott, dich loben wir," inspired many compositions by Baroque German composers, none the least being
J. S. Bach's organ composition of this title (BWV, 725).
Composers of choral setting of the Te Deum Laudamus include Karl H. Graun (1756), Henry Purcell (for St. Cecilia's
Day, 1694), G. F. Handel (for the Peace of Utrecht, 1713,
and for the victory at Dettingin, 1743), F. Mendelssohn (in
the key of A, undated) and A. Bruckner (in C, 1884). Among
20th-century composition of this text are those by Zoltan
Kodály (1936), Ralph Vaughan Williams (1937), Benjamin
Britten (1945) and Ernst Pepping (1956).

> "We praise thee O God: We acknowledge thee to be
> the Lord; All the earth doth worship thee: the Father
> everlasting; To thee all Angels cry aloud; the Heavens,
> and all the Powers therein; To thee Cherubim and
> Seraphim continually do cry, Holy, Holy, Holy, Lord
> God of Sabaoth; Heaven and earth are full of the maj-
> esty of the glory. The glorious company of the Apos-
> tles praise thee. The goodly fellowship of the Prophets
> praise thee. The noble army of Martyrs praise thee.
> The holy Church throughout all the world doth acknow-
> ledge thee; The Father, of an infinite Majesty; Thine
> adorable, true, and only Son; Also the Holy Ghost, the
> Comforter.

> "Thou art the King of Glory, O Christ. Thou art the
> everlasting Son of the Father. When thou tookest upon
> thee to deliver man, thou didst humble thyself to be
> born of a Virgin. When thou hadst overcome the
> sharpness of death, thou didst open the Kingdom of
> Heaven to all believers. Thou sittest at the right hand

of God, in the glory of the Father. We believe that
thou shalt come to be our Judge. We therefore pray
thee, help thy servants, whom thou hast redeemed with
thy precious blood. Make them to be numbered with
thy Saints, in glory everlasting.

"O Lord, save thy people, and bless thine heritage.
Govern them, and lift them up for ever. Day by day
we magnify thee: And we worship thy Name ever,
world without end. Vouchsafe, O Lord, to keep us
this day without sin. O Lord, have mercy upon us,
have mercy upon us. O Lord, let thy mercy be upon
us, as our trust is in thee. O Lord, in thee have I
trusted; let me never be confounded" [BCP].

Julian, John. A Dictionary of Hymnology. New York: Dover
     Publications, 1957. Pp. 1119-1134. (reprint of 1907)
Kahler, E. Studien zum Te Deum zur Geschichte des 24.
     Psalms in der Alten Kirche. Göttingen: Vanderhoeck
     & Rupprecht, 1958.

TENOR (OF. tenour, F. teneur, fr. L. tenor, fr. tenere
     to hold)

     (1) The part to which the principal melody or cantus
firmus is allotted in *plainsong is the tenor.

     (2) In modern usage, the highest natural male voice,
which corresponds in range to the contrapuntal tenor (B-g1)
is the tenor.

     (3) That part which, in four-part writing (c.1450), is
the second-lowest part is referred to as the tenor, the bass
(bassus or countratenor) being the lowest.

     (4) The reciting note of a *psalm-tone is also called
the tenor.

TER SANCTUS (L. ter thrice + sanctus holy)

     The term used for the thrice "holy" of the *Trisagion,
the *Sanctus of the *mass or *service, or the *Te Deum is
Ter Sanctus.

TESTO (It. a text) see HISTORICUS

THOROUGH-BASS (thorough--old spelling for "through"--is
the translation of <u>continuo,</u> i.e., continuing throughout the piece)

The 17th- and 18th-century practice of indicating an
accompanying part of a musical composition by its bass
notes together with numerical figures and signs designating
the harmonies to be played above the bass is commonly
called thorough-bass (in French, <u>basse, chiffre;</u> in German,
<u>Generalbass</u> or <u>bezifferter Bass;</u> in Italian, <u>basso</u> continuo).
It is a type of musical shorthand prevalent during the Ba-
roque and early Classical eras. The realization of this
<u>continuo</u> part requires at least two instruments, a harmony-
type instrument (as the lute, therorbo, harpsichord or organ)
and a bass instrument (as the viol da gamba, violoncello,
bassoon or trombone).

Another term commonly applied to this practice is
"figured bass," descriptive of the bass line and its accompanying figurations. Among these symbols designating corresponding intervals are numbers such as 6 and $^6_4$. Each
simply refers to a first and second inversion triad respectively built upon the given base note. Likewise, seventh
chords are indicated by 7, $^6_5$, $^4_3$ and 2. Accidentals are
placed to the right of the numeral or directly under the note
itself. If a bass note is without any symbol a root position
triad is implied. Frequently, more than one figuration may
appear for a given note, thus, indicating the presence of
some type of non-harmonic tones.

As to the origin of the thorough-bass practice there
is much confusion. However, the turn of the 17th century
is the accepted dating, along with the beginning of the monodic style and its polarity of upper and lower voices. Among
the first works to consistently employ this method of writing
was the <u>Cento Concerti Ecclesiastici</u> (1602) by Ludovico da
Viadana (1564-1645). The basses of these concerti were an
advancement over their predecessors, the old organ basses
(the *<u>basso</u> sequente) of the 16th century, which slavishly
doubled the vocal bass, in that Viadana here incorporated
an occasional independence from the vocal line, furnishing a
foundation of sustained harmonies to it.

Throughout the early Baroque era the thorough-bass
technique found particular popularity in <u>secco</u> recitatives,
sonatas, masses and motets. Originating in Italy, it quickly
spread to England and Germany. In Germany its establishment is seen in volume three of Praetorius' <u>Syntagma Musi-
cum</u> (1615-1619). However, the acceptance of this technique
into German church music was somewhat delayed by the re-

luctance of organists to change from the old German organ
tabulature. Among the first German composers of Protestant church music to employ the use of continuo was Heinrich
Schütz (1585-1672) whose psalms, motets, Cantiones Sacrae,
Symphoniae Sacrae and passions influenced greatly the course
of German church music. This line includes names like
George Muffat, Dietrich Buxtehude, Samuel Scheidt and J. S.
Bach. In England the earliest extant form of a figured
continuo is the Cantiones Sacrae (1617) by Richard Deering
(c.1550-1630), the beginning of a thread leading all the way
to Handelian oratorios and anthems.
        In the early 19th century the only musicians in Eng-
land to maintain the art of realizing the figured bass were
the cathedral organists. Thus, to keep the older music in
the repertory of the English church Vincent Novello published
the first British volume of reprints with fully worked-out
organ parts. This met with violent reaction at first, but
soon was to be copied by other publishers as the art of
continuo playing faded among musicians. With these printed
realizations came many abuses of the practice of realizing;
these resulted, in 1931, in The Art of Accompaniment from
a Thorough-Bass by F. T. Arnold, the result of thirty years
of research. This text has been one of the leading efforts
in the revival of the art of thorough-bass during the mid-20th
century.

Arnold, F. T. The Art of Accompaniment from a Thorough-
    Bass, 1965 (reprint of 1931 ed.).
Bach, Carl Philipp Emanuel. Essay on the True Art of
    Playing Keyboard Instruments, trans. William J. Mitch-
    ell. New York: W. W. Norton, 1949.
Bülow, George J. Thorough-Bass Accompaniment according
    to Johann David Heinichen. Berkeley: University of
    California Press, 1966.
Keller, Herman. Thoroughbass Method, trans. Carl Parrish.
    New York: W. W. Norton, 1965.
Muffat, Georg. An Essay on Thoroughbass, trans. Helmut
    Federhofer. N.p.: American Institute of Musicology,
    1961.
Praetorius, Michael. Syntagma Musicum (1619), Facsimile-
    Nachdruck hrsg. von Willibald Gurlitt. Kassel:
    Bärenreiter, 1959. Vol. III, Chapter 6.
Quantz, Johann Joachim. On Playing the Flute, trans.
    Edward R. Reilly. New York: The Free Press, 1966.
    Chapter 17, section 6.

TOWER MUSIC see BRASS CHOIRS; CARILLON

TRACT (ML. tractus)

A psalm which is chanted antiphonally after the
*epistle and *gradual at the Eucharist during the season of
Lent is called the tract. It replaces the joyous *Alleluia.
Differing from the gradual, the tract often consists of many
verses of a psalm. In the English Hymnal (1906) the tracts
are included with the *introits and *anthems.

Procter, Francis and W. H. Frere. A New History of the
    Book of Common Prayer. London: Macmillan, 1955.
Reed, Luther D. The Lutheran Liturgy. Philadelphia:
    Muhlenberg Press, 1947.

TRISAGION (Gr. fr. trisagios thrice holy, fr. tris thrice + hagios holy)

The trisagion is a short invocation found in Greek
liturgies which has been translated "Holy God, holy Mighty,
holy Immortal, have mercy upon us."

TURBA (L. crowd)

The words of the narratives in *oratorios and *passions spoken by the crowds or groups and assigned to the
choir are referred to as the turba. These were often set
polyphonically. (See, e.g., Victoria's St. Matthew Passion
in Opera omnia, V:117.)

Smallman, Basil. The Background of Passion Music.
    Naperville, Ill.: SCM Book Club, 1957.
Wienandt, Elwyn A. Choral Music of the Church. New
    York: The Free Press, 1965.

TWENTIETH CENTURY CHURCH LIGHT MUSIC GROUP

The British church composers of the mid-20th century who gathered together around Father Geoffrey Beaumont
for the advancement of church music in the "popular" style
called themselves the Twentieth Century Church Light Music
Group. The main work to commence this philosophy was
Beaumont's Folk Mass (1956).
    Others associated with the group are Patrick Apple-
ford, E. C. Blake, John Alldis, Mark Hankey and Malcolm

Williamson. The major publisher of their works is Joseph
Weinberger Ltd., London.

Routley, Erik. Twentieth Century Church Music. London:
      Herbert Jenkins, 1964. Chapter 13.

URANIA (L. fr. Gr. Ourania, fr. ouranios heavenly, fr.
      ouranos heaven)

      The first American collection to contain original
choral music by an American composer was James Lyon's
(1735-1794) Urania; or, A Choice Collection of Psalm-Tunes,
Anthems, and Hymns... (1761). It also contains the first
American imprint of *"fuging tunes".
      With its oblong shape and bulky 198 pages Lyon's col-
lection begins with a detailed set of instructions about music
reading and singing, in an attempt to improve the art of
psalmody throughout the Colonies. It also contains a volu-
minous assortment of music, including 70 textless psalm-
tunes, 12 anthems based on biblical prose and 14 hymns.
The musical contents were exclusively by British composers
with the exception of the six tunes by Lyon.

Lyon, J. Urania; or, a Choice Collection of Psalm-tunes,
      Anthems and Hymns. Philadelphia: H. Dawkins, 1761.
Sonneck, Oscar G. T. Francis Hopkinson and James Lyon.
      New York: Da Capo Press, 1967.

VATER UNSER (G. Our Father)

      The nine-stanza German metrical version of the
*Lord's Prayer is Vater unser im Himmelreich written by
Martin Luther. Its earliest inclusion in a *hymnal was in
1539, in V. Schumann's Geistliche Lieder. (Cf. *Pater
Noster.) The tune to which it is set, bearing some of
Luther's own musical ideas, has been a source of inspira-
tion for many composers of *chorale preludes, including J.
S. Bach, Johann Krieger, Georg Böhm and Johann Pachelbel.
The sixth organ sonata of Felix Mendelssohn is also based
upon this melody.

Venite   306

Leupold, Ulrich S. (ed.). Luther's Works, Vol. LIII.
      Philadelphia: Fortress Press, 1965. Pp. 295-298.

VENITE (L. come, imper. 2nd per. pl.)

      The invitatory psalm (Psalm 95) sung before the set
psalms in the offices of *Morning Prayer and *Matins is
called the Venite from the first words of its Latin translation. It entered the Protestant liturgies from its medieval
use in Matins through Martin Luther's order for morning
office, Matins. The Anglican office of Morning Prayer included it in the first prayer book (1549), but without any
*invitatory. In the American Prayer Book (1789) the last
four verses of the psalm are substituted for Psalm 96:9, 13.
This jubilant summons to the whole world of nature and man
to joyfully worship its Creater is omitted from the Anglican
service on the 19th day of the month when Psalm 95 appears
among the psalms of the day. In Lutheran worship the
Venite remains fixed and Psalm 95 is omitted from the
psalter sequence in regular use at Matins.
      Originally, the psalm was sung by solo voices with
the full choir singing the *invitatory response in Lutheran
liturgy. However, as with the Anglican church it is normally sung to *Anglican chant. Settings of the Venite may
occur in the services of various composers, as it does in
Byrd's Great Service.

      "O come, let us sing unto the Lord: let us make a
      joyful noise to the Rock of our salvation. Let us
      come before his presence with thanksgiving: and make
      a joyful noise unto him with psalms. For the Lord is
      a great God: and a great King above all gods. In his
      hand are the deep places of the earth: the strength of
      the hills is his also. The sea is his and he made it:
      and his hands formed the dry land.

      "O come let us worship, and bow down: let us kneel
      before the Lord our Maker. For he is our God: and
      we are the people of his pasture and the sheep of his
      hand.

      "O worship the Lord in the beauty of holiness; let the
      whole earth stand in awe of him. For he cometh, for
      he cometh to judge the earth; and with righteousness to
      judge the world, and the peoples with his truth" [BCP].

Reed, Luther. The Lutheran Liturgy. Philadelphia: Muh-
      lenberg Press, 1947.

Shepherd, Massey H., Jr. The Oxford American Prayer
   Book Commentary. New York: Oxford University
   Press, 1950.

VERSE (ME. vers, fers, fr. OE. fers combined with F.
      vers; both from L. versus a furrow, row, a line of
      writing, and in poetry, a verse, fr. L. vertere,
      versum, to turn, to turn around)

   (1) The section of service or an anthem sung by solo
voices is called a verse. Therefore, such compositions are
referred to as verse services or *verse anthems, in contradistinction to full services or anthems where the entire choir
sings throughout.

   (2) A single metrical line of poetry, with regard to
a *hymn, is a verse, as opposed to the grouping of the
lines into a *stanza.

VERSE-ANTHEM (ME. vers, fers, fr. L. versus a row,
      a line in writing, a verse + *anthem)

   The *anthem form which is characterized by alternating passages for solo voice (or voices) and instrumental
accompaniment with those passages for full chorus is the
verse anthem. It is considered to be the most significant
Anglican musical form of the 17th century. The four periods
of its development are as follows: I. (c.1580-1625)--
Elizabethan: polyphonic tradition (e.g., O. Gibbons, 1583-
1625). II. (1625-1650)--Transition: transitional styles (e.g.,
H. Lawes, 1595-1662). III. (1650-1700)--Restoration:
homophonic, virtuoso tradition (e.g., H. Purcell, c.1659-
1695). IV. (1700-1775)--Decline: expanded sectional division and increased soloistic virtuosity (e.g., G. F. Handel,
1685-1759).

Mehrle, Brandon. "The Origin of the Verse Anthem and Its
      Evidence among the Works of Tudor Composers." Un-
      published D.M.A. dissertation, University of Southern
      California, Los Angeles, 1963.
Price, Shelby Milburn, Jr. "The Verse Anthem: Its Begin-
      nings, Development and Decline." Unpublished M.A.
      thesis, Baylor University, Waco, Texas, 1963.
Wienandt, Elwyn and Robert Young. The Anthem in England
      and America. New York: The Free Press, 1970.

VERSICLE   (L. versiculus, dim. of versus   see   *verse)

The versicles are passages from the *psalms employed to introduce *collects, *canticles, prayers or psalmody, a practice dating from before the sixth century. The
most common versicle is from Psalm 11:15, "O Lord, open
thou my lips, " which introduces the psalmody in the morning
services of prayer (Anglican and Lutheran).

VESPERS (OF. vespres, fr. ML. vesperae, fr. L. vespera
         evening)

The historical name of the Evening Prayer or Office
of the *Canonical Hours in the Roman and Lutheran rites.
Its roots are in the Jewish evening sacrifice which became
the Christian Office of Lights (Lucernarium). Around 530,
Benedict's order of monasteries divided it into Vespers (for
early evening) and Compline (retiring). With the Reformation it was returned to one service designed for the laity.
The significant mood is one of contemplation, thanksgiving
and prayer to God at the close of the day. (See also
*canticle.)

Order of Vespers (Lutheran)

The Versicles
   "O Lord, open thou my lips" (Psalm 51:15)
   "Make haste to help me" (Psalm 70:1)
   Gloria Patri
The Psalm and Gloria Patri
The Lesson and Response
Sermon
Hymn
Versicle "Let my prayer be set before Thee"
Canticle (Magnificat or Nunc dimittis--the former
        for festal and joyous seasons)
The Prayer
   Prayers
   Kyrie eleison
   The Lord's Prayer
   The Salutation
   The Oremus
   The Collect for the Day
Versicle "The Lord will give strength" (Psalm 19:11)
Collect for Peace
Benedicamus
Benediction (II Corinthians 13:14)

Mander, Albert, ed. Evangelisches Tagzeitenbuch. Kassel:
     Strands, 1967.
Reed, Luther. The Lutheran Liturgy. Philadelphia: Muh-
     lenberg Press, 1947. Pp. 428-449.

VESTMENTS (ME. vestement, vestiment, fr. OF. vest-
     ment, vestiment, fr. L. vestimentum, fr. vestire to
     clothe, fr. vestis a garment, clothing)

The uniform garment worn by choristers during the
religious service is known as the robe or vestment. The
vesting of choir members provides a sense of unity in appearance and oneness for the task of leading the congregation in worship.

Ancient Egyptian religious history provides the
earliest evidence of vestments being used in worship. The
high priests were garbed in simple, flowing robes during
chantings to Isis and Osiris. In ancient Israel David and
all his singers were robed on the festive occasion of bringing the Ark of the Covenant into Jerusalem. This robing of
fine linen continued into the Temple of Solomon, where the
choristers were covered with hooded robes, literally from
head to foot. During the first 400 years of the Christian
church, no special garments were worn in the services,
just the everyday clothing of long white gowns. However,
when trousers were adopted as everyday attire for men in
the sixth century the clergy retained the gowns. Eventually
these gowns were set apart exclusively for church usage,
symbolizing a "purity," a separateness from everyday life.
Thus, this model has continued as the basis for church vestments throughout the centuries.

An important fact must be seen at this point; that is,
most liturgical vestment developed from the common clothing
practices of the Graeco-Roman world. The alb, a long white
garment reaching from neck to feet and held at the waist
with a cincture, was originally the tunica alba of the Roman
gentleman. The alb later developed into the surplice.
Probably derived from the caracalla, a sleeved, fur-lined
outdoor garment of the 11th century, the cassock became
the distinctive outer dress for the clergy. Its cinctured
waist has been replaced by buttons the length of the garment.
Worn over the cassock, the surplice (from Latin, super over
and pellis fur) of linen or cotton was added to clerical attire
for daily offices around 1400. Its color was always white
for purity. The original hemline of the surplice was con-
siderably shortened in the 17th century.

With the Reformation some of the reformers sought
to abolish all vestments related in any way to Roman practice. However, Luther disregarded this thinking and the
cassock and surplice have continued to be used in the Lutheran church. The Reformed tradition adopted the 16th-
century black academic Genevan robe, which is still the
normal garb in many Protestant denominations.

The above mentioned garments remained the exclusive
property of the clergy until the 19th century. With the *Oxford Movement in the Anglican Church, vested choirs of lay-
men in cassocks and surplices began appearing. The vested
choir did not achieve common acceptance in the United States
until the 1880's and then only in urban centers.

Norris, Herbert. Christian Vestments: Their Origin and
    Development. London: J. M. Dent, 1949.
Piepkorn, Arthur Carl. The Survival of the Historical
    Vestments in the Lutheran Church after 1555. St.
    Louis: School of Graduate Studies, Concordia Semi-
    nary, 1956.

VOLUNTARY (L. voluntarius, fr. voluntas will, choice,
    fr. the root velle to will)

An organ solo played in conjunction with a church
service in England has been named a voluntary. It had no
fixed position in the service prior to the 19th century; however, it most generally appeared between the psalms and
the first lesson, or between the conclusion of *Morning
Prayer and the beginning of *communion. During the 19th
century the practice of the opening and closing voluntaries
(*prelude and *postlude) came into vogue. In some churches
an offertory voluntary is performed also.

The musical form of the voluntary is basically free.
Throughout the history of the term it has been molded into
preludes and fugues, variations on hymn tunes, and even
suites and sonatas. When a multi-movement form, the
voluntary generally began with a slow introduction which was
countered by a lively movement. This second movement,
however, could be a fugue. The 18th-century voluntaries
often consisted of three or four movements or even as many
as six. For the most part the voluntary is characterized
by slavish imitation and a two-part texture of a solo versus
a bass.

The earliest extant voluntaries are included in the
Mulliner Book (c. 1550). Three of William Byrd's (1543-

1673) voluntaries appear in My Ladye Nevell's Booke (1591),
while other composers such as Thomas Weelkes (d. 1623) and
Orlando Gibbons (1583-1625) are also known to have composed voluntaries.

Among the 18th-century composers of voluntaries were
Thomas Roseingrave (1690-1766), John Travers (c. 1703-1758),
John Bennett (d. 1284), Augustine Arne (1710-1778), William
Boyce (1710-1779), John Stanley (1713-1786) and Jonathan
Battishill (1738-1801).

During the 19th century the practice of the improvised
voluntary fell into degenerated depths of transcriptions from
other literature (such as *oratorios and instrumental works)
as well as the nondescript original pieces of the period.   It
is from this level that the 20th century has been rising, under the leadership of such men as Healey Willan (1880-1968),
Eric Thiman (b. 1900) and D. N. Johnson (b. 1922).

Beechey, Gwilym. Ten 18th Century Voluntaries. Vol. VI,
      Recent Researches in the Music of the Renaissance.
      Madison, Wis.: A-R Editions, Inc., 1969.
Camburn, Robert A.   "The English Organ: The Development
      and Literature, 1756-1827, Part II," JCM, 12:5:6-9,
      May, 1970.
Conway, M. P. Organ Voluntaries. Church Music Society
      Papers, No. 18. London: Oxford University Press,
      1948.

VORSÄNGER   (G. leader of a choir)

The persons who lead the *congregational singing,
particularly in the Amana Society, the Community of True
Inspiration, are called the Vorsänger. The Vorsänger are
usually four to eight men and women who are seated either
together and apart from the congregation (much as a choir),
or among the members of the congregation. Their main
duty is to establish the key of the melody and to lead the
congregation in the singing of psalms and *hymns.

Farlee, Lloyd. "A History of the Church Music of the
      Amana Society, the Community of True Inspiration."
      Unpublished Ph.D. dissertation, University of Iowa,
      Iowa City, 1966.

VOTUM   (L)

The benediction invoking God's peace upon the faithful

which concludes the Office of the Word (following the sermon)
in the Service of the Lutheran church is termed the votum.
It is reminiscent of the ancient custom of ending the homily
with an ascription of praise.   This term also refers to the
verse of Scripture (Philippians 4:7) read at the beginning of
the *Lord's Supper in the Reformed Church of America.

Reed, Luther D.   The Lutheran Liturgy.   Philadelphia:
      Muhlenberg Press, 1947.   Pp. 306-307.

WITTENBURG GESANGBUCH   see   ACHTLIEDER-BUCH

WORSHIP   (ME. worschipe, wurthscipe, fr. OE. weorthscipe,
      fr. weorth worth + scipe -ship)

      The reverent act of man's adoration in response to
the omnipresence of God in virtually all of life is worship.
In a Christian sense, worship is directed to God the Father
of our Lord Jesus Christ, under the guidance of the Holy
Spirit.
      In the early Christian church the worship was a fusion
of the Jewish synagogue service combined with a love feast,
the *Eucharist, and prophesying.   Incorporated into this act
were the reading of the letters from the apostles and the
reading of the Gospels, even before their authors were
canonized, as well as the singing of *psalms and *hymns.
Thus, the early Christian worship contained many of the
basic elements of worship: praise in song, instruction from
the Scriptures, prayer and communion.   By the third and
fourth centuries the worship of the Christian church was
taking on some basic shape, the service being in two sections: the liturgy of the Word and the liturgy of the upper
room.
      The first complete scheme of worship currently extant
is the Clementine Liturgy (c. 380) which contains the two
basic divisions.   Following the hearing of the Word from the
Scriptures and from the expositors, the catechumens and
other non-believers were dismissed.   The succeeding liturgy
of the upper room, the ancestor of the *mass, was reserved
solely for the faithful.   From this time to the Reformation
the worship of the Christian church grew to extreme propor-
tions in the *Opus Dei of the monastic centers and the expanded musical portions of the mass.

Seeking to rid the church of much extraneous materials in worship, the leaders of the Reformation re-evaluated and reorganized the liturgy into what they thought was more closely akin to the worship of the early Christian church. Martin Luther's (1483-1546) orderly concepts were set down in his *Formulae Missae and *Deutsche Messe, which have been the foundation of all succeeding Lutheran services. These services along with the Roman Mass served as the basis of Archbishop Cranmer's (1489-1556) liturgy for the Church of England as expounded in the *Book of Common Prayer (1549) and in succeeding Anglican revisions. The Reformed Church under the leadership of John Calvin (1509-1564) sought to cleanse the medieval mass of its extraneous materials and to reestablish the primacy of the Scripture and Eucharist with weekly celebrations. However, due to a conflict with the magistrates of Geneva, the communion was observed only once a month from 1538. This was the influence of Huldreich Zwingli (1484-1531) upon the Genevan community; for it was his idea in 1523 to clearly separate the Eucharist from the weekly Sunday worship. In so doing the preaching service began to take on a more predominant role.

Looking more closely at Calvin's reformed service of 1545, which was the principal forerunner of worship procedure among the free congregations, the service opened with a confession of sins, followed by sung praise. Having received instruction from the reading of the Gospel and the sermon, the believer responded with a confession of faith and his offering. Then occurred the intercessory prayers and the Eucharist. In response to the sacrament were prayers of praise and thanksgiving.

Through the influence of Calvin, worship was to be no longer a drama performed for the people, but rather a work or liturgy participated in by the people. (See also *Worship service.)

Ashton, John. Music in Worship. Boston: The Pilgrim Press, 1943.

Egge, Mandus A. (ed.). Liturgy, Worship, Music in the Lutheran Church. N.p.: International Choral Union, 1959.

Maxwell, William D. An Outline of Christian Worship: Its Development and Use. London: Oxford University Press, 1936.

Skoglund, John E. Worship in the Free Churches. Valley Forge, Pa.: Judson Press, 1965.

Underhill, Evelyn. Worship. New York: Harper and Row, 1936.

WORSHIP SERVICE   (*worship + *service)

The orderly procedure employed by the followers of
Christ when assembled together for the adoration of God, the
edification of the soul and the fellowship of the believers is
the worship service.   (For the authorized orders of various
communions see *liturgy, *communion service, *Canonical
Hours and *mass.) In the non-liturgical churches, where
each congregation plans its own order, certain general plans
or procedures have evolved from the Reformation to the
present.   These plans being repeated week after week and
year after year have almost become local "liturgies" in themselves.   Basic to these orders are the common elements of
praise, prayer, instruction and exhortation.

In a reaction to the form and ecclesiasticism of liturgical worship, the non-liturgical churches have traditionally
espoused the principle of freedom in worship.   Prior to the
advent of printed orders of worship, the spontaneity of each
service was at the discretion of the person(s) in charge.
However, with the printed order a certain amount of prior
planning has eliminated some of the impromptu spirit.
Here is a sample order of a worship service:

PRAISE AND CONFESSION

Prelude
Introit
Invocation
Hymn of Praise
Confession of Sin
    Prayer of Confession
    Assurance of Pardon

THE WORD

Old Testament lesson
Gloria Patri
New Testament lesson
Anthem
The sermon

RESPONSE TO THE WORD

Hymn
The Creed
Pastoral prayer
Presentation of offerings
    Offertory
    Doxology
    Prayer of Dedication

Hymn
Benediction
Postlude

Ashton, Joseph N. Music in Worship. Boston: The Pil-
    grim Press, 1943.
Halter, Carl. The Practice of Sacred Music. St. Louis:
    Concordia Publishing House, 1955.

YOUTH CHOIR (ME. youthe, youhthe, zuhethe, zuwethe,
    zeozethe, fr. OE. geoguth, geogoth + *choir)

    In its broadest concept, the choral organization for
young people in their teenage years is a youth choir. However, due to extreme variation in public school grading,
which influences the grading of church activities in various
localities, a church youth choir may encompass young people
from grades 7 to 12 at one extreme to grades 10 to 12 at the
other. In the *graded choir program, if the grades 7 to 12
grouping is divided, the younger-aged choir may be called
an *intermediate or *junior high choir and the older-aged
one the Youth or Senior High Choir. (Cf. *Graded choir
program.)

Easterling, R. B., Jr. Church Music for Youth. Nashville:
    Convention Press, 1969.
Ingram, Madeline D. A Guide for Youth Choirs. New York:
    Abingdon Press, 1967.
Lovelace, Austin C. The Youth Choir. New York: Abingdon
    Press, 1964.

ZWISCHENSPIEL (G., fr. zwischen between + spiel play
    (noun))

    The instrumental *interludes improvised by organists
between *stanzas and *verses of a *hymn or *chorale are
termed Zwischenspiel. (A composed example of a similar
technique is J. S. Bach's "Jesu, Joy of Man's Desiring.")
This practice which developed during the 18th century as an
ornamental exercise soon became a showy nuisance as it
appeared at the end of each verse. By the mid-19th century
the practice subsided somewhat, being employed only at the
end of stanzas. (See also *Organ.)

Liemohn, Edwin. *The Organ and Choir in Protestant Worship*. Philadelphia: Fortress Press, 1968.

INDEX*

Abelard, Peter (1079-1142) 161

Abendmusik (17), 59, 213

Aberdeen Psalter 178

A cappella (18), 26

Accomplished Singer, The (1721) 287

Achtlieder-buch (1523/4) (18), 84, 148, 156, 163

Ackley, B. D. (1872-1958) 141

Ackley, A. H. (1887-1960) 141

Adams, Stephan (1844-1913) 291

Adamson, John (d1653) 265

Addison, Joseph (1672-1719) 166

Addition Hymns 112

Agnus Dei (19), 90, 108, 130, 202, 228, 242

Ahle, Johann Rudolph (1625-73) 58, 100, 109

Ahrens, Joseph (b1904) 93, 154

Aiken, Jesse B. (fl1846) 122, 138, 286

Ainsworth, Henry (1517-1622) 19, 261

Ainsworth Psalter (1612) (19), 266, 272, 296

alb 309

Aldhelm, Bishop of Sherborne 260

Aldrich, Henry (1647-1710) 40

Alexander, Cecil Frances (1823-59) 169

Alexander, Charles H. (19th cent) 95

Alexander, Charles McCallon (1867-1920) 120, 140, 153, 246, 293

Alexander Gospel Songs (1909) 95

Alexander, J. W. (1804-59) 162, 170

Alford, Dean Henry (1810-71) 170

All-African Church Music Association 208, 288

Alldis, John (20th cent) 304

Alleluia (20), 97, 111, 144, 158, 304

Alleluia-jubilus 177

Allen, Sir Hugh (1869-1946) 24

Allen, William Francis (1830-89) 296

Allison, Henry (fl1802) 52

Allison, Richard (fl1600) 23, 117, 261

Allison's Psalter (1599) 23

Altargesang (20)

Alternatum 124, 229

Amana Society 211

Ambrose, Bishop of Milan (340?-397) 102, 160

Amen (20), 21

---

*This is an index both of page locations where a Dictionary main entry is further cited or explained or compared, and of items of information which do not themselves appear as main entries. Page references to main entries are in parentheses; page numbers with an "f" indicate "and following pages."

317